Lecture Notes in Computer Science   9839

Commenced Publication in 1973
Founding and Former Series Editors:
Gerhard Goos, Juris Hartmanis, and Jan van Leeuwen

More information about this series at http://www.springer.com/series/7408

Bedir Tekinerdogan · Uwe Zdun
Ali Babar (Eds.)

Software Architecture

10th European Conference, ECSA 2016
Copenhagen, Denmark, November 28 – December 2, 2016
Proceedings

 Springer

Editors
Bedir Tekinerdogan
Wageningen University
Wageningen
The Netherlands

Ali Babar
University of Adelaide
Adelaide, SA
Australia

Uwe Zdun
University of Vienna
Vienna
Austria

ISSN 0302-9743   ISSN 1611-3349   (electronic)
Lecture Notes in Computer Science
ISBN 978-3-319-48991-9   ISBN 978-3-319-48992-6   (eBook)
DOI 10.1007/978-3-319-48992-6

Library of Congress Control Number: 2016947944

LNCS Sublibrary: SL2 – Programming and Software Engineering

Printed on acid-free paper

This Springer imprint is published by Springer Nature
The registered company is Springer International Publishing AG
The registered company address is: Gewerbestrasse 11, 6330 Cham, Switzerland

Preface

Welcome to the European Conference on Software Architecture (ECSA), which is the premier European software engineering conference. ECSA provides researchers and practitioners with a platform to present and discuss the most recent, innovative, and significant findings and experiences in the field of software architecture research and practice. The tenth edition of ECSA was built upon a history of a successful series of European workshops on software architecture held from 2004 through 2006 and a series of European software architecture conferences from 2007 through 2016.

The technical program included a main research track of accepted papers, three keynote talks, an industry track, a doctoral symposium track, and a tool demonstration track. In addition, we also offered several workshops and tutorials on diverse topics related to the software architecture discipline.

The role of women in the computing area has gained more and more importance with the emerging information age. To this end, the first special track on "Women in Software Architecture" collocated with ECSA 2016 brought together students, young and senior researchers, as well as practitioners to present, share, and celebrate their technical accomplishments and experiences making research and/or working in the software architecture field.

For the main research track, we received 84 submissions in the three main categories: full research and experience papers, short papers for addressing emerging research, and education and training papers. Based on the recommendations of the Program Committee, we accepted 12 papers as full papers, and 11 papers as short papers. Hence the acceptance rate for the full papers was 14.28 % and for both full and short papers 27.38 % for ECSA 2016.

The conference attracted papers (co-)authored by researchers, practitioners, and academia from 17 countries (Australia, Brazil, Canada, Czech Republic, Finland, France, Germany, Israel, Italy, The Netherlands, New Zealand, Norway, Spain, Sweden, Turkey, UK, USA).

It was a great pleasure to have prominent keynote speakers at ECSA 2016. The opening day keynote was delivered by Volker Gruhn from the University of Duisburg-Essen. He spoke on "Engineering Cyber-Physical Systems – A Paradigm Shift in Software Architectures?" The second keynote was presented by Mehmet Aksit from the University of Twente, on "9 C's: A conceptual Framework for Understanding the Trends in Software Technology." The third and final keynote was delivered by Flavio Oquendo. He spoke about "Software Architecture Challenges and Emerging Research in Software-Intensive Systems-of-Systems."

We were grateful to the members of the Program Committee for helping us to seek submissions and provide valuable and timely reviews. Their efforts enabled us to put together a high-quality technical program for ECSA 2016. We would like to thank the members of the Organizing Committee of ECSA 2016 for playing an enormously important role in successfully organizing the event with several new tracks and collocated events. We also thank the workshop organizers and tutorials presenters, who also made significant contributions to the success of ECSA.

Owing to unfortunate events the conference had to be relocated from Istanbul, Turkey, to Copenhagen, Denmark. We are grateful to the local Organizing Committee at Kültür University in Istanbul for the initial organizations. We would like to thank the management of IT University of Copenhagen, Denmark, for taking over the local organization in a smooth way and providing its facilities and professionally trained staff for the organization of ECSA 2016.

The ECSA 2016 submission and review process was extensively supported by the EasyChair Conference Management System. We acknowledge the prompt and professional support from Springer, who published these proceedings in printed and electronic volumes as part of the *Lecture Notes in Computer Science* series.

September 2016   Bedir Tekinerdogan
                                                              Uwe Zdun
                                                     Muhammad Ali Babar

Organization

General Chair

M. Ali Babar   University of Adelaide, Australia and IT University
           of Copenhagen, Denmark

Program Co-chairs

Bedir Tekinerdogan   Wageningen University, The Netherlands
Uwe Zdun   University of Vienna, Austria

Industry Track Co-chairs

Klaus Marius Hansen Microsoft Development Center Copenhagen, Denmark
Mansooreh Zahedi   IT University of Copenhagen, Denmark

Track on Women in Software Architecture

Elena Navarro   University of Castilla-La Mancha, Spain
Elisa Yumi Nakagawa University of São Paulo, Brazil

Workshops Co-chairs

Rainer Weinreich   Johannes Kepler University Linz, Austria
Rami Bahsoon   The University of Birmingham, UK

Doctoral Symposium Chair

Danny Weyns   Katholieke Universiteit Leuven, Belgium

Tool Demo Chair

Konstantinos Manikas University of Copenhagen, Denmark
Liu Yan   Concordia University, Canada

Publicity Chair

Matthias Galster   University of Canterbury, New Zealand

Local Organizing Co-chairs

Yvonne Dittrich	IT University of Copenhagen, Denmark
Aufeef Chauhan	IT University of Copenhagen, Denmark

Web Masters

Lina Maria Garcés Rodriguez	University of São Paulo, Brazil
Tiago Volpato	University of São Paulo, Brazil

Steering Committee

Muhammad Ali Babar	University of Adelaide, Australia
Paris Avgeriou	University of Groningen, The Netherlands
Ivica Crnkovic	Mälardalen University, Sweden
Carlos E. Cuesta	Rey Juan Carlos University, Spain
Khalil Drira	LAAS-CNRS – University of Toulouse, France
Patricia Lago	VU University Amsterdam, The Netherlands
Tomi Männistö	University of Helsinki, Finland
Raffaela Mirandola	Politecnico di Milano, Italy
Flavio Oquendo	IRISA – University of South Brittany, France (Chair)
Bedir Tekinerdogan	Wageningen University, The Netherlands
Danny Weyns	Linnaeus University, Sweden
Uwe Zdun	University of Vienna, Austria

Program Committee

Bedir Tekinerdogan	Wageningen University, The Netherlands
Muhammad Ali Babar	IT University of Copenhagen, Denmark
Uwe Zdun	University of Vienna, Austria
Antonia Bertolino	ISTI-CNR, Italy
Mehmet Aksit	University of Twente, The Netherlands
Eduardo Almeida	CESAR, Brazil
Jesper Andersson	Linnaeus University, Sweden
Paris Avgeriou	University of Groningen, The Netherlands
Rami Bahsoon	University of Copenhagen, Denmark
Thais Batista	Federal University of Rio Grande do Norte, Brazil
Stefan Biffl	TU Wien, Austria
Jan Bosch	Chalmers and Gothenburg University, Sweden
Tomas Bures	Charles University, Czech Republic
Rafael Capilla	Universidad Rey Juan Carlos, Madrid
Roger Champagne	École de technologie supérieure, Canada
Michel Chaudron	Chalmers and Gothenburg University, Sweden
Ivica Crnkovic	Chalmers and Gothenburg University, Sweden
Carlos E. Cuesta	Rey Juan Carlos University, Spain

Rogerio De Lemos	University of Kent, UK
Khalil Drira	LAAS-CNRS, France
Laurence Duchien	University of Lille, France
Matthias Galster	University of Canterbury, New Zealand
David Garlan	Carnegie Mellon University, USA
Ian Gorton	SEI, USA
Volker Gruhn	Universität Duisburg-Essen, Germany
John Grundy	Swinburne University of Technology, Australia
Rich Hilliard	IEEE, USA
Paola Inverardi	Università dell'Aquila, Italy
Anton Jansen	Philips Innovation Services
Wouter Joosen	Leuven University, Belgium
Jens Knodel	Fraunhofer IESE, Germany
Heiko Koziolek	ABB Corporate Research, Germany
Patricia Lago	VU University Amsterdam, The Netherlands
Anna Liu	NICTA/UNSW, Australia
Sam Malek	George Mason University, USA
Tomi Männistö	University of Helsinki, Finland
Raffaela Mirandola	Politecnico di Milano, Italy
Henry Muccini	University of L'Aquila, Italy
Elena Navarro	University of Castilla-La Mancha
Robert Nord	Software Engineering Institute
Flavio Oquendo	IRISA (UMR CNRS) – University of Bretagne-Sud (UBS), France
Mourad Oussalah	University of Nantes, France
Richard Paige	University of York, UK
Claus Pahl	Dublin City University, Ireland
Cesare Pautasso	University of Lugano, Italy
Dewayne Perry	The University of Texas, USA
Hasan Sozer	Ozyegin University, Turkey
Judith Stafford	University of Colorado, USA
Bradley Schmerl	Carnegie Mellon University, USA
Clemens Szyperski	Microsoft, USA
Chouki Tibermacine	Montpellier University, France
Rainer Weinreich	Johannes Kepler University Linz, Austria
Danny Weyns	Linnaeus University, Sweden
Eoin Woods	Artechra
Olaf Zimmermann	HSR FHO, Switzerland
Elisa Yumi Nakagawa	University of Sao Paulo, Brazil
Claudia Raibulet	University of Milano-Bicocca, Italy
Jenifer Perez	Technical University of Madrid, Spain

Contents

Software Architecture Quality and Design Reasoning

Software Architecture Challenges and Emerging Research
in Software-Intensive Systems-of-Systems   3
   Flavio Oquendo

Software Architecture Design Reasoning: A Card Game to Help Novice
Designers. 22
   Courtney Schriek, Jan Martijn E.M. van der Werf, Antony Tang,
   and Floris Bex

A Long Way to Quality-Driven Pattern-Based Architecting 39
   Gianantonio Me, Coral Calero, and Patricia Lago

Diversifying Software Architecture for Sustainability:
A Value-Based Perspective. 55
   Dalia Sobhy, Rami Bahsoon, Leandro Minku, and Rick Kazman

Software Architecture Documentation

Towards Seamless Analysis of Software Interoperability:
Automatic Identification of Conceptual Constraints in API Documentation . . . 67
   Hadil Abukwaik, Mohammed Abujayyab, and Dieter Rombach

Design Decision Documentation: A Literature Overview 84
   Zoya Alexeeva, Diego Perez-Palacin, and Raffaela Mirandola

Task-Specific Architecture Documentation for Developers: Why Separation
of Concerns in Architecture Documentation is Counterproductive
for Developers 102
   Dominik Rost and Matthias Naab

Runtime Architecture

Architectural Homeostasis in Self-Adaptive Software-Intensive
Cyber-Physical Systems. 113
   Ilias Gerostathopoulos, Dominik Skoda, Frantisek Plasil, Tomas Bures,
   and Alessia Knauss

Executing Software Architecture Descriptions with SysADL. 129
   Flavio Oquendo, Jair Leite, and Thais Batista

Towards an Architecture for an UI-Compositor for Multi-OS Environments . . .   138
  Tobias Holstein and Joachim Wietzke

Software Architecture Evolution

Inferring Architectural Evolution from Source Code Analysis:
A Tool-Supported Approach for the Detection of Architectural Tactics   149
  *Christel Kapto, Ghizlane El Boussaidi, Sègla Kpodjedo,
  and Chouki Tibermacine*

Evolution Style: Framework for Dynamic Evolution of Real-Time Software
Architecture   166
  Adel Hassan, Audrey Queudet, and Mourad Oussalah

Retrofitting Controlled Dynamic Reconfiguration into the Architecture
Description Language MontiArcAutomaton   175
  *Robert Heim, Oliver Kautz, Jan Oliver Ringert, Bernhard Rumpe,
  and Andreas Wortmann*

Verification and Consistency Management

Statistical Model Checking of Dynamic Software Architectures.   185
  *Everton Cavalcante, Jean Quilbeuf, Louis-Marie Traonouez,
  Flavio Oquendo, Thais Batista, and Axel Legay*

Consistent Inconsistency Management: A Concern-Driven Approach   201
  *Jasper Schenkhuizen, Jan Martijn E.M. van der Werf, Slinger Jansen,
  and Lambert Caljouw*

Formal Verification of Software-Intensive Systems Architectures Described
with Piping and Instrumentation Diagrams   210
  *Soraya Mesli-Kesraoui, Djamal Kesraoui, Flavio Oquendo,
  Alain Bignon, Armand Toguyeni, and Pascal Berruet*

The Software Architect's Role and Concerns

Architects in Scrum: What Challenges Do They Face?.   229
  Samuil Angelov, Marcel Meesters, and Matthias Galster

An Empirical Study on Collaborative Architecture Decision Making
in Software Teams   238
  *Sandun Dasanayake, Jouni Markkula, Sanja Aaramaa,
  and Markku Oivo*

Architecture Enforcement Concerns and Activities - An Expert Study   247
  Sandra Schröder, Matthias Riebisch, and Mohamed Soliman

Software Architectures for Web and Mobile Systems

The Disappearance of Technical Specifications in Web and Mobile
Applications: A Survey Among Professionals 265
   Theo Theunissen and Uwe van Heesch

Architecture Modeling and Analysis of Security in Android Systems 274
   Bradley Schmerl, Jeff Gennari, Alireza Sadeghi, Hamid Bagheri,
   Sam Malek, Javier Cámara, and David Garlan

Towards a Framework for Building SaaS Applications Operating in Diverse
and Dynamic Environments 291
   Ashish Agrawal and T.V. Prabhakar

Software Architecture Reconstruction

Materializing Architecture Recovered from Object-Oriented Source Code
in Component-Based Languages 309
   Zakarea Alshara, Abdelhak-Djamel Seriai, Chouki Tibermacine,
   Hinde Lilia Bouziane, Christophe Dony, and Anas Shatnawi

Using Hypergraph Clustering for Software Architecture Reconstruction
of Data-Tier Software 326
   Ersin Ersoy, Kamer Kaya, Metin Altınışık, and Hasan Sözer

SeaClouds: An Open Reference Architecture for Multi-cloud Governance . . . 334
   Antonio Brogi, Jose Carrasco, Javier Cubo, Francesco D'Andria,
   Elisabetta Di Nitto, Michele Guerriero, Diego Pérez, Ernesto Pimentel,
   and Jacopo Soldani

Author Index 339

Software Architecture Quality and Design Reasoning

Software Architecture Challenges and Emerging Research in Software-Intensive Systems-of-Systems

Flavio Oquendo[✉]

IRISA – UMR CNRS/Univ. Bretagne Sud, Vannes, France
flavio.oquendo@irisa.fr

Abstract. Software-intensive systems are often independently developed, operated, managed, and evolved. Progressively, communication networks enabled these independent systems to interact, yielding a new kind of complex system, i.e. a system that is itself composed of systems, the so-called System-of-Systems (SoS). By its very nature, SoS is evolutionarily developed and exhibits emergent behavior.

Actually, software architecture research has mainly focused on single systems, mostly large or very large distributed systems whose software architecture is described as design-time configurations of components linked together through connectors. However, it is well known that the restricted characteristics of single (even very large distributed) systems lead to architectural solutions (in terms of theories, languages, tools, and methods) that do not scale up to the case of systems-of-systems.

Indeed, novel architectural solutions are needed to handle the complexity of software-intensive systems-of-systems in particular regarding the software architecture challenges implied by evolutionary development and emergent behavior.

This paper presents the challenges facing software architecture research to address software-intensive systems-of-systems. It analyzes the discriminating characteristics of system-of-systems when compared with single systems from the software architecture perspective and focuses on recent advances in software architecture research to formally describe the architecture of software-intensive systems-of-systems.

Keywords: Software architecture · Software-intensive system-of-systems · Software architecture challenges · Research on formal architecture description · Formal behavioral modeling · Emergent behavior

1 Introduction

The complexity of software and the complexity of systems reliant on software have grown at a staggering rate. In particular, software-intensive systems have been rapidly evolved from being stand-alone systems in the past, to be part of networked systems in the present, to increasingly become systems-of-systems in the coming future [18].

© Springer International Publishing AG 2016
B. Tekinerdogan et al. (Eds.): ECSA 2016, LNCS 9839, pp. 3–21, 2016.
DOI: 10.1007/978-3-319-48992-6_1

De facto, the pervasiveness of the communication networks increasingly has made possible to interconnect software-intensive systems that were independently developed, operated, managed, and evolved, yielding a new kind of complex system, i.e. a system that is itself composed of systems, the so-called System-of-Systems (SoS) [23].

SoSs are evolutionary developed from independent systems to achieve missions not possible to be accomplished by a system alone. They are architected to exhibit emergent behavior [20], i.e. behaviors that stem from the interactions among independent constituent systems which cannot be deduced from the behaviors of the constituent systems themselves. It means that the behavior of the whole SoS cannot be predicted through analysis only of the behaviors of its constituent systems, or stated simply: "the behavior of the whole SoS is more than the sum of the behaviors of its constituent systems".

This is the case of SoSs found in different areas as diverse as aeronautics, automotive, energy, healthcare, manufacturing, and transportation [10, 22]; and application domains that address societal needs as e.g. environmental monitoring, emergency coordination, traffic control, smart grids, and smart cities [18]. Moreover, ubiquitous platforms such as the Internet of Things (generalizing wireless sensor/actuator networks in the Cloud) and nascent classes of SoSs such as Cyber-Physical ones are accelerating the deployment of software-intensive SoSs, i.e. SoSs where software contributes essential influences to their design, construction, deployment, and evolution [17], as depicted in Fig. 1.

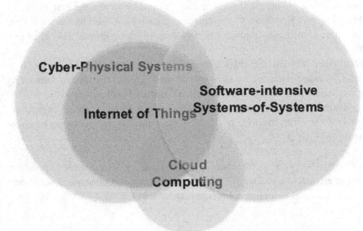

Fig. 1. SoSs and related enabling platforms

Additionally, besides SoSs that are developed in specific localities, e.g. a smart-city, some SoSs are being developed with a world-wide scope, e.g. the Global Earth Observation SoS (GEOSS) [13] that links Earth observation resources world-wide targeting missions for biodiversity and ecosystem sustainability.

It is worth highlighting that complexity is intrinsically associated to SoSs by its very nature that implies emergent behaviors. Note also that in SoSs, missions are achieved through emergent behaviors drawn from the local interactions among constituent systems.

Hence, complexity poses the need for separation of concerns between architecture and engineering [23]: (i) architecture focuses on designing and reasoning about interactions of parts and their emergent properties; (ii) engineering focuses on designing and constructing such parts and integrating them as architected.

Definitely, a key facet of the design of any software-intensive system is its architecture, i.e. the fundamental organization of a system embodied in its constituents, their relationships to each other, and to the environment, and the principles guiding its design and evolution, as defined in the ISO/IEC/IEEE Standard 42010 [17].

In particular, the ISO/IEC/IEEE Standard 42010 states the importance of having software architecture description as an essential first-class citizen artifact (similarly to the case of other architecture fields, e.g. civil architecture and naval architecture). Thereby, Architecture Description Languages (ADLs) are needed to express architecture descriptions. Note that we use the term ADL in the wider meaning defined by the ISO/IEC/IEEE Standard 42010: any form of expression enabling architecture descriptions.

Conceiving ADLs has been the subject of intensive research in the last 20 years resulting in the definition of several ADLs for modeling initially static architectures and then dynamic architectures of (often large or very large) single systems [24, 25, 35]. However, none of these ADLs have the expressive power to describe the architecture of a software-intensive SoS [14, 21].

It is worth to recall here that software intensive systems-of-systems are in general critical and very often safety-critical what is not the case of most of the software-only systems that were the subject of the research on software architecture description. It is also worth noting that among the ADLs proposed in the literature [24], the one that had a widely industrial adoption is AADL, the SAE Standard AS5506 [37], dedicated to safety-critical software-intensive systems in the avionics and automotive domains, where the architecture has a key role to satisfy safety-related requirements.

Therefore, to address the research challenges brought by SoSs, a novel ADL is needed for enabling the formal architecture description of software-intensive SoSs, in particular for the case of critical software-intensive SoSs [14]. This ADL must provide the expressive power to address the challenges raised by SoSs especially regarding correctness properties related to evolutionary development and emergent behavior. SoSs have indeed evolutionary architectures. Moreover, it must enable to prescribe SoS architectures abstractly at design-time without knowing which will be the actual concrete systems that will participate in the SoS at run-time.

The remainder of this paper is organized as follows. Section 2 discusses the notion of software-intensive SoS. Section 3 presents the main roadmaps for SoS research. Section 4 analyzes the distinctive characteristics of SoSs and their implications in terms of software architecture challenges. Section 5 discusses and introduces the essential SoS architectural concepts. Section 6 introduces emerging research on novel formal approaches for describing SoS architectures, focusing on SosADL, an emerging formal ADL for SoS. In Sect. 7, we present a case study, excerpt from a real SoS project, summarizing lessons learnt from the application of SosADL in practice. In Sect. 8, we present related work on SoS architecture description. To conclude we summarize, in Sect. 9, the main contributions of this paper and outline future work.

2   The Notion of System-of-Systems

The notion of system and the related notion of software-intensive system are well known and defined in the ISO/IEC/IEEE Standard 42010. A system is a combination of components organized to accomplish a specific behavior for achieving a mission. Hence, a system exists to fulfill a mission in an environment. A software-intensive system is a system where software contributes essential influences to the design, construction, deployment, and evolution of the system as a whole [17].

The notion of software-intensive system-of-systems is however relatively new, being the result of the ubiquity of computation and pervasiveness of communication networks.

A System-of-Systems (SoS, as stated) is a combination of constituents, which are themselves systems, that forms a more complex system to fulfill a mission, i.e. this composition forms a larger system that performs a mission not performable by one of the constituent systems alone [23], i.e. it creates emergent behavior.

For intuitively distinguishing an SoS from a single system, it is worth to recall that every constituent system of an SoS fulfills its own mission in its own right, and continues to operate to fulfill its mission during its participation in the SoS as well as when disassembled from the encompassing SoS.

For instance, an airport, e.g. Paris-Charles-de-Gaulle, is an SoS, but an airplane alone, e.g. an Airbus A380, is not. Indeed, if an airplane is disassembled in components, no component is a system in itself. In the case of an airport, the constituent systems are independent systems that will continue to operate, e.g. the air traffic control and the airlines, even if the airport is disassembled in its constituents.

Operationally, an airport is an SoS spanning multiple organizations, categorized into major facilities: (i) passenger, (ii) cargo, and (iii) aircraft departure, transfer and arrival. Each facility is shared and operated by different organizations, including air navigation services providers, ground handling, catering, airlines, various supporting units and the airport operator itself. The airport facilities are geographically distributed, managed by independent systems, and fall under multiple legal jurisdictions in regard to occupational health and safety, customs, quarantine, and security. For the airport to operate, these numerous constituent systems work together to create the emergent behavior that fulfill the airport mission.

As a software-intensive SoS, an airport is composed of independent systems that enable passengers, cargo, airplanes, information and services to be at the right place at the right time via the seamless collaboration of these constituent systems, from check-in, to security, to flight information displays, to baggage, to boarding, streamlining airport operations.

It is worth noting that the level of decentralization in the control of the constituent systems of an SoS varies, e.g. regarding airports, the level of subordination in a military airport and in a civil airport are very different. It is also worth noting that in some cases the SoS has a central management, as it is the case of civil and military airports, and in others do not, as it is the case e.g. in a metroplex, i.e. the set of airports in close proximity sharing the airspace serving a city.

SoSs may be classified in four categories according to the levels of subordination and awareness of the constituent systems on the SoS [8, 23]:

- Directed SoS: an SoS that is centrally managed and which constituent systems have been especially developed or acquired to fit specific purposes in the SoS – the constituent systems maintain the ability to operate independently, but their actual operation is subordinated to the central SoS management (i.e. the management system of the coalition of constituent systems); for instance, a military airport.
- Acknowledged SoS: an SoS that is centrally managed and which constituent systems operate under loose subordination – the constituent systems retain their independent ownership; for instance, a civil airport.
- Collaborative SoS: an SoS in which there is no central management and constituent systems voluntarily agree to fulfill a central mission – the constituent systems operate under the policies set by the SoS; for instance, a metroplex.
- Virtual SoS: an SoS in which there is no central management or centrally agreed mission – the constituent systems operate under local, possibly shared, policies; for instance, the airports of a continent such as Europe.

These different categories of SoSs bring the need to architect SoSs where local interactions of constituent systems influence the global desired behavior of the SoS taking into account the levels of subordination and awareness of the constituent systems on the SoS.

3 Roadmaps for the Research on Systems-of-Systems

Currently, the research on software-intensive SoSs is still in its infancy [14, 21]. In addition, SoSs are developed mostly in a case-by-case basis, not addressing neither cross-cutting concerns nor common foundations across SoS application domains [7].

Actually, the relevance and timeliness of progressing the state of the research for developing critical software-intensive SoSs from now on are highlighted in several roadmaps targeting year 2020 and beyond [9, 11, 41]. The needs for research on software-intensive SoSs have been addressed in different studies carried out by the initiative of the European Commission in the H2020 Program, as part of the European Digital Agenda [7].

More precisely, in 2014, two roadmaps for SoSs were proposed (supported by the European Commission) issued by the CSAs ROAD2SoS (Development of strategic research and engineering roadmaps in Systems-of-Systems) [9] and T-Area-SoS (Transatlantic research and education agenda in Systems-of-Systems) [11]. In 2015, the CSA CPSoS [16] presented a research agenda for developing cyber-physical SoSs.

All these roadmaps show the importance of progressing from the current situation, where software-intensive SoSs are basically developed in ad-hoc ways in specific application sectors, to a scientific approach providing rigorous theories, languages, tools, and methods for mastering the complexity of SoSs in general (transversally to application domains).

These roadmaps highlight that now is the right time to initiate research efforts on SoS to pave the way for developing critical software-intensive SoSs in particular regarding architectural solutions for trustworthily harnessing emergent behaviors to master the complexity of SoSs.

Overall, the long-term grand challenge raised by critical software-intensive SoSs calls for a novel paradigm and novel scientific approaches for specifying, architecting, analyzing, constructing, and evolving SoSs deployed in unpredictable open environments while assuring their continuous correctness.

In Europe, this effort started more intensively in 2010 when the European Commission launched a first Call for Research Projects addressing SoS as the main objective of study; in 2013 another Call for Projects had again SoS as an objective and in 2016 the third was opened. The projects funded in the first European Call have now ended: COMPASS (Comprehensive modelling for advanced Systems-of-Systems, from Oct. 2010 to Sept. 2014) [3] and DANSE (Designing for adaptability and evolution in System-of-Systems engineering, from Nov. 2010 to Oct. 2014) [4]. The projects of the second Call started in 2014 [7]: AMADEOS (Architecture for multi-criticality agile dependable evolutionary open System-of-Systems), DYMASOS (Dynamic management of coupled Systems-of-Systems), and LOCAL4GLOBAL (System-of-Systems that act locally for optimizing globally).

Regarding other parts of the world, in the USA, different research programs specifically targets SoS, in particular in the Software Engineering Institute [42] and Sandia National Laboratories [41] among others. In these programs, it is interesting to pinpoint the different research actions that have evaluated current technologies developed for single systems in terms of suitability/limitation for architecting and engineering SoSs. In addition, prospective studies have highlighted the overwhelming complexity of ultra-large-scale SoSs [12].

Note also that different industrial studies and studies from the industrial viewpoint have highlighted the importance, relevance and timeliness of software-intensive SoSs [10, 22].

4   Software Architecture Challenges in Systems-of-Systems

Due to its inherent complex nature, architecting SoSs is a grand research challenge, in particular for the case of critical software-intensive SoSs.

Precisely, an SoS is defined as a system constituted of systems having the following five intrinsic characteristics [23]:

- Operational independence: every constituent system of an SoS operate independently from each other for fulfilling its own mission;
- Managerial independence: every constituent system of an SoS is managed independently, and may decide to evolve in ways that were not foreseen when they were originally combined;
- Geographical distribution: the constituent systems of an SoS are physically decoupled (in the sense that only information can be transmitted between constituent systems, nor mass neither energy);

- Evolutionary development: as a consequence of the independence of the constituent systems, an SoS as a whole may evolve over time to respond to changes in its constituent systems and operational environment; moreover, the constituent systems are only partially known at design-time;
- Emergent behaviors: in an SoS, new behaviors emerge from the local interaction of its constituent systems (i.e. an emergent behavior that cannot be performed by a constituent system alone); furthermore, these emergent behaviors may be ephemeral because the systems composing the SoS evolve independently, which may impact their availability.

The combination of these five defining characteristics turns the architecture of SoSs to be naturally highly evolvable, frequently changing at run-time in unpredictable ways. SoSs have thereby evolutionary architectures (with the meaning that they dynamically adapt or evolve at run-time subject to the evolutionary development of the SoS).

Much work has addressed the issue of describing software architecture (in the sense of architecture of software-only systems as well as software-intensive systems). Most of the work carried out addressed static architectures (architectures which do not change at run-time) and some tackled dynamic architectures (architectures which may change at run-time). Therefore, we must pose the question whether these ADLs provide enough expressive power for describing SoS evolutionary architectures.

To address this question we will first analyze how and why SoSs are different from single systems, then analyze what are the implications of these distinctive characteristics for SoS architecture.

A single system and an SoS are both systems and as such they are developed with the purpose of fulfilling a mission. In both cases, they are themselves constituted of parts that architected together will provide the capabilities of the system as a whole to achieve the specified missions. The distinctive nature of an SoS when compared to a single system derives from its five defining characteristics.

To well understand what in an SoS is different from a single system, it is worth recalling that we are addressing software-intensive systems (not software-only systems) in this comparison. It is also worth noting that, in Systems Engineering, it is well known that the formalisms and technologies for single systems are not suitable to SoSs from a long time [23], SoS having its first dedicated international conference organized 10 years ago: the IEEE International Conference on System-of-Systems Engineering (SoSE), being in its 11th edition in 2016. In particular, the limitations of employing theories, languages, tools, and methods conceived for the architecture of single systems to the architecture of SoSs are well recognized and triggered a new thread of research [18–20, 23].

Let us now enumerate in Table 1 the key differences between both kind of systems (i.e. single systems and SoSs) by analyzing, for each distinctive characteristic, the nature of the constituent parts and the nature of the relationship between the whole and its constituent parts (see [8] for a deeper survey on the distinctive characteristics that differentiate systems-of-systems from single systems and their different graduations).

Table 1. Differences between single system and system-of-systems

Characteristic	Single system	System-of-systems (SoS)
Nature of the constituent parts		
Operational independence of constituents	• *None*: constituent components have no operational independence, i.e. they operate as designed to provide its functionality	• *Partial or Total*: constituent systems have operational independence, i.e. they operate independently (at least partially) from the SoS to fulfill its own mission
Managerial independence of constituents	• *None*: constituent components have no managerial independence, i.e. all decisions are made at the system level	• *Partial or Total*: constituent systems have managerial independence (at least partially) from the SoS to fulfill its own mission, in particular they may decide to evolve in ways that were not foreseen when they were originally combined in the SoS
Geographical distribution of constituents	• *None or Partial*: constituent components may be physically coupled (in the sense that mass and energy can be transmitted between constituent components)	• *Total*: constituent systems of an SoS are physically decoupled, i.e. only information can be transmitted between constituent systems, never mass nor energy
Nature of the relationships between the whole and its constituent parts		
Initial development of system	• *Total*: a single system is architected to meet a mission using constituent components developed or acquired to fit the mission at design-time	• *None or Partial*: an SoS is architected to meet a mission, but very often not knowing the constituent systems that will support the mission at run-time
Evolutionary development of system	• *None or Partial*: after initial development, constituent components may evolve under the control of the system at run-time	• *Total*: an SoS has no (or at most partial) control on how the constituent systems may evolve, in particular as their missions may not be aligned with the SoS mission
Emergent behavior of system	• *None*: constituent components have predictable behaviors from the system perspective as well as system behaviors are predictable from the behavior of the constituent components	• *Partial or Total*: even if the behaviors of constituent systems are predictable, their independence turns the SoS behavior unpredictable from the SoS perspective producing also emergent behaviors from local interactions

Undoubtedly, the main difference between an SoS and a single system is the nature of their constituent systems, specifically their level of independence, and the exhibition of emergent behavior.

Complexity is thereby innate to SoSs as they inherently exhibit emergent behavior: in SoSs, missions are achieved through emergent behavior drawn from the local interaction among constituent systems. In fact, an SoS is conceived to create desired emergent behaviors for fulfilling specific missions and may, by side effect, create undesirable behaviors possibly violating safety, which needs to be avoided. A further complicating factor is that these behaviors may be ephemeral because the systems constituting the SoS evolve independently, which may impact their availability. Additionally, the environment in which an SoS operates is generally known only partially at design-time and almost always is too unpredictable to be summarized within a fixed set of specifications (thereby there will inevitably be novel situations, possibly violating safety, to deal with at run-time).

Overall, major research challenges raised by software-intensive SoSs are fundamentally architectural: they are about how to organize the local interactions among constituent systems to enable the emergence of SoS-wide behaviors and properties derived from local behaviors and properties (by acting only on their interactions, without being able to act in the constituent systems themselves) subject to evolutions that are not controlled by the SoS due to the independent nature of constituents.

Therefore, enabling to describe SoS architectures is a grand research challenge.

5 Enhancing Architectural Concepts for SoS

Remember that a software architecture is defined to be the fundamental organization of a system embodied in its constituents, their relationships to each other, and to the environment, and the principles guiding its design and evolution [17]. In the architecture description of single systems, the core architectural concepts are the one of "component" to represent the constituents, the one of "connector" to represent the interactions among constituents, and the one of "configuration" to represent their composition.

As the restricted meaning of these concepts do not cope with the nature of SoS architectures, it is important to define novel concepts for describing SoS architectures as well as to name the new terms aligned with the SoS terminology.

These SoS concepts are the ones of "constituent system" of an SoS, "mediator" among constituent systems of an SoS, and "coalition" of mediated constituent systems of an SoS.

In addition, SoS architectures must be described in abstract terms at design-time (recall that concrete systems that will become constituents of the SoS are generally not known at design-time). The defined abstract architecture will then be evolutionarily concretized at run-time, by identifying and incorporating concrete systems.

In Table 2 we summarize these concepts and indicate how they are different and extends the ones of single systems.

Table 2. SoS architectural concepts

SoS architectural concepts	
Constituent system	Systems are the constituents of an SoS: a system has its own mission, is operationally independent, managerially independent, and may independently evolve. The concept of constituent system focuses on the capabilities to deliver system functionalities • Note that the concept of constituent system subsumes the concept of component in single systems: a component can be perceived as a "constituent system that is totally subordinated", oppositely to constituent systems in general that are, by definition, generally independent • Constituent systems exist independently of the SoS
Mediator	Mediators mediate the interaction of constituent systems of an SoS: a mediator has the purpose to achieve a specific emergent behavior by mediating the interaction among different constituent systems • Note that the concept of mediator in SosADL subsumes the concept of connector in single systems: mediators have a coordination role, while connectors have basically communication roles • Note that mediators are both operationally and managerially dependent of the SoS, and evolves under the control of the SoS for achieving emergent behaviors (an SoS has total control on mediators: it can create, evolve and destroy mediators at run-time)
Coalition	A coalition constitutes a temporary alliance for coordinated action among constituent systems connected via mediators (it is dynamically formed to fulfill the SoS mission through emergent behaviors) • Coalitions can be recomposed in different ways or with different systems in order to fulfil a specified SoS mission • Coalitions are declared by expressing SoS policies to select and bind existing constituent systems using mediators created by the SoS itself • Note that the SoS totally controls its mediators, but not at all its constituent systems, which are independent from the SoS
Design-time use of the architectural concepts	
Abstract architecture defined by intention	By the nature of SoSs, concrete systems that will actually participate are generally not known at design-time, therefore the SoS architecture needs to be defined abstractly, i.e. specifying constraints to select possible constituent systems and contracts to be fulfilled by constituent systems in mediators • Note that this is the opposite of the case of single systems where almost always the architecture is complete decided at design-time including all its concrete components

(*continued*)

Table 2. (*continued*)

	• Note that the concept of abstract architecture is different and does not have the same purpose as the concept of architectural style or pattern. Both, style and pattern, are codifications of design decisions used as architectural knowledge for designing abstract or concrete architectures. An abstract architecture is the expression of all possible valid concrete architectures in declarative terms. A concrete architecture is the actual architecture that operates at run-time
Run-time use of the architectural concepts	
Concrete architecture defined by extension	Once an SoS is initiated, concrete systems coping with the specified system abstractions needs to be identified to create concrete coalitions at run-time with the assistance of mediators • Note that a concrete system may enter or leave the SoS at run-time by its own decision (the SoS has no control on concrete systems); mediators oppositely are dynamically created and evolve under the control of the SoS

Therefore, in an SoS architecture description:

- Constituent systems are SoS architectural elements defined by intention (declaratively in terms of abstract systems) and selected at run-time (concretized).
- Mediators are SoS architectural elements defined by intention (declaratively in terms of abstract mediators) and created at run-time (concretized by the SoS) to achieve a goal, part of an encompassing mission (note that its architectural role is to mediate the interaction of constituent systems for creating emergent behavior).
- Coalitions are SoS architectural compositions of mediated constituent systems, defined by intention (declaratively in terms of possible systems and mediators and policies for their on-the-fly compositions) and evolutionarily created at run-time (concretized) to achieve an SoS mission in an operational environment.

6   Emerging Research on SoS Architecture Description

To address the research challenge of formally describing SoS architectures, in particular regarding its evolutionary development and the modeling of SoS emergent behaviors, we have started in 2013 a research project in collaboration with industrial SoS architects.

From this research emerged a novel architectural solution in terms of formal languages and supporting tools, especially conceived for formally modeling and analyzing the architecture of software-intensive SoSs. This novel solution for SoS architecture brings the following contributions to the state-of-the-art:

- A novel formal foundation for modeling SoS architectures: we conceived a novel process calculus in the family of the π-Calculus [26], named π-Calculus for SoS (for details on the π-Calculus for SoS see [31] in the proceedings of the 2016 IEEE SoS

Engineering Conference (SoSE 2016) which presents its formal definition and operational semantics).

- A novel formal architectural language embodying the SoS architectural concepts of constituent system, mediator, and coalition: grounded on the π-Calculus for SoS, we conceived a novel ADL based on the separation of concerns between architectural abstractions at design-time and architectural concretions at run-time (for details see [30] in the proceedings of the 2016 IEEE SoS Engineering Conference (SoSE 2016) which presents the concepts and notation of this novel ADL, named SosADL).

- A novel temporal logic for expressing correctness properties of highly dynamic software architectures (including SoS architectures) and verifying these properties with statistical model checking: we conceived a novel temporal logic, named DynBLTL, for supporting analysis of SoS architectures (for details on this temporal logic see [36] in the proceedings of the 2016 International Symposium On Leveraging Applications of Formal Methods, Verification and Validation (ISOLA 2016)); in addition we developed a novel statistical model checking method for verifying properties expressed on DynBLTL on architecture descriptions based on the π-Calculus (for details see [2] in these proceedings of ECSA 2016).

- A novel formalization for checking the architectural feasibility of SoS abstract architecture descriptions and for creating concrete architectures from SoS abstract architectures: it supports automated creation of concrete architectures from an abstract architecture given selected concrete constituent systems as well as supports the evolution of concrete architectures by automated constraint solving mechanisms (for details see [15] in the proceedings of the 2016 IEEE SoS Engineering Conference (SoSE 2016) which presents this novel formal system mechanizing the solving of concurrent constraints of SosADL).

- A novel approach for modeling SoS missions in terms of goals relating them to mediators and required SoS emergent behaviors (for details see [38] in the proceedings of the 2015 IEEE SoS Engineering Conference (SoSE 2015) which presents the SoS mission description notation and the supporting tool).

- The field validation of SosADL and its underlying π-Calculus for SoS drew from a real pilot project and related case study of a Flood Monitoring and Emergency Response SoS, summarized in the next section (for details see [32] in the proceedings of the 2016 IEEE International Conference on Systems, Man, and Cybernetics (SMC 2016)).

Additionally, we have developed an SoS Architecture Development Environment (SosADE) for supporting the architecture-centric formal evolutionary development of SoSs using SosADL and associated analysis languages and tools. This toolset provides a model-driven architecture development environment where the SosADL meta-model is transformed to different analysis meta-models and converted to input languages of analysis tools, e.g. Kodkod for concurrent constraint solving, UPPAAL for model checking, DEVS for simulation, and PLASMA for statistical model checking.

7   Lessons Learnt from Applying SosADL in a Case Study

Formally defined in terms of the π-Calculus SoS, SosADL provides architectural concepts and notation for describing SoS architectures. The notation of SosADL is in particular presented in [30] and formally defined in [31]. Hereafter we will focus on its expressiveness as an ADL for describing SoS architectures by focusing in an excerpt of a case study carried out for architecting an SoS for Flood Monitoring and Emergency Response [32].

Flood Monitoring and Emergency Response SoSs address the problem of flash floods, which raise critical harms in different countries over rainy seasons. This becomes particularly critical in cities that are crossed by rivers such as the city of Sao Carlos, SP, Brazil, crossed by the Monjolinho river as shown in Fig. 2.

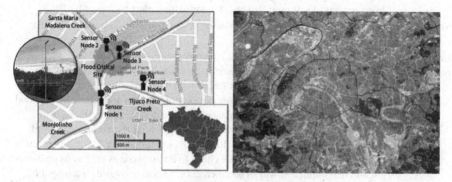

Fig. 2. Monjolinho river crossing the city of Sao Carlos with deployed wireless river sensors

This Flood Monitoring and Emergency Response SoSs has the five defining characteristics of an SoS. Let us now briefly present this in vivo field study in Table 3.

The aim of this field study was to assess the fitness for purpose and the usefulness of SosADL to support the architectural design of real-scale SoSs.

The result of the assessment based on this pilot project shown that the SosADL met the requirements for describing SoS architectures. As expected, using a formal ADL compels the SoS architects to study different architectural alternatives and take key architectural decisions based on SoS architecture analyses.

Learning SosADL in its basic form was quite straightforward; however, using the advanced features of the language needed interactions with the SosADL expert group. The SoS architecture editor and simulator were in practice the main tools to learn and use SosADL and the SoS architecture model finder and model checker were the key tools to show the added value of formally describing SoS architectures.

In fact, a key identified benefit of using SosADL was the ability, by its formal foundation, to validate and verify the studied SoS architectures very early in the application lifecycle with respect to the SoS correctness properties, in particular taking into account emergent behavior in a critical set as the one of flash flood.

Table 3. Field study of SosADL on a flood monitoring and emergency response SoS

Field study for architecting a WSN-based flood monitoring and emergency response SoS	
Purpose	The aim of this field study of a Flood Monitoring and Emergency Response SoS was to assess the fitness for purpose and the usefulness of SosADL and underlying formal foundation to support the architectural design of real-scale SoSs
Stakeholders	The SoS stakeholder is the DAEE (Sao Paulo's Water and Electricity Department), a government organization of the State of Sao Paulo, Brazil, responsible for managing water resources, including flood monitoring of urban rivers. Stakeholders of the constituent systems are the different city councils crossed by the Monjolinho river and the policy and fire departments of the city of Sao Carlos that own Unmanned Aerial Vehicles (UAVs) and have cars equipped with Vehicular Ad-hoc Networks (VANETs). The population, by downloading an App from the DAEE department, are involved as target of the alert actions. They may also register for getting alert messages by SMS
Mission	The mission of this SoS is to monitor potential flash floods and to handle related emergencies
Emergent behaviors	In order to fulfil its mission, this monitoring SoS needs to create and maintain an emergent behavior where sensor nodes (each including a sensor mote and an analog depth sensor) and UAVs (each including communication devices) will coordinate to enable an effective monitoring of the river and once a risk of flood is detected, to prepare the emergence response for warning vehicles with VANETs and drivers with smartphones approaching the flood area as well as inhabitants that live in potential flooding zones. Resilience of the SoS, even in case of failure of sensors and UAVs need to be managed as well as its operation in an energy-efficient way. The emergence response involves warning the policy and fire departments as well
SoS architecture	The architecture of this Flood Monitoring and Emergency Response SoS was described in SosADL as a Collaborative SoS having a self-organizing architecture based on mediators for connecting sensors and forming multihop ad-hoc networks for both flood monitoring and emergency response. The designed SoS architecture allows for continuous connections and reconfigurations around broken or blocked paths, supported by the SoS evolutionary architecture with possible participation of UAVs and VANETs (see [32] for details on the SoS architecture description)

The experimentation and the corresponding assessment have shown that SosADL and its toolset, SosADE, are de facto suitable for formally describing and analyzing real-scale SoS architectures.

8   Related Work on SoS Formal Architecture Description

Software-intensive SoS is a nascent domain. According to [14], ca. 75 % of the publications addressing software-intensive SoSs appeared in the last 5 years and ca. 90 % in the last 10 years.

We carried out a Systematic Literature Review (SLR)[1] to establish the state-of-the-art on architecture description of SoSs [14], which permitted to collect, evaluate, and summarize the research related to the following question: *Which modeling languages (including ADLs) have been used to describe SoS architectures?*

As a result of the SLR [14], the following modeling languages have been identified as the main ones used for SoS architecture description: UML (semi-formal) [40], SysML (semi-formal) [39], and CML [16] (formal). These findings are compatible with the findings of another SLR see [21] conducted independently.

More specifically, SysML was the baseline of two European FP7 projects (COMPASS [3] and DANSE [4]) for which they developed extensions for SoSs.

DANSE did not develop an ADL, but used SysML to semi-formally describe executable architectures that are then tested against interface contracts. The tests are applied to the traces obtained by executing architectures, against interface contracts expressed on GCSL (Goal Contract Specification Language) [4].

COMPASS developed a formal approach, in contrast to DANSE that extended a semi-formal one. In COMPASS, CML [28] was specifically designed for SoS modeling and analysis.

CML is not an ADL. It is a contract-based formal specification language to complement SysML: SysML is used to model the constituent systems and interfaces among them in an SoS and CML is used to enrich these specifications with interface contracts. A CML model is defined as a collection of process definitions (based on CSP/Circus [28]), which encapsulate state and operations written in VDM (Vienna Development Method) as well as interactions via synchronous communications.

CML is a low-level formal language, of which a key drawback (stated by their authors) is that SysML models when mapped to CML produce huge unintelligible descriptions (it was one of the lessons learned from COMPASS [28]).

In contrast to CML, SosADL enables the formal description of an SoS architecture as a whole being a full ADL according to the criteria of ISO/IEC/IEEE Standard 42010 [17], while CML is not, focusing only on contracts of interactions. Moreover, regarding SoS behavioral modeling, SosADL subsumes CML in terms of expressive power by its mathematical foundation based on the π-Calculus for SoS [31], subsuming CSP/Circus.

It is worth to recall here that SosADL as a formal architectural language follows previous work that focused on formalisms for describing software architectures which are dynamic [29] and self-evolving [27] in the scope of single systems. In particular, achievements of the ArchWare European Project [33] (FP5 ICT Program) were presented in a keynote [27] ten years ago in the 1st ECSA concentrating on an active architecture framework for supporting self-evolving software-intensive (single) systems architecturally described in π-ADL [29, 33] and currently supported by modern concurrent languages [1] in the Cloud.

Complementary to ADLs, software architecture models, patterns, and styles as well as software architecture-based frameworks have been studied for different kinds of

---

[1] We conducted automatic searches on the major publication databases related to the SoS domain (IEEE Xplore, ISI Web of Science, Science Direct, Scopus, SpringerLink, and ACM Digital Library), after having the defined the SLR protocol (see [14] for details on the SLR).

single systems exhibiting dynamic architectures, especially for autonomic systems, self-adaptive systems, self-organizing systems and more generally self-* systems. However, these different works have not targeted SoS and in particular have not at all addressed the key issue of emergent behavior as they have de facto limited their scope to single systems, e.g. [5].

Another thread of related work on SoSs is the one of implementation platforms. For the particular case of homogeneous constituent systems, a new generation of component frameworks and modeling languages have been designed to develop a specific class of SoSs, the so-called "ensembles" (an SoS that is only composed of homogeneous systems), e.g. DEECo (Dependable Ensembles of Emerging Components) [44] and SCEL (Service Component Ensemble Language) [44].

It is worth noting that "ensembles" denote a specific implementation style, which may be used to develop the implementation of SoS architectures designed with an SosADL. In this case, SoS homogeneous architectures described and analyzed with SosADL can be transformed to implementation models using SCEL or DEECo.

In summary, based on the study of the state-of-the-art carried out through the SLR, SosADL is positioned as a pioneering ADL having the expressive power to formally describe SoS architectures, no existing ADL being able to express these evolutionary architectures [14, 21]. Regarding detailed design and implementation in specific styles, it is complementary to technologies developed for e.g. "ensembles" as well as more generally to service-oriented architectural styles [43] applied to SoS implementation.

9   Conclusion and Future Work

This paper introduced the notion of software-intensive SoS, raised key software architecture challenges in particular related to SoS architecture description and briefly surveyed emerging research on ADLs for SoS addressing these challenges based on a paradigm shift from single systems to systems-of-systems.

Oppositely to single systems, SoSs exhibit emergent behavior. Hence, whether the behavior of a single system can be understood as the sum of the behaviors of its components, in SoSs, this reductionism fails: an SoS behaves in ways that cannot be predicted from analyzing exclusively its individual constituents. In addition, SoS is characterized by evolutionary development enabling to maintain emergent behavior for sustaining SoS missions.

Software-intensive SoS has become a hotspot in the last 5 years, from both the research and industry viewpoints. Indeed, various aspects of our lives and livelihoods have progressively become overly dependent on some sort of software-intensive SoS.

If SoS is a field well established in Systems Engineering and SoS architecture has been studied for two decades, it is yet in its infancy in Software Engineering and particularly in Software Architecture. Only 3 years ago, the first workshop on the architecture and engineering of software-intensive SoSs was launched: the first ACM Sigsoft/Sigplan International Workshop on Software Engineering for Systems-of-Systems was organized with ECSA 2013 [34] and since 2015 has been organized with ACM/IEEE ICSE, being in 2016 in its fourth edition. The first conference track dedicated to software-intensive SoS, SiSoS, will be organized only in 2017 at ACM SAC.

Beyond these initiatives of scientific forums, it is worth to highlight the increasing number of research initiatives targeting software-intensive SoSs such as the national research networks launched recently in France (CNRS GDR GPL/Research Network on Software-intensive Systems-of-Systems) and UK (VaVaS Research Network for the Verification and Validation of Autonomous SoSs), and the national programs been launched in different countries, e.g. Labex MS2T (Control of Technological Systems-of-Systems) and IRT SystemX (Engineering the Digital Systems of the Future) in France and the SoS Agenda initiative in Sweden.

These different initiatives are paving the way for the future software-intensive SoSs enabling to architect and engineer software-intensive SoSs in different application domains with guaranteed trustworthy properties [6], harnessing emergent behaviors for trustworthily achieving SoS missions in critical SoSs.

Regarding emergent research on SoS and more specifically on SosADL, future work is mainly related with the application of SosADL and its related languages and toolset in industrial-scale projects. They include joint work with DCNS for applying SosADL to architect naval SoSs, with IBM for applying SosADL to architect smart-farms in cooperative settings, and with SEGULA for applying SosADL to architect SoSs in the transport domain.

References

1. Cavalcante, E., Batista, T.V., Oquendo, F.: Supporting dynamic software architectures: from architectural description to implementation. In: Proceedings of the 12th Working IEEE/IFIP Conference on Software Architecture (WICSA), Montreal, Canada, pp. 31–40, May 2015
2. Cavalcante, E., Quilbeuf, J., Traonouez, L.M., Oquendo, F., Batista, T., Legay, A.: Statistical model checking of dynamic software architectures. In: Tekinerdogan, B., et al. (eds.) ECSA 2016. LNCS, vol. 9839, pp. 185–200. Springer, Heidelberg (2016)
3. COMPASS: Comprehensive Modelling for Advanced Systems of Systems. http://www.compass-research.eu
4. DANSE: Designing for Adaptability and Evolution in System-of-Systems Engineering. http://www.danse-ip.eu
5. Lemos, R., et al.: Software engineering for self-adaptive systems: a second research roadmap. In: Lemos, R., Giese, H., Müller, Hausi, A., Shaw, M. (eds.). LNCS, vol. 7475, pp. 1–32. Springer, Heidelberg (2013). doi:10.1007/978-3-642-35813-5_1
6. ERCIM: Special Theme: Trustworthy Systems-of-Systems, ERCIM News, vol. 102, July 2015. http://ercim-news.ercim.eu/en102/
7. European Commission (EC) - Horizon 2020 Framework Program: H2020 Digital Agenda on Systems-of-Systems. https://ec.europa.eu/digital-agenda/en/system-systems
8. Firesmith, D.: Profiling systems using the defining characteristics of systems of systems (SoS), software engineering institute. SEI Technical report: CMU/SEI-2010-TN-001, 87 p., February 2010
9. FP7 CSA Road2SoS (Roadmaps to Systems-of-Systems Engineering) (2011–2013): Commonalities in SoS Applications Domains and Recommendations for Strategic Action. http://road2sos-project.eu/

10. FP7 CSA Road2SoS (Roadmaps to Systems-of-Systems Engineering): Survey on Industrial Needs and Benefits of SoS in Different SoS Domains: Multi-site Industrial Production Manufacturing, Multi-modal Traffic Control, Emergency and Crisis Management, Distributed Energy Generation and Smart Grids. http://road2sos-project.eu/

11. FP7 CSA T-AREA-SoS (Trans-Atlantic Research and Education Agenda on Systems-of-Systems) (2011–2013): Strategic Research Agenda on Systems-of-Systems Engineering. https://www.tareasos.eu/

12. Feiler, F., et al.: Ultra-Large-Scale Systems: The Software Challenge of the Future, Software Engineering Institute – SEI/CMU, 150 p., June 2006

13. GEO (Group on Earth Observations): Global Earth Observation System-of-Systems (GEOSS). http://www.earthobservations.org/geoss.php

14. Guessi, M., Nakagawa, E.Y., Oquendo, F.: A systematic literature review on the description of software architectures for systems-of-systems. In: Proceedings of the 30th ACM Symposium on Applied Computing (SAC), Salamanca, Spain, pp. 1–8, April 2015

15. Guessi, M., Oquendo, F., Nakagawa, E.Y.: Checking the architectural feasibility of systems-of-systems using formal descriptions. In: Proceedings of the 11th System-of-Systems Engineering Conference (SoSE), June 2016

16. H2020 CSA CPSoS (Roadmap for Cyber-Physical Systems-of-Systems) (2013–2016), Roadmap: Analysis of the State-of-the-Art and Future Challenges in Cyber-Physical Systems-of-Systems. http://www.cpsos.eu/

17. ISO/IEC/IEEE 42010:2011: Systems and Software Engineering – Architecture Description, 46 p., December 2011

18. Jamshidi, M.: System-of-Systems Engineering: Innovations for the 21st Century. Wiley, Hoboken (2009)

19. Jaradat, R.M., et al.: A histogram analysis for system-of-systems. Int. J. Syst.-Syst. Eng. **5** (3), 193–227 (2014)

20. Johnson, C.W.: Complexity in design and engineering. Reliab. Eng. Syst. Saf. **91**(12), 1475–1588 (2006)

21. Klein, J., van Vliet, H.: A systematic review of system-of-systems architecture research. In: Proceedings of the 9th International Conference on Quality of Software architectures (QoSA), Vancouver, Canada, pp. 13–22, June 2013

22. Korsten, P., Seider, C.: The World's 4 Trillion-Dollar Challenge: Using a System-of-Systems Approach to build a Smarter Planet, IBM, 20 p., January 2010. ibm.com/iibv

23. Maier, M.W.: Architecting principles for systems-of-systems. Syst. Eng. **1**(4), 267–284 (1998)

24. Malavolta, I., et al.: What industry needs from architectural languages: a survey. IEEE Trans. Softw. Eng. **39**(6), 869–891 (2013)

25. Medvidovic, N., Taylor, R.: A classification and comparison framework for software architecture description languages. IEEE Trans. Softw. Eng. **26**(1), 70–93 (2000)

26. Milner, R.: Communicating and Mobile Systems: The π-Calculus, 174 p. Cambridge University Press, Cambridge (1999)

27. Morrison, R., Balasubramaniam, D., Oquendo, F., Warboys, B., Greenwood, R.M.: An active architecture approach to dynamic systems co-evolution. In: Oquendo, F. (ed.) ECSA 2007. LNCS, vol. 4758, pp. 2–10. Springer, Heidelberg (2007). doi:10.1007/978-3-540-75132-8_2

28. Nielsen, C.B., et al.: Systems-of-systems engineering: basic concepts, model-based techniques, and research directions. ACM Comput. Surv. **48**(2), 1–41 (2015)

29. Oquendo, F.: π-ADL: architecture description language based on the higher-order typed π-calculus for specifying dynamic and mobile software architectures. ACM Sigsoft Softw. Eng. Not. **29**(3), 1–14 (2004)
30. Oquendo, F.: Formally describing the software architecture of systems-of-systems with SosADL. In: Proceedings of the 11th IEEE System-of-Systems Engineering Conference (SoSE), June 2016
31. Oquendo, F.: π-calculus for SoS: a foundation for formally describing software-intensive systems-of-systems. In: Proceedings of the 11th IEEE System-of-Systems Engineering Conference (SoSE), June 2016
32. Oquendo, F.: Case study on formally describing the architecture of a software-intensive system-of-systems with SosADL. In: Proceedings of 15th IEEE International Conference on Systems, Man, and Cybernetics (SMC), October 2016
33. Oquendo, F., Warboys, B., Morrison, R., Dindeleux, R., Gallo, F., Garavel, H., Occhipinti, C.: ArchWare: architecting evolvable software. In: Oquendo, F., Warboys, Brian, C., Morrison, R. (eds.) EWSA 2004. LNCS, vol. 3047, pp. 257–271. Springer, Heidelberg (2004). doi:10.1007/978-3-540-24769-2_23
34. Oquendo, F., et al.: Proceedings of the 1st ACM International Workshop on Software Engineering for Systems-of-Systems (SESoS), Montpellier, France, July 2013
35. Ozkaya, M., Kloukinas, C.: "Are we there yet? Analyzing architecture description languages for formal analysis, usability, and realizability. In: Proceedings of the 39th Euromicro Conference on Software Engineering and Advanced Applications (SEAA), Santander, Spain, pp. 177–184, September 2013
36. Quilbeuf, J., Cavalcante, E., Traonouez, L.-M., Oquendo, F., Batista, T., Legay, A.: A logic for the statistical model checking of dynamic software architectures. In: Margaria, T., Steffen, B. (eds.) ISoLA 2016. LNCS, vol. 9952, pp. 806–820. Springer, Heidelberg (2016). doi:10.1007/978-3-319-47166-2_56
37. SAE Standard AS5506-2012: Architecture Analysis & Design Language (AADL), 398 p., September 2012
38. Silva, E., Batista, T., Oquendo, F.: A mission-oriented approach for designing system-of-systems. In: Proceedings of the 10th IEEE System-of-Systems Engineering Conference (SoSE), pp. 346–351, May 2015
39. SysML: Systems Modeling Language. http://www.omg.org/spec/SysML
40. UML: Unified Modeling Language. http://www.omg.org/spec/UML
41. US Sandia National Laboratories, Roadmap: Roadmap for the Complex Adaptive Systems-of-Systems (CASoS) Engineering Initiative. http://www.sandia.gov/
42. US Software Engineering Institute/Carnegie Mellon University: System-of-Systems Program. http://www.sei.cmu.edu/sos/
43. Wirsing, M., Hölzl, M.: Rigorous Software Engineering for Service-Oriented Systems, 748 p. Springer, Heidelberg (2015)
44. Wirsing, M., et al.: Software Engineering for Collective Autonomic Systems, 537 p. Springer, Heidelberg (2015)

Software Architecture Design Reasoning: A Card Game to Help Novice Designers

Courtney Schriek[1], Jan Martijn E.M. van der Werf[1(✉)],
Antony Tang[2], and Floris Bex[1]

[1] Department of Information and Computing Science,
Utrecht University, P.O. Box 80.089, 3508 TB Utrecht, The Netherlands
c.j.schriek@students.uu.nl, {j.m.e.m.vanderwerf,f.j.bex}@uu.nl
[2] Swinburne University of Technology, Melbourne, Australia
atang@swin.edu.au

Abstract. Software design is a complicated process, and novice designers have seldom been taught how to reason with a design. They use a naturalistic approach to work their way through software design. In order to impart the use of design techniques, a card game was developed to help design reasoning. This game was tested on groups of students and resulted in noticeable differences between the control and test groups. Those who used the cards produced better design arguments: the groups with the card game on average perform 75 % more reasoning than the control groups. The results show that the design strategy used by the groups is a clear indicator for how many and what kind of design problems are designed, while the cards influence how the designers solve these problems.

1 Introduction

Software architecture design is a complicated process, mostly revolving around problem-solving activities. Within software development many things have to be taken into consideration, not least being the requirements, but also what available technologies there are, the needs of stakeholders, and those of the developers and future redesign teams. This is known as a wicked problem, meaning that problem and solution are intertwined so that understanding the problem depends on how the designer wants to solve it. Such problems are inherently ill-defined and have no standard solution [17]. As a result it is the design decisions made at this stage that have the greatest influence on the eventual product. But people do not always use logical thinking, instead making decisions based on instinct, what is known as naturalistic decision making [10]. This can cause flawed reasoning, especially when the problem is complex and/or new, combined with the designers lack of expertise.

In order to resolve these problems, designers need to move from naturalistic decision making to logical reasoning decision making, especially when designers are not experienced with either the problem domain or the solution domain.

B. Tekinerdogan et al. (Eds.): ECSA 2016, LNCS 9839, pp. 22–38, 2016.
DOI: 10.1007/978-3-319-48992-6_2

There has been some software design reasoning research, but there is no simple and comprehensive method that can be used in practice. In this paper, we propose a card game for this purpose. The card game combines techniques in a simple form, and is developed to help novice designers to consider certain reasoning steps during design. This card game has been tested in an experiment involving students of a Software Architecture course. The aim of the experiment is to assess any obvious differences among control and test groups, and to establish if the card game had a positive influence on the logical reasoning process using qualitative analysis.

The card game is based on the reasoning techniques described in Tang and Lago [25]. The main reasoning techniques are the identification of assumptions, risks and constraints. The students also need to carry out trade-offs and articulate the contexts, problems, and solutions. Novice designers can forget that they need to reason about certain things. Razavian et al. [15] proposed to use a reflection system to remind designers. In their experiment, reflective thinking was applied using reasoning techniques to trigger student designers to use logical reasoning. In our experiment, cards were used to remind novice designers to use reasoning techniques. The choice for cards instead of a software tool was made because many software tools, such as those used for Design Rationale, have been developed but are not prevalently used in the design world. The most common reason for this is that the adoption and use of these systems take too much time and are too costly to be effectively used [24]. The cost-effectiveness of such a system isin fact the most important characteristic for consideration by software companies [12]. Cards do not cost much to produce or to use, and depending on the rules do not needextensive time to learn. Additionally, cards are not unfamiliar in software design, as already several card games exist and designers are familiar with their uses. For example, IDEO method cards are used for stimulating creativity [8], Smart Decisions card are used for learning about architecture design [3], and planning poker is played during release planning to estimate the time needed to implement a requirement [5]. Our card game additionally includes several reflection periods during the experiment to encourage participants toexplicitly reason with the design.

We compare novice designers equipped with reasoning techniques to the control groups using natural design thinking. The results show that the test groups came up with many more design ideas than the control group.

In the following sections more background information on design reasoning are given, together with reasoning techniques which stimulate logical reasoning (Sect. 2). Next, we introduce the student experiment, how it has been performed, and how validation of the results has been reached (Sect. 3). After this the results of the experiment will be explained, ending with an analysis of the results and further discussion on how the card game can be used for further experiments (Sect. 4). Threats to validity are discussed in Sect. 5. Section 6 concludes the paper.

2   Design Reasoning

Design reasoning depends on logical and rational thinking to support arguments and come to a decision. In a previous research, it has been found that many designers do not reason systematically and satisfice results easily [29]. Designers often use a naturalistic process when making decisions where experience and intuition play a much larger role [31]. As such, people need to be triggered to consider their decisions in a more rational manner. This can be done by using reasoning techniques. Previous research has shown that supporting designers with reasoning analysis techniques can positively influence design reasoning [15, 27,28]. There are other issues with design thinking, which can be categorized as: cognitive bias, illogical reasoning, and low quality premises.

Cognitive bias occurs when judgments are distorted because the probability of something occurring is not inferred correctly or there is an intuitive bias. This can be seen with representativeness bias and availability bias, where the probability of an event is mistaken because it either looks more typical, or representative, or because it is more easily envisioned. An example is anchoring, where software designers choose solutions for a design problem based on familiarity, even when it is ill-suited to solve the problem [21,23].

Illogical reasoning is when the design reasoning process is not used and problems occur with identifying the relevant requirements. The basis premises and arguments being used in the design discussion are not based on facts.

Low quality premises for design argumentation can be caused by missing assumptions, constraints or context. Premises of poor quality can be caused by either an inaccurate personal belief or the premise being incomplete or missing. Much of reasoning depends on the quality of the premises themselves, if these are not explicitly stated or questioned, software designers are more likely to make incorrect decisions [23,26]. The basis of how such reasoning problems can develop lies in the difference between the two design thinking approaches: the naturalistic decision making, and the rational decision making. This is sometimes referred to as a dual thinking system: System 1 is fast and intuitive with unconscious processes, i.e., naturalistic decision making. System 2 is slow and deliberate with controlled processes, i.e., rational decision making [9]. People naturally defer to System 1 thinking, and so in the case of software design designers need to be triggered to use System 2 thinking for decision making. This is done by invoking reflective thinking or prompting, which in the simplest sense is thinking about what you are doing, meaning that the person consciously evaluates their ideas and decisions [18,22].

2.1   Design Reasoning Techniques

In order to trigger logical reasoning several design reasoning techniques can be implemented during design, such as risk analysis [14], trade-offs [1], assumption analysis [11], and problem structuring [16]. These reasoning techniques support logical reasoning by means of analysis of various aspects of design decisions. These techniques are well known. However, to combine these techniques in a simple form to teach and remind students to consider certain reasoning steps during design is new.

The reasoning techniques chosen for this experiment are not exhaustive and are instead a selection of common techniques already used in software architecture: problem structuring, option generation, constraint analysis, risk analysis, trade-off analysis and assumption analysis.

Problem structuring is the process of constructing the problem space by decomposing the design into smaller problems. These then lead to reasoning about requirements and the unknown aspects of the design [19]. This reasoning technique focuses on identifying design problems and how these can be resolved when the situation is one the designer is unfamiliar with. It is used to identify the problem space and the key issues in design by asking questions related to the problem, such as what are the key issues. Its aim is to prevent the designer from overlooking key issues because of unfamiliarity with the problem. The more time spend on problem structuring the more rational an approach the designer uses.

Solution Option generation is a technique specifically directed at the problem of anchoring by designers, in which the first solution which comes to mind is implemented without considering other options. With option analysis the designer looks at each decision point at what options are available to solve a design problem.

Constraint analysis looks at the constraints exerted by the requirements, context and earlier design decisions and how they impact the design. These constraints are often tacit and should be explicitly expressed in order to take them into account. Trade-offs can come from conflicting constraints.

Risk analysis is a technique to identify any risks or unknowns which might adversely affect the design. Risks can come from the designer not being aware if the design would satisfy the requirements, in which case the design needs to be detailed in order to understand these risks and mitigate them. Or the design might not be implementable because designers are unaware of the business domain, technology being used and the skill set of the team. These risks should be explicated and estimated.

Trade-off analysis is a technique to help assess and make compromises when requirements or design issues conflict. It can be used for prioritization of problems and to weigh the pros and cons of a design which can be applied to all key decisions in a design [25].

Assumption analysis is a technique used to question the validity and accuracy of the premise of an argument or the requirements. It focusses mainly on finding hidden assumptions. It is a general technique which can be used in combination with the other reasoning techniques [23].

We propose a simple method that combines the main design reasoning techniques, and use a card game to prompt novice designers. In our research, we test the effectiveness of this technique.

3   Student Experiment

The theory studied in this paper is that applying reasoning techniques, through the use of a card game, has a positive influence on design reasoning with software designers. This theory is tested using an experiment focusing on inexperienced designers or novices. This experiment involved test and control groups carrying out a design. The results of the two groups are compared to one another. We use simple descriptive statistics and qualitative analysis to analyse the results.

The subjects for the experiment are 12 teams of Master students from the University of Utrecht, following a Software Architecture course. These were split into 6 control teams and 6 test teams, with most having three designers working together, two teams with two designers, and one team with four designers. Based on an earlier assessment, the teams were ranked, from which they were randomly selected for the test or control groups to ensure an equal amount of skill.

3.1   Experiment Design and Pilot Testing

Before the student experiment, a pilot study was run to test the card game and refine it by finding any major flaws or misunderstandings. The pilot study was performed by two Master students whom had already completed the course. The results of the pilot resulted in several important changes being made to the card game. Firstly, the cards were simplified and reduced to 7 cards, to simplify card play as the initial number of cards made it difficult to choose from them. The final card game is show in Fig. 1. The pilot showed that card play tapered off towards the end of the design session. To enforce card play, three reflective

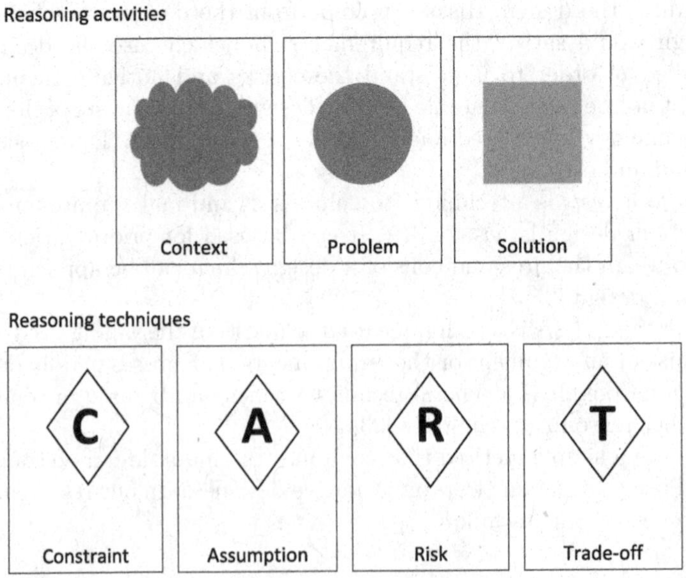

Fig. 1. Final cards of the card game

periods were added evenly spread throughout the session when cards have to be played. Lastly, the card rules were simplified to remove restrictions on fluid discussion. This resulted in the following set of playing rules:

1. The game is played in terms of a discussion;
2. The discussion starts when you play a card;
3. Others contribute to the discussion by playing their own cards;
4. When a decision is made the cards related to that topic can be removed.

The assignment used in the experiment is the same as used in the Irvine experiment performed at the University of California [30]. This assignment is well known in the field of design reasoning, as participants to the workshop analysed the transcripts made and submitted papers on the subject [13]. The assignment is to design a traffic simulator. Designers are provided with a problem description, requirements, and a description of the desired outcomes. The design session takes two hours. The assignment was slightly adjusted to include several viewpoints as end products in order to conform to the course material [1]. The sessions were recorded with audio only and transcribed by two researchers.

The card game is constructed based on an earlier experiment [15] which incorporated the reasoning techniques as reflective questions by an external observer who served as a reflection advocate to ask reflective questions. The card game replaces these questions with cards. Four of the reasoning techniques previously given were made directly into cards; *constraint, assumption, risk* and *trade-off*. Problem structuring and option generation would be triggered by using these techniques and looking at the design activities; context, problem and solution.

Three reflection periods were created at 15 min, 45 min and 1 h and 45 min. In these pre-set times, the students in the test groups were asked to use the cards to prompt discussion and support collaboration. The cards were paired with a table showing suggested questions to ask. Combining the cards enables different questions, such as: *which constraints cause design problems?* The control groups performed the same assignment without the card game, nor having pre-set reflection periods to revise their discussions.

A deductive analysis approach is used for coding the transcripts. The coding scheme is based on the design activities and reasoning techniques. The results of the experiment are analysed using qualitative measures, in this case with discourse analysis performed on the transcripts.

3.2   Results

In this section the results of the experiment are shown. The results show that there are significant differences between the control and test groups, supporting the theory that reasoning techniques influence design reasoning in a positive manner by having them use these techniques more.

Design Session Length. The first and most obvious difference is the time taken for the design session between the control and test groups. Though all groups were given two hours to complete their session, it is mostly the test group which took full advantage of this (Table 1). Half of the control groups finished their design before the 1.5 h mark. Only one test group did the same. From the audio recording, we conclude that this was due to a misunderstanding, as the group believed they had already breached the two hour mark. One test group even surpassed the two hour mark by almost half an hour.

Table 1. Design session times

Control group	Time		Test group	Time
C1	1:43:51		T1	2:01:23
C2	1:57:15		T2	1:23:00
C3	1:22:47		T3	1:59:56
C4	1:13:39		T4	2:24:42
C5	1:17:20		T5	1:54:48
C6	2:05:33		T6	1:51:34

Card Game Influence. To establish if there are any noticeable differences in the use of the reasoning techniques, the frequencies in which these were used are measured and compared (Table 2). The results show that there is a noticeable difference in the frequencies in which the reasoning techniques are used. From the techniques directly influenced by the cards especially assumption and risk analysis are consistently more used by the test groups.

Table 2. Design reasoning techniques frequencies

Analysis techniques	T1	T2	T3	T4	T5	T6	Total
Assumption analysis	14	6	9	5	8	7	49
Constraint analysis	7	9	2	7	8	10	43
Risk analysis	6	7	6	5	5	5	34
Trade-off analysis	5	2	2	4	2	1	16
Option generation	19	2	11	6	6	8	52
Problem structuring	33	19	24	25	20	25	146
Total	84	45	54	52	49	56	340

Analysis techniques	C1	C2	C3	C4	C5	C6	Total
Assumption analysis	2	0	2	3	1	3	11
Constraint analysis	4	6	10	7	7	5	39
Risk analysis	2	2	3	4	1	3	15
Trade-off analysis	1	1	0	3	0	1	6
Option generation	1	3	4	6	9	7	30
Problem structuring	15	20	18	12	15	13	93
Total	25	39	37	35	33	32	194

Option generation and problem structuring, which are indirectly influenced by the cards, are also more prevalent with the test groups. The test groups on average perform 75 % more reasoning than the control groups.

Constraint analysis on the other hand is about even among the test and control groups, and does not show the same rise in use of reasoning techniques. To better understand these results, we examine the distinct values of the individual reasoning elements. The reasoning techniques themselves are overarching and can contain several elements, and elements can be repeated. The distinct number of design elements identified by the two groups is given in Table 3. The groups can repeatedly discuss the same assumption for instance, but the number of distinct assumptions identified shows that the reasoning techniques help designers find new design information. The distinct design elements are shown in the grey columns in Table 3. The percentage difference shows 77 % more identification of distinct reasoning elements by the test groups.

Table 3. Design reasoning elements – no. of distinct identification

Design reasoning elements	T1		T2		T3		T4		T5		T6		Total distinct elements identified
Assumption	15	15	6	6	10	6	5	5	11	8	7	7	47
Constraint	9	8	17	8	5	4	9	7	13	8	18	7	42
Risk	6	6	7	6	7	5	7	7	7	7	8	6	37
Total													126

Design reasoning elements	C1		C2		C3		C4		C5		C6		Total distinct elements identified
Assumption	2	2	1	1	2	2	5	5	1	1	3	3	14
Constraint	4	4	12	8	17	9	9	5	22	8	16	8	42
Risk	2	2	2	2	3	3	4	4	1	1	3	3	15
Total													71

Our results show that assumptions and risks occur with a similar frequency as with their reasoning techniques. The constraints are shown to have an even more similar frequency across the test and control groups, there is hardly any difference at all. Although trade-off analysis shows an obvious difference, it is the lowest in frequency with both test and control groups. This is a surprising result as option generation shows a much greater difference in frequency. However, trade-off analysis, which concerns options, does not. To investigate these results we need to look at the elements which make up trade-offs; pros and cons (Table 4). Taking a closer look towards the results, the differences between the test and control group becomes more obvious. The frequencies of pros and cons more closely match that of option generation. More pros and cons for various options are given; only the combination of both pro and con is scarce. As the coding scheme used requires a trade-off to have both a pro and a con for an option explains why trade-off analysis has such low frequencies. Interestingly, in

comparison to the control groups, the test groups use both more pro with 53 %
more, but also far more cons to argue about their options, tripling the amount
with 269 % compared to the control group.

Table 4. Trade-off analysis, pros and cons elements

	T1	T2	T3	T4	T5	T6	Total
Tradeoff analysis	5	2	2	4	2	1	16
Pros	17	4	10	8	4	3	46
Cons	10	2	8	13	9	6	48
	C1	C2	C3	C4	C5	C6	Total
Tradeoff analysis	1	1	0	3	0	1	6
Pros	2	4	5	12	3	4	30
Cons	1	2	0	4	2	4	13

Table 5. Design problem, option and solution elements

	T1	T2	T3	T4	T5	T6	Total
Design problems	29	10	17	17	8	13	94
Design options	42	9	33	28	18	18	148
Design solutions	29	10	17	17	8	11	92
	C1	C2	C3	C4	C5	C6	Total
Design problems	3	8	13	19	16	11	70
Design options	5	10	14	18	25	23	95
Design solutions	4	9	13	20	17	11	74

Looking at the identified design problems, options and solutions we find that
mostly the design options have increased in the test groups compared to the
control group, with a percentage difference of 56 % (Table 5). This corroborates
with the increase in option generation established before. The identified design
problems and solutions have increased with the test groups, but not by much: a
percentage difference of 34 % in design problems, and 24 % with design solutions.

4   Discussion

The results of the experiment show significant differences in applying reasoning between the control and test groups. The cards overall trigger more design
reasoning in the test groups. More assumptions and risks are identified, more
options are generated and more key issues are defined with problem structuring.
In this section we analyse the results and discuss their meaning.

4.1   Thorough Reasoning vs Satisficing

A first result is the marked difference in the time spent in design. The test groups took longer for their design session, while the control groups took less time overall.

The test groups found more things to discuss and reason using the cards, whereas the control group is more partial to satisficing behaviour, which is a phenomenon where designers do not look exhaustively for every potential solution to a problem, but go with the first solution that is satisfying [20,29]. This suggests that due to the cards, the test groups were reminded to reason with the reasoning topics, and were encouraged to explore more about the design. This supports our finding that **the card game leads to applying more reasoning techniques.**

The test groups were less easily satisfied with their decisions since they found more issues that they had to address. We can see this difference in attitude by examining the transcripts. The test groups often mention how they have run out of time before they are completely satisfied with their design. As can be seen in the extract of T5 (Fig. 2), a new design issue was mentioned, but there was no time to solve it.

The control groups on the other hand, especially those which did not reach the two hour mark, simply ran out of issues to resolve. In the extract of C5 (Fig. 2) they were touching on design issues that they needed to solve, but they convinced themselves that what they had was good enough (satisficing). They did not go further into detail to explore more about that decision but instead ended the discussion. Hence, **the card game combats satisficing behaviour.**

The control groups were easier satisfied with their decisions and design, even when they had not reached the full two hours given. For the test groups, the card game stimulated the designers to keep refining their design and consider their decisions, and often the time given was too short for these groups to fully explore the design.

4.2   How Cards Influence Design Discourse

The cards directly influence the design discourse in two ways. Firstly, the cards provide inspirations for students to investigate a certain topic. Secondly, the students use the cards to reassess their previous discussion by classifying it in card terms, e.g. a system rule is later identified as having been a constraint. Examples like the extract from T3 show how these cards are used for inspiration (Fig. 2). Person 2 was looking over the cards searching for issues to discuss and came up with a risk, which needed to be clarified for the other person. This risk made the designers reconsider an earlier assumption, that the program is a web-based application, which later turned into a nearly 5 minute long trade-off discussion.

With the extract from T2 we can see the cards being used for classification (Fig. 2). Here they had just discussed a problem and found a solution for it. But when they reassessed the discussion as a problem, they realized that in order to solve the problem, they had also identified risks and used assumptions.

T5 (1:52:06-1:52:15)
PERSON 2: So we have we got everything. I think maybe only the traffic light is not taken into account and that's connected to intersection.
PERSON 1: Yeah. Definitely need to be there just make it here. And do we also model dependencies.
PERSON 2: Okay I think we don't have the time to put in. Maybe we can sketch it.

C5 (1:16:38 1:17:19)
PERSON 2: Oh ok. Do we have to say something more? Are we done actually? Or do they actually also wanna know how we include the notation and such, because-
PERSON 1: No they also get the documents, so they can see
PERSON 2: Yeah ok, but maybe how we come up with the- I dont know. No? isnt necessary?
PERSON 3: Mm
PERSON 1: Its just use UML notation, for all
PERSON 2: For all?
PERSON 1: No, and lifecycle model, and petri net. No, no petri net
PERSON 2: Perhaps petri net. Ok, shall we- shall I just?
PERSON 1: Yeah
PERSON 2: Ok

T3 (0:20:31-0:21:10)
PERSON 2: HTML 5 yeah? Information would of course [inaudible] constraints or risk or trade-offs, we have to make- a risk might be of course that- of course there is a [inaudible] so while you are travelling. For example, when you have an older device that could be a problem of course. So then you couldnt use the navigation maybe, the- well, [inaudible] right?
PERSON 1: What do you mean exactly? For example.
PERSON 2: Yeah well, for example, if you are travelling and you want to use the
application. You want to use the traffic simulator, then of course that might be the case that your device is not suitable for it. For example. So, on the other hand

T2 (0:28:14-0:28:28)
PERSON 1: So this was a problem
PERSON 3: This was a problem
PERSON 1: Yeah
PERSON 2: Yeah. Because [inaudible]
PERSON 1: And a risk right
PERSON 2: A constraint? Yeah but it was also like an assumption that you have a minimum length. That is our assumption right or-
PERSON 3: Yeah we created that now, and thats ok because its our own system

T4 (1:25:13-1:26:05)
PERSON 1: So that's the trade-off. The other side is good to have in the cloud because you can easily push a new update every hour if you want but you need really really strong server for all this simulations. Now professor did not say how much money she has. So it can be also. There can be also an option to pay for usage of this server for every simulation or for every hour of simulation.
PERSON 2: I don't think so.
PERSON 1: There can be an option. But it can be also very expensive so when I think about everything I think that is cheaper and easier to have local stand-alone version.
PERSON 2: Yeah.
PERSON 3: Yeah.

Fig. 2. Transcript extracts

4.3 Reasoning with Risk, Assumption and Trade-Off

A main purpose of the reasoning card game is to prompt the students to consider design elements. The results of the experiment show that especially risks and assumptions are considered more by the test groups. Trade-off analysis does not show much difference, whereas constraint remained the same.

In many cases, the test groups considered the design scope to be clear at first glance. But when they started using the cards and thought more about the design topics, they found out that it actually is more complicated than they first realized. The designers reflect on their previous ideas, discuss and redefine them, which clearly shows that the cards trigger reasoning in designers.

For the control groups it is clear that considering assumptions and risks for decision making about the design is not at the forefront of their minds, as indicated by their low distinct element frequencies. With the test groups, the cards remind the designers to take these considerations into account, as again can be seen in T3 where person 2 lists the cards, which prompts him to identify a risk (Fig. 2).

For the trade-off analysis few pros and cons were discussed, contributing to the low number of trade-offs. However, the test groups generated many pros, and especially more cons to argue against the solution options than the control group. The control groups also generate many pros, but fewer cons (Table 4). This suggests that the control groups are more concerned with arguments that support their options, or arguing why these are good, instead of looking at potential problems that could invalidate their options (cons). The test groups are more critical of their choices and look at options from different viewpoints. The extract of T4 shows part of a larger trade-off analysis in which several options are heavily discussed: mostly to have either a standalone program, or one which is cloud or web-based (Fig. 2). In this part, person 1 mentions that a pro for a cloud based program would be that you can update every hour, but a con is that a strong server is necessary which would be costly. The person then proceeds to suggest another option to ask users to pay for the usage of the server. This is not well-received by the group and person 1 admits that this option would still be a very expensive one and gives a pro to their first option: a local standalone version to which the others agree.

Even though the group eventually went with their first option, they took the time to explore multiple options and critically assess them by providing both pros and cons. The control groups had fewer of such discussions.

4.4 Reasoning with Design Context, Problems and Solutions

The effect of the card game is to combat satisficing behaviour and lack of design reasoning by stimulating the designers to reconsider their options and decisions, ultimately taking more time to delve into the issues. And yet, when we look at the design problems and design solutions identified by both groups, the percentage difference is much lower than that of the other elements, such as options and problems structuring. The cards prompt designers to consider their problems and explore more of the design, but problems are not identified as much by the test groups, as the other reasoning techniques are used.

Design problems identification can be influenced by other factors, such as design strategy and designer experience. Design strategies such as problem-oriented, or solution-oriented can influence the information seeking behaviour of designers [16]. The approach used for problem-solving, whether to focus on finding problems or solutions first, seems to have more of an impact on the design problems being identified. When comparing groups with similar strategies, the influence of the cards becomes clearer.

As an example, we have groups T2 and C1. Both use a satisficing strategy, where they actively avoided going into the details. They preferred to view a problem as being outside of their scope. Their option generation and trade-off analysis results are very similar. But the problem structuring, risk, assumption and constraint analysis of T2 is at least double of that of C1. Despite their adherence to a minimum satisficing strategy, the cards prompted T2 to recognize problems which often resulted from identified risks and constraints, for which they made assumptions to simplify the problem and solution.

It seems that the design strategy used by the groups is a clearer indicator for how many and what kind of design problems are identified, while the cards influence how the designers solve these problems. This supports our finding that **problem identification depends more on the design strategy than on the card game.**

4.5   Constraint Identification

The card game seems to have no influence on constraint analysis. The individual constraints identified by both groups are the same. This result in itself is interesting, considering the effect of the cards on the other reasoning techniques. The question here is why constraint analysis is different. One possible explanation for this is that the very nature of constraints, i.e. limitations on the design, as seen by novice designers, is intrinsically bound to the requirements. When thinking about design and what the system must accomplish, novice designers think of what is required, and what is not required. As a result both test and control groups identify constraints as things that are not allowed or rules that the system must follow. What is interesting here is that both groups identify much of the same constraints, with many coming directly from the requirements in the assignment, even taking on the same wording.

We find that both test and control groups frequently take over the literal requirements presented in the text as constraints. To give a more detailed representation of this, for the test groups there are 11 identified constraints which are shared in various degrees amongst the groups. There are 11 other constraints which they do not share and had to be inferred from the assignment, with 5 of these being identified by only one group. The control groups share 12 constraints from the text, and only 5 are other.

This then goes to explain the similar results when it comes to constraint analysis, many of them are found literally in the text of the assignment and require minimal effort to find. It is easy to see why these constraints would be in the text as requirements, as it is to the clients benefit to give clear instructions on what the program should and should not do. This means that constraints are easier to identify, causing the cards to have little influence, as these are given as requirements. **The card game provides no noticeable difference in constraint identification.** The other techniques, such as assumptions and risks, must all be inferred from the text and are not clearly given. The effect of the cards is more obviously shown there.

5   Threats to Validity

We recognise the threats to validity in this research, especially those revolving around generalization. For the transcripts, discourse analysis was used to interpret the text, which in itself is subjective and reliant on the view of the researcher [7]. This paper is an empirical research in the form of an experiment involving an example assignment. Empirical research is one of the main research methods within the software architecture research field, relying on evidence to support the research results. We address the internal and external validity of the results acknowledging any limitations which may apply [4].

5.1   Internal Validity

Internal validity is about how far a valid conclusion can be made from the experiment and data collected. Firstly, this research makes use of the Irvine assignment which has been used and tested in other research and is well-known in the field of design reasoning [13]. This limits the results of this research to those applicable to this kind of design assignment.

Secondly, participants were randomly selected for their situational representativeness, as students of software architecture, and the result of this research is limited to novice designers in the Netherlands. However, we have found convincing results to show that the card game made a difference to the reasoning capability of novice designers. We argue that these two limitations do not impose a major threat to the interpretation of the evidence that the cards have a positive effect on design reasoning by novices.

5.2   External Validity

External validity is about to what extent the results from the case study can be generalized across other published design reasoning articles. The results of this case study are supported by similar experiments [6, 15, 27, 28], showing that in the case of novice designers, being made aware of reasoning techniques actively counteracts satisficing behaviour and results in performing more design reasoning.

But the results also show a discrepancy when it comes to constraints, which did not show any difference across test and control groups. There are two possibilities for this discrepancy, either a requirement naturally leads to constraints, or the assignment itself is too clearly defined by explicitly including constraints. Whether the constraint card would have any influence on an assignment which did not mention constraints in their requirements cannot be proven at this point.

For the design problems and solutions there seems to be a design strategy component which has an influence on the amount of design problems being identified. This makes it unclear how much of an influence the cards have.

5.3 Reliability

Reliability is about ensuring that the results found in the study are consistent, and would be the same if the study is conducted again. To ensure that the coding of the transcripts is reliable it was tested for inter-reliability using Cohens kappa coefficient [2] to measure the level of agreement. The transcripts were each coded by two researchers using Nvivo 10. The average kappa coefficient of each of the transcripts was above 0.6 which is considered to show a good level of agreement. The average of all transcripts combined is 0.64.

6   Conclusions

Software design is a complicated problem-solving process, which due to its effect on the later stages of software development, is one of the most important stages to consider. Problems occurring at this stage which are not solved immediately will result in problems later during development or implementation, costing money and time. Problems with software design can result from problematic design decisions, which are easily influenced by designer biases. These biases can be avoided by using more logical reasoning.

In this paper, we propose a simple card game to help novice designers? use design reasoning. Design reasoning means using logic and rational thinking in order to make decisions, something which people as a whole find difficult due to the usual way they think. In order to prompt design reasoning several common reasoning techniques were chosen to be represented by the card game. These techniques are; problem structuring, option generation, constraint analysis, risk analysis, trade-off analysis, and assumption analysis.

To study the effect of the card game, we designed an experiment based on 12 student groups following a software architecture course. These 12 groups were divided into 6 control and 6 test groups. The 12 groups were asked to construct a software design. The transcripts of these experiments were analysed using discourse analysis. The results show a notable difference between the test and control groups on nearly all technique usages. The effect of the cards is to trigger the designers to use design reasoning techniques to reason with different aspects of design, to prompt new discussion topics, or to reconsider previous discussions. In all manners, the cards trigger reasoning and lead to more discussion and reconsideration of previous decisions. Those who use the card game generally identify more distinct design elements and spend more time reasoning with the design. Only the constraint analysis technique shows no obvious difference.

Further research includes to study the effect of the card game to professional designers, i.e., those who are experienced in the field. Professionals have more experience. Therefore, it would be interesting to observe how such a simple card game works with people who are more aware of design techniques. The card game could also be used as a learning tool for novice designers, to further their understanding of software architecture and learn design issues from the reasoning angles.

References

1. Bass, L., Clements, P., Kazman, R.: Software Architecture in Practice. Series in Software Engineering. Addison Wesley, Reading (2012)
2. Cohen, J.: Weighted kappa: nominal scale agreement with provision for scaled disagreement or partial credit. Psychol. Bull. **70**, 213–220 (1968)
3. Smart Decisions: A software architecture design game. http://smartdecisionsgame.com/
4. Galster, M., Weyns, D.: Emperical research in software architecture. In: 13th Working IEEE/IFIP Conference on Software Architecture, Italy, Venice, pp. 11–20. IEEE Computer Society (2016)
5. Grenning, J.: Planning poker or how to avoid analysis paralysis while release planning. Hawthorn Woods Renaiss. Softw. Consult. **3**, 1–3 (2002)
6. van Heesch, U., Avgeriou, P., Tang, A.: Does decision documentation help junior designers rationalize their decisions? A comparative multiple-case study. J. Syst. Softw. **86**, 1545–1565 (2013)
7. Horsburgh, D.: Evaluation of qualitative research. J. Clin. Nurs. **12**, 307–312 (2003)
8. IDEO: IDEO Method Cards. https://www.ideo.com/by-ideo/method-cards/
9. Kahneman, D.: Thinking, Fast and Slow. Penguin Books, London (2012)
10. Klein, G.: Naturalistic decision making. Hum. Factors J. Hum. Factors Ergon. Soc. **50**, 456–460 (2008)
11. Lago, P., van Vliet, H.: Explicit assumptions enrich architectural models. In: 27th International Conference on Software Engineering, ICSE 2005, pp. 206–214. ACM (2005)
12. Lee, J.: Design rationale systems: understanding the issues. IEEE Expert. Syst. Appl. **12**, 78–85 (1997)
13. Petre, M., van der Hoek, A.: Software Designers in Action: A Human-Centric Look at Design Work. CRC Press, Boca Raton (2013)
14. Poort, E.R., van Vliet, H.: Architecting as a risk- and cost management discipline. In: 9th Working IEEE/IFIP Conference on Software Architecture, WICSA 2011, pp. 2–11. IEEE Computer Society (2011)
15. Razavian, M., Tang, A., Capilla, R., Lago, P.: In two minds: how reflections influence software design thinking. J. Softw. Evol. Process **6**, 394–426 (2016)
16. Restrepo, J., Christiaans, H.: Problem structuring, information access in design. J. Des. Res. **4**, 1551–1569 (2004)
17. Rittel, H.W.J., Webber, M.M.: Dilemnas in a general theory of planning. Policy Sci. **4**, 155–168 (1973)
18. Schön, D.A.: The Reflective Practitioner: How Professionals Think in Action. Basic Books, New York (1983)
19. Simon, H.A.: The structure of ill structured problems. Artif. Intell. **4**, 181–201 (1973)

20. Simon, H.A.: Rationality as process and as product of a thought. Am. Econ. Rev. **68**, 1–16 (1978)
21. Stacy, W., MacMillan, J.: Cognitive bias in software engineering. Commun. ACM. **38**, 57–63 (1995)
22. Stanovich, K.E.: Distinguishing the reflective, algorithmic, autonomous minds: is it time for a tri-process theory? In: Two Minds: Dual Processes and Beyond, pp. 55–88. Oxford University Press (2009)
23. Tang, A.: Software designers, are you biased? In: 6th International Workshop on SHAring and Reusing Architectural Knowledge, pp. 1–8. ACM, New York (2011)
24. Tang, A., Babar, M.A., Gorton, I., Han, J.: A survey of architecture design rationale. J. Syst. Softw. **79**, 1792–1804 (2006)
25. Tang, A., Lago, P.: Notes on design reasoning techniques. SUTICT-TR.01, Swimburne University of Technology (2010)
26. Tang, A., Lau, M.F.: Software architecture review by association. J. Syst. Softw. **88**, 87–101 (2014)
27. Tang, A., Tran, M.H., Han, J., Vliet, H.: Design reasoning improves software design quality. In: Becker, S., Plasil, F., Reussner, R. (eds.) QoSA 2008. LNCS, vol. 5281, pp. 28–42. Springer, Heidelberg (2008). doi:10.1007/978-3-540-87879-7_2
28. Tang, A., Vliet, H.: Software architecture design reasoning. In: Babar, M.A., Dingsøyr, T., Lago, P., van Vliet, H. (eds.) Software Architecture Knowledge Management, pp. 155–174. Springer, Heidelberg (2009)
29. Tang, A., Vliet, H.: Software designers satisfice. In: Weyns, D., Mirandola, R., Crnkovic, I. (eds.) ECSA 2015. LNCS, vol. 9278, pp. 105–120. Springer, Heidelberg (2015). doi:10.1007/978-3-319-23727-5_9
30. UCI: Studying professional software design. http://www.ics.uci.edu/design-workshop/
31. Zannier, C., Chiasson, M., Maurer, F.: A model of design decision making based on empirical results of interviews with software designers. Inf. Softw. Technol. **49**, 637–653 (2007)

A Long Way to Quality-Driven Pattern-Based Architecting

Gianantonio Me[1,2](✉), Coral Calero[1], and Patricia Lago[2]

[1] Universidad de Castilla La Mancha, Ciudad Real, Spain
{gianantonio.me,coral.calero}@uclm.es, g.me@vu.nl
[2] Vrije Universiteit Amsterdam, Amsterdam, The Netherlands
p.lago@vu.nl

Abstract. The relation between architectural patterns (or styles) and quality attributes has been widely addressed in the literature. However, the knowledge is fragmented over a wide range of heterogeneous studies. Our aim is to build a systematic body of knowledge to support architectural decision-making and design. If available, this knowledge helps architects in addressing quality requirements consciously and more explicitly, i.e. in *quality-driven pattern-based design.* In order to build that body of knowledge we carried out a systematic literature review. We identified 99 primary studies for the analysis. The resulting data shows a wide spectrum of approaches encompassing patterns and quality attributes. In this study we (1a) present in which way patterns and quality attributes interact and (1b) provide quantitative data on the frequency of appearance for both patterns and quality attributes; (2) give an overview of the approaches we elicited from the analysis; and (3) provide our insights regarding a specific challenge (combination of patterns). Our analysis is a first step toward a theory on the architectural patterns and quality attribute interaction.

Keywords: Architectural patterns · Architectural styles · Quality attributes · Decision making

1 Introduction

Architectural patterns and styles are recurrent solutions to common problems. Among others, they include knowledge on quality attributes (QAs) [1]. For the sake of simplicity, throughout the paper we use the term architectural pattern to mean both. In fact, according to Buschmann [2], patterns and styles are very similar as every architectural style can be described as an architectural pattern. However, some differences can be considered as essential, the most relevant being that patterns are more problem oriented, while styles do not refer to a specific design situation [2]. Accordingly, in our analysis we make explicit if and why authors adopt the term pattern or style. We observe a similar problem with the definition of quality attribute. Again, for the sake of simplicity, we adopt the term quality attribute. In our analysis, if necessary, we make explicit the term

© Springer International Publishing AG 2016
B. Tekinerdogan et al. (Eds.): ECSA 2016, LNCS 9839, pp. 39–54, 2016.
DOI: 10.1007/978-3-319-48992-6_3

used by the authors such as non-functional requirement, quality property, quality dimension, etc. Architectural patterns include knowledge on quality attributes. Architects rely on that knowledge for effective architectural decision-making. Increasing that knowledge means increasing the role of patterns in satisfying quality attributes. The aim of this paper is to present our results of the Systematic Literature Review (SLR), hence providing some conceptual building blocks on patterns and quality attributes interaction. Those conceptual blocks can be used for building a systematic theoretical framework. We also aim to encourage the discussion in the software architecture community.

Paper Overview: Section 2 offers a description of background knowledge and related work. Section 3 presents our study design. Section 4 presents our analysis and results, while Sect. 5 includes threats to validity. Section 6 summarizes conclusions and future work.

2   Background and Related Work

In the literature there are several works that, to various degrees, address the interaction between architectural patterns and quality attributes. Many have been included as primary studies of our SLR. In this section, we focus on two additional works, Buschmann [2] and Harrison and Avgeriou [1], holistic in nature and hence providing an excellent starting point for our SLR. Buschmann [2] is the cornerstone of architectural patterns and many later publications refer to its taxonomy of patterns. The approach is holistic. Firstly, software architecture design is considered more than a simple activity with a limited scope. Software architecture design has system-wide goals. Secondly, it aims at providing systematic support beyond that of a single pattern. As the title of the book suggests, patterns are framed in a *system of patterns*. For our purpose, we have considered the work of Buschmann in a pattern-quality interaction perspective, i.e. with a special focus on such interaction. In particular, the relationship between patterns and quality is based on a quality model that includes Changeability, Interoperability, Reliability, Efficiency, Testability and Reusability. Several quality attributes (called in [2] non-functional properties) present one or more sub-characteristics. Each quality attribute has been exemplified by means of scenarios. Some good fitting solutions (pattern-quality attribute) are given, for instance an example of fitting solution for changeability is the pattern Reflection. Trade-off and prioritization of quality properties have been mentioned. Non-functional properties can be classified according to the architectural techniques for their achievement. Patterns provide a support for building high-quality software system in a systematic way given some quality properties and functionalities. According to [2], the final assessment of quality properties in software architecture is still a difficult task. Indeed, although quality properties are crucial for the design, we still have to solve problems in their measurement. The lack of quantification makes the choice mostly based on the intuition and knowledge of software architects [2]. Similar to [2], Harrison and Avgeriou [1] holistically cover architectural patterns; differently, they propose to extend patterns with the knowledge about their impact on quality attributes: by knowing the consequences of adopting a certain pattern, architects would ideally make better-informed design decisions. The authors provide some evidence regarding the impact of patterns and quality attributes. Their ultimate goal is to organize a body of knowledge in a way that is accessible and informative for architects, in order to support an architectural decision making process. This goal is shared with ours. There are other studies that aimed to address the interaction between architectural patterns and quality attributes. For instance, Babar [3] focuses on the synergy between architectural patterns, quality attributes and scenarios. He provided a framework for collecting and representing the knowledge of that synergic interaction. His motivation is the lack of systematic knowledge about that synergy that might support software design. Babar proposes a valuable template, but he does not go beyond a methodological proposal, without bringing experimental evidence. In [4], Zdun focuses on pattern combinations. He proposes a pattern language grammar in order to keep track of patterns relationships. The formalized pattern language grammar has been considered also with effects to quality goals. This work fits with our purpose. However the level of analysis is on design patterns; as such it does not qualify as primary study for our SLR, because, we decided to explore only the highest level of abstraction (patterns and styles) excluding design and idiom level. This decision was necessary to scope the amount of information to a manageable size within a single SLR. The rationale is the amount of information would have been difficult to manage in a single systematic review study. Weyns [5] explains how patterns capture expert knowledge in the domain of multi-agent systems. The knowledge accumulated over years of practice and research has been represented by a pattern language. The interaction between patterns and quality attributes appear in a primary representation that includes quality attributes, constituent elements, responsibilities, interfaces explaining how elements have been used together and design rationale behind the architectural choices. Finally, Costa et al. [6] built a collection of scenarios useful for a particular architectural style evaluation. Such methodological approach can be extended to other patterns, or pattern combinations (system of patterns).

3 Study Design

Our systematic literature review has been carried out according to Kitchenham guidelines [7]. Few studies focus exactly on the interaction between quality attributes and architectural patterns. Therefore, we have decided to carry out this SLR with the motivation of detecting the widespread knowledge and build it in a systematic theoretical framework.

3.1 Research Questions

It is widely known that architectural patterns and quality attributes are not independent by implying (explicitly or not) significant interactions [8]. Such interactions can be represented as reusable knowledge elements. In this line of reasoning, for instance, Layered architecture presents a trade-off between efficiency and maintainability, where the second quality attribute is better fit [1]. Architects in search for assuring a high maintainability for their software architecture might take decisions on the basis of the knowledge reported above, and hence adopt a Layered pattern, but sacrificing something regarding efficiency. In this light, the knowledge on the interaction between patterns and quality attributes is a foundation for architectural decisions. Therefore, this study aims to assess if that type of reusable knowledge elements is widely accepted in the literature or if there are substantial differences in evaluating which pattern is more adequate for achieving specific quality attributes (QAs). Accordingly, we will address the following research questions (RQs):

- RQ1: What types of relations exist between architectural patterns and quality attributes?
  This research question has two goals. Firstly, it aims to explore the characterization of those relations (e.g., impact, dependencies, interaction, synergies or quantitative). Secondly, the type of relations can be evaluated and classified according to frequency of various patterns and QAs and related combinations.
- RQ2: What types of approaches address the relations between architectural patterns and quality attributes?
  This research question aims to understand and classify the various methodologies, frameworks, models, etc. available in the literature that addresses the relation between pattern and QAs.
- RQ3: What are the most important challenges for a quality-driven and pattern-based design?
  This research question aims to identify the most important challenges for building a theory of pattern-QAs interaction. We consider challenges as specific issues that emerge from the primary studies and for which better/explicit knowledge can help in addressing them better.

3.2   Data Sources and Search Strategy

Piloting the review protocol is essential [9]. We identified a set of 12 pilot studies. This set includes key studies we knew upfront as relevant and expected to find back in our systematic search, and at least one study on every single architectural pattern considered for the analysis. In this way it is possible to assess if the generic term architectural pattern can catch specific patterns (for instance *Layered*). Firstly, we have been collecting keywords for shaping the search string from the following studies. In case authors keywords were not available, we selected keywords by reading the abstract. Secondly, the search string has been tested on Google Scholar and other customary search engines in order to verify if the pilot studies would be detected. Our final search string is: (*architecture pattern* **OR** *architectural pattern* **OR** *architecture style* **OR** *architectural style*) **AND** (*quality attribute* **OR** *quality characteristic* **OR** *quality properties* **OR** *non-functional requirement* **OR** *no functional requirement* **OR** *quality dimension*).

3.3   Study Selection

We run the search string on the following search engines with the corresponding results: ACM Digital Library (422 studies); IEEE eXplore (129); SpringerLink (1395); Scopus (499); Web of Science (79) and Science Direct (418). The total was of 2942 hits collected in November 2015, covering a time span of 26 years (1990–2015). Subsequently we merged the hits in a reference manager database (Mendeley). SpringerLink has been analyzed on a spreadsheet due to some technical difficulties in importing references to Mendeley. The primary-study selection was organized in four rounds (Round 1: based on title and abstract; Round 2: skimming reading; Round 3: Full reading; Round 4: Snowballing. One level of Snowballing has been performed on the citations of the included studies). The Round 1 and Round 2 were aimed to clear the set of studies from out of scope works and duplicates. We started the Round 3 with 283 studies and we applied the Inclusion and Exclusion criteria. Inclusion and exclusion used the following criteria. Inclusion criteria are: (1) A study that offers knowledge elements on the interaction between at least one architectural patterns and at least one quality attribute; (2) A study that is carried out by either academics or practitioners; (3) A study that is written in English. Exclusion criteria are: (1) A study that does not provide directly or indirectly any description for the quality attributes taken into account; (2) A study that does not provide directly or indirectly any description for the architectural patterns taken into account; (3) A study that does not focus on architectural patterns of applications; (4) A study that focuses on pre-pattern or anti-patterns; (5) A study that the analysis is at design or idiom level. We focus only on a higher level of abstraction (patterns/styles) and (6) A study that is not available, or is a book or a workshop note. After applying inclusion and exclusion criteria through a skimming reading we had back 160 studies that where reduced to 88 after a whole reading. By snowballing we retrieved other additional 11 studies. So doing, study selection resulted in a total of 99 primary studies.

4   Analysis and Results

We extracted the data from all the primary studies by using a structural coding procedure. Structural coding captures a conceptual area of the research interest [10]. All the knowledge has been classified in four main categories: Decision-Making, Patterns, Quality Attributes and Patterns-QAs Interaction. We decided for four categories according to our previous work [11]. Subsequently, data analysis has been reported with a descriptive approach. Due to the extensive amount of knowledge gathered, for the focused scope of promoting the discussion in the community, in this work we present our most interesting preliminary results.

4.1   RQ1: On Pattern-QA Relations

As previously stated, RQ1 has a dual goal. First we want to uncover how the various studies characterize the interaction between patterns and quality attributes.

That interaction remains mostly undefined. Other main important characterizations are indirect by means of tactics and according to quantitative measures. In the first case the interaction between patterns and quality is supported by tactics. In the second case quantitative models shape the interaction according to specific QAs measures. Table 1 shows the summary of this analysis part. In particular, it shows the various ways of addressing the interaction between quality attributes and patterns.

Table 1. Interaction patterns-quality attributes

Number of studies per type	Type of interaction described	Total number of studies
35	Undetermined	35
12	Tactics	12
8	Measurability	8
7	Fitness & satisfaction	7
6	Interaction as knowledge	5
5	Trade-offs	5
3	Scenario-based; characterization of patterns with a QA	6
2	Functional-Non-functional; Markov Model; Views and Viewpoint; Materialization; Technical; Real world requirements (QAs)-Systems specification (Patterns);	12
1	Responsibilities; Appropriateness; Capturing; Actors and dependencies; Relationship; Representability; Softgoals; Problem space-Solution space interaction; Transformation	9

The highest frequency is the category Undetermined. In this case it was not possible to identify one specific type of interaction. Category Tactics provides an intermediate mechanism between quality attributes and patterns. Category Trade-offs focuses on specific techniques for comparing and assessing several quality attributes at the same time. Different types of interactions work at different levels of abstraction. For instance: while Scenario-based provides the (external) context for analyzing the interaction, Measurability addresses the (internal) quantification of such interaction. In other words, we may have types of interactions relating to the external context and others capturing the internal functioning of a certain system. A type of interaction pursues another goal: assessing the quantitative value of a quality attribute inside a specific system solution (pattern). The second goal of RQ1 is to single out how patterns and quality attributes interact as witnessed in the primary studies. Firstly we have

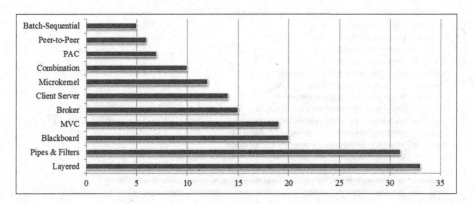

Fig. 1. Most frequent architectural patterns

gathered the frequency of both patterns and attributes. Figure 1 shows the patterns identified in the primary studies with the related frequency of appearance.

According to Fig. 1, the most frequent patterns (with a frequency of five or higher) are those 10 enlisted patterns plus a set of pattern combinations (see Combination). In fact, there are 44 additional patterns (not displayed in the figure) with frequency between 1 to 5. Among these less frequent patterns, multi-agent system patterns show a good potential for further research. Our online protocol provides the frequency table for the full list of patterns.

We performed a similar analysis about the found quality attributes, which provide a similar picture with an extended landscape of exotic quality attributes. In this case we have found 43 quality attributes (plus a residual category of not recognizable QAs) with a frequency mean of 15,6. Figure 2 includes only the quality attributes that appear at least 13 times in our primary studies. Like for patterns, the less frequent QAs are available in the online protocol[1]. Finally we have combined the two data pools (Patterns-QAs Frequency, see Table 2). In particular, we identified 711 couples pattern-QA. Of these, 422 (62 %) are couples composed by one of the most frequent patterns and one of the most frequent quality attributes. Interestingly, 166 couples out of 711 (23 %) are composed by one of the most frequent quality attributes listed in Fig. 2. Other combinations are much lower, for instance the couple "most frequent patterns-less frequent quality attributes" appears just in 62 cases (9 %) and expectably the couple "less frequent patterns-less frequent QAs" appears in even less cases (41, corresponding to 6 %).

Regarding the frequency of patterns and QAs, we observe that the set of most frequent quality attributes covers 85 % of all identified couples pattern-QA. Only 70 % of the identified couples are composed by a pattern belonging to the set of most frequent patterns. This might suggest that the set of most frequent QAs is mature enough to be considered as a backbone for an architectural quality model. On the other hand, patterns as a category is to be considered as

---

[1] www.s2group.cs.vu.nl/gianantonio-me/.

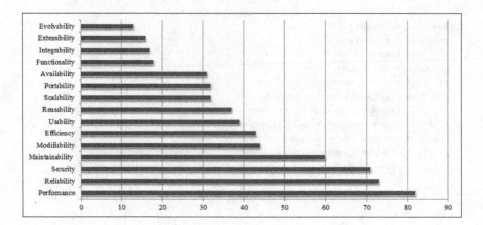

Fig. 2. Most frequent quality attributes

Table 2. Patterns and quality attributes combinations

Combinations	Most frequent QAs	Less frequent QAs	Total
Most frequent patterns	62 %	9 %	71 %
Less frequent patterns	23 %	6 %	29 %
Total	85 %	15 %	100 %

potentially unlimited: combinations of patterns or new patterns might be continuously created. This poses a challenge on how to capture the heterogeneity in a continuum, and represent it in a body of reusable knowledge.

4.2 What Do We Learn? (Answer to RQ1)

We identified several ways of characterizing patterns and QAs interaction. The highest frequency belongs to an Undetermined interaction, which means that the elements provided by the study were not clear or sufficient for defining the patterns-QAs interaction. One important mechanism for addressing quality in patterns, however, is the architectural tactic. Other studies focus on how to measure the interaction between patterns and quality, by offering quantitative knowledge for supporting architectural decisions. We also identified both a set of most frequent patterns and QAs. We discovered that most quality attributes frequent cover the large part of the couples pattern-QA we identified in the literature.

4.3 RQ2: On Classifying the Approaches

Table 3 provides an overview of the types of approaches identified in the 99 primary studies. We clustered the different approaches according to the characterizing elements for each study. For instance, Decision-Making approaches highlight the role of architectural decisions. Tactics might belong to the Decision-Making category because they highlight a specific mechanism for design decision-making. Studies that focus on quantitative modeling for prediction aim to support architectural decisions by measuring the QAs. Therefore, overlaps of approaches are very likely to arise.

Table 3. Types of approaches

Type of approach	Nr. of studies	Focus on
Decision-making	22	How to support architectural decisions: e.g. hierarchies of QAs for prioritizing decisions
Quantitative-prediction and/or formal model	16	Support of architectural choice with quantitative assessment of QAs Design Method 8 Holistic method, focus on the process of designing systems architecture
Knowledge based	8	Reusable and well-known knowledge on patterns and QAs
Evaluation method	7	The focus is on the process of evaluating architecture Pattern QA characterization 7 Patterns are characterized by a single QA (e.g. Security Broker)
Ontology-pattern language topology-taxonomy	6	The focus is on the description and definition both of patterns, or quality attributes (Taxonomies)
Specific domain method	6	Those studies focus on a specific context, e.g. multi-agent system
Views-scenario based	6	Those studies extract information on patterns-QAs interaction using scenarios as particular instance of the system
Quality driven method	5	Those studies consider the entire process of architecting as achieving quality
Business process-real world oriented	3	Those studies explore how patterns and QAs can effectively address specific real world challenges
Functionality oriented	3	Those studies explore the link between functionalities and quality
Technical method	2	Those studies explore the patterns and QAs in terms of how to capture technological complexity

Basically, each type of approach represents an element potentially common to other approaches. For instance, studies that focus on Business Processes and/or

Real World needs shed light on an intrinsic goal of the other methodologies, namely to design systems that match business processes needs.

We have identified 13 different types of approaches. However, overlaps are very common (e.g. knowledge-based and decision-making). A reason for this overlap is that the approaches are at different levels of abstraction. For instance, scenario-based approaches provide the space were patterns and quality will be assessed; functionality-oriented approaches zoom in how the considered pattern both satisfies functionality and quality, zooming in implementation level. Overall we noticed that Decision-Making elements are widespread in all the identified approaches. Many studies have the goal to provide support for decisions, so decision-making can be considered as a cross-characterizing element for all the methodologies. In the same line of reasoning, knowledge-based approaches present a body of reusable knowledge for adopting decisions. In general, we observe redundant elements proposed as new/different methodologies. Table 4 proposes a possible key of reading the holistic relation we uncovered in the 13 approaches we identified.

Table 4. Unified framework for pattern-quality based architecting

Type of approach	Meaning	
Decision-making	Goal	
(Pattern) quality driven method	Rationale	
Design method	General framework	
Evaluation method	General framework	
Specific domain method	Context	
Business process-real world oriented	Context	
Knowledge-based		Support for decision-making
Knowledge-based contents	Quantitative-prediction formal model	Architectural knowledge element
	Pattern QA characterization	Architectural knowledge element
	Ontology-pattern language topology-taxonomy	Architecture description technique
	Views- scenario based	Architectural evaluation technique
	Functionality oriented	Architectural knowledge element
	Technical method	Architectural implementation technique

The essence of architecting is taking decisions. Therefore, (effective) *Decision-Making* represents the main goal of the overall process of architecting. From top to bottom:

- We aim to a unified framework where the rationale behind *Decision-Making* is quality- and pattern-driven. There are two ways to organize decision-making in a methodological framework: evaluation and design method.
- *Evaluation methods* focus on assessing how and how much system architectures achieve quality.
- *Design methods* focus on the process of architecting, defining the system architecture.
- Those methodological frameworks are intertwined. Architecting is contextualized into a specific domain (see Specific Domain Method), a Business Process or in general into a Real World need.
- Concrete support for decision-making is provided by reusable knowledge. Knowledge-based approaches encompass several knowledge elements or techniques. They can be used in combination or in isolation, according to the needs of the system in focus. Knowledge-based contents does consider the type of interaction between patterns and quality attributes, but mostly implicitly.

4.4   What Do We Learn? (Answer to RQ2)

We identified 13 main types of approaches. Each of them is characterized by a specific element. We observed multiple overlaps of approaches. For instance, Decision-Making aspects can be identified in all other approaches, although they focus on other specific elements. Our proposal, rather than invent a new approach, is to unify in a holistic framework all the essential and shared elements widespread in several, apparently different, approaches. We offered a prototype of that holistic approach, by isolating and highlighting the characterizing aspects of each single approach.

4.5   RQ 3-Challenges: Combination of patterns

In looking for the interaction between architectural patterns and QAs it emerged that a quality-driven combination of architectural patterns is among the most important challenges in developing modern software systems. We zoomed into the effect that combining multiple patterns may have on the overall quality delivered by the combination. I.e., while individually two patterns may contribute (or hinder) a certain quality attribute, their combination might have a positive (or conflicting) impact on the same. "Combination of patterns" can find a place in our Unified Framework among the Knowledge-based elements. Interestingly enough, among our 99 primary studies, we found only 8 papers mentioning such a combination, as described in the following.

Background Works on Combination of Patterns. Study [1] considers the research on combination of patterns as a great challenge, considering the lack of knowledge we have on the interaction between combinations of architectural patterns and quality attributes. In [2] combinations of patterns are considered crucial: patterns do not operate in isolation. However, according to [2] a combination of patterns is not software architecture yet because more refinements are required. Finally in [4] the focus is also on pattern combinations. In order to keep track of patterns relationship a pattern language grammar has been proposed. The formalized pattern language grammar has been considered also with effects to quality goals. Relationships between patterns are also in [12]. However those last two studies work on design pattern level of abstraction that, at least for the moment, is out of scope for our research.

Examples of Combinations of Patterns. The best source of information for combination of patterns is [13]. The study offers a wide list of combinations of patterns and some quantitative data. Table 5 summarizes the knowledge on the interaction between combination of architectural patterns and quality attributes.

4.6   Combination of Patterns

Lee et al. [14] present a method for evaluating quality attributes. This uses conjoint analysis in order to quantify QAs preferences. It can be used in combination with the ATAM. In this study the decision of a Layered+ MVC architecture is the result of a composition of customers needs. The approach of [14] suggests a conceptual building block where combinations of patterns reflect the result of negotiation between stakeholders.

In [15] the authors provided a knowledge base for architecting wireless services. They propose a knowledge-based model with a service taxonomy, a reference architecture and basic services as backbone. Regarding combinations of patterns, in [15] the focus is on service sub-domain. Combinations of patterns are solutions to achieve quality attributes in specific sub-domain. They are applied to basic services and shape the reference architecture. The approach of [15] selects the Layered as a main pattern for building the software architecture. The rationale is in the type of quality attributes supported and the popularity among engineers. This study offers the conceptual idea that a combination of patterns can be classified according the main pattern.

In [17] the authors are aiming for an architectural pattern language for embedded middleware systems. The core architecture is a Layered+ Microkernel.

In [18] the authors proposed a framework for early estimation of energy consumption, according to particular architectural styles, in distributed software systems. In their experiment styles have been tested in isolation. Further, one combination of them has been assessed regarding energy consumption. The combination of patterns (called in the study hybrids) showed less energy consumption and overhead with the same amount of data shared respect to each single pattern. In that case the impact on the quality attributes is not merely addictive; indeed combining patterns reduces the energy consumption of a single pattern.

In [16] a full model for architectural patterns and tactics interaction has been analyzed, with the aim of linking strategic decisions (decisions that affect the

Table 5. Pattern combinations and quality attributes

N	Combination of patterns	Quality Attributes	Study	Approach and/or type of interaction according to Tables 1 and 2
1	Layered, model view controller	Performance, usability, availability, modifiability and security	[14]	Measurability; quantitative-prediction formal model
2	Model view controller, broker	Modifiability, interoperability and reusability	[15]	Interaction as knowledge; knowledge based
3	Layered, blackboard, presentation abstraction control	Interoperability, integrability, portability and modifiability	[15]	Idem
4	Pipes & Filters, presentation abstraction control	Simplicity and integrability	[15]	Idem
5	Broker, repository, layered	Performance (capacity, response time), reliability (availability and fault tolerance)	[16]	Tactics; decision-making
6	Layered+, microkernel	A wide set of QAs	[17]	Measurability; quantitative-prediction formal model
7	Public subscribe, client server	Energy efficiency	[18]	Undetermined; quantitative-prediction-formal model
8	Pipes & Filters, model view controller	Flexibility	[19]	Undetermined; evaluation method
9	Reflective blackboard	Performance, maintainability, manageability and reusability	[20]	Undetermined; specific domain

overall architecture) and tactics (clear-cut implementations that achieve specifically a quality attribute). Regarding combination of patterns the study shows a Broker combined with a Repository and a Layered. In the case study the overall level of performance has been augmented by the introduction of a new component. The new component allows Broker to bypass some Layers and this increases performance. Tactics for Fault Tolerance can be implemented in the Broker, without changing the overall structure. The valuable knowledge element from this study is that tactics can support pattern combinations.

Study [19] focuses on a specific software architecture style for applications performing distributed, asynchronous parallel processing of generic data streams. The combination of patterns here presented highlights data stream and user interactivity. This leads to increased flexibility. Unfortunately, the study does not provide enough information to support generalization about combinations of patterns. Finally, study [20] shows an interesting motivation for combination of patterns. The analysis is framed in the context of multi-agent systems. The combination of Reflection pattern and Blackboard allows effective separation of concerns, contributing to high manageability of several agents.

4.7   What Do We Learn? (Answer to RQ3)

In spite of its systematic nature, the SLR does not provide enough knowledge for building either univocal types of interactions between given couples pattern-QA or pattern combinations. Usually, if a given pattern addresses a particular QA positively that interaction would be replicated in the combination. Generally all the combinations reported above address QAs in the same way of each single pattern. That means, for instance, that a Layered pattern addresses positively Portability (according to [1]) also when Layered is combined with other patterns. Similarly, combination 3 [15] supports portability as well. The only clear (reported) exception regards Energy Efficiency, for which the QA measure seems better if the patterns are combined instead of implemented in isolation. More evidence is needed to confirm this result [21]. Finally, an interesting and promising research path is to consider combinations of patterns as specific design-solutions for real world problems.

5   Threats to Validity

As customary, for the analysis we followed a SLR protocol. However, there are potential threats to validity. Firstly, the search string might not catch all the relevant papers available. We mitigated this risk by adding a snowballing phase, checking references of primary studies. Secondly, the process of inclusion and exclusion criteria applications has been conducted by only one researcher. Thirdly, there are almost no studies that explicitly address the focus of our analysis. This means that the knowledge is widespread in a heterogeneous spectrum of studies. Relevant information might be hidden in studies not detectable by a sound search string. To cope with this issue we performed a pilot study for testing and refining the search string. Finally, the threats to validity for the analysis results and conclusions might be considered as a problem of generalization. Since we are in search of a theory, our results should be generalizable to different contexts. Our strategy mitigation for this issue has been the adoption of a coding procedure. However, the context specifications still represent an important challenge for this research work.

6   Conclusion

We performed a systematic literature review in order to shed light on the interaction between architectural patterns and quality attributes. We answered three
main research questions. For the first research question we identified the ways
of addressing the interaction between quality attributes and patterns. We discovered that relation remains mainly unexplored, with a high number of studies
showing an Undetermined type of interaction. We also analyzed the frequency
of recurring patterns and recurring quality attributes. The main finding was
that the set of most frequent quality attributes covers 85 % of the identified
couples patterns-QAs. We can conclude that the set of quality attributes we
found can act as backbone for a quality model. The second research question
was answered by identifying different types of approaches for addressing quality
through architectural patterns. We observed redundancy and overlapping, so we
described basic elements for a pattern-quality driven architecting and we unified
them in a holistic framework. The third research question, about challenges in
quality and patterns interaction, allowed us to explore combinations of patterns.
We realized that we still lack extended knowledge on this specific challenge in
particular. Overall, the knowledge gathered so far puts the basis for a further
development of a theory for pattern-quality driven architecting. However, in spite
of architectural patterns and quality attributes being both widely explored and
practiced, there is still a lot to learn on their interaction—a long way to go.

Acknowledgement. This work is part of the GINSENG (TIN2015-70259-C2-1-R)
project (funded by the Spanish Ministerio de Economía y Competitividad and by
FEDER-Fondo Europeo de Desarrollo Regional) and by VILMA (PEII11-0316-2878)
project (funded by the Junta de Comunidades de Castilla-La Mancha and by FEDER-
Fondo Europeo de Desarrollo Regional).

References

1. Harrison, N.B., Avgeriou, P.: Leveraging architecture patterns to satisfy quality attributes. In: Oquendo, F. (ed.) ECSA 2007. LNCS, vol. 4758, pp. 263–270.
   Springer, Heidelberg (2007). doi:10.1007/978-3-540-75132-8_21
2. Buschmann, F., Meunier, R., Rohnert, H., Sommerlad, P., Stal, M.: A System of
   Patterns. Wiley, Hoboken (1996)
3. Babar, M.A.: Scenarios, quality attributes, and patterns: capturing and using their
   synergistic relationships for product line architectures. In: Software Engineering
   Conference, 11th Asia-Pacific, pp. 574–578. IEEE (2004)
4. Zdun, U.: Systematic pattern selection using pattern language grammars and
   design space analysis. Softw.-Pract. Exp. **37**(9), 983 (2007)
5. Weyns, D.: Capturing expertise in multi-agent system engineering with architectural patterns. In: Weyns, D. (ed.) Architecture-Based Design of Multi-Agent Systems, pp. 27–53. Springer, Heidelberg (2010)
6. Costa, B., Pires, P.F., Delicato, F.C., Merson, P.: Evaluating rest architectures?
   Approach, tooling and guidelines. J. Syst. Softw. **112**, 156–180 (2016)

7. Kitchenham, B., Charters, S.: Procedures for performing systematic literature reviews in software engineering. Keele University & Durham University, UK (2007)
8. Harrison, N.B., Avgeriou, P.: How do architecture patterns and tactics interact? A model and annotation. J. Syst. Softw. **83**(10), 1735–1758 (2010)
9. Brereton, P., Kitchenham, B.A., Budgen, D., Turner, M., Khalil, M.: Lessons from applying the systematic literature review process within the software engineering domain. J. Syst. Softw. **80**(4), 571–583 (2007)
10. Saldaña, J.: The Coding Manual for Qualitative Researchers. Sage, Thousand Oaks (2015)
11. Me, G., Calero, C., Lago, P.: Architectural patterns and quality attribute interaction. In: Working IEEE/IFIP Conference on Qualitative Reasoning about Software Architectures (QRASA), WICSA 2016. IEEE (2016)
12. Zimmer, W., et al.: Relationships between design patterns. Pattern Lang. Prog. Des. **57** (1995)
13. Harrison, N.B., Avgeriou, P.: Analysis of architecture pattern usage in legacy system architecture documentation. In: Seventh Working IEEE/IFIP Conference on Software Architecture, WICSA 2008, pp. 147–156. IEEE (2008)
14. Lee, K.C., Choi, H.-J., Lee, D.H., Kang, S.: Quantitative measurement of quality attribute preferences using conjoint analysis. In: Gilroy, S.W., Harrison, M.D. (eds.) DSV-IS 2005. LNCS, vol. 3941, pp. 213–224. Springer, Heidelberg (2006). doi:10.1007/11752707_18
15. Niemela, E., Kalaoja, J., Lago, P.: Toward an architectural knowledge base for wireless service engineering. IEEE Trans. Softw. Eng. **31**(5), 361–379 (2005)
16. Harrison, N.B., Avgeriou, P., Zdun, U.: On the impact of fault tolerance tactics on architecture patterns. In: Proceedings of the 2nd International Workshop on Software Engineering for Resilient Systems, pp. 12–21. ACM (2010)
17. Wu, C., Chang, E.: Comparison of web service architectures based on architecture quality properties. In: 2005 3rd IEEE International Conference on Industrial Informatics, INDIN 2005, pp. 746–755. IEEE (2005)
18. Seo, C., Edwards, G., Malek, S., Medvidovic, N.: A framework for estimating the impact of a distributed software system's architectural style on its energy consumption. In: Seventh Working IEEE/IFIP Conference on Software Architecture, WICSA 2008, pp. 277–280. IEEE (2008)
19. Francois, A.R.: A hybrid architectural style for distributed parallel processing of generic data streams. In: Proceedings of the 26th International Conference on Software Engineering, pp. 367–376. IEEE Computer Society (2004)
20. Silva, O., Garcia, A., Lucena, C.: The reflective blackboard pattern: architecting large multi-agent systems. In: Garcia, A., Lucena, C., Zambonelli, F., Omicini, A., Castro, J. (eds.) SELMAS 2002. LNCS, vol. 2603, pp. 73–93. Springer, Heidelberg (2003). doi:10.1007/3-540-35828-5_5
21. Procaccianti, G., Lago, P., Vetrò, A., Fernández, D.M., Wieringa, R.: The green lab: experimentation in software energy efficiency. In: Proceedings of the 37th International Conference on Software Engineering-Volume 2, pp. 941–942. IEEE Press (2015)

Diversifying Software Architecture for Sustainability: A Value-Based Perspective

Dalia Sobhy[1,2]([✉]), Rami Bahsoon[1], Leandro Minku[3], and Rick Kazman[4]

[1] University of Birmingham, Birmingham, UK
{dms446,r.bahsoon}@cs.bham.ac.uk
[2] Arab Academy, Alexandria, Egypt
dalia.sobhi@aast.edu
[3] School of Computer Science, University of Leicester, Leicester, UK
leandro.minku@leicester.ac.uk
[4] SEI/CMU, University of Hawaii, Honolulu, USA
kazman@hawaii.edu

Abstract. We use real options theory to evaluate the options of diversity in design by looking at the trade-offs between the cost and long-term value of different architectural strategies under uncertainty, given a set of scenarios of interest. As part of our approach, we extend one of the widely used architecture trade-offs analysis methods (Cost-Benefit Analysis Method) to incorporate diversification. We also use a case study to demonstrate how decision makers and architects can reason about sustainability using a diversified cost-value approach.

1 Introduction

Design Diversity is *"the approach in which the hardware and software elements that are to be used for multiple computations are not copies, but are independently designed to meet a system's requirements"* [2]. It is the generation of functionally equivalent versions of a software system, but implemented differently [2]. Design diversification has the potential to mitigate risks and improve the dependability in design for situations exhibiting uncertainty in operation, usage, etc. On the other hand, architecture sustainability is *"the architecture's capacity to endure different types of change through efficient maintenance and orderly evolution over its entire life cycle"* [1]. In this paper, we argue that we can link diversity and sustainability from a value-based perspective. The link can summarize the success of engineering and evolution decisions in meeting the current and future changes to users, system, and environment requirements. We are concerned with how to employ diversity in the architecture as a mechanism to better support future changes. This requires rethinking architecture design decisions by looking at their link to long-term value creation in enabling change and reducing their debt, etc. The focus is on how we can sustain the architecture, which requires treatment for not only short-term costs and benefits but also for long-term ones and their likely debts. As the valuation shall take into consideration uncertainty, we appeal to options thinking [7] to answer the above question. Our novel contribution is an architecture-centric method, which builds

© Springer International Publishing AG 2016
B. Tekinerdogan et al. (Eds.): ECSA 2016, LNCS 9839, pp. 55–63, 2016.
DOI: 10.1007/978-3-319-48992-6_4

on Cost-Benefit Analysis Method (CBAM) [5] and options theory [7] to evaluate and reason about how architectural diversification decisions can be employed and their augmentation to long-term value creation. In particular, the approach uses real options analysis [7] to quantify the long-term contribution of these decisions to value and determine how that value can assist decision-makers and software architects in reasoning about sustainability in software. Our exploratory case analysis is based on provisional data gathered from the GridStix prototype, deployed at River Ribble in the North West England [4].

2 Background

CBAM: A Cost-Benefit Analysis Method that intends to develop an economic model of software and systems that helps a designer select amongst different architectural options at design-time [5]. CBAM extends ATAM with explicit focus on the costs and benefits of the architecture decisions in meeting scenarios related to quality attributes (QA) as illustrated in Fig. 1. Interested reader can refer to [5] for more details.

Real Options Analysis: We view architecting for sustainability through diversification as an option problem. Real options analysis is well-known paradigm used for strategic decision-making [7]. It emphasizes the value-generating power of flexibility under uncertainty. An option is the right, but not the obligation, to make an investment decision in accordance to given circumstances for a particular duration into the future, ending with an expiration date [7]. Real options are typically used for real assets (non-financial), such as a property or a new product design. We used call options, which give the right to buy an uncertain future valued asset for the strike price by a specified date. In this paper, we consider different architectural strategies and different options, and use the Binomial option pricing model [7] to value real options. The choice of this model gives the architect the freedom to estimate the up and down in the value over time, backed up by their experience.

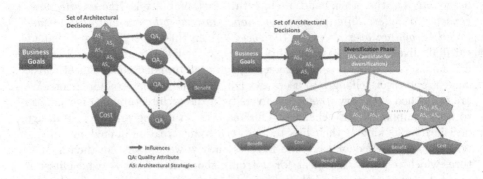

Fig. 1. Steps of classical CBAM [5]   **Fig. 2.** Proposed approach

GridStix: We present a case study based on the GridStix prototype, a grid-based technique to support flood prediction by implementing embedded sensors with diverse networking technologies [4]. The water depth and flow rate of the river are continuously observed using sensors located along the river. Data are collected in real-time and dispatched over GPRS to a prediction model [4] for flood anticipation. GridStix has a highly dynamic environment, and is influenced by numerous QAs and different architectural components [4]. Our evaluation, shown in Sect. 5, is performed using hypothetical data, aiming to measure the long-term impact of implementing a diversified vs non-diversified design decisions on system QAs, cost, and value.

3 Architecture Diversification as a Real Options Problem

Diversified software architecture is composed of architectural strategies (ASs). It can meet some quality goals of interest and trade-offs by implementing a set of diversified ASs. At run-time, switching between diversified AS is allowed. Suppose that k denotes a particular capability, including connectivity, routing technology, data management, etc., as depicted in GridStix. AS_{ka} indicates the software architectural component a implementing capability k. Some of the following ASs are envisioned as a way to implement diversification in GridStix: AS_{11}, AS_{12}, AS_{13} are connect node with gateway via *Wifi*, *Bluetooth (BT)*, and *GPRS* respectively; AS_{21}, AS_{22} are search for the best path between gateway and node using *Fewest Hop (FH)*, *Shortest Path (SP)* routing algorithm, respectively.

Inspired by options theory [7], we consider each different possible diversified architecture as an option. Therefore, we refer to them as Diversified Architecture Options (DAOs). An example of DAO would be $DAO_1 = (AS_{11}, AS_{12}, AS_{21})$, meaning that the system can switch between AS_{11} and AS_{12} at run-time. Another example would be $DAO_2 = (AS_{11}, AS_{12}, AS_{13}, AS_{21}, AS_{22})$, meaning that the system can switch between AS_{11}, AS_{12} and AS_{13}, and between AS_{21} and AS_{22} at run-time.

The value of these options is long-term and can cross-cut many dimensions. In particular, the valuation of the options can be performed in accordance to sustainability dimensions, which can be technical, individual, economics, environment, and social [3]. In this paper, we attempt to link technical decision to cost and long-term value. When evolving an existing system, the current implementation of the system has a direct ramification on the selection of a DAO. It could provide an intuitive indication about whether the current system architecture needs to grow, alter, defer, etc. To exemplify, if the current system architecture has low long-term value, hence it is obvious that another DAO should be employed instead.

The goal of our approach is to help the architect to choose a DAO that provides a good trade-off between cost and long term value, given some quality goals. This is done by evaluating a portfolio of DAOs.

4 The Approach

The proposed approach is a CBAM-based method for evaluating diversified architectural options (DAO) with real options theory, as illustrated in Fig. 2.

Step 1: Choosing the business goals, Scenarios and DAOs. Our method focuses on QAs and their responses with respect to scenarios of interest that are related to sustainability. DAOs are the architectural options that deal with these scenarios. In our approach, DAOs are represented as a portfolio of options. Exercising each DAO can be formulated as call option [7], with an exercise price and uncertain value. We aim to provide a good trade-off between the benefit and cost of applying diversified options on system's QA over time, given the following: *1 - A set of diversified architectural options* $\{DAO_1, DAO_2, DAO_n\}$, *where each DAO is composed of integrated architectural strategies among candidate diversified ones* $\{AS_1, AS_2, AS_m\}$. *2 - One or more ASs are selected as candidates for diversification* AS_k, *as shown in figure 2. 3 - The diversified ASs are denoted by* AS_{ka}, *where* $0 <= k <= x, 0 <= a <= y$. *4 - Each DAO comes with a cost* $Cost_{DAO_i}(t)$ *and a benefit* $Benefit_{DAO_i}(t)$, *which may vary over time.*

Among the business goals, which we consider to illustrate our approach are the accuracy of flood anticipation and reasonable warning time prior to the flood. In our method, we mainly test and evaluate the application of diversity versus no diversity. Therefore, $non-diversified-option = Wifi + FH$, $DAO_1 = Wifi + BT + FH$, and the following scenario *Messages transmission between any given sensor node and gateway should arrive in* ≤ 30 ms *(addressing the performance QA)* are employed for evaluation. We set 60 % target for improvement of average network latency backed up by [4].

Step 2: Assessing the relative importance of QAs (Elicit QAWeight$_j$). The architect assigned a weight to the QA according to equation in Table 1.

Step 3: Quantifying the benefits of the DAOs (Elicit ContribScore$_j$). The impact of *Non-diversified option* and DAO_i on the QAs are elicited from the stakeholders with respect to $Benefit_{DAO_i}$ equation in Table 1.

Step 4: Quantifying the costs of DAOs and Incorporating Scheduling implications. Classical CBAM uses the common measures for determining the costs, which involves the implementation costs only. Unlike CBAM, our approach embraces the switching costs between decisions, which is equivalent to the primary payment required for purchasing a stock option. This is in addition to the costs of deploying DAOs, configuration costs, and maintenance costs, similarly to the exercise price, denoted by $Cost(DAO_i)$. It is essential to note that CBAM implements the ASs with high benefit and low cost [5]. On the other hand, we believe that some ASs could provide high cost with low benefit initially or high cost with high benefit, but a much higher benefit in the long-term that outweighs the cost. The long-term benefit is the key factor for ASs evaluation.

Table 1. Approach notations

Variable	Description	Formulation/application on GridStix
DAO_i	Diversified architectural options	DAOs as a portfolio of call options
QA	Quality attribute	Performance (Perf), Reliability (Rel), Availability (Ava), Security (Sec), Scalability (Sca), & Energy Efficiency (Ene)
$QAWeight_j$	The relative importance of QAs	Should satisfy $\sum_j QAWeight_j = 100$, Perf(20), Rel(30), Ava(20), Sec(5), Sca(5), & Ene(15)
$ContribScore_j$	Impact of each DAO on QAs	DAO_1: Perf(1), Rel(1), Ava(0.8), Sec(0.5), Sca(0.7), Ene(-0.4), Cost(60)
$Benefit_{DAO_i}$	Benefit of a DAO	$Benefit_{DAO_i} = \sum_j QAWeight_j * ContribScore_{i,j}$
$Cost(DAO_i)$	Switching, deployment, configuration, & maintenance costs	$\forall i : Cost(DAO_i) \leqslant Budget$
S_{DAO_i}	System value	$S_{DAO_i} = V_s + Benefit_{DAO_i}$
$S_{DAO_i}(t)$	System value over time t	$S_{DAO_i}(t) = V_s + Benefit_{DAO_i}(t)$
u, d	System value (corresponding to stock price) benefiting/being hurt from DAO i.e. value rise	Should satisfy $d < 1 + r < u$ [6]
r	Risk-free interest rate	0.5 %
f_u	The likely rise of payoff from implementing a DAO	$f_u = max(0, uS_{DAO_i}(t) - Cost(DAO_i))$
f_d	The likely fall of payoff from implementing a DAO	$f_d = max(0, dS_{DAO_i}(t) - Cost(DAO_i))$
p	Risk-adjusted probability	$p = \frac{1+r-d}{u-d}$
f	Option price	$f = \frac{pf_u+(1-p)f_d}{1-r}$

Step 5: Calculate the Return of each DAO for the scenarios. We used binomial option pricing calculation [7] and steps inspired by [6]. Binomial option pricing model is a constructive aid aiming to show the suitable time slot for exercising an option i.e. the cost-benefit of diversified options over time. For each step of the binomial tree, the up and down node values are important in determining the system value rise and fall, which is ultimately used to calculate the option price. Our method aims to determine the impact of applying each DAO (i.e. utility) on the system QAs, which is computed at every time slot t,

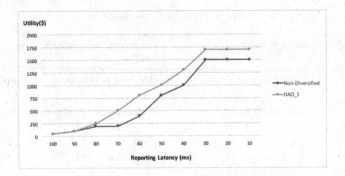

Fig. 3. Enhanced Utility versus Reporting Latency in case of implementing additional nodes for *non-diversified and diversified* decisions

where $t = l$ indicates that the time equals to l unit time of interest i.e. months in GridStix. For example, currently, the approximate number of deployed gridstix nodes is 14 [4]. It is likely that adding extra nodes may improve the system's safety due to the presence of backup nodes and providing wider network coverage. This in turn promotes the accuracy of flood prediction, satisfying our main business driver, thus sustaining the GridStix software. Figure 3 envisages the enhanced utility gained with/without diversification versus reporting latency in accordance to offering up to 20 nodes, based on the graphs in [4]. The following steps are necessary for valuation of options using the binomial option pricing model.

1. *Calculate the system value after factoring diversification into the decisions:* As a start, S_{DAO} is evaluated with respect to the initial system value denoted by V_s and resultant benefit of deploying DAO as shown in Table 1. Also $S_{DAO}(t)$ is the system value after implementing a particular DAO causing either incremental improvement or degradation at time t, which is equivalent to the uncertain stock price when modeling an American call option.
2. *Calculate the likely rise and fall of payoff with DAOs:* f_u and f_d are computed using equations depicted in Table 1.
3. *Calculate the option price of exercising a DAO:* This step reveals at what time t, it is favorable to take the decision i.e. exercise an option using f as seen in Table 1. It also illustrates the long-term performance of a system, which in turn aids in promoting sustainability.

5   Preliminary Evaluation

Without Diversification Outcome: A preliminary analysis of the method without diversifying ASs is necessary. The architecture comprising *Wifi* and *FH* was evaluated. The utility values for the implementation of the latter architecture is depicted in Fig. 4 along with utilities of other DAOs, which are elicited from

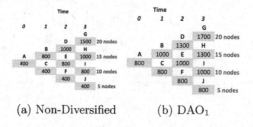

(a) Non-Diversified   (b) DAO$_1$

Fig. 4. Anticipated values for the utility of non-diversified and DAO$_1$

stakeholders. Decision makers can vary the base value at cell A (guided by the chart in Fig. 4a) to perform what-if analysis. In this example, possible values range from \$400 to \$1500. The likely value of each architecture is different. The valuation of non-diversified option over varying time slots for uncertainty of implementing additional nodes is clearly shown in Fig. 5. In this example, V_s is \$1750. For detailed analysis, consider cell D for the evaluation of two-unit time as presented in Fig. 5, which is the upper cell value: $S_{non-div}(2) = V_s + Benefit_{non-div}(2) = 1750 + 1000 = \$2750$. The lower cell value is computed as follows: $f_{non-div}(2) = max(0, S_{uu} - Cost_{non-div}) = max(0, 2750 - 1250) = \$1500$. The option price formula f of non-diversified is: $f_{non-div} = f_{DAO_{non-div_1}} + f_{non-div_2} + f_{non-div_3} = 905.47 + 910.79 + 915.60 = \$2732.22$.

Diversification Outcome: DAO$_1$ is employed for method evaluation. The predicted utility values for the implementation of DAO$_1$ are revealed in Fig. 4b, which is elicited from stakeholders. By applying the same logic used to calculate the option value for non-diversified decision, the valuation of DAO$_1$ over varying time slots for uncertainty of implementing additional nodes is shown in Fig. 6, where the orange cells represent $f_{DAO_i}(t)$ and green cells denote the $S_{DAO_i}(t)$. For detailed analysis, Consider cell D for the evaluation of two-unit time as presented in Fig. 6, which is the upper cell value: $S_{DAO_1}(2) = V_s + Benefit_{DAO_1}(2) = 1750 + 1300 = \$3050$. The lower cell

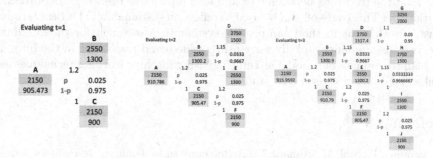

Fig. 5. Valuation of *non-diversified* option staged over 3 time periods

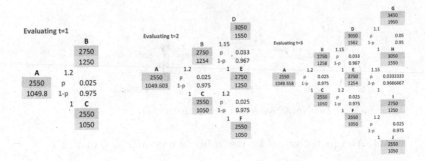

Fig. 6. Valuation of diversified option (DAO_1) staged over 3 time periods

value is computed as follows: $f_{DAO_4}(2) = max(0, S_{uu} - Cost(DAO_4)) = max(0, 3050 - 1500) = \$1550$. Therefore, the option price formula f of DAO_1 is: $f_{DAO_1} = f_{DAO_{1.1}} + f_{DAO_{1.2}} + f_{DAO_{1.3}} = 1049.8 + 1049.60 + 1049.56 = \$3148.91$.

Summary of Evaluation: From the above, the value of non-diversified is \$2750 and the value of DAO_1 is \$3150. The costs are \$2732.22 and \$3148.91, respectively. Although DAO_1 has higher cost than non-diversified option, yet it has higher long-term benefit. This proves that implementing high cost options would provide higher long-term benefit i.e. high option value.

6   Conclusion

We have described an approach, which makes a novel extension of CBAM. The approach reasons about diversification in software architecture design decisions using real options. The fundamental premise is that diversification embeds flexibility in an architecture. This flexibility can have value under uncertainty and can be reasoned using Real Options. In particular, the approach can be used by the architect and the decision maker to apprise the value of architecting for sustainability via diversification based on binomial trees. For instance, the method can be used to inform whether an architecture decision needs to be diversified and what the trade-offs between cost and long term value resulting from diversification are. This trade-off can be used to reflect on sustainability. Our case study illustrates that the method can provide systematic assessment for the interlink between sustainability and diversity using value-based reasoning. In the future, we plan to evaluate our model at run-time using machine learning techniques as well as apply it on several case studies.

References

1. Avgeriou, P., Stal, M., Hilliard, R.: Architecture sustainability [guest editors' introduction]. IEEE Softw. **30**(6), 40–44 (2013)
2. Avizienis, A., Kelly, J.P.J.: Fault tolerance by design diversity: concepts and experiments. Computer **17**(8), 67–80 (1984). http://dx.doi.org/10.1109/MC.1984.1659219

3. Becker, C., Chitchyan, R., Duboc, L., Easterbrook, S., Mahaux, M., Penzenstadler, B., Rodriguez-Navas, G., Salinesi, C., Seyff, N., Venters, C., et al.: The Karlskrona manifesto for sustainability design (2014). arXiv preprint arXiv:1410.6968
4. Grace, P., Hughes, D., Porter, B., Blair, G.S., Coulson, G., Taiani, F.: Experiences with open overlays: a middleware approach to network heterogeneity. ACM SIGOPS Oper. Syst. Rev. **42**(4), 123–136 (2008)
5. Kazman, R., Asundi, J., Klein, M.: Quantifying the costs and benefits of architectural decisions. In: Proceedings of 23rd International Conference on Software Engineering, pp. 297–306. IEEE Computer Society (2001)
6. Ozkaya, I., Kazman, R., Klein, M.: Quality-attribute based economic valuation of architectural patterns. In: 1st International Workshop on Economics of Software and Computation, ESC 2007, p. 5. IEEE (2007)
7. Trigeorgis, L.: Real Options: Managerial Flexibility and Strategy in Resource Allocation. MIT Press, Cambridge (1996)

Software Architecture Documentation

Towards Seamless Analysis of Software Interoperability: Automatic Identification of Conceptual Constraints in API Documentation

Hadil Abukwaik[✉], Mohammed Abujayyab, and Dieter Rombach

University of Kaiserslautern,
Gottlieb-Daimler-Straße 47, 67663 Kaiserslautern, Germany
{abukwaik,rombach}@cs.uni-kl.de, mohabujayyab@gmail.com

Abstract. Building successful and meaningful interoperation with external software APIs requires satisfying their conceptual interoperability constraints. These constraints, which we call the COINs, include structure, dynamic, and quality specifications that if missed they lead to costly implications of unexpected mismatches and running-late projects. However, for software architects and analysts, manual analysis of unstructured text in API documents to identify conceptual interoperability constraints is a tedious and time-consuming task that requires knowledge about constraint types. In this paper, we present our empirically-based research in addressing the aforementioned issues by utilizing machine learning techniques. We started with a multiple-case study through which we contributed a ground truth dataset. Then, we built a model for this dataset and tested its robustness through experiments using different machine learning text-classification algorithms. The results show that our model enables achieving 70.4 % precision and 70.2 % recall in identifying seven classes of constraints (i.e., Syntax, Semantic, Structure, Dynamic, Context, Quality, and Not-COIN). This achievement increases to 81.9 % precision and 82.0 % recall when identifying two classes (i.e., COIN, Not-COIN). Finally, we implemented a tool prototype to demonstrate the value of our findings for architects in a practical context.

Keywords: Interoperability analysis · Conceptual constraints · Black-box interoperation · API documentation · Empirical study · Machine learning

1 Introduction

Interoperating with externally developed black-box Web Service or Platform APIs is restricted with their Conceptual interoperability constraints (COINs), which are defined as the characteristics controlling the exchange of data or functionalities at the following conceptual classes: Syntax, Semantics, Structure,

© Springer International Publishing AG 2016
B. Tekinerdogan et al. (Eds.): ECSA 2016, LNCS 9839, pp. 67–83, 2016.
DOI: 10.1007/978-3-319-48992-6_5

Dynamics, Context, and Quality [2]. Hence, to build a successful interoperation, software architects and analysts need to identify and fulfil these conceptual constraints of the external APIs. Otherwise, unexpected conceptual mismatches can prevent the whole interoperation or make its results meaningless. Consequently, this causes resolution expenses at later stages of projects [8]. Therefore, it is necessary to perform effective conceptual interoperability analysis for shared documents about a software API of interest to identify its conceptual constraints. This in turn offers a basis for analyzing interoperability on other levels, which are out of our research scope, like organizational level (e.g., privacy concerns), managerial level (e.g., budget restrictions), and technical level (e.g., network protocols).

Current analysis approaches relies on manual investigation of shared API documents [9]. However, such manual reading and inspection of natural language text in these documents to find constraints is an exhausting, time-consuming, and error-prone task [19]. Add to this, it requires knowledge about the different conceptual constraints along with linguistic analysis skills.

In this paper, we elaborate on and extend our proposed conceptual interoperability analysis framework [2]. In particular, we automate the identification of COINs in API documentations' text by employing machine learning (ML) techniques. Our goal is to assist software architects and analysts in performing effective and efficient conceptual interoperability analysis. We followed a systematic empirically-based research methodology, which has two main parts. In the first part, we conducted a multiple-case study that yielded our first contribution, which is a ground truth dataset. This dataset is a community-reusable asset in the form of a repository of textual sentences that we collected from multiple API documents and manually labeled them with a specific COIN class. In the second part, we contributed a classification model for the COINs in the ground truth dataset, and we evaluated it through experiments using different ML text-classification algorithms. Our experiments revealed promising results towards automating the identification of COINs in text of API documents. We achieved up to 70.4 % precision and 70.2 % recall for identifying seven classes of constraints (i.e., Syntax, Semantics, Structure, Dynamics, Context, Quality, and Not-COIN). This increased to reach 81.9 % precision and 82.0 % recall for identifying two classes (i.e., COIN, Not-COIN). Finally, we developed a tool prototype that demonstrates the value of our ideas in serving software architects during their interoperability analysis task. In specific, the tool allows architects to select sentences from API document webpages, and it checks and reports the existence of COINs along with their types. Such a classification service would enhance the interoperability analysis results, especially for inexperienced architects, as it helps in understanding the constraints' impact and how to satisfy them.

The rest of this paper is organized as follows. Section 2 introduces a background, Sect. 3 overviews the related works, and Sect. 4 outlines our research methodology. Sections 5 and 6 detail our first and second research parts. Section 7 presents our tool support and Sect. 8 is the conclusion.

2   Background

In this section we present a brief introduction to conceptual interoperability constraints and the used machine learning techniques in our research.

2.1   Conceptual Interoperability Constraints

The presented work in this paper is based on the Conceptual Interoperability Constraints (COIN) model [2], which focuses on the non-technical constraints of interoperable software systems and can be applied to different types of software systems (e.g., information systems, embedded systems, mobile systems, etc.). COINs are the conceptual characteristics that govern the software systems interoperability with other systems. Therefore, missing or wrong understanding of COINs may defect the desired interoperability by leading to conceptual inconsistencies or meaningless results. There are six classes of COINs that we summarize as the following: (1) *Syntax COINs* that state the constraints packaging (e.g., used terminology or modeling language). (2) *Semantic COINs* that express meaning-related constraints (e.g., goals of methods). (3) *Structure COINs* that depict the systems elements, their relations, and arrangements affecting the interoperation results (e.g., data distribution). (4) *Dynamic COINs* that restrict the behavior of interoperating elements (e.g., synchronization feature). (5) *Context COINs* that pertain to external settings of the interoperation (e.g., user and usage properties). (6) *Quality COINs* that capture quality characteristics related to exchanged data and services (e.g., interoperation response time).

2.2   Machine Learning for Text Classification

In order to enable the automatic detection of COINs in text, we employed ML text-classification algorithms (e.g., NaïveBayes [10] and Support Vector Machine [18]). The accuracy results of such algorithms depend on the quality and the size of the dataset [4] that consists of manually labeled sentences with one of the predefined classification classes. Text classification process consists of:

- *Building the classification model*, in which all features of the sentences in the dataset are identified and modeled mathematically. In our research, we used popular techniques for building our model: (1) Bag of Words (BOWs) [6] that considers each word in a sentence as a feature, and accordingly a document is represented as a matrix of weighted values; (2) N-Grams [16] that considers each N adjacent words in a sentence as a feature, where $(N > 0)$.
- *Evaluating the classification model*, in which the manually labeled dataset is divided into a training and testing sets. The training set is used for training the ML classification algorithm on the features captured in the model, while the testing set is for evaluating the classification accuracy. For our research, we used *k-fold Cross-validation* [11], in which our ground truth dataset (i.e., COINs Corpus) is divided into k folds. Then, $(k-1)$ folds are used for training and one fold is used for testing. Finally, an average of k evaluation rounds is computed.

3   Related Work

A number of previous works proposed automating the identification of some interoperability constraints from API documents. Wu et al. [19] targeted parameters dependency constraints, Pandita et al. [13] inferred formal specifications for methods pre/post conditions, and Zhong et al. [20] recognized resource specifications. We complement these works and elaborate on Abukwaik et al. [2] idea of extracting a comprehensive set of conceptual interoperability constraints.

On a broader scope, other works proposed retrieving information to assist software architects in different tasks. Anvaari and Zimmermann [3] retrieved architectural knowledge from documents for architectural guidance purposes. Figueiredo et al. [7] and Lopez et al. [12] searched for architectural knowledge in emails, meeting notes, and wikis for proper documentation purposes. Although, these are important achievements, they do not meet our goal of assisting architects in interoperability analysis tasks.

In general, our work and the aforementioned related works intersect in the utilization of natural language processing techniques in retrieving specific kind of information from documents. However, they used rule-based and ontology-based retrieval approaches, while we explored ML classification algorithms that are helpful for information retrieval in natural language text. Add to this, our systematic research contributed a reusable ground truth dataset for *all COIN types* that enables related research replication and results' comparison.

4   Research Methodology

In this research, we systematically revealed the potentials of automating the extraction of COINs from API documents using ML techniques. Our research goal formulated in terms of GQM goal template [5] is: *to* support the conceptual interoperability analysis task *for the purpose of* improvement *with respect to* effectiveness and efficiency *from the viewpoint of* software architects and analysts *in the context of* analyzing text in API documentation within software integration projects. We translate this goal into the following research questions:

RQ1: *What are the existing conceptual interoperability constraints, COINs, in the text of API documentation?*
This question explores the current state of COINs in real API documents. It also aims at building the ground truth dataset (i.e. COINs Corpus representing a repository of sentences labeled with their COIN class). This forms a main building block towards the envisioned automatic extraction idea.

RQ2: *How effective and efficient would it be to use ML techniques in automating the extraction of COINs from text in API documentations?*
This question explores the actual benefits of utilizing ML in supporting software architects and analysts in analyzing the text. It aims at building a classification model that will be evaluated through well-known ML classification algorithms.

In order to achieve the stated goal and answer the aforementioned questions, we performed our research in two main parts as follows:

Research Part 1 (Multiple-case study). In this part, we systematically explored the state of COINs in six cases of API documentations. The result of this part is a ground truth dataset (i.e., COINs Corpus). We detail the study design and results in Sect. 5.

Research Part 2 (Experiments). In this part, we started with using the ground truth dataset, which resulted from the previous part, in building the COIN Classification Model. Afterwards, we investigated the accuracy of different ML classification algorithms in identifying the COINs in text by using our model. We detail the process and results of this research part in Sect. 6.

Our systematic research provided us with traceability between the different activities and their results. Moreover, it enables future researchers to independently replicate our work and to compare the results.

5   Multiple-Case Study: Building the Ground Truth Dataset for COINs

In this section, we describe our multiple-case study design, execution, and results.

5.1   Study Design

Study Goal. We aim at answering the first research question RQ1 that we stated in Sect. 4. In order to do so, we needed to examine real-world API documentations to discover the state of conceptual interoperability constraints in them.

Research Method. We decided to perform a multiple-case study with literal replication of cases from different domains. Such a method aids in collecting significant evidences and drawing generalizable results.

Case Selection. For systematic selection of cases of API documentations, we considered the following selection criteria:

SC1: Mashup Score. This is a published statistical value[1] for the popularity of a Web Service API in terms of its integration frequency into new bigger APIs.
SC2: API Type. This can be either Web Service API or Platform API.
SC3: API Domain. This is the application domain for the considered API document (e.g., social blogging, audio, software development, etc.).

Analysis Unit. Our case study has a holistic design, which means that we have a single unit of analysis. This unit is "the sentences in API documents that

---

[1] Programmable web: http://www.programmableweb.com/apis/directory.

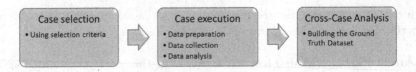

Fig. 1. Multiple-case study process

include COIN instances". To document and maintain the analyzed sentences, we designed a data extraction sheet that we implemented as an MS Excel sheet. This sheet consists of demographic fields (i.e., API name, date of retrieval, mashup score, API type, API domain, and no. of sentences) and analysis fields (i.e., case id, sentence id, sentence textual value, and the COIN class).

Study Protocol. Our multiple-case study protocol includes three main activities that are adapted from the process proposed by Runeson [17]. The study activities are case selection, case execution, and cross-case analysis as we summarize in Fig. 1 below and describe in details within the next subsection.

5.2   Study Execution and Results

Based on our predefined case selection criteria, in August 2015 we chose six API documentations. Four API documents from the Web Services type (i.e., SoundCloud, GoogleMaps, Skype, and Instagram) and two from the Platform type (i.e., AppleWatch and Eclipse-Plugin Developer Guide). These cases cover different application domains (i.e., social micro-blogging, geographical location, telecommunication, social audio, and software development environment). With regards to the mashup criteria, our four cases of Web Service APIs are chosen to cover a wide range of scores starting from 30 for Skype and ending with 2582 for GoogleMaps. After selecting our cases, we executed each case as the following:

Data Preparation. We started this step with fetching the API documentation for the selected case from its online website. Then, we read the documents and determined the webpages that had textual content offering conceptual software description and constraints (e.g., the Overview, Introduction, Developer Guide, API Reference, Summary, etc.). Subsequently, we started processing the text in chosen webpages by performing the following:

- *Automatic Filtering*. We implemented a simple PHP code using Simple HTML DOM Parser[2] library to filter out the text noise (i.e., headers, images, tags, symbols, html code, and JavaScript code). Thus, we passed the URL link of the chosen webpage (input) to our implemented code. Then, we got back a .txt file containing the textual content of the webpage (output).
- *Manual Filtering*. The automatic filtering fells short in excluding specific types of noise (e.g., text and code mixture, references like "see also", "for more information", "related topics", copyrights, etc.). These sentences could mislead the machine learning in our later research steps, so we removed them manually.

---

[2] Simple HTML DOM: http://simplehtmldom.sourceforge.net/.

Data Collection. In this step, we cut the content of the text file resulted from previous step into single sentences within our designed data extraction sheet (.xsl file) that we described in Subsect. 5.1. We completed all the fields of the data sheet for each sentence except for the "COIN class" filed that we did within the next step. *Note that,* we maintained a data storage, in which we stored the original HTML webpages of the selected API documentations, their text file, and their excel sheet. This enables later replication of our work by other researchers as documentations get changed so frequently.

Data Analysis. We manually analyzed each collected sentence in the extraction sheet and carefully assigned it a COIN class. This classification was based on an interpretation criteria, which is the COIN Model with its six classes (i.e., Syntax, Semantic, Structure, Dynamic, Context, and Quality). We added a seventh class for sentences with no COIN instance (i.e., Not-COIN class). For example, a sentence like "A user is encapsulated by a read-only Person object." was classified as a "Structure COIN". While, "You can also use our Sharing Kits for Windows, OS X, Android or iOS applications" was classified as a "Not-COIN" as it did not express a conceptual constraint, but rather a technical information.

The result of this step was a very critical point towards our envisioned automatic COIN extraction idea. Hence, the data analysis was performed by two researchers, who independently classified all sentences for each case. Then, in multiple discussion sessions, the two researchers compared their classification decisions and resolved conflicts based on consensus.

Obviously, the case execution process consumed time and mental effort, especially in the data analysis step. Table 1 summarizes the distribution of our collected 2283 sentences among the cases along with the effort (in terms of hours) that we spent in executing them. Noticeably, SoundCloud and Instagram have small documents, and consequently they have the smallest share of sentences included in our study (i.e., 9.5 % and 11 %). Meanwhile, Eclipse documentation is the largest and consequently has the highest share of sentences (i.e., 28.5 %).

Table 1. Case-share of sentences and execution effort

API document	Total number of sentences	Total execution efforts (Hours)
Sound cloud	219	7.7
GoogleMaps	473	6.5
AppleWatch	360	8.0
Eclipse plugin	651	12.0
Skype	325	4.5
Instagram	255	4.8
Total	2283	43.5

Cross-Case Analysis (Answering RQ1: What are the Types of Existing Conceptual Interoperability Constraints, COINs, in the Text of Current API Documentations?). After executing all cases, we arranged the incrementally classified sets of sentences from all cases (i.e., 2283 sentences) into one repository that we call the *ground truth dataset* or *the COINs Corpus* as called in ML. We have developed two versions of this dataset as the following:

Seven-COIN Corpus, in which, each sentence belongs to one of the seven classes (i.e., Not-COIN, Dynamic, Semantic, Syntax, Structure, Context, or Quality). *Two-COIN Corpus*, in which, each sentence belongs to one of two classes rather than seven (i.e., COIN or Not-COIN). In fact, the Two-COIN Corpus is derived from the Seven-COIN Corpus by abstracting the six COIN classes into one class. Table 2 shows the difference between the two Corpora with example sentences.

Table 2. Example of content in the Seven-COIN and Two-COIN Corpus

Sentence ID	Sentence	Seven-COIN class	Two-COIN class
s1	You can also use ou Sharing Kits for Windows, OS X, Android or iOS applications	Not-COIN	Not-COIN
s2	When it is finished mainpulating the object, it releases the lock	Dynamic	COIN
s3	A user is encapsulated by a read-only Person object	Structure	COIN
s4	A user's presence is a collection of information about the users' availability, their current activity, and their personal note	Synatx	COIN
s5	A dynamic notification interface lets you provide a more enriched notification experience for the user	Semantic	COIN
s6	This service is not designed to respond in real time to user input	Context	COIN
s7	Your interfaces need to display information quickly and facilitate fast navigation and interactions	Quality	COIN

The aim of building these two versions of the corpus is to better investigate the performance results of the ML algorithms in the later research experiments. We explain this in more details in Sect. 6.

COIN-Share in the Contributed Ground Truth Dataset. In Fig. 2, we illustrate the distribution of sentences among the COIN classes within the Seven-COIN Corpus (on the left) and the Two-COIN Corpus (on the right). It is noticed that the Not-COIN class, which expresses technical constraints rather than conceptual ones, is the dominant among the other six classes (i.e., 42 %). The Dynamic and Semantic classes have the second and third biggest shares. Remarkably, the Structure, Syntax, Quality, and Context instances are very few with convergent shares ranging between 1 % and 5 % of the dataset.

COIN-Share in the Cases. On a finer level, we have investigated the state of COINs in each case rather than in the whole ground truth dataset. We found that the content of each API document was focused on the Not-COIN, Dynamic and Semantic classes similarly as in the aggregated findings on the complete dataset seen in Fig. 2. For example, in the case of AppleWatch documentation, 40.8 % of

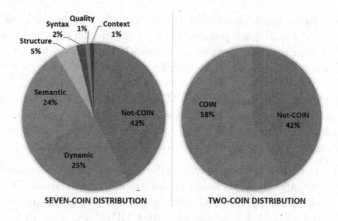

Fig. 2. COIN-share in the ground truth dataset

the content is for Not-COIN, 26.1 % for Dynamic, and 25 % for Semantic. Add to this, all cases had less than 10 % of its content to the Structure, Syntax, Quality, and Context classes (e.g., Eclipse-Plugin gave them 8.5 %).

5.3 Discussion

Technical-Oriented API Documentations. The Not-COIN class reserves 42 % of the total sentences in the investigated parts of the API documents that were supposed to be conceptual (i.e., overview and introduction sections). A noteworthy example is the GoogleMaps case, which took it an extreme level of focus on the technical information (i.e., 63 % of its content was under the Not-COIN class, 11.2 % for Dynamic class, 13.1 % for Semantic class, and the rest is shared by the other classes). Accordingly, it is important to raise a flag about the lack of sufficient information about the conceptual aspects of interoperable software units or APIs (e.g., usage context, terminology definitions, quality attributes, etc.). This concern needs to be brought to the notice of researchers and practitioners who care about the usefulness and adequacy of content in API documentations. This obviously has a direct influence on the effectiveness of architects and analysts in the conceptual interoperability analysis related activities.

Considerable Presence of Dynamic and Semantic Constraints. Our study findings reveal that the Dynamic and Semantic classes have apparently big shares in current API documents (i.e., 25 % and 24 % of the dataset). This reflects the favorable awareness about the importance of proper and explicit documenting of the API semantics (e.g., data meaning, service goal, conceptual input and output, etc.) and dynamics (e.g., interaction protocol, flow of data, pre- and post- conditions, etc.). Nevertheless, based on the tedious work we went through our manual analysis for the six cases, we believe that it would be of great help for architects and analysts to have clear boarders between these two classes of constraints within the verbose of text. For example, it would be easier to skim the text, if the API goal get separated from its interaction protocol, rather than blending them into long paragraphs. This would offer architects and analysts a better experience and it would consequently enhance their analysis results.

COIN-Deficiency in Platform and Web Service API Documents. From our investigated cases, we perceived a convention on assigning insignificant shares for the Structure, Syntax, Quality, and Context classes. Interestingly, the cases varied with regards to what they chose to slightly cover out of these four classes.

On one hand, the cases of Web Service APIs were the main contributors to the Context, Quality, and Syntax classes in the ground truth dataset. That is, the documents of GoogleMaps, SoundCloud, Skype, and Instagram provided 82.5 % of the Syntax COINs, 70.4 % of the Quality COINs, and 92 % of the Context COINs. Such a contribution cannot be related to the nature of Web Service APIs, as Platfrom ones need also to share these COINs explicitly. For example, it is critical for a FarmerWatch application to know the offered response time by the Notification service of AppleWatch APIs.

On the other hand, the Platform API documents participated with 56.1 % of the Structure COINs in the ground truth dataset, while the Web Service API documents participated with 43.9%. Note that, this is not related to the larger amount of sentences that these two documents contributed to the dataset, but rather due to the internal case share of Structure COINs. On average, the Platform API documents allocate about 6 % of their content to structural constraints, while Web Service API documents allocate about 3.6 % for these constraints.

Observed Patterns for the Dominant Classes in the Ground Truth Dataset. From the considerable amount of sentences for the Not-COIN, Semantic, and Dynamic classes, we observed a number of patterns in terms of frequently occurring terms and sentences. We envision that using the patterns in combination with the BOW in future experiments would enhance the results of the automatic COIN identification. Below we describe some of these patterns.

- *Patterns of the Not-COIN Class.* We observed the presence of "Technical Keywords", which are abbreviations of software technologies (e.g., XML, iOS, XPath, JavaScript, ASCII, etc.). With further analysis, we found that 30.7 % of the Not-COIN instances have technical keywords. Another pattern for this class is variables with special format (e.g., "XML responses consist of zero or more <route> elements."). Also, sentences starting with specific terms (e.g., "for example", "for more information", "see", etc.) recurred in 12.8 % of the Not-COIN instances.
- *Patterns of the Dynamic Class.* We found a number of recurrent terms related to actions and data/process flow thae we gathered into a list called the "Action Verbs", which includes: create, use, request, access, lock, include, setup, run, start, call, redirect, and more. In fact, 35.8 % of the sentences with Dynamic COINs have one or more of these terms. Furthermore, 24 % of the Dynamic COIN sentences contain a conditional statement expressing a pre- or post- condition. For example, the sentence "If a command name is specified, the help message for this command is displayed" has a Dynamic COIN that states a pre-condition.

- *Patterns of the Semantic Class.* We noticed repeated terms and organized them into: "Input/Output Terms" (e.g., return, receive, display, response, send, result, etc.) that are in 18.8 % of the Semantic COIN sentences and "Goal Terms" (e.g., allow, enable, let, grant, permit, facilitate, etc.) that are in 16.4 %. For example, the sentence "A dynamic notification interface lets you provide a more enriched notification experience for the user" has a Semantic COIN stating a goal.

5.4   Threats to Validity

Case Bias. To obtain significant results and draw generalizable conclusions, we included multiple cases for building the ground truth that plays prominent role in our research. We literally replicated six API documents (i.e., Sound-Cloud, GoogleMaps, Skype, Instagram, AppleWatch and Eclipse-Plugin Developer Guide) from two different types (Web Service and Platform APIs).

Completeness. Due to resource limitations (i.e., time and manpower), we were unable to analyze the large API documents completely. However, we were careful with respect to selecting inclusive parts of such large documents. For example, out of the huge document of Eclipse APIs, we covered the Plugin part.

Researcher Bias. To build our ground truth dataset in a way that guarantees results accuracy and impartiality, we replicated the manual classification of the cases sentences by two researchers separately based on the COINs Model as an interpretation criteria. In multiple discussion sessions, the researchers compared their classification decisions and resolved conflicts based on consensus.

6   Experiments: Automatic Identification of COINs Using Machine Learning

In this section, we detail the experiments design, execution, and results.

6.1   Experiments Design

Experiments Goal. This part of our research aims at answering the second research question RQ2 that we stated in Sect. 4. In order to do so, we needed to examine ML techniques to discover their potentials in supporting architects and analysts in automatically identifying the COINs in text of API documents.

Research Method. We built a classification model and ran multiple experiments employing different ML text-classification algorithms. This method enables comparing the algorithms results and drawing solid conclusions about the ML advantages in addressing the challenges of manual interoperability analysis.

Evaluation Method and Metrics. We used k-fold Cross-validation, which we explained in the background section, with $k = 10$. For evaluation metrics of classification accuracy, we used the following commonly used measures [14]:

Precision: the ratio of correctly classified sentences by the classification algorithm to the total number of sentences it classifies either correctly or incorrectly.
Recall: the ratio of correctly classified sentences by the classification algorithm to the total number of sentences in the corpus.
F-Measure: the harmonic mean of precision and recall that is calculated as: $(2 * Precision * Recall)/(Precision + Recall)$.

Experiments Protocol. Our experiments protocol includes three main activities that are: feature selection, feature modeling, and ML algorithms evaluation. We illustrate this protocol in Fig. 3, and we describe it in details within the next subsection. We ran this protocol twice, once for the Seven-COIN Corpus and another for the Two-COIN Corpus.

6.2   Experiments Execution and Results

We performed all our execution on Weka v3.7.11[3], which is a suite of ML algorithms written in Java with result visualization capabilities. The execution started with processing the textual sentences in our contributed dataset (i.e., COINs Corpus) using natural language processing (NLP) techniques. The processing included tokenizing sentences into words, lowering cases, eliminating noise words (e.g., is, are, in, of, this, etc.), and stemming words into their root format (e.g., encapsulating and encapsulated are returned as encapsulate).

Feature Selection. After processing the text, we identified the most representative features or keywords for the COIN classes within the COINs Corpus using the Bag-of-Words (BOWs) and N-Gram approaches, which we explained in the background section. That is, each sentence was represented as a collection of words. Then, each single word and each n-combination of words in the sentence were considered as features, where N was between 1 and 3. For example, in a

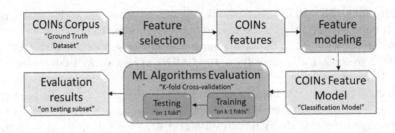

Fig. 3. Experiments process

---
[3]   Weka: http://www.cs.waikato.ac.nz/ml/weka.

sentence like "A user is encapsulated by a read-only Person object", the word "encapsulate" and the combination "read-only" were considered as two of its features. The output of this step was a set of features for the COINs Corpus.

Feature Modeling. In this stage, the whole COINs Corpus was transformed into a mathematical model. That is, it was represented as a matrix, in which headers contained all extracted features from the previous phase, while each row represented a sentence of the corpus. Then, we weighted the matrix, where each cell [row, column] held the weight of a feature in a specific sentence. For weighting, we used the Term Frequency-Inverse Document Frequency (TF-IDF) [15], which is often used for text retrieval. The result of this was the COINs Feature Model (or the classification model), which is a reusable asset reserving knowledge about conceptual interoperability constraints in API documents.

ML Algorithms Evaluation. We selected a number of well-known ML text-classification algorithms (e.g., NaïveBayes versions, Support Vector Machine, Random Forest Tree, K-Nearest Neighbor KNN, and more). Then, we ran these algorithms on the classification model resulted from the modeling activity.

Table 3. COINs identification results using different ML algorithms

ML algorithm	Seven-COIN Corpus			Two-COIN Corpus		
	Precision	Recall	F-measure	Precision	Recall	F-measure
ComplementNaïveBayes	70.4%	70.2%	70.0%	81.9%	82.0%	81.9%
NaïveBayesMutinomialupdatable	66.0%	65.1%	65.4%	81.9%	82.0%	81.8%
Support vector machine	59.3%	60.0%	59.0%	75.7%	75.7%	75.7%
Random forest tree	60.4%	56.3%	52.3%	73.7%	73.9%	73.7%
Simple logistic	52.5%	54.4%	52.4%	68.2%	68.4%	67.2%
KNN K=1	54.8%	45.5%	40.8%	64.2%	52.3%	47.8%
KNN K=2	49.8%	36.1%	30.1%	64.4%	48.7%	40.6%

Evaluation Results (Answering RQ2: How Effective and Efficient Would it be to Use ML Techniques in Automating the Extraction of COINs from Text in API Documentations?).

Effectiveness of Identifying the COINs using ML Algorithms. Here we report the effectiveness results in terms of accuracy metrics in two cases:

- *Seven-COIN Corpus Case.* The evaluation results showed that the best accuracy in automatically identifying seven classes of interoperability constraints in text was achieved by the ComplementNaïveBayes algorithm (see Table 3). It achieved 70.4% precision, 70.2% recall, and 70% F-measure. In the second place came NaïveBayesMutinomialupdatable algorithm with about 5% less accuracy than the former algorithm. The other algorithms had accuracy, F-measure, between 62.8% and 59.0%. The worst results were from the KNN algorithms.
- *Two-COIN Corpus Case.* By applying the same algorithms on the Two-COIN Corpus, we obtained better results. In particular, the accuracy increased

with almost 11 % compared to the results in the Seven-COIN case with the ComplementNaïveBayes algorithm. That is, the precision increased to 81.9 %, recall to 82.0 %, and F-measure to 81.9 %. Similar to the previous case, NaïveBayesMutinomialupdatable came in the second rank and the 2-Nearest Neighbor algorithm had the worst results as seen in Table 3. Note, we have achieved an improvement in accuracy compared to our preliminary investigation results [1], in which we had F-measure of 62.2 % using the NaïveBayes algorithm.

Efficiency of Identifying the COINs Using ML Algorithms. Obviously, the machine beats the human performance in terms of the spent time in analyzing the text. As we mentioned earlier, analyzing the documents costed us about 44 working hours, while, it took the machine way less time. For example, training and testing the NaïveBayesMultinominalupdate took about 5 s on our complete corpus with 2283 sentences). This efficiency would enhance when using machines with faster and more powerful CPU (we ran the experiments on a machine with Intel core i5 460 M CPU with 2.5 GHZ speed).

6.3 Discussion and Limitations

Towards Automatic Conceptual Interoperability Analysis. The achieved effectiveness in the automatic identification of constraints (e.g., 81.9 % F-measure) is promising and shows the potentials of our ML classification model in serving architects through their interoperability analysis tasks. We consider this accuracy high, as we compared the algorithms' results to our complete sentence-by-sentence manual analysis for the API documents, which we did for the sake of building a robust corpus. However, in practice, sentences are not examined in such a heavy way, especially when projects are limited in time and manpower. Hence, our model and its provided results in this work are a step towards achieving a good level of automation intelligence for the classic software engineering practices that are both error-prone and resource-consuming.

Larger Corpus, Better Accuracy Results. It is known in ML that the more classification classes you want to train the machine on identifying, the more training data it requires to be fed with. This explains the higher accuracy we achieved using the Two-COIN Corpus compared to the Seven-COIN Corpus even with the same amount of sentences in both. Therefore, we plan to enlarge our corpus, to achieve better accuracy in identifying the seven COIN classes.

Unbalanced Amount of Instances for Each Class in the Corpus. As noticed, the number of instances for the COIN classes is not balanced in the corpus. That is, dominant classes (i.e., Not-COIN, Dynamic, and Semantic) contribute with the majority of sentences in the data set (i.e., 91 %). While, the other classes (i.e., Structure, Syntax, Quality and Context) are smaller and share the left 9 % of the corpus. This affects the classification accuracy of the classes with fewer instances. Therefore, in future work we intend to increase the number of instances for these minor classes in the training data to achieve higher accuracy results.

7 Tool Support (A Prototype)

To bring our ideas to practical life, we designed a tool as a web browser plugin that aims at assisting software architects and analysts in their conceptual interoperability analysis task. The tool takes sentences from API documents, recognizes if they have any conceptual interoperability constraint, and reports their COIN classes within seconds. We implemented an easy-to-use prototype for the tool, in which the architect can highlight a sentence in a webpage for an API document to examine if it has any COIN (see Fig. 4).

The tool encapsulates our contributed classification model and mirrors its efficiency and accuracy that we described in Subsect. 6.2. That is, the tool saves time and manual effort by automatically identifying and classifying the conceptual constraints from text in seconds. This functionality offers critical input for architects to understand the impact of the identified constraints and to satisfy them based on their class. Hence, the tool has potentials to improve the effectiveness of interoperability analysis, especially for inexperienced architects.

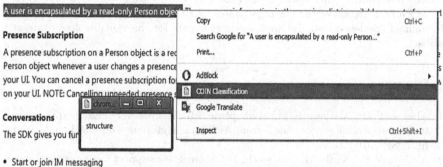

Fig. 4. Example of the tool identification for a Structure COIN in an API document

We implemented the prototype as a plugin for the Chrome web browser using Java and JavaScript languages. The functionality is offered as a Web Service and all communication is over the Simple Object Access Protocol (SOAP). The tool design includes: (1) *Front-End component* that we developed using JavaScript to provide the graphical user interface. (2) *Back-End component* that we developed using Java and Weka APIs to be responsible for locating our service on the server, passing it the input sentence, and carrying back the response.

8 Conclusion and Future Work

In this paper, we have presented our ideas about supporting software architects in performing seamless conceptual interoperability analysis. The contribution

pursued by this work was to utilize ML algorithms for effective and efficient identification of conceptual interoperability constraints in text of API documents.
Our systematic empirically-based research included a multiple case study that
resulted in the ground truth dataset. Then, we built a ML classification model
that we evaluated in experiments using different ML algorithms. The results
showed that we achieved up to 70.0 % accuracy for identifying seven classes of
interoperability constraints, and it increased to 81.9 % for two classes.

In the future, we plan to automate the manual filtering part of the data
preparation. We will also analyze further API documents to advance the generalizability of our results. This would enrich the ground truth dataset as well,
allowing better training for the ML algorithms and accordingly better accuracy
in identifying the conceptual interoperability constraints. With regards to the
tool, we will extend it to generate full reports about all interoperability constraints in a webpage and to collect instant feedback from users about automation results. In addition, we plan to empirically evaluate our ideas in industrial
case studies.

Acknowledgment. This work is supervised by Prof. Dieter Rombach and funded
by the Ph.D. Program of the CS Department of Kaiserslautern University. We thank
Mohammed Abufouda and the anonymous reviewers for the valuable comments and
feedback.

References

1. Abukwaik, H., Abujayyab, M., Humayoun, S.R., Rombach, D.: Extracting conceptual interoperability constraints from API documentation using machine learning.
In: ICSE 2016 (2016)
2. Abukwaik, H., Naab, M., Rombach, D.: A proactive support for conceptual interoperability analysis in software systems. In: WICSA 2015 (2015)
3. Anvaari, M., Zimmermann, O.: Semi-automated design guidance enhancer
(SADGE): a framework for architectural guidance development. In: Avgeriou, P.,
Zdun, U. (eds.) ECSA 2014. LNCS, vol. 8627, pp. 41–49. Springer, Heidelberg
(2014). doi:10.1007/978-3-319-09970-5_4
4. Banko, M., Brill, E.: Scaling to very very large corpora for natural language dis-
ambiguation. In: Proceedings of 39th Annual Meeting of the Association for Computational Linguistics (2001)
5. Caldiera, V., Rombach, H.D.: The goal question metric approach. Encyclopedia
Softw. Eng. **2**, 528–532 (1994)
6. Chu, W., Lin, T.Y.: Foundations and advances in data mining (2005)
7. Figueiredo, A.M., Dos Reis, J.C., Rodrigues, M.A.: Improving access to software
architecture knowledge an ontology-based search approach (2012)
8. Garlan, D., Allen, R., Ockerbloom, J.: Architectural mismatch or why it's hard to
build systems out of existing parts. In: ICSE 1995 (1995)
9. Hallé, S., Bultan, T., Hughes, G., Alkhalaf, M., Villemaire, R.: Runtime verification
of web service interface contracts. Computer **43**(3), 59–66 (2010)
10. John, G.H., Langley, P.: Estimating continuous distributions in Bayesian classifiers.
In: Conference on Uncertainty in Artificial Intelligence (1995)

11. Kohavi, R., et al.: A study of cross-validation and bootstrap for accuracy estimation and model selection. In: Ijcai, vol. 14 (1995)
12. López, C., Codocedo, V., Astudillo, H., Cysneiros, L.M.: Bridging the gap between software architecture rationale formalisms and actual architecture documents: an ontology-driven approach. Sci. Comput. Program. **77**, 66–80 (2012)
13. Pandita, R., Xiao, X., Zhong, H., Xie, T., Oney, S., Paradkar, A.: Inferring method specifications from natural language API descriptions. In: ICSE 2012 (2012)
14. Powers, D.M.: Evaluation: from precision, recall and F-measure to ROC, informedness, markedness and correlation (2011)
15. Robertson, S.: Understanding inverse document frequency: on theoretical arguments for IDF. J. Documentation **60**(5), 503–520 (2004)
16. Oakes, M.P., Ji, M. (eds.): Quantitative Methods in Corpus-Based Translation Studies: A Practical Guide to Descriptive Translation Research, vol. 51. John Benjamins Publishing, Amsterdam (2012)
17. Runeson, P., Höst, M.: Guidelines for conducting and reporting case study research in software engineering. Empirical Softw. Eng. **14**(2), 131–164 (2009)
18. Tong, S., Koller, D.: Support vector machine active learning with applications to text classification. J. Mach. Learn. Res. **2**, 45–66 (2001)
19. Wu, Q., Wu, L., Liang, G., Wang, Q., Xie, T., Mei, H.: Inferring dependency constraints on parameters for web services. In: WWW 2013 (2013)
20. Zhong, H., Zhang, L., Xie, T., Mei, H.: Inferring resource specifications from natural language API documentation. In: ASE 2009 (2009)

Design Decision Documentation: A Literature Overview

Zoya Alexeeva[1]([⊠]), Diego Perez-Palacin[2], and Raffaela Mirandola[2]

[1] Industrial Software Systems, ABB Corporate Research, Ladenburg, Germany
{zoya.alexeeva}@de.abb.com
[2] Dip. di Elettronica, Inf. e Bioingegneria, Politecnico di Milano, Milano, Italy
{raffaela.mirandola,diego.perez}@polimi.it

Abstract. Despite the abundance of research on methodologies for the documentation of design decisions and the evidence linking documentation to the improvement in the systems evolution, their practical adoption seems to be sparse. To understand this issue, we have conducted an overview of state-of-the-art on documentation of design decisions. We pursue an identification of characteristics of the different techniques proposed in the literature, such as the final goal of the documentation, the quantity of information attached to each decision documentation, the rigour of the proposed technique or its level of automation. To unveil these, we propose six classification dimensions, relevant for the industrial application, and use them to structure and analyse the review results. This work contributes with a taxonomy of the area, a structured overview covering 96 publications and a summary of open questions, which can be addressed by future research to facilitate practical adoption.

1 Introduction

Software architecture is comprised of non-trivial design decisions, and their documentation is crucial for improved system evolution [1–6]. However, while there is usually at least some kind of architectural model available, the underlying design decisions are seldom documented in practice [7–9]. From the other side, there is plenty of research work on documentation of design decisions, which practical adoption seems to be still sparse [8, 10–15]. To understand this issue we have conducted a literature review on documentation of design decisions covering 96 publications dating from 2004 to 2015.

In this work, we treat "software architecture" and "software design" as synonyms. Under software architecture we understand *"a set of principal design decisions made about the system"* [2], and is *"a structure or structures of the system, which comprise software elements, the externally visible properties of those elements, and the relationships among them"* [16]. *Architectural design decision* is *"an outcome of a design process during the initial construction or the evolution of a software system, which is a primary representation of architecture"* (adopted from Tyree and Akerman [17], Jansen and Bosch [18] and Kruchten [19]).

B. Tekinerdogan et al. (Eds.): ECSA 2016, LNCS 9839, pp. 84–101, 2016.
DOI: 10.1007/978-3-319-48992-6_6

To structure the overview results, we propose 6 classification dimensions relevant for the industrial applicability: Goal, Formalisation, Context, Extension, Tool-support, and Evaluation (definitions are provided in Sect. 3). The dimensions were inspired by the conclusions of related reviews provided in Sect. 2. We than analyse resulting research area taxonomy to propose further research directions to understand and close the gap between the state of research and its industrial application.

To summarize, the contributions of this paper are (1) a taxonomy of the area, (2) a structured overview covering 96 publications and (3) a summary of open questions, which can be addressed by future research to facilitate practical adoption. In depth evaluation of selected approaches was out of scope of the review and is a subject of future work.

The remainder of this paper is structured as follows: Sect. 2 provides overview of the related reviews, Sect. 3 outlines our overview method, including proposed classification dimensions. Section 4 presents the results: Structured overview of 96 publications and summary of open research questions. Limitations of the work and lessons learned are discussed in Sect. 5. Finally, Sect. 6 concludes the paper.

2   Related Literature Reviews

This section provides an overview of related reviews in a chronological order.

A survey by Regli et al. [20] provides an overview of design rationale research area, focusing on prototype systems from different domains. While the survey was published over a decade ago, the observed problems are still relevant nowadays: Little information on successful application of rationale documentation in industry and a limited adoption of design rationale systems.

Babar et al. [15] provide an overview of 8 approaches for architectural knowledge management, four of which are relevant for decision documentation and are also included into our review. Additionally, the authors categorize approaches between codification (knowledge capturing and sharing via repositories) and personalization (knowledge sharing via individuals). They observe that while the research mostly focuses on codification, industry seems to unintentionally rely on personalization strategies.

Kruchten et al. [3] describe "evolution" of the decision's view, provide a brief overview of tools supporting the design rationale, and observe that documentation process is not yet fully integrated into software engineering practice.

Shahin et al. [21] provide an overview and comparison of several design decision models and tools using the criteria for effective tool support defined by Farenhorst et al. [22]. The latter provide observations on knowledge sharing from an industrial organisation, define the criteria and apply these criteria to 6 software architecture tools.

Bu et al. [23] analyse several approaches from three perspectives: Knowledge modelling, decision making and rationale management. Findings include: Scarce support of the identification of architecture-significant requirements, deficits in support of cross-cutting decisions, provided decision processes and software-lifecycle, and sometimes incomplete modelling of architectural knowledge. Henttonen and Matinlassi [24] provide a framework to evaluate knowledge sharing tools and apply to three tool examples.

Tang et al. [14] provide evaluation and a comprehensive comparison of 5 knowledge management tools. The authors confirm the observation by Babar et al. [15] on the preference in personalization approaches to knowledge management (knowledge is passed between individuals, rather than via repositories). Previous work by Tang et al. [5] provides an overview of architecture design rationale state-of-the-practice by surveying 81 practitioners. Lack of methodology and tool support are listed between the main findings of the survey.

Hoorn et al. [25] report on a study on sharing architectural knowledge with 279 architects. The results provide several valuable insights on the architecting process and architect's desires in regard to knowledge sharing support.

Our overview extends on the related work described above, providing an extended overview of design decision documentation research area and proposing possible future research directions.

3   Overview Methodology

Our overview is based on methodology described in Kitchenham [26], de Boer and Farenhorst [27], Koziolek [28] and Aleti et al. [29]. The overview covers publications from 2004 to 2015, as Kruchten et al. [3] referred to 2004 as a starting date for research area growth. The work was finished in Q1 of 2016, therefore, some of the more recent publications could be skipped due to the missing indexation in search engines. The goal of this work is to provide an overview of the design decision documentation research and to identify further research directions, rather than to evaluate single approaches for their industrial applicability. Such an evaluation is subject of future work.

The rest of this section describes the classification dimensions, process (incl. venues, keywords and search string), and inclusion and exclusion criteria.

3.1   Classification Dimensions

To structure the overview, classification dimensions are required that are (1) relevant for the industrial adoption of the decision documentation approaches, and (2) obtainable from publications. Inspired by the related work Sect. 2, we propose 6 following dimensions: **1. Goal** – what is the goal of decision documentation. **2. Formalisation** – what formalisation approach is used in the publication. **3. Extent** – does the work attempt to capture all the decisions or it applies some selection criteria. **4. Context** – what additional artefacts or trace links to other artefacts are captured together with the decisions. **5. Tool-support** – is there any tool-support, and if yes what kind of. **6. Evaluation** – what type of evaluation is described in the publication (Table 1).

Table 1. Literature sources

AES	Elsevier Advances in Engineering Software	ESEC FSE	Eu. Sw. Eng. Conf. and the ACM SIGSOFT Symposium on the Found. of Sw. Eng.
Comp	IEEE Computer	Europlop	Conference of pattern languages
JSA	Elsevier Journal of Systems Architecture	FASE	International Conference on Fundamental Approaches to Software Engineering
JSME	Journal of Software: Evolution and Process	ICMS	IEEE International Conference on Software Maintenance
JSS	Elsevier Journal of Systems and Software	ICSR	International Conference on Software Reuse
SE	Wiley Journal of Systems Engineering	IWPSE	EVOL
SoSyM	Springer Journal on Software and Systems Modelling	Models	International Conference on. Model Driven Engineering Languages and Systems
SW	IEEE Software	QOSA	International ACM Sigsoft Conference on the Quality of Software Architectures
TOSEM	ACM Transactions on Software Engineering and Methodology	RE	IEEE International Requirements Engineering conference
TSC	IEEE Transactions on Services Computing	SHARK	SHaring and Reusing Architectural Knowledge
TSE	IEEE Transactions on Software Engineering	SPLC	International Software Product Line Conference
ASE	IEEE/ACM International Conference. Automated Sw. Engineering	TOOLS	International Conference on Objects, Models, Components, Patterns
CBSE	Int. ACM Sigsoft Symposium on Component-Based Sw. Eng.	TwinPeaks	International Workshop on the Twin Peaks of Requirements and Architecture
CSMR	European Conference on Sw. Maintenance and Reengineering		

While there might be other relevant dimensions, such information is not necessarily present in publications. For example, information on quality of documented decisions or supported project development phases is seldom in texts.

3.2 Overview Process

In out work, we have followed the following process:

S1. Identification of literature sources, whereby we focused on the main venues in software engineering, software evolution and software architecture research fields to limit the overall review effort. The venues were selected based on conference rankings available in [30], and are listed in Fig. 1.

S2. Definition of classification dimensions to structure the search and to derive results taxonomy. Section 3.1 presented the outcome of this step.

S3. Selection of the keywords and definition of the search string. We have defined a set of keywords, and have conducted a manual search through the series of *ECSA (European Conference on Software Architecture)* to be able to verify keywords for correctness. We than defined a search string and checked whether it was capable of finding most of the ECSA publications that we have identified manually. More general conferences like ICSE and FSE seemed less suitable for a manual check, as overall number of publications was too high to manage with a reasonable effort.

The logical representation of the search string is: *("Design*" OR "Architecture*") AND ("Decision" OR "Documentation" OR "Knowledge" OR "Architectural specification" OR "Rationale").* The search engines used are: IEEE [31], DBLP [32] and ACM [33]. We did not use Google as all selected venues are covered by the other search engines. **S4. Automated search** through the literature sources using the search engines and search string defined in step 3. Manual filtering of publications based on the information contained in the title, abstract, introduction and conclusion to discard the false-positives of the search.

S5. Full-text analysis of publications selected in step 4. Definition of a taxonomy comprising categories for each of the dimensions identified in step 2. Final structuring and analysis of the results.

3.3   Inclusion and Exclusion Criteria

Documentation of design decisions is a broad research area. While it is related to architectural knowledge management, only some of the publications in the field are concerned with documentation of decisions as such. Thus, *only publications that explicitly cover documentation of design decisions and explain the process are included into the overview.* This criteria also applies to publications on product-lines, feature and architecture models, reference architectures, code and others.

Publications on support or documentation of decision making process, architecture recovery and visualisation of design decisions were excluded from the overview unless design decision documentation was explicit.

Furthermore, we define a set of publications on evolution of one approach over several years as a *"publication-line"*. Such set is merged to one publication entry in the result tables, and the most recent publication is taken as a reference.

4   Overview Results

We have found 432 publications that matched our keywords and the search string. The preliminary evaluation in process step 4 reduced the number to 160 publications, and a full-text evaluation in step 5 reduced the number to 96 publications that truly matched the overview scope. The top-represented venues are (Fig. 1): ECSA (29), SHARK (19), WICSA (15) and QoSA (10). Furthermore, 56 papers were identified as "publication-lines" and clustered to 18 main representative publications. Thus, in overall, we report on 58 unique approaches in the remainder of this section. The unique publication does not mean unique authors, but the approach presented in the publication.

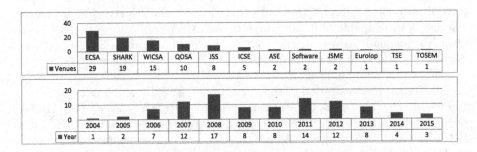

Fig. 1. Distribution of publications between venues and years

The distribution of publication between years on Fig. 1 could suggest that the popularity of the topic is gradually reducing over the last years, which could mean that the research area has achieved a certain maturity degree and the next step would be a transfer of the research results into practical adoption. However, the latter remains a challenging step as observed by [8, 10, 13–15].

4.1   Results Taxonomy and Structured Overview

The obtained taxonomy and structured overview of design decision documentation publications are provided in Table 2. The detailed results are explained in the following.

Table 2. Taxonomy and structured overview of decision documentation publications

Goal	Formalisation	Tool-Support	Extent	Context	Evaluation
Documentation/Capture	Formal	Commercial addon	All	Decisions	Industrial Case Study
Consistancy/Compliance	Semi-Formal	Eclipse-Based	Selected by Type	Rationale	Real-life Case Study
Evolution	Informal	Web-based	Selective by Quality/Number	Requirements	Research Case Study
Extraction		Other		Other	Research Example
Impact Anaysis		Not available			Empirical
Reuse					Not available
Sharing					
Traceability					
Visualisation					

Goals	Publications
Documentation/ Capture	[6, 8, 11, 15, 88, 27, 17–21, 23, 25, 26, 29, 30, 32, 34–40, 47, 46, 44, 49, 53, 56, 58, 60, 62, 22, 66, 72–74, 78, 80, 82, 81, 83, 85, 86, 75, 89–94]
Consistency/ Compliance	[10, 29, 30, 47, 44, 49, 54, 58, 60, 63, 66, 80]
Decision/ Rationale Extraction	[23, 46, 60, 63]
Evolution	[21, 28, 35, 40, 53, 54, 57, 58, 66, 94]
Impact Analysis	[30, 35, 44, 58, 66, 82]
Reuse	[32, 11, 20, 38, 49, 92, 94]
Sharing	[6, 10, 8, 18, 19, 27, 31, 47, 44, 60, 66, 72, 74, 93, 94]
Traceability	[10, 13, 18, 28, 35, 47, 44, 54, 57, 58, 60, 63, 22, 72, 78, 85, 86, 89, 91, 27, 94]
Visualisation	[7, 56, 60, 66, 72]
Formalization	
Informal	[11, 73]
S-F, Template	[30, 32, 36, 37, 39, 57, 63, 86, 94]
S-F, Ontology	[7, 8, 53, 56]
S-F, Meta-Model	[10, 13, 17–21, 23, 28, 31, 35, 47, 49, 54, 62, 22, 66, 72, 74, 80, 89, 92, 93]
S-F, Other and ADLs	[6, 14, 25, 27, 40, 46, 44, 58, 78, 90, 91]
S-F, Other	[34, 38, 75]
Formal	[29, 60, 81–83, 85]
Extent	
All	[6, 10, 7, 8, 11, 13, 14, 27, 17–21, 23, 25, 28, 31, 34, 35, 38, 47, 46, 44, 49, 53, 54, 56, 57, 60, 22, 66, 72, 74, 75, 78, 83, 85, 91–94]
Selective by Decision Type	[29, 36, 37, 39, 40, 58, 62, 63, 73, 80, 89, 90]
Selective by Qual./ #	[30, 32, 81, 82, 86]

Context	Publications
Decision	All
Rationale	[6, 8, 13, 14, 27, 17–21, 23, 25, 28, 30–32, 38, 40, 47, 53, 54, 56, 60, 62, 63, 22, 66, 72–74, 78, 86, 89, 94]
Requirements	[6, 8, 13, 14, 17–21, 23, 25, 28, 31, 35, 40, 47, 44, 60, 62, 22, 66, 75, 85, 86, 89, 91, 94]
Other	[6, 10, 8, 11, 13, 14, 17–21, 23, 25, 28–31, 34, 36, 35, 38–40, 47, 46, 44, 54, 56, 58, 60, 62, 63, 22, 66, 73, 75, 78, 80–82, 85, 86, 89, 91, 93, 94]

Tool-Support	Publications
Commercial Addon	[19, 31, 49, 78, 94]
Eclipse-Based	[13, 14, 25, 28, 47, 44, 54, 58, 60, 22, 81, 90, 93]
Web-Based	[6, 18, 66]
Other (Wiki, Word plugin)	[7, 8, 11, 29, 53, 56, 62, 63, 72, 73, 75, 80, 92]
Not available	[10, 27, 17, 20, 21, 23, 30, 32, 34–40, 46, 57, 74, 82, 83, 85, 86, 89, 91]

Evaluation	Publications
Industrial Case Study	[10, 8, 18, 19, 21, 30, 31, 38, 56, 58, 60, 75, 78, 92–94]
Real-Life Case Study	[7, 23, 38, 22, 57]
Research Case Study	[10, 20, 47, 46, 54, 60, 63, 66, 74]
Research Example	[13, 14, 17, 25, 28, 34, 36, 37, 40, 47, 49, 72, 73, 80, 82, 85, 86, 89–91]
Empirical	[18, 32, 40, 44, 58, 78, 83]
Not available	[6, 11, 27, 35, 39, 53, 62, 81]

1. Goal. While all the publications deal with documentation of design decisions, they follow different goals: *a. Documentation/Capture* – focus solely on documentation of architectural knowledge including decisions, only on design decisions and/or on design rationale. *b. Consistency/Compliance* – documentation of decisions in order to enable architecture consistency or compliance checks.

c. Evolution – documentation of decisions in order to manage and support evolution of a system, including managing evolution of decisions in some of the cases. Publications dealing with the evolution only implicitly were not included into the category. *d. Extraction* – focus on extraction of information in order to support documentation of design decisions, rationale and/or trace links. *e. Impact Analysis* – documentation of decisions in order to run impact analysis in architecture on decision changes, and in some cases, to estimate effort required for implementation of changes. *f. Reuse* – documentation of decisions in order to facilitate design reuse. *g. Sharing* – documentation of decisions in order to facilitate explicit sharing of architectural knowledge. *h. Traceability* – documentation of decisions in order to explicitly facilitate traceability between design artefacts. *e. Visualisation* – focus on documentation and improved visualisation of documented decisions.

If a publication followed on several goals, it was assigned to several categories in the result tables. Obviously, the majority of publications (80 %) focus on the documentation as their primary goal, closely followed by traceability (36 %), knowledge sharing (26 %) and consistency checks (21 %).

Although such brown-field scenario is predominant in an industrial setting, there is a low number of approaches on decision and rationale extraction out of already existing artefacts (7 %). The evolution of the system, including the evolution of decisions as such, is also important in industrial context [11,34]. But, only few approaches consider system evolution as their goal (10 %), and even less approaches foresee a possibility of a decision to evolve (4 approaches, comprising only 7 % of the overall number).

2. Formalisation. Classification of publications by Formalisation is the following: *a. Formal* – use of formal methods, such as repertory grids, formal ADLs and others. *b. Semi-Formal* – use of semi-formal methods, such as meta-models, ADLs, ontologies, text-based templates and others. *c. Informal* – use of informal methods, such as free text or white board cards and photos.

There is a good balance between formal and informal approaches. The predominance of meta-modelling formalisation approaches (40 %) may be explained via benefits of tool-chain generation. However, at the moment of our analysis, 9 approaches did not use presumed meta-modelling benefits for the tool-support. Only 3 of these approaches offered a decision documentation and management add-on to a commercial tool [35–37], 6 offered an Eclipse pug-in [38–43], and 5 offered some other tool-support [44–48].

3. Extent. Extent of decision documentation can be divided into: *a. All* – all design decisions are documented and if multiple decision types are defined – all of the types are documented. *b. Selected by decision type* – focus on one or several decision types and documentation is limited to these types. *c. Selected by quality or number* – documentation only of some design decisions, e.g. based on decision quality or relevance for certain components.

In large systems, there might be hundreds of design decisions evolving over time, and not all decisions are important to be documented. Assumptions shall be made on what decisions must be documented and to what extent. Moreover, manual documentation and management of such number of decisions is infeasible and a tool-support on documentation generation or automatic documentation would be required. However, selective decision documentation based on decision number or quality is considered only by 5 publications (9 %), and 13 (22 %) publications consider filtering decisions by type.

4. Context. Classification of publications is the following: *a. Decisions* – focus on documentation of design decisions, no documentation of other project artefacts. *b. Requirements* – requirements are co-documented with decisions as part of the proposed approach. In some cases, these requirements are captured as triggers or rationale for a decision. *c. Rationale* – decision rationale is co-documented with decisions. In some cases, requirements are linked as part of the rational, but usually the rationale is captured as a free-text explanation. *d. Other* – other artefacts, e.g. decision alternatives, solutions, tracelinks, and others are co-documented with decisions.

If a publication proposed co-documentation of multiple items, it was assigned to several categories in the result tables. Most of the approaches document not only design decisions but also other related artefacts, such as triggering requirements (47 %), rationale (60 %) and other (80 %), such as code, thus providing a comprehensive context to a decision.

5. Tool-Support. Tool-support of documentation of decisions can be classified as: *a. Commercial Add-on* – an add-on to a commercial tool, such as an architecting tool (i.g., Enterprise Architect), requirements management tool (i.g., Polarion), and others. *b. Eclipse-Based* – an Eclipse-based research tool. *c. Web-Based* – a Web-based research tool, often with a goal to support a collaborative work on architecture. *d. Other (Wiki, Word plug-in)* – a research tool based on other technologies, e.g. Wikis, Word plug-ins, and others. *e. n/a* – no tool-support or no information on tool-support is available.

While tool-support is crucial for industrial application, 24 approaches (41 %) have no tool-support or provide no information on it, and 5 publications (9 %) describe an extension to a commercial tool, such as Enterprise Architect. While we do not have a statistical information on which exact tools are widespread in industry, we do know that these are usually commercial tools. The low number of tool-support suitable for integration into the industrial tool-chain may be an impediment for the industrial applicability of approaches.

6. Evaluation. Evaluation of approached can be classified as: *a. Industrial Case Study* – an industrial application, executed at industrial site, e.g. by a company or in a company project. *b. Real-Life Case Study* – a real-life case study, executed at the research site or provided details were insufficient to categorize it as a pure industrial case study. *c. Research Case Study* – a research case study. *d. Research Example* – a research example, on the contrary to the case study meaning a smaller application, usually in a de-attached context. *e. Empirical* – an empirical evaluation of the proposed approach. *f. Not available* – no evaluation or no information available.

Publication reporting several types of evaluation were added to multiple categories. While evaluation is important, publications with no evaluation or with evaluation based on a research example comprise 48 %. About 28 % of the publications report evaluation in industrial context and 7 % real-life case studies, which is a prerequisite towards industrial applicability. However, despite the reported positive feedback, there seem to be no follow-up actions or reports on a more long-term application by the involved companies. We can conclude that the adoption of approaches in organisations likely remains a problem even if the first positive results were achieved.

4.2   Research Area Open Questions

Analysing the selected publications, we have identified several potential directions for further research in the area. We list the suggestions based on assumed importance, where the first point is evaluated as more urgent, and the last as less urgent.

Q1. Industrial Applicability Requirements. We found only few reports on industrial experience or listing requirements on approaches coming from the industry. Several few examples are: Work by Manteuffel et al. [7], Zimmermann et al. [34] and Dragomir et al. [11], where the authors focus on the situation in an individual company. Survey Tang et al. [5] from 2006 reports on design rationale practices based on perception of 81 practitioners. Work by Farenhorst et al. [22] reports observations on knowledge sharing from an individual company. In addition, Falessi et al. [12], Tang et al. [14] and Babar et al. [15] list several possible requirements for the area.

A systematic survey of state-of-the-practice on decision documentation and definition of industrial applicability requirements would be a significant contribution to the research area.

Q2. Brownfield Support. Few publications explicitly define whether they target a new system development or an existing system. Implicitly, the majority of the approaches deal with new development (so-called "greenfield" development), except for [49–51]. To our best knowledge, system development in industry often includes brownfield. Therefore, we see the support of legacy systems as a highly reasonable research direction ("brownfield" support).

Q3. Evolution of Decisions. Design decisions pass through different stages and evolve over time together with system development. While documentation of stages of design decisions is a common feature (e.g. via status as new, accepted or deprecated), documentation of decision evolution is not sufficiently covered. Some exclusions are work by Zimmermann et al. [34], Dragomir et al. [11], van Heesch et al. [52], Szlenk et al. [53] and Nowak and Pautasso [54].

Q4. Quality and Extent of Captured Decisions. Quality evaluation of captured design decisions was addressed by few publications, such as [12,17,55], and most of the approaches seem to focus on capturing all design decisions. Many do not specify which attributes are mandatory and which are optional. As large systems potentially include 100s of design decisions that address various aspects of a system at different levels of granularity, a more refined approach would be required. The scalability of extensive documentation for larger systems requires further investigation.

Q5. Tool-Support. Approaches extending commercial tools for architectural modelling are [34–37,56]. We suggest to address the following related open research questions: "What (architectural) tools are used in industry?"; "Can the proposed approaches be meaningfully integrated into such tools?", and "What organisational changes are required for the approach and tool adoption?".

Q6. Industrial Evaluation. Evaluation presented in publications is mostly performed on research examples or case studies. Few publications report on evaluation in an industrial setting, however, there are no follow up reports on the long-term application. Investigation of latter could provide insights on what aspects are to be addressed by the future research.

Q7. Overhead Connected to Documentation. Work by Capilla and Ali Babar [57] is one of the few examples addressing a question on how much extra overhead is actually caused by decision documentation. Further investigation of overhead associated with the approaches versus the obtained benefit seems relevant to us.

Q8. Reuse of Design Decisions Between Projects and Systems. Considering the effort required to prepare and document a decision, reuse of such knowledge between projects and systems would seem beneficial for practical adoption. Only few approaches from address this issue, e.g. [12,34,48,58]. Here, open research questions could be: "In what cases could reuse be beneficial?", "How could design decisions could be captured for reuse?", "Are there expert systems on software architecting available, and are they applied on practice?".

Q9. Common Terminology Definition. The terminology in the area of architectural research is not yet completely established. Terms are often overloaded or used to describe different concepts, such as architecture, design, model, component, interface and others. The majority of publications neither defines what is understood under architecture and design, nor defines design decision and related attributes as such. This observation matches with the observation of de Boer and Farenhorst [27] for the architectural knowledge. An action needs to be taken to define and to agree on a common glossary for the research area. In our opinion, such discussion could be best carried as a panel discussion in a larger conference on software architecture, such as ECSA.

5   Discussion

This section discusses limitations of the overview and the lessons learned.

5.1   Limitations

In the following, we discuss the limitations of the literature overview presented in this paper.

Scope Limitation. This overview structures scientific work on design decision documentation that was published in recognized journals and conferences. The overview does not include overview or evaluation of commercial tools unless the information on them was published as scientific work. Evaluation of approaches proposed in scientific publications or their quality is also out of scope and is subject of future work.

Completeness of the Results. The overview provides a comprehensive view on the research area, however, an absolute completeness cannot be warranted. The overview is based on the automatic venue search and relies on keywords, which were derived from a selective manual search. Filtering of the publications according to the overview scope was conducted by two persons, nevertheless, a mistake of false-negative evaluation cannot be excluded.

We limit relevant publications years starting from 2004 up to 2015, based on reference by Kruchten et al. [3], which is also a common practice in the literature overviews. In addition, some related research areas, e.g. code generation from models or decision-making support, can be also seen as a way to capture design decisions, but our overview does not include these. It follows the inclusion and exclusion criteria provided in Sect. 3.

Dimension Limitations. The dimensions, that are proposed to structure the literature overview, may be subjective to our opinion. There may be other industry-relevant dimensions, however, we did not discover any other information manageable in a systematic way.

Categorisation Validity. All publications were carefully analysed, but a human mistake cannot be excluded completely.

5.2   Lessons Learned

We have learned several lessons that we would like to share with community:

Keywords are Venue-Specific. This observation is opposite to the common review practice that we have also followed on. However, keywords are often venue-specific and the search string shall be defined per venue with venue-specific keywords. Such definition would significantly improve the accuracy of search.

Terms are Used Differently. We have encountered significant differences in terms usage e.g., "evolution of decisions" could mean evolution of decisions as such, evolution of system design with decisions only implicitly evolving, evolution of requirements leading to new decisions or evolution of a general system.

Automated Search Accuracy Cannot Be 100 %. As we used selective manual search to define our keywords, we could compare our manual search results with automated search results. An accuracy of 100 % could not be achieved, no matter how we modified the keywords and the search string. Moreover, some engines had problems with indexation of some conferences and workshops (i.g., SHARK workshop was partially absent from previous version of DBLP). Our final conclusion is that the *manual search might be quicker and more precise than the automated search.*

DBLP is Sufficient as a Search Engine. We could obtain the best search results using the DBLP search, especially after a new version of DBLP was rolled-out in 2015. It allowed quick access to the materials of multiple publishers, in addition to easy definition of keywords and rich filter criteria. DBLP only allows to search through the meta-information, such as title or keywords (if available). However, it proved to be enough and led to comparably low number of false-positives if compared to i.e. IEEE search in our observation. Based on this experience, we would prefer a manual search over the automatic search, but in cases where automatic search is beneficial, e.g. high number of publications across many venues, we would choose to use DBLP as the only engine.

Classification of Approaches May Be Non-trivial. Presentation of information may strongly vary between publications, and, in some cases, the available information cannot be compared without a direct approach application or detailed case study reports. For example, industrial evaluation vs. evaluation described as real-life case study was challenging to classify and compare due to sparse information provided.

6   Conclusion and Future Work

This paper presents a structured overview of 96 publications covering 58 unique approaches on documentation of design decisions. Despite the high number of research and evidence linking decision documentation to improved system evolution, the industrial adoption of design decision documentation approaches seems still sparse. Our observations suggest that the following factors may be responsible for this gap: Absence of industrial applicability requirements, only marginal support of brownfield development (legacy systems), insufficient consideration of the additional overhead produced by the extensive documentation of decisions, simplified or often missing perspective on evolution of systems and involved design decisions, and lack of tool-support and integration with commercial tools. We also see definition of common terminology in the software architecture research field and reuse of design decisions between projects and systems as two important research challenges.

Our future work focuses on systematic investigation of industrial applicability requirements and definition of generic applicability guidelines. The investigation shall include consolidation of currently available experience reports and review results, such as by Zimmermann et al. [34], Tang et al. [14], Savolainen et al. [59], Miksovic and Zimmermann [60], Lago et al. [61], and Komiya [62]. We also plan to investigate into additional industrial applicability dimensions. In the long term, future work shall include evaluation of the most mature approaches and definition of application guidelines for practitioners.

Acknowledgement. The authors would like to thank Ralf Reussner for his valuable input. The work has been partially supported by the FP7 European project Seaclouds.

References

1. Ozkaya, I., Wallin, P., Axelsson, J.: Architecture knowledge management during system evolution: observations from practitioners. In: SHARK (2010)
2. Taylor, R.N., Medvidovic, N., Dashofy, E.M.: Software Architecture: Foundations, Theory, and Practice. Wiley, New York (2009)
3. Kruchten, P., Capilla, R., Dueas, J.: The decision view's role in software architecture practice. IEEE Softw. **26**, 36–42 (2009)
4. Burge, J.E., Carroll, J.M., McCall, R., Mistrik, I.: Rationale-Based Software Engineering. Springer, Heidelberg (2008)
5. Tang, A., Babar, M.A., Gorton, I., Han, J.: A survey of architecture design rationale. J. Syst. Softw. **79**, 1792–1804 (2006)
6. Babar, M., Tang, A., Gorton, I., Han, J.: Industrial perspective on the usefulness of design rationale for software maintenance: a survey. In: 2006 6th International Conference on Quality Software (QSIC), pp. 201–208 (2006)
7. Manteuffel, C., Tofan, D., Koziolek, H., Goldschmidt, T., Avgeriou, P.: Industrial implementation of a documentation framework for architectural decisions. In: WICSA (2014)
8. Nkwocha, A., Hall, J.G., Rapanotti, L.: Design rationale capture for process improvement in the globalised enterprise: an industrial study. Softw. Syst. Model. **12**, 825–845 (2013)

9. Burge, J.E., Brown, D.C.: Software engineering using RATionale. J. Syst. Softw. **81**, 395–413 (2008)
10. Anvaari, M., Zimmermann, O.: Semi-automated Design Guidance Enhancer (SADGE): a framework for architectural guidance development. In: Avgeriou, P., Zdun, U. (eds.) ECSA 2014. LNCS, vol. 8627, pp. 41–49. Springer, Heidelberg (2014). doi:10.1007/978-3-319-09970-5_4
11. Dragomir, A., Lichter, H., Budau, T.: Systematic architectural decision management: a process-based approach. In: WICSA (2014)
12. Falessi, D., Briand, L.C., Cantone, G., Capilla, R., Kruchten, P.: The value of design rationale information. ACM Trans. Softw. Eng. Methodol. **22**(3), 21 (2013)
13. Tofan, D., Galster, M., Avgeriou, P.: Difficulty of architectural decisions – a survey with professional architects. In: Drira, K. (ed.) ECSA 2013. LNCS, vol. 7957, pp. 192–199. Springer, Heidelberg (2013). doi:10.1007/978-3-642-39031-9_17
14. Tang, A., Avgeriou, P., Jansen, A., Capilla, R., Babar, M.A.: A comparative study of architecture knowledge management tools. J. Syst. Softw. **83**, 352–370 (2010)
15. Babar, M., de Boer, R., Dingsoyr, T., Farenhorst, R.: Architectural knowledge management strategies: approaches in research and industry. In: SHARK (2007)
16. Rozanski, N., Woods, E.: Software Systems Architecture: Working with Stakeholders Using Viewpoints and Perspectives. Addison-Wesley Professional, Upper Saddle River (2009)
17. Tyree, J., Akerman, A.: Architecture decisions: demystifying architecture. IEEE Softw. **22**(2), 19–27 (2005)
18. Jansen, A., Bosch, J.: Software architecture as a set of architectural design decisions. In: 5th Working IEEE/IFIP Conference on Software Architecture, WICSA (2005)
19. Kruchten, P.: An ontology of architectural design decisions in software intensive systems. In: 2nd Groningen Workshop on Software Variability (2004)
20. Regli, W., Hu, X., Atwood, M., Sun, W.: A survey of design rationale systems: approaches, representation, capture and retrieval. Eng. Comput. **16**, 209–235 (2000)
21. Shahin, M., Liang, P., Khayyambashi, M.: Architectural design decision: existing models and tools. In: WICSA/ECSA (2009)
22. Farenhorst, R., Lago, P., Vliet, H.: Effective tool support for architectural knowledge sharing. In: Oquendo, F. (ed.) ECSA 2007. LNCS, vol. 4758, pp. 123–138. Springer, Heidelberg (2007). doi:10.1007/978-3-540-75132-8_11
23. Bu, W., Tang, A., Han, J.: An analysis of decision-centric architectural design approaches. In: SHARK (2009)
24. Henttonen, K., Matinlassi, M.: Open source based tools for sharing and reuse of software architectural knowledge. In: WICSA/ECSA (2009)
25. Hoorn, J.F., Farenhorst, R., Lago, P., van Vliet, H.: The lonesome architect. J. Syst. Softw. **84**(9), 1424–1435 (2011)
26. Kitchenham, B.: Procedures for performing systematic reviews. Keele University Technical report TR/SE-0401 and NICTA Technical report 0400011T.1 (2004)
27. de Boer, R.C., Farenhorst, R.: In search of 'architectural knowledge'. In: SHARK (2008)
28. Koziolek, H.: Performance evaluation of component-based software systems: a survey. Perform. Eval. **67**, 634–658 (2010)
29. Aleti, A., Buhnova, B., Grunske, L., Koziolek, A., Meedeniya, I.: Software architecture optimization methods: a systematic literature review. IEEE Trans. Softw. Eng. **39**, 658–683 (2013)

30. University of Illinois: Software Engineering Conferences (2014)
31. IEEE: IEEE Digital Library. http://ieeexplore.ieee.org/search/advsearch.jsp
32. DBLP: Search DBLP Computer Science Bibliography. http://dblp.uni-trier.de/search/
33. ACM: ACM Digital Library. http://dl.acm.org/advsearch.cfm
34. Zimmermann, O., Wegmann, L., Koziolek, H., Goldschmidt, T.: Architectural decision guidance across projects - problem space modeling, decision backlog management and cloud computing knowledge. In: WICSA (2015)
35. Capilla, R., Zimmermann, O., Zdun, U., Avgeriou, P., Küster, J.M.: An enhanced architectural knowledge metamodel linking architectural design decisions to other artifacts in the software engineering lifecycle. In: Crnkovic, I., Gruhn, V., Book, M. (eds.) ECSA 2011. LNCS, vol. 6903, pp. 303–318. Springer, Heidelberg (2011). doi:10.1007/978-3-642-23798-0_33
36. Eloranta, V.P., Hylli, O., Vepsalainen, T., Koskimies, K.: TopDocs: using software architecture knowledge base for generating topical documents. In: WICSA/ECSA (2012)
37. Könemann, P., Zimmermann, O.: Linking design decisions to design models in model-based software development. In: Babar, M.A., Gorton, I. (eds.) ECSA 2010. LNCS, vol. 6285, pp. 246–262. Springer, Heidelberg (2010). doi:10.1007/978-3-642-15114-9_19
38. Buchgeher, G., Weinreich, R.: Automatic tracing of decisions to architecture and implementation. In: WICSA (2011)
39. Durdik, Z., Reussner, R.: On the appropriate rationale for using design patterns and pattern documentation. In: QoSA (2013)
40. Jansen, A., van der Ven, J., Avgeriou, P., Hammer, D.K.: Tool support for architectural decisions. In: WICSA (2007)
41. Küster, M.: Architecture-centric modeling of design decisions for validation and traceability. In: Drira, K. (ed.) ECSA 2013. LNCS, vol. 7957, pp. 184–191. Springer, Heidelberg (2013). doi:10.1007/978-3-642-39031-9_16
42. Navarro, E., Cuesta, C., Perry, D.: Weaving a network of architectural knowledge. In: WICSA/ECSA (2009)
43. Zimmermann, O., Miksovic, C., KüSter, J.M.: Reference architecture, metamodel, and modeling principles for architectural knowledge management in information technology services. J. Syst. Softw. **85**, 2014–2033 (2012)
44. Boer, R.C., Farenhorst, R., Lago, P., Vliet, H., Clerc, V., Jansen, A.: Architectural knowledge: getting to the core. In: Overhage, S., Szyperski, C.A., Reussner, R., Stafford, J.A. (eds.) QoSA 2007. LNCS, vol. 4880, pp. 197–214. Springer, Heidelberg (2007). doi:10.1007/978-3-540-77619-2_12
45. Miller, J.A., Ferrari, R., Madhavji, N.H.: An exploratory study of architectural effects on requirements decisions. J. Syst. Softw. **83**, 2441–2455 (2010)
46. Shahin, M., Liang, P., Khayyambashi, M.R.: Improving understandability of architecture design through visualization of architectural design decision. In: SHARK (2010)
47. That, M.T.T., Sadou, S., Oquendo, F.: Using architectural patterns to define architectural decisions. In: WICSA/ECSA (2012)
48. Zimmermann, O., Koehler, J., Leymann, F., Polley, R., Schuster, N.: Managing architectural decision models with dependency relations, integrity constraints, and production rules. J. Syst. Softw. **82**, 1249–1267 (2009)
49. Cui, X., Sun, Y., Mei, H.: Towards automated solution synthesis and rationale capture in decision-centric architecture design. In: WICSA (2008)

50. Miesbauer, C., Weinreich, R.: WICSA/ECSA (2012)
51. Mirakhorli, M., Cleland-Huang, J.: Transforming trace information in architectural documents into re-usable and effective traceability links. In: SHARK (2011)
52. van Heesch, U., Avgeriou, P., Tang, A.: Does decision documentation help junior designers rationalize their decisions? A comparative multiple-case study. J. Syst. Softw. **86**(6), 1545–1565 (2013)
53. Szlenk, M., Zalewski, A., Kijas, S.: Modelling architectural decisions under changing requirements. In: WICSA/ECSA (2012)
54. Nowak, M., Pautasso, C.: Goals, questions and metrics for architectural decision models. In: SHARK (2011)
55. Eklund, U., Arts, T.: A classification of value for software architecture decisions. In: Babar, M.A., Gorton, I. (eds.) ECSA 2010. LNCS, vol. 6285, pp. 368–375. Springer, Heidelberg (2010). doi:10.1007/978-3-642-15114-9_30
56. Tang, A., Jin, Y., Han, J.: A rationale-based architecture model for design traceability and reasoning. J. Syst. Softw. **80**, 918–934 (2007)
57. Capilla, R., Ali Babar, M.: On the role of architectural design decisions in software product line engineering. In: Morrison, R., Balasubramaniam, D., Falkner, K. (eds.) ECSA 2008. LNCS, vol. 5292, pp. 241–255. Springer, Heidelberg (2008). doi:10.1007/978-3-540-88030-1_18
58. Bortis, G.: Informal software design knowledge reuse. In: ICSE (2010)
59. Savolainen, J., Kuusela, J., Männistö, T., Nyyssönen, A.: Experiences in making architectural decisions during the development of a new base station platform. In: Ali Babar, M., Gorton, I. (eds.) ECSA 2010. LNCS, vol. 6285, pp. 425–432. Springer, Heidelberg (2010). doi:10.1007/978-3-642-15114-9_37
60. Miksovic, C., Zimmermann, O.: Architecturally significant requirements, reference architecture, and metamodel for knowledge management in information technology services. In: WICSA (2011)
61. Lago, P., Avgeriou, P., Capilla, R., Kruchten, P.: Wishes and boundaries for a software architecture knowledge community. In: WICSA (2008)
62. Komiya, S.: A model for the recording and reuse of software design decisions and decision rationale. In: Software Reuse: Advances in Software Reusability (1994)
63. Babar, M.A., Gorton, I.: A tool for managing software architecture knowledge. In: SHARK (2007)
64. de Boer, R., Van Vliet, H.: Experiences with semantic wikis for architectural knowledge management. In: WICSA (2011)
65. Wang, W., Burge, J.E.: Using rationale to support pattern-based architectural design. In: SHARK (2010)
66. Capilla, R., Dueñas, J.C., Nava, F.: Viability for codifying and documenting architectural design decisions with tool support. J. Softw. Maint. Evol. **22**, 81–119 (2010)
67. Carignano, M., Gonnet, S., Leone, H.: A model to represent architectural design rationale. In: WICSA/ECSA (2009)
68. Che, M.: An approach to documenting and evolving architectural design decisions. In: Proceedings of the 2013 International Conference on Software Engineering, ICSE (2013)
69. de Silva, L., Balasubramaniam, D.: A model for specifying rationale using an architecture description language. In: Crnkovic, I., Gruhn, V., Book, M. (eds.) ECSA 2011. LNCS, vol. 6903, pp. 319–327. Springer, Heidelberg (2011). doi:10.1007/978-3-642-23798-0_34

70. Díaz, J., Pérez, J., Garbajosa, J., Wolf, A.L.: Change impact analysis in product-line architectures. In: Crnkovic, I., Gruhn, V., Book, M. (eds.) ECSA 2011. LNCS, vol. 6903, pp. 114–129. Springer, Heidelberg (2011). doi:10.1007/978-3-642-23798-0_12

71. Egyed, A., Wile, D.: Support for managing design-time decisions. IEEE Trans. Softw. Eng. **32**, 299–314 (2006)

72. Garcia, A., Batista, T., Rashid, A., Sant'Anna, C.: Driving and managing architectural decisions with aspects. SIGSOFT Softw. Eng. Notes **31**, 6 (2006)

73. Gerdes, S., Lehnert, S., Riebisch, M.: Combining architectural design decisions and legacy system evolution. In: Avgeriou, P., Zdun, U. (eds.) ECSA 2014. LNCS, vol. 8627, pp. 50–57. Springer, Heidelberg (2014). doi:10.1007/978-3-319-09970-5_5

74. Gu, Q., Lago, P.: SOA process decisions: new challenges in architectural knowledge modeling. In: SHARK (2008)

75. Gu, Q., van Vliet, H.: SOA decision making - what do we need to know. In: SHARK (2009)

76. Habli, I., Kelly, T.: Capturing and replaying architectural knowledge through derivational analogy. In: SHARK (2007)

77. Harrison, N.B., Avgeriou, P., Zdun, U.: Using patterns to capture architectural decisions. IEEE Softw. **24**, 38–45 (2007)

78. Jansen, A., Bosch, J., Avgeriou, P.: Documenting after the fact: recovering architectural design decisions. J. Syst. Softw. **81**, 536–557 (2008)

79. Jansen, A., Avgeriou, P., van der Ven, J.S.: Enriching software architecture documentation. J. Syst. Softw. **82**, 1232–1248 (2009)

80. Lee, L., Kruchten, P.: A tool to visualize architectural design decisions. In: Becker, S., Plasil, F., Reussner, R. (eds.) QoSA 2008. LNCS, vol. 5281, pp. 43–54. Springer, Heidelberg (2008). doi:10.1007/978-3-540-87879-7_3

81. Lytra, I., Tran, H., Zdun, U.: Supporting consistency between architectural design decisions and component models through reusable architectural knowledge transformations. In: Drira, K. (ed.) ECSA 2013. LNCS, vol. 7957, pp. 224–239. Springer, Heidelberg (2013). doi:10.1007/978-3-642-39031-9_20

82. Cuesta, C.E., Navarro, E., Perry, D.E., Roda, C.: Evolution styles: using architectural knowledge as an evolution driver. J. Softw. Evol. Process **25**(9), 957–980 (2013)

83. Sinnema, M., van der Ven, J.S., Deelstra, S.: Using variability modeling principles to capture architectural knowledge. SIGSOFT Softw. Eng. Notes **31**, 5 (2006)

84. Soliman, M., Riebisch, M., Zdun, U.: Enriching architecture knowledge with technology design decisions. In: WICSA (2015)

85. Tibermacine, C., Zernadji, T.: Supervising the evolution of web service orchestrations using quality requirements. In: Crnkovic, I., Gruhn, V., Book, M. (eds.) ECSA 2011. LNCS, vol. 6903, pp. 1–16. Springer, Heidelberg (2011). doi:10.1007/978-3-642-23798-0_1

86. Tibermacine, C., Dony, C., Sadou, S., Fabresse, L.: Software architecture constraints as customizable, reusable and composable entities. In: Babar, M.A., Gorton, I. (eds.) ECSA 2010. LNCS, vol. 6285, pp. 505–509. Springer, Heidelberg (2010). doi:10.1007/978-3-642-15114-9_51

87. Tofan, D., Galster, M., Avgeriou, P.: Capturing tacit architectural knowledge using the repertory grid technique (NIER track). In: ICSE (2011)

88. Trujillo, S., Azanza, M., Diaz, O., Capilla, R.: Exploring extensibility of architectural design decisions. In: SHARK (2007)

89. Wu, W., Kelly, T.: Managing architectural design decisions for safety-critical software systems. In: Hofmeister, C., Crnkovic, I., Reussner, R. (eds.) QoSA 2006. LNCS, vol. 4214, pp. 59–77. Springer, Heidelberg (2006). doi:10.1007/11921998_9

90. Zdun, U., Avgeriou, P., Hentrich, C., Dustdar, S.: Architecting as decision making with patterns and primitives. In: SHARK (2008)

91. Zhu, L., Gorton, I.: UML profiles for design decisions and non-functional requirements. In: SHARK (2007)

92. Li, Z., Liang, P., Avgeriou, P.: Architectural technical debt identification based on architecture decisions and change scenarios. In: WICSA (2015)

93. de Boer, R., Lago, P., Telea, A., van Vliet, H.: Ontology-driven visualization of architectural design decisions. In: WICSA/ECSA (2009)

94. Burge, J.E., Brown, D.C.: SEURAT: integrated rationale management. In: Proceedings of the 30th International Conference on Software Engineering, ICSE (2008)

Task-Specific Architecture Documentation for Developers

Why Separation of Concerns in Architecture Documentation is Counterproductive for Developers

Dominik Rost[(⊠)] and Matthias Naab

Fraunhofer IESE, Kaiserslautern, Germany
{dominik.rost,matthias.naab}@iese.fraunhofer.de

Abstract. It is widely agreed that architecture documentation, independent of its form, is necessary to prescribe architectural concepts for development and to conserve architectural information over time. However, very often architecture documentation is perceived as inadequate, too long, too abstract, too detailed, or simply outdated. While developers have tasks to develop certain features or parts of a system, they are confronted with architecture documents that globally describe the architecture and use concepts like separation of concerns. Then, the developers have the hard task to find all information of the separated concerns and to synthesize the excerpt relevant for their concrete task. Ideally, they would get an architecture document, which is exactly tailored to their need of architectural information for their task at hand. Such documentation can however not be created by architects in reasonable time. In this paper, we propose an approach of modeling architecture and automatically synthesizing a tailored architecture documentation for each developer and each development task. Therefore architectural concepts are selected from the model based on the task and an interleaving of concepts is done. This makes for example all interfaces explicit, which a component has to implement in order to comply with security, availability, etc. concepts. The required modeling and automation is realized in the tool Enterprise Architect. We got already very positive feedback for this idea from practitioners and expect a significant improvement of implementation quality and architecture compliance.

Keywords: Architecture documentation · Architecture knowledge · Architecture realization · Developers · Implementation · Task · Separation of concerns

1 Introduction

It is widely accepted that architecture documentation is necessary to prescribe architecture concepts and preserve architecture knowledge over time. This is particularly true in complex project settings: When systems are large and have long lifecycles, architecture documentation serves as a tool to preserve the most important design decisions, and to facilitate communication between stakeholders. Also, software

© Springer International Publishing AG 2016
B. Tekinerdogan et al. (Eds.): ECSA 2016, LNCS 9839, pp. 102–110, 2016.
DOI: 10.1007/978-3-319-48992-6_7

development becomes a more and more distributed and globalized activity, often delaying or even making direct communication impossible. In such settings, architecture documentation is a vital communication vehicle to allow a consistent realization of the architecture.

Architecture documentation for such systems can become large. In our experience, for large-scale projects several hundreds of pages are realistic. Working with such documentation can be difficult, in particular for developers, who use it as the basis for their implementation activities, for two main reasons:

First, the perspectives of architects and developers on the system diverge. Architects focus on the system as a whole, designing the overall principles of the system for a multitude of stakeholders. They break down the big and complex problem of the complete system into smaller parts, i.e. apply the principles of divide and conquer and separation of concerns, to create concepts that address architecture drivers in a consistent and uniform way. Examples are concepts for exception handling, validation, scaling, etc. For a medium sized project this can easily lead to 20–50 different concepts.

Our central insight is that *while separation of concerns is vital for architects, who deal with a problem too large to handle as a whole, it is actually counter-productive for a developer working on a task with a narrow focus on single entities, because the separated concerns need to be located and synthesized again.* When developers implement single modules, they need to know and consider several architecture concepts and realize them in their specific context. Such concepts are normally not explicitly described for every element that needs to realize it, but once, in a general way and then instantiated throughout the system (e.g. which interfaces to implement in which way for the security concepts, for transaction handling, ...). This means, every single developer needs to be aware of or search for relevant concepts for the development task at hand (cf. Fig. 1).

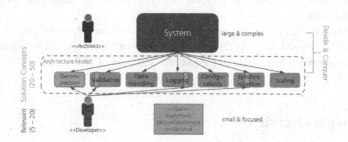

Fig. 1. Architect developer perspective difference

The second aspect is related to the architecture-code-gap [1]. When architects design the system, they reason about the system in terms of components, layers, or decisions. Developers on the other hand work with classes, packages, and interfaces. While it is reasonable for the different roles to work with the elements that best suit their needs, their inherent difference creates an obstacle for architecture realization: There is an additional cognitive step to transform architecture concepts, to the code level.

Both aspects lead to an architecture realization that is on the one hand less efficient, because developers are required to search and identify relevant concepts in a large amount of architecture information. On the other hand, it is error prone because developers under high time pressure might not take the time to consult the architecture documentation, causing architecture violations and consequently architecture erosion [2].

To address these problems, we propose an approach of automatically generating architecture documentation specific for tasks of individual developers. An overview of the approach is presented in Sect. 3 before we describe its details in Sect. 4. To get a better understanding, we present an example in Sect. 5 and conclude in Sect. 6 with validation and future work.

2   Related Work

The approach we present in this paper is built on the foundations of architecture documentation and architecture views. Several different works cover these topics and have presented their own documentation approaches and view sets: [3, 4], etc. Views are a tool for separation of concerns during the design of a software system, but can also be used to tailor information towards the readers [5]. This, however normally refers to types of stakeholders, like developers in general, not more specific.

The idea of considering design decisions as an integral part of architecture and documentation started the whole new research field Architecture Knowledge Management (AKM) Capilla et al. published a comprehensive analysis of the work done in AKM in the past ten years [6]. Our approach is closely related to these approaches, in particular those that provide some kind of personalization mechanism, i.e. making AK specific for a target group. EAGLE [7], ADDM [8], and Decision Architect [9] are examples.. However, none of them tackles the described challenges, either they focus on personalization for stakeholder types, not individuals, or their goal of personalization is different.

The approach we present in this paper is the advancement of the preliminary and basic ideas we outlined in [10]. To align our work with the needs of industry we also performed a comprehensive state of the practice analysis of architecture documentation in industry in [11].

3   Approach Overview

3.1   Task-Specific Architecture Documentation

We frequently experience the challenges we describe in Sect. 1 in industrial projects with our customers. For this reason, we developed an approach for creating architecture documentation that is not only specific for a certain group of stakeholders, but for individual developers and each of their individual development tasks. The resulting architecture documentation centers around the specific architectural elements that developers need to change, create, or delete. It provides detailed information on these *focus elements*, together with all relevant information from architecture concepts that need to be considered. Besides the elements, "relevant information" includes their internal structure, interfaces to provide, location in the source code, and relations to create. These pieces of information are combined, so that a meaningful view on a very specific part of the system is created. Thus, the architecture documentation for developers contains only a minimum of overhead information, and in a form that allows direct realization. Manually creating such documentation is economically impossible, hence, task-specific architecture documentation needs to be created fully automated with a tool.

3.2   Development Setting and Tooling

Task-specific architecture documentation is not bound to a particular development process, but works best with highly iterative approaches with small increments, like agile development. In each iteration, a user story or use case is selected for realization. For the selected user story, a project manager, architect or even the team derive development tasks. For each of these development tasks, the architect generates the corresponding task-specific architecture documentation, which is used by developers when they carry out the task. Normally, an architect has created an architecture design for all relevant concepts in a previous iteration, so that it is ready for realization in the next.

The architecture model is based on UML and the documentation generator is created as an add-in for the widely used modeling tool Enterprise Architect (cf. Fig. 2). The add-in works on task specifications, that reference elements from the architecture model. Therefore, task specifications are created as elements in the architecture model as well (in future versions an integration with issue tracking systems is planned). The resulting documentation is created as a read-only document. In future versions, the result can be generated as a small, tailored architecture model, that can be integrated with a viewer in the IDE developers normally work with. This allows more interactive working the documentation and more sophisticated linking between documentation and code.

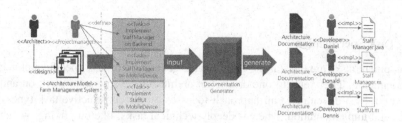

Fig. 2. Development setting and tooling

3.3   Foundational Principles of the Modeling Approach

Our modeling approach has several similarities to many others, it is based on the ISO/IEC/IEEE 42010 standard, uses UML, views, etc. Therefore, transferring the idea to other architecture approaches should be simple. However, two aspects we need to highlight, that are specific and have an influence on the documentation generation approach. First, when we design architectures, we explicitly *differentiate between runtime and development time*. We often see people drawing boxes and lines, mixing the two arbitrarily, without understanding the differences. Runtime elements (components) can be multiply instantiated and deployed. They are realized with development time entities (modules), which for example represent classes. Different mappings are possible between these entities. Components are normally realized by multiple modules; to optimize reuse, one module can be used for the realization of many components.

The second aspect is *template elements*. They result from the idea of making architecture modeling more efficient by grouping similarities. To eliminate the necessity to describe a concept every time it is applied in the system, template elements are used to describe a concept once. For example, if, as a part of the *validation concept* in a system, we wanted to express that for every *backend service* in the system, there has to be a corresponding *validator* component to validate the data received from clients, we could model the template components *T_Backend Service* and *T_Backend Service Validator* as shown in Fig. 3 and link them to concrete instances. With this idea, the required amount of modeling to describe the architecture concepts of the system can be reduced.

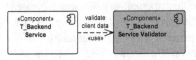

Fig. 3. Service validator concept

Fig. 4. Example of a task specification

4 Detailed Approach

The documentation generation process realized in the documentation generator can be divided into four distinct parts, which are explained in the following sections.

4.1 Task Specification

Development tasks are the starting point for the generation of task-specific architecture documentation. They refer to one or a set of architecture elements to work on and are carried out by a developer. Our approach focusses on the constructive task types, like design and implementation, whereas deeply technical tasks, like bug fixing, which are hardly covered in an architecture model, are out of scope.

Architects model task specifications in the architecture model, so that architecture elements to which the task refers can be directly linked, traced and processed. A task element has a name and a description. It references architecture elements, the *focus elements*, with either a create, change, or delete relationship. And, a task is assigned to a concrete developer who is responsible for carrying it out. Figure 4 shows an example of a task specification in an architecture model.

4.2   Selection

Selection is the automatic process of analyzing the architecture model and identifying model elements that are relevant to consider for the subsequent steps. The starting point for selection is always one or more focus elements. The following elements are included in the selection processes: Developers need to know all details about the *focus elements,* so all occurrences are included with their properties and description. The hierarchy of the element's *template elements* need to be included because all concepts involving the templates are relevant for the focus elements as well. The *mapped development-time elements* are included because they describe how an element needs to be realized. In our modeling approach, *design decisions* are created in the architecture model as well and relevant ones are included in the selection process. Finally, descriptions of all elements and diagrams are included as well.

4.3   Concept Interleaving

Concept Interleaving is the central automatic processing step of integrating all pieces of information, to create the task-specific architecture documentation. It takes the elements from the selection step and extracts relevant information from them to merge it with the focus elements. This includes the following elements, which are first shifted to development time and then interleaved: *Child elements* describe the internal structure of the element to implement and are normally depicted as within an element or have an explicit "part of"-relationship. Child elements of the focus element, its templates and development time elements are considered. *Relation target elements* refer to any element being the target of an outgoing relation. This denotes, which elements to use and create a relationship to. *Interfaces* show the functionality to provide t other elements. Finally, *DT parent elements* denote the location in the source code project.

4.4   Development Time Shift

The collected information should be presented according to the developer's perspective, to facilitate instant realization. The main idea of the Development Time (DT) Shift is to translate elements from an architecture and runtime level to the code and development time level. This is applied for all selected and elements of interleaved concepts.

We differentiate two ways of doing that: DT-Shift with *explicit development time mappings* or *implicit shifting rules*. To ensure uniformity and a clean code structure and to facilitate reuse, architects might decide to prescribe where in the source code the elements of an architecture concept should be created. In this case, an element is mapped with an *explicit* relation to development time elements, e.g. one component to be realized by three classes. The documentation generator simply replaces such elements by the mapped development time elements for the resulting documentation.

In other cases, to save time and reduce complexity, he may also decide to rely on a set of standard shifting rules. Table 1 provides an overview of these.

Table 1. Implicit shifting rules

Runtime element	Development time element
Component (without Subcomponents)	Class
Component (with Subcomponents)	Package
Component (template)	Abstract module
Interface	Interface
Connector	Class
Data	Class

5 Example

The following example illustrates the main ideas of the approach. The context is a farm management system, a system with which farmers manage and plan machines, grain supply, etc. [12]. The next user story to be implemented in the project is managing staff. This includes the tasks to create the according database structure, the user interfaces, etc. One task for a developer is to implement the backend service (cf. Fig. 4).

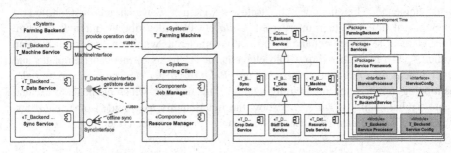

Fig. 5. Example system services   **Fig. 6.** Example dev. time mappings

Figure 5 shows an overview of the different kinds of services that are provided by the backend. The services that provide the different kinds of data to the applications running on the Farming Client are represented by the template component T_Data Service.

The relevance of this template becomes clear when looking at Fig. 6. The diagram shows the different kinds of services used in the application and an explicit mapping to DT. In this case, for every service, an according package in the services package, together with the processor and configuration classes have to be created. As one example of an architecture concept, Fig. 3 shows a simple validation concept that prescribes every backend service to use an according validator component.

The result of the generation process is depicted in Fig. 7. Colors denote corresponding elements. The focus element Staff Data Service has been shifted to DT according to the explicit mapping shown in Fig. 6, resulting in the Staff Data Service package with the two contained modules. The relation target elements of these two modules, the two framework interfaces have been integrated. The interface provided by the T_Data Service has been shifted and integrated with a realization relation. The validation concept has been interleaved by adding the shifted validator module. Where possible, the names of templates have been replaced by the name of the focus element.

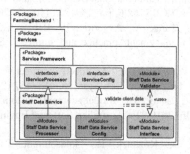

Fig. 7. Example generation result

6 Validation and Future Work

As an applied research organization we work with many industry customers in architecture and development projects. Our experience in these projects and first feedback to the approach gives us good confidence that it will be beneficial to developers in complex development settings. The discussions with our partners show the high demand and positive feedback when we presented our approach. To acquire more formal validation data, we are currently working on a controlled experiment to conduct later this year at Technical University of Kaiserslautern. In this experiment, we will gather data from groups of computer science students, working with task-specific and generic architecture documentation. We will measure the time it takes to identify relevant architecture information for a given development task, as well as errors made when trying to understand the relevant architecture concepts.

In terms of tooling, we are currently developing a prototype according to the conceptual approach presented in this paper and hope to have a running version ready by the end of this year. In the future this is the basis for many possible extensions. For example, IDE integration and feedback mechanisms to architects will provide the opportunity to bring architecture and source code closer together.

References

1. Fairbanks: Just Enough Software Architecture: A Risk-Driven Approach. Marshall & Brainerd (2010)
2. Perry, D.E., Wolf, A.L.: Foundations for the study of software architecture. ACM SIGSOFT Softw. Eng. Notes **17**, 40–52 (1992)

3. Clements, P., Bachmann, F., Bass, L., Garlan, D., Ivers, J., Little, R., Merson, P., Nord, R., Stafford, J.: Documenting Software Architectures: Views and Beyond. Addison-Wesley Professional, Boston (2002)
4. Hofmeister, C., Nord, R., Soni, D.: Applied Software Architecture. Addison-Wesley Professional, Boston (1999)
5. Bayer, J., Muthig, D.: A view-based approach for improving software documentation practices. In: 13th Annual IEEE International Symposium and Workshop on Engineering of Computer-Based Systems, ECBS 2006, pp. 269–278 (10 p.) (2006)
6. Capilla, R., Jansen, A., Tang, A., Avgeriou, P., Babar, M.A.: 10 years of software architecture knowledge management: practice and future. J. Syst. Softw. **116**, 191–205 (2015)
7. Farenhorst, R., Lago, P., van Vliet, H.: EAGLE: effective tool support for sharing architectural knowledge. Int. J. Coop. Inf. Syst. **16**, 413–437 (2007)
8. Chen, L., Babar, M.A., Liang, H.: Model-centered customizable architectural design decisions management. In: 2010 21st Australian Software Engineering Conference, pp. 23–32. IEEE (2010)
9. Manteuffel, C., Tofan, D., Koziolek, H., Goldschmidt, T., Avgeriou, P.: Industrial implementation of a documentation framework for architectural decisions. In: 2014 IEEE/IFIP Conference on Software Architecture, pp. 225–234. IEEE (2014)
10. Rost, D.: Generation of task-specific architecture documentation for developers. In: Proceedings of the 17th International Doctoral Symposium on Components and Architecture - WCOP 2012, p. 1. ACM Press, New York (2012)
11. Rost, D., Naab, M., Lima, C., Flach Garcia Chavez, C.: Software architecture documentation for developers: a survey. In: Drira, K. (ed.) ECSA 2013. LNCS, vol. 7957, pp. 72–88. Springer, Heidelberg (2013). doi:10.1007/978-3-642-39031-9_7
12. Naab, M., Braun, S., Lenhart, T., Hess, S., Eitel, A., Magin, D., Carbon, R., Kiefer, F.: Why data needs more attention in architecture design - experiences from prototyping a large-scale mobile app ecosystem. In: 2015 12th Working IEEE/IFIP Conference on Software Architecture, pp. 75–84. IEEE (2015)

Runtime Architecture

Architectural Homeostasis in Self-Adaptive Software-Intensive Cyber-Physical Systems

Ilias Gerostathopoulos[1,2]($\boxtimes$), Dominik Skoda[2], Frantisek Plasil[2],
Tomas Bures[2], and Alessia Knauss[3]

[1] Fakultät fur Informatik, Technische Universität München, Munich, Germany
gerostat@in.tum.de
[2] Charles University in Prague, Faculty of Mathematics and Physics,
Prague, Czech Republic
{skoda,plasil,bures}@d3s.mff.cuni.cz
[3] Department of Computer Science and Engineering,
Chalmers University of Technology, Gothenburg, Sweden
alessia.knauss@chalmers.se

Abstract. Self-adaptive software-intensive cyber-physical systems (sasiCPS) encounter a high level of run-time uncertainty. State-of-the-art architecture-based self-adaptation approaches assume designing against a fixed set of situations that warrant self-adaptation; as a result, failures may appear when sasiCPS operate in environment conditions they are not specifically designed for. In response, we propose to increase the homeostasis of sasiCPS, i.e., the capacity to maintain an operational state despite run-time uncertainty, by introducing run-time changes to the architecture-based self-adaptation strategies according to environment stimuli. In addition to articulating the main idea of architectural homeostasis, we describe three mechanisms that reify the idea: (i) collaborative sensing, (ii) faulty component isolation from adaptation, and (iii) enhancing mode switching. Moreover, our experimental evaluation of the three mechanisms confirms that allowing a complex system to change its self-adaptation strategies helps the system recover from runtime errors and abnormalities and keep it in an operational state.

Keywords: Cyber-physical systems · Software architecture · Run-time uncertainty · Self-adaptation strategies

1 Introduction

Cyber-Physical Systems (CPS) [1] are large complex systems that rely more and more on software for their operation—they are becoming *software-intensive* CPS [2, 3]. Such systems, e.g., intelligent transportation systems, smart grids, are typically comprised of several million lines of code. A high level view achieved via focusing on *software architecture* abstractions is thus becoming increasingly important for dealing with such scale and complexity during development, deployment, and maintenance.

These systems continuously sense physical properties in order to actuate physical processes. Due to the close connection to the physical world that is hard to predict at design time and control at run-time, they encounter a high level of uncertainty in their

© Springer International Publishing AG 2016
B. Tekinerdogan et al. (Eds.): ECSA 2016, LNCS 9839, pp. 113–128, 2016.
DOI: 10.1007/978-3-319-48992-6_8

operating conditions—*run-time uncertainty* [4]. Such kind of uncertainty is typically rooted in (i) unexpected changes in the run-time infrastructure (e.g., communication latencies, disconnections, sensor malfunctioning); (ii) unexpected changes in the environment (e.g., harsh weather conditions); (iii) the evolution of other cyber or physical systems that interface with the CPS in question; and (iv) the randomness introduced by human interaction. Run-time uncertainty can cause numerous failures ranging from temporary service unavailability to complete system crash [4].

A promising way to tackle run-time uncertainty is to endow software-intensive CPS with self-adaptive capabilities, i.e., with capabilities of adjusting their own structure and behavior at run-time based on their internal state and the perceived environment, while considering their run-time goals and requirements [5]. In our work, we focus on self-adaptation approaches implemented at the architectural level (e.g. Stitch [6–10]). One of the limitations in the state-of-the-art architecture-based self-adaptation approaches is that they assume designing against a fixed set of situations that warrant self-adaptation [11]. However, when run-time uncertainty is high, anticipating all potential situations upfront (i.e. at design time) and designing corresponding actions is a costly, lengthy, and sometimes not even a viable option [4, 12].

In our work, instead of trying to identify all potential situations and corresponding actions (*strategies* in architecture-based self-adaptation), we propose to engineer flexibility in the strategies of a self-adaptive software-intensive CPS (*sasiCPS* further on) in the form of run-time changes to these strategies. This way we try to increase the software homeostasis of sasiCPS, i.e. the capacity for the system to maintain its normal operating state and implicitly repair abnormalities or deviations from expected behavior [13], by specifically focusing at the architectural level—*architectural homeostasis*.

We claim that supporting architectural homeostasis at run-time helps tackle the run-time uncertainty in sasiCPS. The underlying assumptions of our approach are that (i) fixed architecture-based self-adaptation strategies result in brittle systems in domains with high run-time uncertainty; (ii) allowing the components of a complex system to change their self-adaptation strategies in a slightly different way while still aiming at a common goal can have positive results in the overall utility of a self-adaptive system. The last point is common in other domains (e.g., communication protocols that try to reestablish a connection in some random manner in order to avoid a flood of reconnections).

The main contribution of this paper lies in presenting three concrete homeostatic mechanisms that operate at the architectural level and effectively increase the capacity of a sasiCPS to maintain an operational state despite run-time uncertainty. The secondary contribution lies in implementing the proposed mechanisms in a development and run-time framework for sasiCPS—*DEECo* component framework [14]—and in evaluating their feasibility and effectiveness in a controlled experiment. In the experimental setup, the mechanisms worked both independently and in combination with each other. The results show that using the proposed mechanisms increase in the overall utility of the system in face of runtime errors and abnormalities (high-level exceptions).

The rest of the paper is structured as follows. Section 2 presents our running example and the background of our work. Section 3 presents the main idea of architectural homeostasis, together with its reification into three concrete homeostatic mechanisms. Section 4 details our evaluation based on implementing the mechanisms and quantifying their effects in the running example, together with discussing the interesting points, extensions, and limitation of our approach. Finally, Sect. 5 compares our work to existing ones in the literature and Sect. 6 concludes.

2 Running Example and Background

2.1 Cleaning Robots Example

In the scenario used throughout the paper, four Turtlebots (http://www.turtlebot.com/) are deployed in a large 2D space with the task to keep it as clean as possible. The space is covered by tiles that can get dirty at some arbitrary points in time. Each robot is able to move around, identify dirty tiles via its downwards-looking camera and humidity sensor, and clean them. Each robot also works on a specific energy budget; before it expires, the robot needs to reach a docking station and recharge. Several docking stations exist in the space. Figure 1 depicts a scenario with three robots and two docking stations.

The robots communicate with each other to exchange information about the lastly cleaned tiles to avoid unnecessary trips. They also communicate with the docking stations to determine the most convenient station for recharging.

This example, although a toy one, comprises a number of situations where run-time uncertainty creeps in. These include situations where a robot loses the ability of reliably detecting dirty tiles (e.g. due to a failure in its humidity sensor) or loses the ability of communicating with the docking stations. Docking stations may also stop working. Run-time uncertainty is also manifested in the unpredictable pace and position where dirt appears in the space.

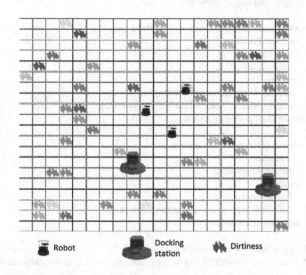

Fig. 1. Cleaning robots example (screenshot from the tool).

2.2   DEECo Model of Cleaning Robots – Running Example

DEECo is a development and run-time framework for sasiCPS [14]. In DEECo, a component is an independent entity of development and deployment. Two component types were identified in our running example: Robot and DockingStation. Every DEECo component contains data (knowledge) and functionality in the form of periodically invoked processes which map input knowledge to output knowledge; each process is associated with one or more component mode(s). In the running example, each Robot comprises knowledge about its position, dirtinessMap, etc. (Figure 2, lines 9–14), and several processes, e.g. clean (lines 25–31), move, and charge. A process belongs to one or more modes – e.g., the Robot's clean process belongs to cleaning mode (line 25). The modes of each component are switched at run-time according to the component's mode-state machine (Fig. 7). A component in DEECo has a number of roles, each allowing a subset of knowledge fields to become subject to component interaction. In the running example, each Robot features the Dockable and Cleaner roles (lines 1–4, 8).

```
1.    role Dockable:
2.      id, assignedDockingStationPosition
3.    role Cleaner:
4.      id, position, targetPosition, dirtinessMap
5.    role Dock:
6.      position, dockedRobots
7.
8.    component Robot1 features Dockable, Cleaner
9.      knowledge:
10.       id = 2
11.       position = { 16, 02}
12.       dirtinessMap = {}
13.       targetPosition = null
14.       assignedDockingStationsPosition = null
15.
16.     process move in mode Cleaning, Searching
17.        in targetPosition
18.        inout position
19.        inout dirtinessMap
20.        function:
21.           position ← move (targetPosition)
22.           dirtinessMap ← update(position, dirtinessMap)
23.        scheduling: periodic( 100ms )
24.
25.     process clean in mode Cleaning
26.        in position
27.        inout dirtinessMap
28.        function:
29.           if dirty(position)
30.              dirtinessMap ← clean(position, dirtinessMap)
31.        scheduling: periodic( 1000ms )
32.
33.     /* similar spec for other processes of Robot1 */
34.     /* similar spec for Robot2 and Robot3, DockingStation1, and DockingStation2 */
```

Fig. 2. Excerpt from DSL of DEECo components of the cleaning robots example.

Components do not interact with each other directly. Their interaction is dependent on their membership in dynamic groups called ensembles. An ensemble is dynamically created/disbanded depending on which components satisfy its membership condition. The key task of an ensemble is to periodically exchange knowledge parts between its coordinator and member components (determined by their roles). At design-time, an ensemble specification consists of (i) ensemble roles that the member and coordinator components should feature, and (ii) a membership condition prescribing the condition under which components should interact (Fig. 3, lines 45–51), and (iii) a knowledge exchange function, which specifies the knowledge exchange that takes place between the components in the ensemble (lines 52–53). For instance, the components featuring the Dockable role (e.g. Robot) can form an ensemble with components featuring the Dock role (i.e. with a DockingStation) to coordinate on the docking activity (lines 36–37).

Matching of a component role and an ensemble role can be interpreted as establishing a connector in a classical component model; such a connector lasts only until the next evaluation of the membership condition. This semantics provides for software architecture that is dynamically adapted to the current components' knowledge values.

Self-adaptation in DEECo. The semantics of switching modes within a component reflects the idea of the MAPE-K self-adaptation loop (Monitor-Analyze-Plan-Execute over Knowledge) [15]: Consider a component C and its associated mode-state machine M_C. In M_C, the transition guards from the current state are periodically evaluated based on monitoring the variables (knowledge parts featured in the guards) of C; then it is analyzed which of the eligible transition should be selected by so that the next mode is planned. Finally, the next mode is brought to action (executed).

```
35.   ensemble DockingInformationExchange:
36.     coordinator: Dock
37.     member: Dockable
38.     membership:
39.       coordinator.dockedRobots.size() <= 3
40.     knowledge exchange:
41.       coordinator.dockedRobots ← member.id
42.       member.assignedDockingStationPosition  ← coordinator.position
43.     scheduling: periodic( 1000ms )
44.
45.   ensemble CleaningPlanExclusion:
46.     coordinator: Cleaner
47.     member: Cleaner
48.     membership:
49.       coordinator.targetPosition == member.targetPosition
50.         and distance(coordinator.position, coordinator.targetPosition)
51.           < distance(member.position, member.targetPosition)
52.     knowledge exchange:
53.       member.targetPosition ← null
54.     scheduling: periodic( 1000ms )
```

Fig. 3. Excerpt from DSL of DEECo ensembles of the cleaning robots example.

The semantics of ensembles also reflects the idea of MAPE-K: Consider an ensemble E. The membership condition MC of E is evaluated (analyzed) periodically, requiring systematic monitoring of the variables (knowledge parts) in all components featuring E's roles. From all of these components considered in a particular MC evaluation, only those satisfying MC are planned to be the members/coordinator of E. This plan is then executed and communication of the members/coordinator via knowledge exchange is then realized.

Overall, in DEECo, self-adaptation is performed by two mechanisms applied in parallel: (i) mode-switching at the level of individual components, (ii) dynamic participation of components in ensembles. In principle, each instance of a self-adaptation mechanism defines a particular self-adaptation strategy (in the sense of [6]), being characterized in each component by a specific mode-state machine, and in each ensemble instance by a specific membership condition and knowledge exchange function. Technically, this is realized by an Adaptation manager (part of the runtime framework of DEECo [14]), which takes the specification of mode-state machines and ensembles as definition of self-adaptation strategies and invokes them accordingly.

3   Homeostasis at the Architectural Level

Our approach modifies/adds/removes self-adaptation strategies at run-time when the system requirements and/or environment assumptions which the strategies have been designed for are not met anymore. Our approach realizes this in an additional adaptation layer (*homeostasis layer*). Conceptually, the three layers presented in Fig. 4 follow the three-layered architecture for evolution of dynamically adaptive systems proposed by Perrouin et al. [16]. Contrary to their work, however, we do not use an evolution layer to switch between self-adaptation strategies. Instead, we propose the top layer to change the employed self-adaptation strategies by *homeostatic mechanisms* (*H-mechanisms*) based on a MAPE-K loop governed by an H-Adaptation Manager (Fig. 4).

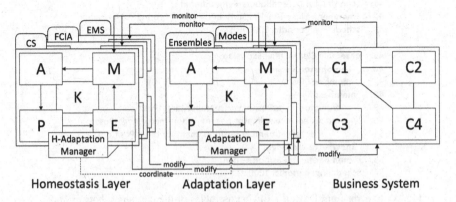

Fig. 4. Three-layered architecture with homeostasis layer

To illustrate the concepts of the Homeostasis Layer, we present three H-mechanisms. H-Adaptation manager coordinates monitoring of exceptional/ unanticipated situations at the Adaptation Layer and reacts by activation of a selected H-mechanism, which, in turn, modifies a self-adaptation strategy at the Adaptation Layer. Technically, the Adaptation Manager coordinates the application of self-adaptation mechanisms (to avoid conflicts in adaptation); a similar coordination role has the H-Adaptation Manager with respect to application of H-mechanisms. Moreover, the H-Adaptation manager can force the Adaptation Manager to postpone any adaptation based on the self-adaptation strategy being modified.

In principle the Homeostasis Layer could be avoided by enhancing the Adaptation Layer to handle all the exceptional situations; however, this would make their specification clumsy and error prone. Therefore we hoist the handling of these exceptional situations to the architectural level and modify the Adaptation Layer by the Homeostasis Layer at run time. Moreover, the adoption of such an architecture style provides more design flexibility by the allowing incremental tuning up of the Adaptation Layer.

As a reference implementation, the Adaptation Layer in our running example is built upon the self-adaptation mechanisms in DEECo (mode-state machines, ensembles), by modifying/adding/removing the self-adaptation strategies defined by their instances at run-time.

3.1   H-Mechanism #1: Collaborative Sensing

sasiCPS are often large data-intensive systems with components that perform sensing of physical properties via hardware sensors (e.g. GPS, accelerometer, thermometer) with various reliability margins. When components rely on sensor readings for satisfying important functional requirements (e.g. a robot needs to know its position in order to plan its path to a destination), it becomes extremely important to deal with sensor malfunctioning to still enable environment sensing at run-time.

A way to overcome the problem of sensor malfunctioning is to take advantage of the data dependencies and redundancies that may exist in sasiCPS due to components sensing the same or similar property P. Collaborative sensing (CS) H-mechanism provides an adequate approximation of property P for a faulty component. CS is based on defining a new self-adaptation strategy on the fly – technically, in DEECo, by creating an additional ensemble specification with knowledge exchange function providing the desired approximation.

CS involves two computational steps: (i) *CS Analysis*—identification of data dependencies and (ii) *CS Plan*—approximation of P. While CS Plan is relatively easy to realize once a dependency relation is identified, for the two main tasks of CS Analysis (Fig. 5), there are multiple alternatives involving different trade-offs: A major issue is the computational overhead of data collection vs. the readiness of dependency relation when the need for applying CS is acute.

For illustration of CS Analysis, in the following we consider the subtasks (a)-(i)-(I) and (b)-(i). Let us assume that the H-Adaptation Manager collects the values of preselected knowledge fields of the set of components of the same type in the latest time

> **a. Data collection**
>   (i) On a real system
>   I. Preventively
>   II. Ex-post
>   (ii) By simulation
> **b. Acquiring dependency relation**
>   (i) Regression/machine learning
>   (ii) Empirical knowledge

Fig. 5. Alternative subtasks of CS analysis (identification of data dependencies).

instances $t = 1..n$. Furthermore, for acquiring the dependency relation, CS Analysis checks all the aggregated knowledge to find out which knowledge fields are dependent on others. Let $C_i.k_l^t$ be the value of knowledge field k_l of component C_i at a time instance t, and $\{C_i.k_l\}_1^n$ denote the time series of the knowledge field k_l of component C_i at time instances 1 to n. Further let $\mu_{k_l}(C_i.k_l^t, C_j.k_l^t)$ be the distance between two knowledge values of k_l^t in components C_i and C_j measured by metric μ specific to k_l. Then, for all component pairs $C_i, C_j; i \neq j$, having the fields k_l and k_m, CS Analyze computes the boundary Δ_{kl} such that the implication $\mu_{k_l}(C_i.k_l^t, C_j.k_l^t) < \Delta_{k_l} \Rightarrow \mu_{k_m}(C_i.k_m^t, C_j.k_m^t) < T_{k_m}$ for the time instances $t = 1..n$ is satisfied in (at least) the specified percentage of all the cases (confidence level a_{k_m}, e.g. 90 %). Here T_{k_m} represents the tolerable distance threshold and is provided for each k_m. The CS Analysis concludes that the value of $C_i.k_m^t$ is close to the value of $C_j.k_m^t$ (and vice versa) for t such that the values of $C_i.k_l^t$ and $C_j.k_l^t$ are close as well.

Thus, when a component C_f fails to sense the values of k_m, an approximation of this property has to take place. This is done by CS Plan by creating an ensemble with the exchange function $C_f.k_m := C_j.k_m$ and membership condition $\mu_{k_l}(C_f.k_l, C_j.k_l) < \Delta_{k_l}$. If more than one C_j satisfies the membership condition, an arbitrary one is selected. The ensemble is deployed and started by CS Execute.

The task to compute the boundary Δ_{k_l} is resource and time demanding but there are techniques that can lower the time needed to finish, such as sorting the data according to $\mu_{k_m}(C_i.k_m^t, C_j.k_m^t)$ or using sampling of the gathered data to obtain a statistically significant answer. There are of course a number of other methods to detect dependencies between data such as linear regression, k-nearest neighbors, neural networks, etc.

For illustration, consider the situation where the downwards-looking camera of a robot R starts failing and consequently R loses the ability to detect dirtiness on the floor (and, to update its `dirtinessMap`). This situation will trigger the CS H-mechanism which will create a `DirtinessMapExchange` ensemble, the membership condition of which states that R becomes the coordinator and the other robots that are closer to R than the given threshold (obviously, when their positions are close, their maps are "close") become its members. By knowledge exchange, R adopts the dirtinessMap of the closest member (Fig. 6) and can resume its cleaning operation.

```
55.  role DirtinessMapRole:
56.    position, dirtinessMap
57.
58.  ensemble DirtinessMapExchange:
59.    coordinator: DirtinessMapRole
60.    member: DirtinessMapRole
61.    membership:
62.      // Member and coordinator must be "close" to form the ensemble
63.      // The robot with broken sensor becames the coordinator
64.      close(coordinator.position, member.position)
65.        and obsolete(coordinator.dirtinessMap)
66.    knowledge exchange:
67.        coordinator.dirtinessMap ← member.dirtinessMap
68.    scheduling: periodic( 1000ms )
```

Fig. 6. DSL excerpt from specification of collaborative sensing ensemble of the cleaning robots.

3.2 H-Mechanism #2: Faulty Component Isolation from Adaptation

The idea of the faulty component isolation from adaptation (FCIA) H-mechanism is rooted in the well-known fault-tolerance mechanism: When a component starts malfunctioning it has to be isolated from the rest of the system and its activity taken over by another non-faulty component providing the same functionality. In essence, FCIA addresses the situation where a component A starts emitting faulty values of its property P. In such a case, FCIA modifies the adaptation strategies that count on P in order to prevent the "contamination" of other components with faulty values of P.

For illustration, consider a situation where a docking station DS due to some error or malfunction is not able of having docked robots charge anymore, while still being advertised as operational to robots, which are technically members of the DockingInformationExchange ensemble associated with DS (Fig. 3). As a result, a Robot may still queue at the faulty DS. This is a trigger for applying the FCIA H-mechanism by the H-Adaptation Manager. In essence, FCIA modifies the DockingInformationExchange specification in such a way that DS is excluded from being the coordinator of one of its instances. Technically, this can be done by modifying the membership condition to make it not satisfiable for DS.

3.3 H-Mechanism #3: Enhancing Mode Switching

The motivation behind the enhancing mode switching (EMS) H-mechanism is that there are cases where the behavior of a component specified by its mode-state machine is over-constrained. Thus, instead of being stuck in situations that have not been anticipated at design time, it can be beneficial to relax the constraints and enlarge the space of actions that can be tried out to handle such situations. Building on this idea, the EMS H-mechanism adjusts the self-adaptation strategy implemented as a mode-state machine associated with a particular component. Specifically, EMS (i) creates new probabilistic transitions from every mode to every other one, and (ii) introduces probabilities to the existing mode transitions (in Fig. 7 the introduced probabilities have a value of 0.01; however, the actual probability learned in our experiments is much smaller). The resulting mode-state machine is represented by a fully connected probabilistic graph. An important part of EMS is a fitness function assessing the impact of a specific modification to the mode-state machine (e.g. by evaluation of system performance). EMS monitors the value of the fitness function and triggers the change of probabilities when the value is low. This change is subject to iterations to tune the fitness value to the desired threshold (e.g. by simulated annealing).

For illustration, consider the unanticipated situation that there are far more Robots than DockingStations. Assuming similar energy depletion and similar initial energy budgets, if all Robots follow the mode-state machine depicted in Fig. 7, they might all switch to Charging mode at similar points in time (when their energy falls below 20 %). This would result in an increase in the average charging time, since robots will need to queue up at the docking stations. The situation when the queuing and consequently charging time of robots takes longer than usual will act as a trigger for EMS. It will change the mode-state machine of affected robots by adding new transitions and guards (depicted in green in Fig. 7). The new transitions have a probability of 0.01. This is just for illustration; the actual probabilities learned in our experiments are much smaller (see Sect. 4.2). It is important to realize that each component may find itself in the triggering situation of EMS at a different time and that the mode-state machine evolution is also specific to an individual component.

The EMS H-mechanism effectively allows the transition from every mode to every other mode with a given probability. This, however, can be dangerous when there exist modes that should be entered only under certain circumstances (e.g., because they involve operations with non-revertible effects). To address this issue, we assume that there is a way to specify such forbidden transitions in the mode-state machine.

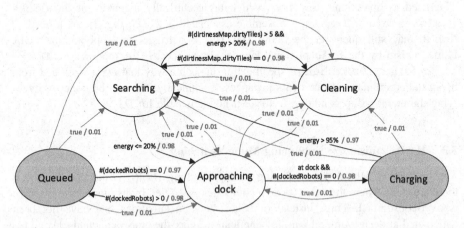

Fig. 7. Mode-state machine capturing the mode switching logic of the Robot component. Each state (mode) is associated with several processes. Transitions are guarded by conditions upon the Robot's knowledge. Changes introduced by the EMS H-mechanism are marked in (bold) green – transitions are now guarded by a condition/probability pair. States that are not allowed to have incoming transitions are marked in grey background. (Color figure online)

4 Evaluation and Discussion

4.1 Experiment Design and Testbed

In order to quantitatively assess the effects of the three H-mechanisms, we applied them to the running example (Sect. 2.1) in its JDEECo implementation (JDEECo is a Java implementation of the DEECo component model [14]). We implemented them as plugins to the JDEECo framework, taking advantage of its modeling and simulation capabilities. All these realizations of H-mechanisms[1] are governed by the H-Adaptation Manager implemented as an isolated DEECo component.

To show that the application of the H-mechanisms increases the overall utility of the system in case of faults, a controlled experiment was designed and conducted. This was based on a number of simulation runs of predefined scenarios, each being a combination of deliberatively introduced faults to be addressed by a particular H-mechanism (or their combination). In total, we considered the 8 different scenarios, each of them containing four robots, depicted in Fig. 8. To measure the overall utility of a system run, we used an application-specific metric returning the 90th percentile of the time required for a tile that got dirty until it is cleaned.

Scenario	Fault	Mechanism	Number of docking stations
1	-	-	3
2	A robot's dirtiness sensor malfunctions	-	3
3	A robot's dirtiness sensor malfunctions	CS	3
4	A docking station emits wrong availability data	-	3
5	A docking station emits wrong availability data	FCIA	3
6	Too many robots w.r.t. docking stations	-	1
7	Too many robots w.r.t. docking stations	EMS	1
8	All above	-	2
9	All above	CS+FCIA+EMS	2

Fig. 8. Scenarios considered in the controlled experiment. Simulation duration is 600 s (with extra 300 s "learning phase" in scenarios 7 & 9), environment size is 20 × 20, number of robots is 4.

4.2 Results and Discussion

Results. Each scenario was run in 100 iterations. Figure 9 shows the values of the overall system utility in the form of boxplot diagrams where the number associated with the red line denotes the median of the sample. System utility is expressed by the time needed to clean a tile after it gets dirty, the smaller the time the better.

---

[1] Available at: https://github.com/d3scomp/uncertain-architectures.

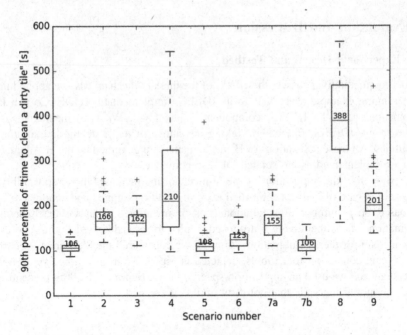

Fig. 9. Simulation results. Smaller values are better.

Scenario 1 represents the vanilla case (no faults – no H-mechanism active), acting as the baseline. Not surprisingly, in other scenarios the 90th percentile of the time to clean a tile increases when a fault occurs and is not counteracted by an H-mechanism (scenarios 2, 4, 6, 8). When an H-mechanism counteracts the fault (scenarios 3, 5, 7, 9), the overall utility improves, but does not reach the baseline scenario. Below we comment more on CS and EMS, since the application of FCIA was straightforward.

As to the application of CS (scenario 2), a dependency relation (Sect. 3.1) was identified such that the closeness of the `positions` of Robot components implied similar values in their `dirtinessMaps`. This resulted in the creation and deployment of the `DirtinessMapExchange` of Fig. 6. The used metrics, tolerable distances, and confidence levels are depicted in Fig. 10.

The effect of EMS is illustrated in scenarios 6 and 7. In both scenarios, only a single docking station is active, corresponding to the situation that one of the two docking stations gets unavailable at run-time. When EMS is applied (scenario 7), due to the introduced probabilistic mode switching, the robots started visiting the docking station

Knowledge field	Distance metric (μ)	Tolerable distance (T)	Confidence level (α)
position	Euclidean	3	0.9
battery	difference	0.005	0.95
dirtinessMap	In Fig. 11	3	0.9

Fig. 10. Distance metrics, tolerable distances, and confidence levels in Robot knowledge fields.

```
1.   def dirtinessMapDistance(map1, map2):
2.     dist = 0
3.     // for each node in the global map, if visited in
4.     // same-ish time add penalty if needed
5.     for n in DirtinessMap.getNodes():
6.        if(map1.getVisited().get(n) -
7.          map2.getVisited().get(n) <= timeWindow):
8.           dirt1 = map1.getDirtinessIn(n)
9.           dirt2 = map2.getDirtinessIn(n)
10.          if(dirt1 - dirt2 > dirtWindow):
11.             dist = dist + differencePenalty
12.    return dist
```

Fig. 11. Distance metric for dirtinessMap field of Robot component.

at different times. Hence, the overall queueing time was reduced and the overall utility increased. EMS needs time to auto-calibrate (set to 300 s) as it searches for the probability value for the added transitions that yields the highest fitness value following a simulated annealing algorithm. In Fig. 9, the results have been split into the learning phase (7a) and the execution run with learned values (7b). The solution naturally underperforms in the learning phase compared to the case without EMS (6) because of the trial and error that the learning involves. However, once the learning period is over and EMS uses the learned values, it yields a significantly better behavior compared to (6). The fitness value was calculated as the inverse of the average time it takes the robot to clean a tile since it discovered the dirt. Since EMS was running independently for each robot, the local searches returned different optimal probabilities for each robot found by the search (with values close to 0.0001).

In scenario (8) all the faults are introduced and in (9) they are handled by all the three H-mechanisms; this illustrates that all of them can be active at the same time without worsening the overall utility of the system. Since the fitness function in EMS was selected in such a way that it does not depend on the faults triggering CS and FCIA, all the three H-mechanisms behaved as orthogonal.

Discussion. We use two distinct architectural layers—"standard" self-adaptation and adaptation of self-adaptation strategies (the task of H-mechanisms). Hence, our solution basically follows the principle of architectural hoisting [17] —separating concerns by assigning the possibility for a global system property (here self-adaptation) to system architecture. Even though the H-mechanisms layer can be interpreted as (high-level) exception handling in self-adaptation settings and can be implemented at the same level of abstraction as the self-adaptation itself, achieving the same functionality without the H-mechanism layer would make the code of ensembles and components very clumsy. Architectural hoisting makes the separation of these concerns much easier and elegant.

Depending on the particular fitness function applied, EMS may be triggered in a situation that is also covered by other H-mechanisms (e.g. by CS). In such a case it is important to address this interference and state which H-mechanism has precedence in order to avoid unnecessary side effects. This is the task of the H-Adaptation Manager.

Limitations. In general, the extra layer demands additional computational load, since monitoring of the triggering events is inherent to all three H-mechanisms. Even though it is minor for CS and FCIA, in the case of EMS it depends on the complexity of the associated fitness function. Obviously, the most computationally demanding step is the data collection in CS if done preventively at runtime. This can be reduced by limiting the time window for collecting data, or by starting it ex-post, i.e. when a need be.

Another limitation of the work presented in this paper is that the proposed H-mechanisms have been only evaluated so far with DEECo self-adaptation strategies. Investigating the generalizability of our homeostasis concept with other self-adaptation approaches (e.g. Stitch) is an interesting topic of our future work.

5   Related Work

In this paper we focus on handling run-time uncertainty in the context of sasiCPS engineered as self-adaptive systems. We thus discuss related literature on the topics of handling uncertainty in cyber-physical as well as self-adaptive systems, in addition to works on solving run-time architecture problems.

Managing uncertainty has been identified as one of the major challenges in engineering software for self-adaptive systems [5]. Self-adaptive systems can be affected by different kinds of uncertainty: Requirements, design and run-time uncertainty [4]. We reflect on the major works in uncertainty affecting self-adaptive systems. On the requirements uncertainty level, Ramirez et al. have introduced the RELAX language which allows to make requirements more tolerant to environmental uncertainty [18]. Esfahani et al. propose POISED – an approach based on possibility theory for handling internal uncertainty that affects the system in making adaptation decisions [19]. Internal uncertainty is caused by the difficulty of determining the impact of adaptation on the system's quality objectives. Knauss et al. contribute with ACON – a learning based approach to deal with unpredictable environment and sensor failure [20]. It uses machine learning to keep the context in which contextual requirements are valid up-to-date. In contrast to the approaches discussed on handling uncertainty in self-adaptive systems, only ACON focuses on the same kind of uncertainty as we do in this paper – the run-time uncertainty. However, in this paper we take an architectural view and focus on ways to evolve self-adaptive logic at run-time to counteract run-time uncertainty, while ACON focuses on keeping requirements up to date.

On architecture-based run-time adaptation, the works by Oreizy et al. [21] on the adaptation and evolution management and Garlan et al. on the Rainbow framework [22] are important. Rainbow supports the reuse of adaptation strategies and infrastructure to apply them. A running system is monitored for violations and appropriate adaptation strategies are employed to resolve them. However, only predesigned strategies are used, which also do not evolve at run-time.

Elkhodary et al. present FUSION that allows a self-adaptive system to self-tune its adaptation logic in case of unanticipated conditions [23]. It uses a feature-oriented system model and learns the impact of feature selection and feature interaction. In contrast to this, we do not use a learning-based approach, but advocate introducing flexibility in self-adaptation strategies as a method to deal with run-time uncertainty.

Villegas et al. focus on supporting context-awareness in self-adaptive systems [24]. Their DYNAMICO reference model supports dynamic monitoring and requirements variability to allow satisfying system goals under highly changing environments. DYNAMICO supports adaptation at the model level (i.e., control objectives, context, and context monitors). We focus on supporting self-adaptation at the architectural level.

6 Conclusions

This paper focused on tackling uncertainty in the operating conditions of self-adaptive software-intensive cyber-physical systems. The general idea is to equip such a system with architecture homeostasis – the ability to change its self-adaptation strategies at run-time according to environment stimuli. This idea was exemplified in three concrete homeostatic mechanisms, which, when triggered, adjust self-adaptation strategies that work at the software architecture level. The conducted experiments showed that hoisting modification of self-adaptation strategies at the architectural level is a viable option.

In our future work, we intend to conduct further research on the classification algorithms to effectively determine situations that trigger homeostatic mechanisms, and investigate, concretize, and experiment with more homeostatic mechanisms.

Acknowledgements. This work was partially supported by the project no. LD15051 from COST CZ (LD) programme by the Ministry of Education, Youth and Sports of the Czech Republic; by Charles University institutional fundings SVV-2016-260331 and PRVOUK; by Charles University Grant Agency project No. 391115. This work is part of the TUM Living Lab Connected Mobility project and has been funded by the Bayerisches Staatsministerium für Wirtschaft und Medien, Energie und Technologie.

References

1. Kim, B.K., Kumar, P.R.: Cyber-physical systems: a perspective at the centennial. Proc. IEEE **100**, 1287–1308 (2012)
2. Hölzl, M., Rauschmayer, A., Wirsing, M.: Engineering of software-intensive systems: state of the art and research challenges. In: Wirsing, M., Banâtre, J.-P., Hölzl, M., Rauschmayer, A. (eds.) Software-Intensive Systems. LNCS, vol. 5380, pp. 1–44. Springer, Heidelberg (2008)
3. Beetz, K., Böhm, W.: Challenges in engineering for software-intensive embedded systems. In: Pohl, K., Hönninger, H., Achatz, R., Broy, M. (eds.) Model-Based Engineering of Embedded Systems, pp. 3–14. Springer, Heidelberg (2012)
4. Ramirez, A.J., Jensen, A.C., Cheng, B.H.: A taxonomy of uncertainty for dynamically adaptive systems. In: SEAMS 2012, pp. 99–108. IEEE (2012)
5. Cheng, B.H.C.: Software engineering for self-adaptive systems: a research roadmap. In: Cheng, B.H.C., de Lemos, R., Giese, H., Inverardi, P., Magee, J. (eds.) Self-adaptive Systems. LNCS, vol. 5525, pp. 1–26. Springer, Heidelberg (2009)
6. Cheng, S.-W., Garlan, D., Schmerl, B.: Stitch: a language for architecture-based self-adaptation. J. Syst. Softw. **85**, 1–38 (2012)

7. Iftikhar, M.U., Weyns, D.: ActivFORMS: active formal models for self-adaptation. In: SEAMS 2014, pp. 125–134. ACM Press (2014)
8. Weyns, D., Malek, S., Andersson, J.: FORMS: a formal reference model for self-adaptation. In: Proceedings of the 7th International Conference on Autonomic Computing, pp. 205–214. ACM, New York (2010)
9. Floch, J., Hallsteinsen, S., Stav, E., Eliassen, F., Lund, K., Gjorven, E.: Using architecture models for runtime adaptability. IEEE Softw. **23**, 62–70 (2006)
10. Brun, Y., et al.: Engineering self-adaptive systems through feedback loops. In: Cheng, B.H., de Lemos, R., Giese, H., Inverardi, P., Magee, J. (eds.) Self-adaptive Systems. LNCS, vol. 5525, pp. 48–70. Springer, Heidelberg (2009)
11. Gerostathopoulos, I., Bures, T., Hnetynka, P., Hujecek, A., Plasil, F., Skoda, D.: Meta-adaptation strategies for adaptation in cyber-physical systems. In: Weyns, D., Mirandola, R., Crnkovic, I. (eds.) ECSA 2015. LNCS, vol. 9278, pp. 45–52. Springer, Heidelberg (2015). doi:10.1007/978-3-319-23727-5_4
12. Cheng, B.H.C., Sawyer, P., Bencomo, N., Whittle, J.: A goal-based modeling approach to develop requirements of an adaptive system with environmental uncertainty. In: Schürr, A., Selic, B. (eds.) MODELS 2009. LNCS, vol. 5795, pp. 468–483. Springer, Heidelberg (2009). doi:10.1007/978-3-642-04425-0_36
13. Shaw, M.: "Self-healing": softening precision to avoid brittleness. In: Proceedings of the First Workshop on Self-healing Systems, pp. 111–114. ACM (2002)
14. Bures, T., Gerostathopoulos, I., Hnetynka, P., Keznikl, J., Kit, M., Plasil, F.: DEECo – an ensemble-based component system. In: Proceedings of CBSE 2013, pp. 81–90. ACM (2013)
15. Kephart, J., Chess, D.: The vision of autonomic computing. Computer **36**, 41–50 (2003)
16. Perrouin, G., Morin, B., Chauvel, F., Fleurey, F., Klein, J., Traon, Y.L., Barais, O., Jezequel, J.-M.: Towards flexible evolution of dynamically adaptive systems. In: Proceedings of ICSE 2012, pp. 1353–1356. IEEE (2012)
17. Fairbanks, G.: Architectural hoisting. IEEE Softw. **31**, 12–15 (2014)
18. Ramirez, A.J., Cheng, B.H., Bencomo, N., Sawyer, P.: Relaxing claims: coping with uncertainty while evaluating assumptions at run time. In: France, R.B., Kazmeier, J., Breu, R., Atkinson, C. (eds.) MODELS 2012. LNCS, vol. 7590, pp. 53–69. Springer, Heidelberg (2012)
19. Esfahani, N., Kouroshfar, E., Malek, S.: Taming uncertainty in self-adaptive software. In: Proceedings of SIGSOFT/FSE 2011, pp. 234–244. ACM (2011)
20. Knauss, A., Damian, D., Franch, X., Rook, A., Müller, H.A., Thomo, A.: ACon: a learning-based approach to deal with uncertainty in contextual requirements at runtime. Inf. Softw. Technol. **70**, 85–99 (2016)
21. Oreizy, P., Medvidovic, N., Taylor, R.N.: Architecture-based runtime software evolution. In: Proceedings of ICSE 1998, pp. 177–186. IEEE (1998)
22. Cheng, S., Huang, A., Garlan, D., Schmerl, B., Steenkiste, P.: Rainbow: architecture-based self-adaptation with reusable infrastructure. IEEE Comput. **37**, 46–54 (2004)
23. Elkhodary, A., Esfahani, N., Malek, S.: FUSION: a framework for engineering self-tuning self-adaptive software systems. In: Proceedings of FSE 2010, pp. 7–16. ACM (2010)
24. Villegas, N.M., Tamura, G., Müller, H.A., Duchien, L., Casallas, R.: DYNAMICO: a reference model for governing control objectives and context relevance in self-adaptive software systems. In: de Lemos, R., Giese, H., Müller, H.A., Shaw, M. (eds.) Self-adaptive Systems. LNCS, vol. 7475, pp. 265–293. Springer, Heidelberg (2013)

Executing Software Architecture Descriptions with SysADL

Flavio Oquendo[1]([⊠]), Jair Leite[2], and Thais Batista[2]

[1] IRISA – Université de Bretagne Sud, Vannes, France
flavio.oquendo@irisa.fr
[2] UFRN – Federal University of Rio Grande do Norte, Natal, Brazil
{jair,thais}@dimap.ufrn.br

Abstract. Most Software Architecture Description Languages (ADLs) lack explicit support for executing an architecture description. In the execution view, the runtime behavior of an architecture is simulated to validate its logic regarding satisfaction of behavioral requirements. In this paper, we present the executable viewpoint of SysADL, a SysML Profile for modeling the architecture of software-intensive systems, which brings together the expressive power of ADLs for architecture description with a standard modeling language widely accepted by the industry, i.e. SysML. SysADL encompasses three integrated viewpoints: structural, behavioral, and executable. This paper focuses on the executable viewpoint that enables the description of the execution model of a software architecture. In this viewpoint, SysADL provides an extended action language subsuming the ALF action language based on fUML, adapted for SysML. In this paper, we use a Central Conditioner System as a case study to illustrate SysADL execution views.

Keywords: Architecture Description Language · Execution viewpoint · SysML · ALF action language

1 Introduction

Architecture Description Languages (ADLs) describe a software architecture as a configuration of components whose interactions are mediated by connectors [4]. Although more than 120 ADLs [1] have been proposed since the 1990s, most ADLs do not support multiple viewpoints, which are essential for the stakeholders in the industry. In addition, none of them have a broad adoption in the industry according to the survey presented by Malavolta et al. [3], even if a few ADLs were adopted in the industry for particular application domains. On the other hand, the Unified Modeling Language (UML)[1] is very popular in the software development community and industry, however it has limitations for describing software architectures. Moreover, the Systems Modeling Language (SysML)[2], an evolution of UML for systems engineering,

---

[1] http://www.omg.org/spec/UML/.
[2] http://www.omg.org/spec/SysML/.

© Springer International Publishing AG 2016
B. Tekinerdogan et al. (Eds.): ECSA 2016, LNCS 9839, pp. 129–137, 2016.
DOI: 10.1007/978-3-319-48992-6_9

has been increasingly used by systems engineers, inheriting the popularity of UML. It enriches UML with new concepts, diagrams, and it has been widely adopted to design software-intensive systems. However, in terms of architectural description, SysML inherits the limitations of UML: architectural constructs are basically the same as UML with the exception of richer features for the definition of ports.

The abovementioned problems motivated us to define SysADL as a specialization of SysML to the architectural description domain, with the aim of bringing together the expressive power of ADLs for architecture description with a standard language widely accepted by the industry, which itself provides hooks for specialization. SysADL, reconciles the expressive power of ADLs with the use of a common notation in line with the SysML standard for modeling software-intensive systems, while also coping with the ISO/IEC/IEEE 42010 Standard in terms of multiple viewpoints.

SysADL has a rigorous operational semantics, which allows the analysis (in terms of verification of both safety and liveness properties) and execution (in terms of simulation for validation) of the architecture. It is structured according to three viewpoints: (i) structural; (ii) behavioral; and (iii) executable. In a previous paper [2], we presented the profile for the structural viewpoint with stereotypes to represent the well-known architectural concepts of component, connector, port, and configuration. In another previous paper [7], we presented the behavioral viewpoint, which complements the structural viewpoint with the specification of behaviors for each structural element of the architecture. However, these descriptions are not executable. To be able to execute the architecture description, an *action semantics* is needed for all of them. In fact, most ADLs lack explicit support for executing an architecture description. In the execution view, the runtime behavior of an architecture is simulated to validate its logic regarding satisfaction of behavioral requirements. Thus, an architecture description can be executed, debugged, tested, and analyzed.

In this paper our focus is on the SysADL executable viewpoint that provides the constructs to describe the execution of a software architecture. SysADL provides its executable viewpoint by defining the execution semantics of the structural constructs (components, connectors, and configurations), and of the behavioral constructs (actions and activities). It also defines the data and control flow concepts for describing the body of actions and activities. For this viewpoint, SysADL provides an extended action language subsuming the ALF action language[3] based on fUML[4], adapted for SysML. We use a *Room Temperature Controller (RTC)* system as a case study to illustrate the concepts. We investigated the applicability of SysADL through two case studies and interviews with software architecture specialists.

This paper is structured as follows. Section 2 briefly summarizes the SysADL structural and behavioral viewpoints. Section 3 presents the executable viewpoint of SysADL. Section 4 presents related work. Section 5 contains our concluding remarks.

---

[3] http://www.omg.org/spec/ALF/.

[4] http://www.omg.org/spec/FUML.

2   Overview of SysADL Structural and Behavioral Viewpoints

SysADL defines three architectural viewpoints to communicate the architecture to the involved stakeholders. They express the architecture from a high-level conceptual model to an executable model. In this section we overview the structural and behavioral viewpoints presented in previous papers, i.e. [2, 7] respectively. Section 2.1 gives an overview of the structural viewpoint. Section 2.2 summarizes the behavioral viewpoint. To illustrate the use of SysADL in practice, we design a software architecture to control the temperature of a room: a *Room Temperature Controller (RTC) system*. It has two temperature sensors to capture the current temperature in different areas. A user sets the desired temperature. A central controller receives the values from the temperature sensors, compares them with the desired temperature and turns the cooler or the heater on or off. It also has a presence sensor to detect if there is someone in the room. In case of presence, the system operates to provide the desired temperature. Otherwise, it maintains 22 °C.

2.1   Structural Viewpoint Overview

The SysADL structural viewpoint specializes the SysML model elements to describe the well-known architectural elements: component, connector, and configuration.

Component. In SysADL, a component is represented using a block classifier with a stereotype «component» and its name and type. A component uses ports to interact with its environment. A component can have *in* ports, to required data, and *out* ports, to provided data. In Fig. 1 the central component of the RTC System, *RoomTemperatureControllerCP*. is connected to two *TemperatureSensorCP* components that give the temperature in Fahrenheit values in their *FTemperatureOPT* ports. The *PresenceCheckerCP* informs a Boolean value in the *PresenceOPT* port. *UserInterfaceCP* delivers the user-defined temperature value in Celsius. The *CoolerCP* and *HeaterCP* components receive the command values in their respective ports.

Port. A port is a part of a component. The data flow is represented using an arrow inside the port square indicating its direction. For instance, the *s1* and *s2* components (Fig. 1) has a *current* out port of the type *FTemperatureOPT*.

Connector. A connector links ports of components, allowing data to flow between them. In SysADL, a connector type is defined as an association block with a «connector» stereotype followed by its name and two port types as participants. The association specifies that it can connect any component that has compatible with the participant ports, as shown in Fig. 1, which illustrates the connectors that link each component to the central controller. Also, in Fig. 1, most connectors are direct links that transmit the data from an *out* port to an *in* port except for the *FahrenheitToCelsiusCN* connector that has the responsibility of converting values from Fahrenheit to Celsius value units.

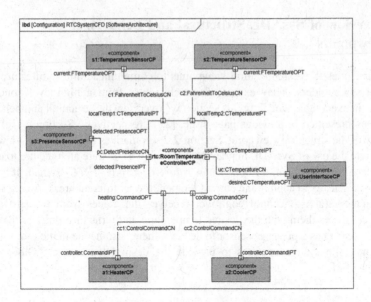

Fig. 1. The software architecture configuration of RTC System

Configuration. A configuration refers to the structural organization of an architecture, a composite component or a composite connector in terms of other components and connectors. Figure 1 shows the definition of the architecture configuration of our RTC.

Diagram. In SysADL two diagrams organize the structural view: the *block definition diagram* (*bdd*) and the *internal block diagram* (*ibd*). Types are defined using *bdd*, architecture configurations are represented using *ibd*. The complete definition of the RTC System is available at http://consiste.dimap.ufrn.br/sysadl/.

2.2   Behavioral Viewpoint Overview

The basic concepts used to represent the behavior are: activity, action, and equation. The behavioral viewpoint includes: (i) the definition and use of activities and actions and their data parameters; (ii) the definition and use of equations that specifies the semantics of activities and actions by defining constraints, i.e. pre- and post-conditions, on the data parameters. In the executable viewpoint we define the executable construct to specify the execution body of an action.

Activity. An activity depicts the behavior of a software architecture element by expressing: (i) how the element consumes and produces data; (ii) the basic actions that execute that process; and (iii) the control and data that flow through the actions. An activity type describes its *pins*, *actions* and *flows*. *Pins* are representations of parameters and specify a stream of data. *In* pins represent input parameters, while *out* pins represent output parameters. *Flows* represent the control and data flows. It must link *in* and *out* pins, as they represent how the data flows and control flows concurrently progress from an action to another within an activity. *Actions* are atomic behaviors that execute from beginning to end receiving parameters and returning a result. The behavior also encompasses the protocol of ports and constraints.

Protocol. The behavioral specification of a port is expressed by a protocol in an activity diagram. For instance, in the case of energy management of the temperature sensor in the RTC System, the *CTemperatureOPT* port is specified to notify when the energy level is low (represented by a threshold value).

The behavior of the *SensorsMonitorCP* component, depicted in Fig. 2, is defined in terms of an activity, *CalculateAverageTemperatureAC*, specified in the behavioral view. It declares the input and output parameters that are directly associated to the ports of the component. This activity itself calls an action, *CalculateAverageTemperatureAN*. The behavior of this component is: it repeatedly waits to receive a value of temperature in °C from port *S1* and another value from port *S2* (in any order) and after calculating the average by calling action *CalculateAverageTemperatureAN, it* sends the result through its port *average*. Both the activity and the action are specified in the behavioral view. In the execution view, we need to complement it with the body implementing the action specified in terms of pre- and post-conditions.

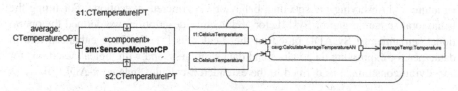

Fig. 2. A component and its corresponding specified activity

Action. An action is specified by its parameters, its pre-conditions expressed in terms of input parameters, and its post-conditions expressed in terms of input and output parameters. Pre- and post-conditions are expressed using *equations*. An example of a post-condition is the equation expressing that the average between two temperatures is the sum of them divided by 2 (or that 2 times the average is equal to their sum). Figure 3. An action and its corresponding equation shows the specification of the *CalculateAverageTemperatureAN* action type with three parameters (*t1, t2, averageTemp*), and the *CalculateAverageTemperatureEQ(t1,t2, averageTemp)* equation.

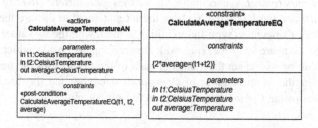

Fig. 3. An action and its corresponding equation

Equation. An equation specifies the constraints that must satisfy all executions of actions and activities. It is defined by a logical expression using the input/output parameters, where an output parameter is calculated using the input parameters. SysADL extends OCL (part of UML adapted to SysML) to express equation constraints.

3   SysADL Executable Viewpoint

After having overviewed the structural and behavioral viewpoints in the previous section, we now present the executable viewpoint of SysADL. In the behavior viewpoint we saw how to express the activities and interactions to achieve the required system functionality. However, that behavior is not executable. To make an architecture executable, the executable viewpoint provides the SysADL constructs to describe the execution semantics of the body of actions. It comprises the data and control flow concepts. The executable viewpoint is expressed by describing the body of the actions expressing the computation. The SysADL notation to represent the body of the actions is based on ALF (See footnote 3), part of UML and SysML. The architect will, then, be able to run the executable architecture description for understanding the dynamics of the structure and observing the specified behavior via concrete executions. For filling the behavioral semantic gap of SysML for architecture description, we defined the operational semantics of SysADL based on the π-calculus [5]. We have enhanced it with datatypes for expressing data values and data structures, and with logical assertions for specifying constraints, as defined in the extended π-calculus, named π-ADL [6].

3.1   The Executable Element

In SysADL, we apply the *executable* construct to specify the body of actions. An executable depicts the action body by expressing: its *parameters*: the pins that consume and produce data; its *body*: the statements that execute how the output pin is computed from the input pins.

Figure 4 shows two examples of executables. In the left, the *CalculateAverageTemperatureEX* executable is defined to the *CalculateAverageTemperatureAN* action described in the previous section. The specification includes its *parameters (t1, t2, result)* and the *body* that calculates the average of temperatures coming from the inputs pins and returns the result in the output pin (*result*). A more complex example is the *CompareTemperatureEX* executable. It defines *parameters (averageTemp, targetTemp, result)* and the *body* that: (i) uses the **let** statement to declare the *heater* and *cooler* variables of *Command* type and to initialize them with the *off* value; (ii) uses the **if** statement to compare *averageTemp* with *targetTemp* to decide which commands must be set to *on* or *off* and set the values of each of them; (iii) uses the **new** statement to create a value that is an instance of *Commands* datatype; and (iv) uses the **return** statement to return the *Commands* instance in the output pin.

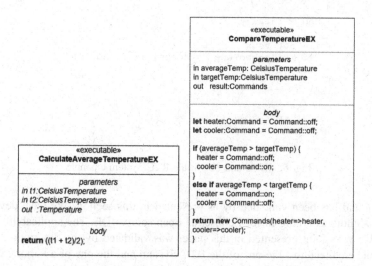

Fig. 4. Two examples of executable specifications

3.2   Action Language

The action language of the executable viewpoint allows the definition of the executable action body providing statements such as assignment, for, while, if, return among others. We will illustrate hereafter some of these statements with the *RTC System*. We first illustrate variable declarations (Fig. 5). They require the specification of a type and an optional expression that returns a value.

```
defaultTemperature : CelsiusTemperature = 22;
targetTemperature = defaultTemperature - 2;
temperatures : CelsiusTemperature[] = new CelsiusTemperature[]{20,22};
```

Fig. 5. Variable declaration in the RTC System example

In Fig. 6 we show two examples of executable body. In the first example in this figure, a search for an element (*searchedTemp*) is performed in a sequence of temperature values in the RTC System, knowing that the sequence is stored in a variable named *temps*. *while* is used to allow the searching loop until the searched temperature is found. *if* is used to evaluate if the searched element is found. In the second example in the same figure, it computes the sum of a sequence of temperature values in the RTC System, stored in a variable named *temps*. A *for* declares a *t* to iterates over all the elements of the *temps* sequence. In each iteration, t refers to an element of the sequence (from the first to the last), and its value is added to the current sum.

SysADL provides a complete action language for describing the executable body of actions. It is worth noting that the execution view is given by the interleaving of the operational semantics of the description of structure, behavior and executable bodies. The executable viewpoint, jointly with the structural and behavioral ones, is supported

```
found = false;
i = 1;
while(not found) {
    if (searchedTemp == temps[i]) found = true;
    else i++;
}

sum = 0;
for (t in temps) {
    sum = sum + t;
}
```

Fig. 6. *While* and *For* in the RTC System example

by a tool and has been validated by as presented in this section. We have developed SysADL Studio as a plug-in for Eclipse, an open source IDE. The applicability of the executable viewpoint presented in this paper was validated by the description of two executable architectures: the one of the RTC System and the one of a Parking system. More details about can be found at http://consiste.dimap.ufrn.br/sysadl.

4 Related Work

The importance of executable architecture descriptions is recognized in several works as a means of early validating the design of software architectures. This is also the general trend of modeling languages, in particular with the Executable Foundational UML (fUML), an intermediary between UML models and platform executable languages. fUML allows the building of executable models. Its declarative semantics is specified in first order logic and based on Process Specification Language. It is more verbose than the SysADL executable language as it mixes architectural abstractions and code that is not proper for architectural descriptions. There are several related works on simulation of UML or SysML design models. Most of them rely on converting UML/SysML models in other executable model, such as Petri Nets and Modelica. This approach is different from ours that provides execution as a first-class property of architectural elements and specializes ALF for providing the action language.

5 Conclusion

In this paper we presented the executable viewpoint of SysADL, defined as a specialization of SysML based on its profile mechanism and filling the semantic variation gaps needed for architecture description. SysADL, as a lightweight extension of an existing standard, can be easily adopted by the software and systems community, both from academy and industry. In addition, as SysADL enriched SysML with ADL-related concepts, it benefits both ADL and SysML skilled architects.

References

1. ADLs: current architectural languages, June 2016. http://www.di.univaq.it/malavolta/al/
2. Leite, J., Oquendo, F., Batista, T.: SysADL: a SysML profile for software architecture description. In: Proceedings of 7th European Conference on Software Architecture (ECSA), Montpellier, France, pp. 106–113 (2013)
3. Malavolta, I., Lago, P., Muccini, H., Pelliccione, P., Tang, A.: What industry needs from architectural languages: a survey. IEEE Trans. Softw. Eng. **39**(6), 869–891 (2013)
4. Medvidovic, N., et al.: A classification and comparison framework for software architecture description languages. IEEE Trans. Softw. Eng. **26**(1), 70–93 (2000)
5. Milner, R.: Communicating and Mobile Systems: The π-Calculus. Cambridge University Press, Cambridge (1999)
6. Oquendo, F.: π-ADL: an architecture description language based on the higher-order typed π-Calculus for specifying dynamic and mobile software architectures. ACM SIGSOFT SEN **29**(3), 1–14 (2004)
7. Oquendo, F., Leite, J., Batista, T.: Specifying architecture behavior with SysADL. In: Proceedings of 13th Working IEEE/IFIP Conference on Software Architecture (WICSA), Venice (2016)

Towards an Architecture for an UI-Compositor for Multi-OS Environments

Tobias Holstein[1,2(✉)] and Joachim Wietzke[3]

[1] Department of Computer Science, University of Applied Sciences,
Darmstadt, Germany
[2] School of Innovation, Design and Engineering, Mälardalen University,
Västerås, Sweden
[3] Faculty of MMT, University of Applied Sciences, Karlsruhe, Germany

Abstract. Separation through hardware/software virtualization on operating system (OS) layer reduces complexity in automotive software. Automotive software is categorized into domains (e.g. comfort, safety related features, driver assistance) and each domain is handled by a separate OS, which contains domain-specific applications. A common user interface (UI) for all applications from all domains is created through an UI-Compositor, which composites and manages the different input/output modalities.

While interactions with a single OS with multiple applications and input/output modalities are well known, we find that a composition of applications from different OSs or a composition of multiple OSs into a single UI is challenging. In this paper we investigate architectural patterns for an UI-Compositor for Multi-OS environments and suggest a new architecture that supports the concept of separation.

1 Introduction

Automotive UIs have changed a lot over the last decades. Comparing car dashboards from 30 years ago to today's dashboards leaves no doubt about the significance and impact of modern UIs. The complexity of automotive software rises with every new generation [3]. Up to 70 % of newly introduced features are software related [1] and categorized into domains: safety related features (e.g. ASP, ESP), driver assistance (e.g. distance checking, lane assist) and comfort (e.g. entertainment, navigation).

The increasing amount of features hence influences the dashboards of current and future cars, which is possible through advances in technology (e.g. freely programmable instrument clusters (FPKs), touch-screens, etc.). System and software architectures have to cope with the correlated complexity and increasing dependencies. A current approach is the separation through hardware/software virtualization to reduce complexity and dependencies and to mitigate the risks of interferences by separating safety critical and non-safety critical applications.

A domain represents an OS, which encapsulates domain-specific applications and services. This is also known as Multi-OS environment. When applications from different domains share resources, such as a common UI, a component called

© Springer International Publishing AG 2016
B. Tekinerdogan et al. (Eds.): ECSA 2016, LNCS 9839, pp. 138–145, 2016.
DOI: 10.1007/978-3-319-48992-6_10

UI-Compositor handles the actual composition. As an example, when multiple applications share a single screen, the screen is the shared resource and the UI-Compositor handles the interaction with those applications and e.g. places the graphical user interfaces (GUIs) on the screen. This central component allows to unify interactions and provide a homogeneous user experience towards all applications.

However, there are problems with compositing UIs from different OSs, such as different interaction styles, different input (e.g. multi-touch instead of mouse) or output devices (e.g. different display resolution). An UI-Compositor has to solve those problems.

Current approaches propose software architectures that require applications to be developed for a certain target environment and set strict rules about how applications are connected with and composed into a unified UI. Therefore specialized frameworks or software development kits (SDKs) are used for the development of applications for Multi-OS environments, which support various ways of inter-VM-communication. This provides high flexibility and rich UIs, but breaks previously intended separation concepts [7].

Considering the previous effort in the development of Multi-OS environments, which is the separation into domains to increase security and to decrease complexity and dependencies, we find that current approaches actually introduce new issues by raising the complexity and dependencies in the overall UI.

Our contributions in this paper are: (1) a universal description of an UI-Compositor; (2) an investigation into the tasks and problems of an UI-Compositor; (3) a comparison of current approaches and (4) the proposal of a new software architecture for an UI-Compositor, that complies with the concept of separation.

2 Related Work

One of the strongest motivations for virtualization in embedded systems is probably security [4]. Embedded systems are highly integrated and their subsystems have to cooperate to contribute to the overall function of the system. Heiser [4] states that "isolating them from each other interferes with the functional requirements of the system". While isolation, i.e. the separation through virtualization, increases security, it is still necessary to control or interact with subsystems.

Multi-OS environments use a type one hypervisor to run different OS types concurrently on a multi-core hardware [10, p. 167]. If OSs of mixed criticality are used it is categorized as a mixed-criticality system. A Hypervisor assigns hardware resources, such as peripheral devices or hardware components, to a certain OS. Accessing resources of other OSs is therefore only possible via inter-VM-communication. Multi-OS environments aim to improve the software architecture attributes modifiability, security, availability and testability. Interoperability is required to some extent, but every interconnection might mitigate the encapsulation of an OS and lead to a security risk [9].

Compositing can take place in different layers, such as Hardware, OS, Application or UI layer. Higher layers depend on lower layers and lower layers define constraints to higher layers, which causes a variety of challenges, especially when a homogeneous UI has to be created [6].

The compositing of GUIs of a partitioned in-vehicle infotainment system (IVIS) is shown in [8]. Each partition, i.e. domain, provides multiple applications, which are combined in a GUI using a compositor. Applications and compositor communicate via inter-VM-communication and exchange pixel data and touch events via shared memory (SHM). Plain pixel data "obviates the need to interpret information and hence mitigate security issues such as code injection" [8]. A homogeneous UI is integrating applications, all with their respective UI, from different domains. These applications combined form the actual homogeneous UI. In order to differentiate between the overall UI and the UI provided by an application, we call the latter UI-Artefact (cmp. [8]).

3   UI-Compositor

An UI-Compositor assembles, i.e. blends, scales or places, and provides user interaction with the different UI-Artefacts. This includes the redirection of input events to one or more designated applications and the composition of different types of output.

If multiple applications use the same type of UI, the UI-Compositor has to decide how the composition is done. Figure 1 depicts a composition of multiple UI-Artefacts based on an example of three UIs.

The UI-Compositor is also responsible to provide the primary UI-Logic, which includes for example the mapping of input events to a certain application. When a GUI is displayed and a user clicks inside one of many displayed GUIs, the UI-Compositor has to calculate/map the actual position of the mouse click to an relative coordinate of the GUI. The application does not know, whether its GUI is displayed in an UI-Compositor or not.

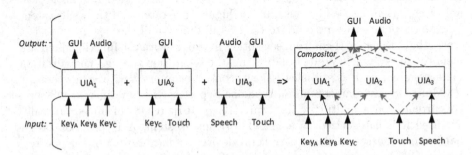

Fig. 1. Abstract representation of tasks of a compositor; UIA: User-Interface Artifact; Key: hard-/soft-keys and/or keyboard; Red/dashed lines show decisions to be made by the compositor. (Color figure online)

3.1 Layers of Decision Making

If two applications on the same hierarchical layer have to negotiate about priorities of each other, e.g. who's window is to be displayed topmost, it usually concludes in a tie. It also requires interconnections among all participating applications, which raises the complexity and dependencies.

A solution is a delegation of the decision to a higher instance (e.g. a UI-Compositor, window manager, etc.), where contextual information is available. This can be achieved through an implementation of UI-Logic. In case of the Windows Icon Menu Pointer (WIMP) interaction style, the UI-Logic inside the window manager handles all windows, including the current active window. Storing the information about the currently active window allows to determine where keyboard events have to be sent.

3.2 Hierarchies in Multi-OS Environments

In a single OS the highest instance is determined by the OS itself. In Multi-OS environments this is different. There is a hypervisor, which as a lower layer manages all OS and their dedicated resources. As soon as resources, such as input or output devices, are shared among multiple OSs, a delegation is required.

This means, that all OSs with non-shared input and output devices therefore have no dependencies to other OSs, which is a rare case. However, in a Multi-OS environment there are two delegations commonly made.

An input event is received in the UI-Compositor, which is the delegate of all OSs. The UI-Compositor knows all domains and therefore the event can be redirected to one (or more) of the given domains, which are represented by OSs. When an OS receives an event, it redirects the event to an application.

A similar procedure has to be followed for the composition of outputs of all applications. When an application e.g. uses an audio output, the audio stream is mixed or regulated through the OS. The OS redirects its audio output to an UI-Compositor, which again mixes or regulates all audio streams from all domains.

3.3 Influence of Modalities

The amount and diversity of available interaction techniques, devices and interaction styles affect the UI-Compositors decision making. The following enumeration provides some examples, that outline the general problem.

Pointing Devices. Pointing devices like mouse or touch screens depend on the actual GUI output. A mouse click is associated with a GUI element, by comparing mouse coordinates with the geometry of the GUI. If the OS sends its complete desktop to the UI-Compositor, which is similar to a remote desktop session, then the UI-Compositor can send back a mouse event relative to its size. The decision of which application will receive this mouse event is thus already made and the OS only needs to execute it.

Hard-Keys or Keyboard. For key events in the WIMP interaction style, the decision making already requires contextual information: the current active window. A user selects a window and then uses the keyboard to enter text. Another variant would be to assign a key directly to an application. This e.g. could be a hard key to always start the navigation program. In this case the compositor would always redirect this specific input event directly to the respective OS.

Stream Based Input. Stream-based input types, such as an interaction via voice or speech, have no clear action points, such as e.g. button pressed or button released, and are more difficult to handle. A microphone records sound waves and whether or not those sound waves include a voice or speech has to be determined by a speech recognition component. This component translates or interprets the given raw data continuously. Delegating would require to pre-interpret the raw data to determine its meaning. In order to select a certain domain, a user would have to say a keyword to choose the domain. Afterwards, an OS might use an own speech recognition to handle incoming raw data.

Another variant would be to only have one speech recognition component for all domains. However, this would cause more dependencies, because a common protocol or interface between this component and each application would be necessary. Applications would have to define, which speech commands they expect, so that an UI-Compositor could redirect those commands. Nevertheless, multiple applications could use the same speech command, which again causes a delegation.

3.4   Other Approaches

While all of the previous variants enforce an actual decision, there are also patterns that allow an alternative approach.

Hard Coded Presets. Instead of a component that decides how events are distributed/redirected, all input and output events could be assigned fixed or part of a specification. For example Key_X is assigned to App_Y and thus it will always be redirected to this single application. Conflicts are avoided by specification, but this also results in less flexibility.

Priority Based. The chain of responsibility pattern for example could be used to redirect an input event to a certain domain. Therefore all domains have to be sorted based on their assigned priority. An input event is always send to the domain with the highest priority first. Domains may consume an event, which causes the event not to be send to another domain. Therefore high priority applications always receive events.

Broadcast. Another approach could be a broadcast of all input events to all domains at the same time. Multiple applications may expect and receive the same input events and trigger functions simultaneously. This will cause the UI to be unusable, because an user looses the ability to make distinct decisions for a certain application.

Those approaches require a predefined specification of mappings between input event and each application. Conflicts have to be ruled out from the beginning, otherwise certain events might never reach an application through priority conflicts or multiple applications might be triggered concurrently.

4   Architecture

In the previous sections we introduced Multi-OS environments, the definition of an UI-Compositor and showed how the hierarchic structure of an Multi-OS environment influences the distribution of input events and the composition of outputs. In this section we compare a standard client/server architecture with our new architecture and show advantages as well as disadvantages in both architectures.

4.1   Client/Server Architecture

Current implementations use a client/server architecture, where the application as a client connects to a compositor as a server. Protocols, such as Wayland or the X Window System, are based on this architecture.

A client/server architecture can be implemented in a Multi-OS environment, where inter-VM-connections are used as communication channels to allow clients from one OS to connect to a server on another OS. Applications as clients must be aware of the compositor as a server to some extent, because a connection has to be established.

Therefore SDKs and frameworks integrate and provide interfaces to lower layers for inter-VM-communication. A common way is the use of virtual network adapters, which provide access to a virtual network among all virtual machines (VMs). Usually those networks are protected by firewalls, which are based on a set of rules and configuration files. However, network stacks are basically re-implemented to provide inter-VM-communication and therefore re-introduce the same problems and complexity from standard network connections.

Interconnections between multiple applications and multiple UI-Compositors would also create a network of dependencies among multiple OSs. They also increase the chance of fault propagation.

Another problem in client/server architecture is that data is transferred between client and server via serialization. This copying requires the data to be synchronized. Multi-OS environments can actually use SHM to share data between two OSs without serialization and copying. Synchronization mechanisms between two OSs are the only dependency actually required.

4.2   Publish/Subscribe and Data-Container Architecture

Publish/subscribe [2, p. 242] is a concept for loosely coupled communication partners in a network. Here, client and server do not communicate directly. Instead both use an intermediary message broker for dispatching messages.

Client(s) and server(s) can subscribe to messages as well as publish messages at the same time. The format of the message is the common base. Message subscribers are notified via the message broker as soon as new messages are available.

Data container [11, p. 349] is another architecture that describes the use of SHM between two processes. The data container is an area in a SHM that contains data. The architecture defines that data is never sent to another process via serialization or copying. Instead a data container contains the data, and the process, that is supposed to receive this data, is notified via update events and then reads data from the SHM. Therefore data is not copied and the receiver will always read up-to-date data.

In our architecture we combine both architectures. A data container in Multi-OS environments can be placed in SHM, which is shared among multiple OSs. The SHM is partitioned and each OS owns, i.e. can write into, its assigned partition, but may read from all other partitions. In order to provide a loose coupling between all OSs, we introduce the publish/subscribe architecture to notify OSs about changes in a certain data container. This allows an inherently many-to-many asynchronous communication, which is fault resilient, thus supporting the concept of separation on OS layer.

However some changes on each OS have to be made to be able to use this concept for an UI-Compositor. Applications have to publish their UI output to the SHM and subscribe to input events.

Publishing UI output from applications to a SHM has to be implemented for each OS. A local OS specific window manager could be modified to achieve that.

The data container should contain information about the provided data in such a way, that a subscriber can determine the type of UI used. This information is necessary to implement an UI-Logic in an UI-Compositor. This includes the expected input (e.g. sound, multi-touch, etc.) for an application and depending on the interaction style it might be necessary to include application states (e.g. key stroke expected).

5 Conclusion

Interaction styles play an important role in architecture of Multi-OS environments. They define the common interfaces between application, OS and Compositor. Without knowing the type of UI used by an application, an unwanted flexibility in protocols has to be implemented. An exact definition of an application's UI, in terms of its inputs and outputs, allows to use minimal inter-connections and well-defined interfaces, which reduces the overall complexity.

In Multi-OS environments the separation and secure encapsulation of domains is the primary goal. Inter-connections between domains cause unwanted dependencies and raise the complexity, which was supposed to be decreased through separation.

Using the herein proposed compositor architecture allows a loose coupling between UI-Compositor and applications from all domains by applying the publish/subscriber and data container architecture. Therefore applications are not directly connected to a server, but write content to a data container in a SHM. Inter-VM-communication is only used to report/send notifications about changes in certain data containers. It is therefore lightweight and neither serialization nor copying has to be used.

The proposed architecture supports the concept of separation in Multi-OS environments while providing loosely coupled interconnections for an UI-Compositor.

6 Future Work

Based on our research basic prototypes to verify the suggested approach were implemented [5]. However, a fully working UI-Compositor for Multi-OS environments with support for different interaction styles for applications from different OSs, is a complex task that will be implemented in the future. Also examples for voice controlled UIs in a Multi-OS environment are subject of further research.

References

1. Bosch, J.: Continuous software engineering: an introduction. In: Bosch, J. (ed.) Continuous Software Engineering. Springer, Heidelberg (2014)
2. Coulouris, G., Dollimore, J., Kindberg, T., Blair, G.: Distributed Systems: Concepts and Design, 5th edn. Addison-Wesley Publishing Company, Hoboken (2011)
3. Ebert, C., Jones, C.: Embedded software facts, figures, and future. Computer 42(4), 42–52 (2009)
4. Heiser, G.: The role of virtualization in embedded systems. In: Proceedings of the 1st Workshop on Isolation and Integration in Embedded Systems, IIES 2008, pp. 11–16. ACM, New York (2008)
5. Holstein, T., Weißbach, B., Wietzke, J.: Towards a HTML-UI-compositor by introducing the wayland-protocol into a browser-engine. In: IEEE/IFIP Conference on Software Architecture (WICSA), April 2016
6. Holstein, T., Wallmyr, M., Wietzke, J., Land, R.: Current challenges in compositing heterogeneous user interfaces for automotive purposes. In: Kurosu, M. (ed.) HCI 2015. LNCS, vol. 9170, pp. 531–542. Springer, Heidelberg (2015). doi:10.1007/978-3-319-20916-6_49
7. Holstein, T., Wietzke, J.: Contradiction of separation through virtualization and inter virtual machine communication in automotive scenarios. In: Proceedings of the 2015 European Conference on Software Architecture Workshops, ECSAW 2015, pp. 4:1–4:5. ACM, New York (2015)
8. Knirsch, A.: Improved composability of software components through parallel hardware platforms for in-car multimedia systems. Ph.D. thesis, Plymouth University, Plymouth, UK (2015)
9. Schnarz, P., Wietzke, J.: It-sicherheits-eigenschaften für eng gekoppelte, asynchrone multi-betriebssysteme im automotiven umfeld. In: Halang, W.A. (ed.) Funktionale Sicherheit. Informatik aktuell, pp. 29–38. Springer, Heidelberg (2013)
10. Wietzke, J.: Embedded Technologies: Vom Treiber bis zur Grafik-Anbindung. Springer, Heidelberg (2012)
11. Wietzke, J., Tran, M.T.: Automotive Embedded Systeme - Effizientes Framework - Vom Design zur Implementierung. Springer Xpert.press, Heidelberg (2005)

Software Architecture Evolution

Inferring Architectural Evolution from Source Code Analysis

A Tool-Supported Approach for the Detection of Architectural Tactics

Christel Kapto[1], Ghizlane El Boussaidi[1(⊠)], Sègla Kpodjedo[1],
and Chouki Tibermacine[2]

[1] Department of Software and IT Engineering, École de Technologie Supérieure,
Montreal, Canada
ghizlane.elboussaidi@etsmtl.ca
[2] LIRMM - CNRS and University of Montpellier II, Montpellier, France

Abstract. Several approaches have been proposed to study and provide information about the evolution of a software system, but very few proposals analyze and interpret this information at the architectural level. In this paper, we propose an approach that supports the understanding of software evolution at the architectural level. Our approach relies on the idea that an architectural tactic can be mapped to a number of operational representations, each of which is a transformation described using a set of elementary actions on source code entities (e.g., adding a package, moving a class from a package to another, etc.). These operational representations make it possible to: (1) detect architectural tactics' application (or cancellation) by analyzing different versions of the source code of analyzed systems, and (2) understand the architectural evolution of these systems. To evaluate the proposed approach, we carried out a case study on the JFreeChart open source software. We focused on the modifiability tactics and we analyzed a number of available releases of JFreeChart. The results of our analysis revealed inconsistencies in the evolution of the system and some erratic applications and cancellations of modifiability tactics.

Keywords: Software evolution · Architectural evolution · Architectural tactics · Tactics detection

1 Introduction

Throughout the life of a software system, developers and maintainers will modify the source code in order to add new features, correct or prevent defects. In doing so, they will apply many simple coding techniques and patterns but they will also occasionally introduce higher level elements that will be meaningful at an architectural level. While there are many proposals concerned about evolution data at a low level [1], few approaches have been proposed to analyze and interpret this information at the architectural level. Even though several approaches that tackle the understanding and formalization of architecture evolution have emerged (e.g., [2–8]), there exist very few

© Springer International Publishing AG 2016
B. Tekinerdogan et al. (Eds.): ECSA 2016, LNCS 9839, pp. 149–165, 2016.
DOI: 10.1007/978-3-319-48992-6_11

tools to help designers track and group a set of low-level source code changes and translate them into a more concise high-level architectural intention. A key challenge is that some architectural elements may not be traced easily and directly to code elements (e.g., architectural constraints). In fact, architectural elements include extensional elements (e.g., module or component) and intensional ones (e.g., design decisions, rationale, invariants) while source code elements are extensional [9, 10]. This contributes to the absence of the architectural intention at the source code level and the divergence of the source code from this intention. Moreover, architectural decisions are non-local [9] and often define and constrain the structure and the interactions of several code elements. If the developer is aware of the architectural decisions and constraints, the changes she made to the source code will be consistent with these. In fact, some of these changes may derive from the architecture evolution of the software and they reveal some intentions at the architectural level.

Thus, in this work, we hypothesize that some of the architectural intentions can be inferred from the analysis of the evolution of the source code. Clustering a set of changes made to the source code and analyzing the results may reveal a high level decision. We focus on object-oriented (OO) systems and modifiability tactics [11, 12] as they involve changes that can be detected through the analysis of different releases of a software system. Thus we propose an approach that enables detecting tactics' application (or cancellation) in an OO system and inferring an architectural evolution trend through the system's evolution. To do so, we map high level descriptions of tactics, as introduced in [11], to a number of operational representations (i.e., source code transformations). Tactics are intensional and thus may have several operational representations. An operational representation is a pattern of evolution described using elementary actions on source code entities (e.g., adding a class to a package, moving a class from a package to another, etc.) and a set of constraints describing the structure of the system before or after these actions. Using these operational representations, we analyze available evolution data about the source code to retrieve architectural tactics that were applied or cancelled during development or maintenance. We developed a prototype tool that supports our approach and experimented on a set of modifiability tactics and a number of versions of a Java open source project.

The paper is organized as follows. Section 2 proposes some background and related work about architectural tactics and evolution. Section 3 presents an overview of our approach while Sects. 4 and 5 detail two key aspects of our proposal: the definition of operational representations of tactics and the detection of their occurrences respectively. Section 6 proposes a case study for our approach and discussion of the obtained results. Finally Sect. 7 summarizes our proposal and outlines future work.

2   Background and Related Work

2.1   Architectural Tactics

Architectural tactics are design decisions that achieve quality attributes [11, 12]. Quality attributes are measurable properties that indicate how well a given system supports specific requirements [11]. Examples of these attributes include performance, availability and security. Bass et al. [11] introduced the concept of an architectural tactic as an architecture transformation that supports the achievement of a single quality attribute. They catalogued a set of common tactics that address availability, interoperability, modifiability, performance, security, testability and usability. This catalog of tactics aims to support systematic design. For instance, performance tactics aim at ensuring that the system responds to arriving events within some time constraints while security tactics aim at resisting, detecting and recovering from attacks [11]. Examples of performance tactics include increasing computational efficiency, managing the event rate and introducing concurrency. Common security tactics include authenticating users and maintaining data confidentiality. The designer chooses the appropriate tactics according to the system's context and trade-offs, and the cost to implement these tactics.

2.2   Related Work

Developing approaches and tools that support the designers in understanding architectural evolution involves many theoretical and practical challenges [20]. Several approaches were proposed to tackle the architectural evolution of software systems. These approaches can be classified according to their goal: (1) supporting architects in building software evolution plans at the architectural level (e.g., [2, 3]); (2) understanding and visualizing the evolution [5, 6, 13, 14]; and (3) evaluating architectural stability [4, 8]. With the goal of supporting architects in building software evolution plans at the architectural level, the concept of evolution paths was introduced in [2, 3]. An evolution path is a sequence of intermediate architectures starting from the initial architecture of the system and leading to the desired architecture once the evolution is complete. These evolution paths can be represented in an evolution graph where nodes are (intermediate) architectures and edges are transitions among these architectures. To support the architect in finding the optimal path, the authors propose analysis based on constraints on the path evolution and functions that evaluate the path qualities. Even if our focus is on tactics' detection, our work can be seen as complementary as we analyze existing software systems to infer architectural decisions that were applied through the evolution of these systems and to check if the changes made to a given system represent a consistent pattern of evolution.

In [6], the authors propose a method for differencing and merging component and connector architecture views by comparing the structural elements composing these views. The comparison and matching between different views may help to identify architectural violations and synchronize the views. The proposed approach does not tackle the particular problem of identifying architectural tactics when comparing architecture views. The case studies presented in their paper are related to the synchronization of an implementation-level architecture view (obtained using architecture recovery) with a conceptual one (described using an ADL). This feature can be perceived as complementary to our work. With the focus on visualization, both [5, 13] propose techniques that exploit source code modifications to understand software evolution at architectural level. In particular, McNair et al. [5] propose a diagram, called architectural impact view, which is basically an entity-relationship diagram enhanced with colors to depict the impact of the code changes under study on the entities and relationships of the system (e.g., added, deleted, etc.). D'Ambros et al. [13] describe a general schema to analyze software repositories for studying software evolution. This schema includes three essential steps: (1) modeling various aspects of the software system and its evolution, (2) retrieving and processing the information from the relevant data sources, and (3) analyzing the modeled and retrieved data using appropriate techniques depending on the targeted software evolution problem. Though we do not target the visualization of architecture evolution, our approach follows this general schema and we also aim to help designers and developers understand and be aware of the architectural evolution of a given system.

Le et al. [8] propose an approach called ARCADE (Architecture Recovery, Change, And Decay Evaluator) which relies on various architecture recovery techniques to build different views of the analyzed system and three metrics for quantifying architectural changes at the system-level and component-level. ARCADE was used in an empirical study. An interesting outcome of this study was that considerable architectural change is introduced both between two major versions and across minor versions. In [4], a metric-based approach is proposed to evaluate architectural stability. To do so, the approach starts by analyzing different releases of the system under study and extracting facts from these releases. These facts are then analyzed using some software metrics that are indicators of architectural stability (e.g., change rate, growth rate, cohesion and coupling). Our approach can be complementary to these metric-based approaches as it relies on the detection of tactics applications or cancellations to assess the architectural evolution of software systems.

Kim et al. [14] proposed Ref-Finder, an Eclipse plug-in, that automatically detects refactorings that were applied between two versions of a given program. To do so, Ref-Finder extracts logic facts from each program version and used predefined logic queries to match program differences with the constraints of the refactorings under study. This approach is more focused on the refactorings introduced in Fowler's book [15]. Unlike Ref-Finder, our goal is to detect evolution patterns that match architectural tactics and to support the designer in defining any evolution pattern that might be of interest in her context/domain.

3   An Approach for Inferring Architectural Evolution from Source Code

In this paper, we propose an approach that supports the detection of architectural tactics' application (or cancellation) and the inference of the architectural trend through the system's evolution. Our approach assumes that high level descriptions of tactics, as introduced in [11], can be mapped to a number of operational representations, i.e., source code transformations described using elementary actions on source code entities (e.g., adding a package, moving a class from a package to another, etc.). Once these operational representations are identified and precisely defined, it becomes possible to use evolution data about the source code to retrieve architectural tactics that were applied or cancelled during development or maintenance.

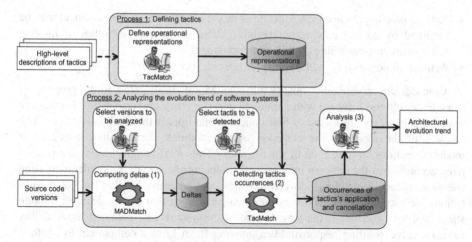

Fig. 1. Overview of the approach

Figure 1 presents an overview of our approach which defines two processes. The first enables the designer to specify operational representations of a given tactic; this process is described in Sect. 4. The second process aims at supporting the designer in analyzing the evolution trend of a software system. It uses the operational representations of tactics and the available versions of the system under study and proceeds in three steps (numbered 1 to 3 in Fig. 1). In the first step, a differencing tool is applied to multiple versions of the system and generates deltas that are expressed using a number of source code changes (e.g., removed package, added package, added class, removed class, moved class, etc.). For this purpose, our approach uses MADMatch [16] a tool that enables a many-to-many approximate diagram matching approach. The second step matches the generated deltas to the operational representations of tactics to detect applied or cancelled tactics. We designed and implemented a tool TacMatch which generates on the fly detection algorithms from the operational representations of tactics and executes these detection algorithms to find occurrences of tactics in the analyzed delta of the source code. In the third step, the resulting occurrences are analyzed by the designer to infer the architectural evolution trend of the analyzed system. The whole process is described in detail in Sect. 5.

4 Defining Operational Representations of Tactics

4.1 High-Level Descriptions of Tactics

As stated above, a tactic can be seen as a transformation undergone by software architecture to satisfy a specific quality attribute. Thus a tactic can be described as a set of actions that may change the structure and behavior of the components of the system. The type and magnitude of these actions depend on the tactic and the current architecture of the system to which the tactic is to be applied. We roughly divide these actions into two types:

- Actions on components: create, delete or modify components. A component may be modified by adding new responsibilities, deleting its responsibilities or moving some of its responsibilities to another component.
- Actions on connectors: add, modify or remove a connector.

Consider the modifiability quality attribute. Modifiability refers to the property of changing easily the software with a minimal cost (i.e., time and resources). Tactics that ensure this property are linked to four concerns that impact the modifiability [11, 12]: the size of the modules, the cohesion of the modules, the coupling between the modules, and the binding time of modification. Thus modifiability tactics are categorized according to the concern they address: reducing the size of a module, increasing cohesion, reducing coupling between modules, and deferring binding time of modification. We focus on these tactics as they involve actions that can be detected through static analysis of different releases of a software system; i.e., common modifiability tactics involve splitting responsibilities, moving them from a component to another, introducing intermediaries between components and encapsulating components.

For instance, the modifiability tactic "Abstract Common Services" (ACS) states that common services should be abstracted so that modifications to them would be localized to a single module. Figure 2 gives a high level representation of this tactic. A and B are responsibilities that can be split respectively to A' and A", and B' and B" and where A' and B' provide a variant of a similar service to A" and B", respectively. In this case, the ACS tactic merges A' and B' into a more general and common service (called C in the figure) and updates A" and B" to depend on the general service. Applying the ACS tactic enables to localize modifications of the common services and to prevent ripple effects as changes made to a module using the common services will not impact other modules [11, 12].

Fig. 2. A high level representation of Abstract Common Services, adapted from [12].

Table 1 presents the high level description of the ACS tactic in terms of actions on architectural components and connectors.

Table 1. High-level description of Abstract Common Services

Type of action	High-level description
Actions on components	Create C
Actions on components	Move A' from A to C
Actions on components	Move B' from B to C
Actions on connectors	Modify A" to depend now on C
Actions on connectors	Modify B" to depend now on C

4.2 Operational Representations of Tactics: Actions and Constraints

High-level descriptions of tactics must be refined in order to generate concrete design/implementation strategies, while taking into consideration the system's context. In this paper, we target the analysis of object oriented (OO) systems. Thus, architectural components involved in tactics' application are matched with the entities of the system such as packages and classes. The responsibilities of a given component are mapped to fields and methods implemented by the classes that are part of this component. This mapping introduces multiple possible concrete instances for a given tactic; e.g., we may map the modules of the ACS tactic to packages in a concrete instance and to classes in another instance. As for architectural connectors, they are not explicitly supported by typical OO languages [17]; they are indirectly specified through method calls, references and events. Thus our operational representations of tactics are expressed as a set of **actions** (i.e., adding, deleting, modifying and moving) on packages, classes, methods, fields, object references, method calls and events.

Furthermore, the same set of actions may be common to different tactics. For instance, both Split Responsibility (SR) and Abstract Common Service (ACS) tactics involve moving responsibilities from a module (i.e., package or class in our context) to another. However, in case of ACS, the moved responsibilities belonged to different modules before applying the tactic while in SR the moved responsibilities belonged to the same module before applying the tactic. To distinguish these tactics, we added a set of constraints on the elements or actions involved in a given tactic. Thus we express an operational representation as a set of actions on architectural elements and a set of constraints relating these elements or actions. Once an operational representation is defined, its cancellation is simply derived by reversing the source and destination of the different actions and constraints used in its definition. For example, if a tactic definition involves adding a class, its cancellation would involve deleting a class. Table 2 lists some examples of operational representations for four modifiability tactics in the context of an object oriented system. For instance, Table 2 lists three different operational representations of the ACS tactic.

4.3 Tool Support

To support the developer in defining the operational representations of tactics or any other relevant evolution pattern, we use a language that resembles the natural language and eases the translation of the concrete representations into detection algorithms. In fact, we wanted to provide a way for a user to specify the tactics (or any targeted evolution pattern) without having to know a specific language to do so. The user has only to know the actions of the tactic (or any targeted evolution pattern) on architectural elements and how these elements are constrained.

Thus, to define operational representations of tactics, we designed and implemented a custom interface that was inspired by query languages such as SQL and QBE (Query By Example). Figure 3 displays the TacMatch interface for defining operational representations of tactics. This interface is divided into four parts: (1) the name of the tactic and the variant if there are many variants of the tactic; (2) a selector zone that enables the user to select the type of changes/actions the tactic introduces (i.e., a set of predefined actions are provided to the user); (3) a filter zone that enables the user to

Table 2. Examples of operational representations

Tactic	Concrete representation (s)	Tactic	Concrete representation (s)
Abstract common services (ACS)	**P**: added or existing package **C**: moved classes to **P** Classes in **C** did not belong to the same package in the previous release	Split responsibilities (SR)	**P**: added package **C**: moved classes to **P** All classes in **C** belonged to the same package in the previous release
Abstract common services (ACS)	**C**: added class or existing class **M**: moved methods to **C** Methods in **M** did not belong to the same class in the previous release	Split responsibilities (SR)	**C**: added class **E**: moved elements (attribute and method) to **C** All elements in **E** belonged to the same class in the previous release
Abstract common services (ACS)	**C**: added class **Inherits C**: added inheritance All classes involved in "**Inherits C**" existed in the previous release These classes belong to at least two different packages in next release	Use encapsulation (UE)	**C**: added class **Inherits C**: added inheritance All classes involved in "**Inherits C**" existed in the previous release These classes belong to the same package in the next release
Increase cohesion (IC)	**C**: moved classes to package **P$_{dest}$** All classes in **C** belonged to the same package (**P$_{src}$**) in the previous release **P$_{dest}$** existed Cohesion of **P$_{src}$** increased	Increase cohesion (IC)	**E**: moved elements (attribute and method) to class **C$_{dest}$** **C$_{dest}$** existed All elements in **E** belonged to the same class (**C$_{src}$**) in the previous release Cohesion of **C$_{src}$** increased

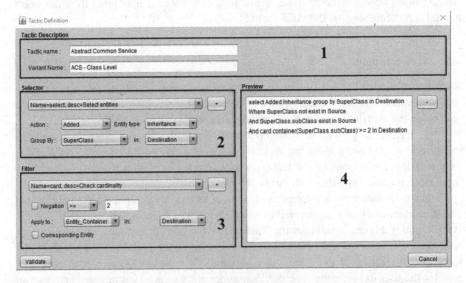

Fig. 3. Defining an operational representation of a tactic using TacMatch

specify the constraints on the selected elements; and (4) the preview zone that displays the tactic's specification in a form similar to an SQL query[1]. Figure 3 displays an example of the ACS tactic (i.e., the variant described in row 3 of Table 2) where multiple constraints were defined by the user using the filter zone (the "+" button enables to add a constraint at a time to the specification). These declarative specifications are used by our tool TacMatch to generate on the fly (when the user launches an analysis of a given system) the algorithm that retrieves the set of elements (from deltas) that match the tactic's application. This process is described in detail in Sect. 5.2.

5 Detecting Tactics Occurrences in Software Systems

Using the operational representations of tactics and two different versions of the software system under study, TacMatch supports the designer in detecting occurrences of these tactics in the system. To do so, TacMatch relies on MADMatch [16], a tool that enables diagram matching, to compute the deltas between two different versions of the same system. TachMatch uses the operational representation to generate on the fly detection algorithms for the tactics selected by the designer in the current analysis of the system. TachMatch executes these algorithms on the analyzed delta of the system and returns tactics' occurrences or cancellations. These occurrences can be used by the designer to carry out different types of analysis and to evaluate the architectural evolution of the analyzed system.

5.1 Computing and Storing Deltas Between Versions

Our approach relies on differencing tools able to supply our technique with elementary source code changes that we can then analyze, regroup and possibly match to architectural tactics. One such tool is MADMatch [16], which is a recent tool that takes as input graph representations of two different versions of the source code and generates the delta between these versions. In our case, these graphs represent class diagrams that were recovered using the Ptidej tool suite [18]. A generated delta describes the source code changes that occurred between the two analyzed versions (e.g., removed package, added package, added class, moved class, etc.). Deltas are serialized in CVS files. Our proposed tool TacMatch analyzes these CVS files to extract relevant information on the delta and saves this information in a database to which we will ultimately send customized queries to detect tactics' occurrences.

5.2 Detecting Tactics Occurrences

Given a generated delta from the system under study and a set of tactics chosen by the user for her current analysis, TacMatch retrieves corresponding tactics specifications and generates the corresponding detection algorithms on the fly and then execute them

---

[1] For lack of space, we do not discuss in this paper the predefined actions and constraints that TacMatch provides, nor the specification language used to describe the tactics.

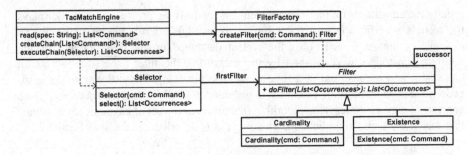

Fig. 4. Generating the detection algorithms using a chain of responsibility

on the delta. To generate the detection algorithms, TacMatch relies on a set of classes that read the specification of a tactic and generate different parts of the corresponding algorithm. Figure 4 gives an excerpt of the core classes of TacMatch, which were organized using the Chain of Responsibility (CoR) design pattern [19]. The Selector class enables to select occurrences of the changes undergone by the system and that correspond to those specified in the Select clause of the operational representation of the tactic (e.g., see the first line of the preview in Fig. 3). The Filter type defines an interface for filtering occurrences of the changes undergone by the system according to a given constraint; i.e., sub-classes of Filter implement different constraints. We used the CoR design pattern so that we can instantiate and configure, at runtime, the subset of filters that correspond to the constraints defined by the tactic at hand. Moreover, using the CoR design pattern makes it easy to add new filters (i.e., constraints).

TacMatch's entry point is the class TacMatchEngine which reads the tactic's specification as entered by the designer and generates a collection of commands corresponding to the lines of the specification. These commands are then used to create an ordered list of objects that starts with an instance of the Selector class followed by a chain of the appropriate subset of the filters. This is done using the createChain method which relies on the FilterFactory class to instantiate and set the appropriate filter for each command[2]. The appropriate selector object and chain of filters are instantiated and ordered in a dynamic way according to the operational representation of a tactic. This corresponds to generating on the fly the skeleton of the detection algorithm for the given tactic. For instance, given the operational representation described in the preview zone of Fig. 3, TacMatch generates a selector object that is set to retrieve inheritance relationships grouped by their superclass followed by a chain of two instances of the Existence filter[3] and one instance of the Cardinality filter.

The method executeChain enables execution of the detection algorithm related to a given tactic. This method takes as input the selection object corresponding to the tactic and it calls first the select() method of this object to retrieve the relevant occurrences of

---

[2] Both the Selector and the filter classes have their own fields which are set during their respective instantiation using the command parameter received by their respective constructor.

[3] In some tactics, the same filter class can be instantiated more than once using different parameters (i.e., commands). Moreover, we use a filter class to instantiate a constraint or its opposite depending on the tactic's definition.

changes from the delta. These occurrences are then sent to the first filter referenced by the selector object and from one filter to its successor in the chain; each filter filters the occurrences according to the constraint it implements (i.e., using the doFilter() method) and passes the resulting occurrences to its successor in the chain.

6 Case Study: Analyzing the Architectural Evolution Trend of JFreeChart

Our approach aims at mapping high-level descriptions of tactics to operational representations that can be detected at the source-code level, and inferring the architectural evolution trend of a software system by analyzing its available versions and detecting occurrences of the operational representations. To evaluate the effectiveness of our approach, we implemented a prototype tool that supports the definition and detection of operational representations and we conducted a retrospective case study using an open source software system.

In particular, the goal of our case study was to answer the following research questions:

- **RQ1: How effective is our technique at detecting applied tactics?** To answer this question, we used our prototype tool to analyze a number of versions of an open source Java system in order to detect a common set of the modifiability tactics. These tactics are: Split Responsibility (SR), Abstract Common Services (ACS), Use Encapsulation (UE) and Increase Cohesion (IC). We focused on these tactics as they involve actions that can be detected through static analysis of different releases of a software system. We computed the precision and recall of the obtained results by manually analyzing the changes made to the versions under study as reported by the differencing tool MADMatch.
- **RQ2: Are we able to derive an architectural evolution trend using our approach and interpret this trend at the architectural level?** To answer this question, we studied the detected applications and cancellations of tactics to check if the changes made to the system follow a comprehensible pattern of architectural evolution. We also compared the results of our detection process when applied to major releases versus minor releases versus revisions.

Our case study is focused on the analysis of JFreeChart, a Java open source framework which was previously studied in many publications, including the MAD-Match paper [16]. JFreeChart is a library that supports developers in displaying various charts in their applications and it was used to develop a number of open-source and commercial products. We analyzed 37 versions of JFreeChart including revisions, minor and major releases starting from version 0.5.6[4] till version 1.0.6. The size of the analyzed versions varies from 26 to 141 packages and from 100 to 1196 classes.

---

[4] In this three sequence-based schema, the first sequence is the major number (incremented when there are significant changes to the system), the second sequence is the minor number (incremented when there are minor changes to the system or significant bug fixes) and the last sequence is the revision number (incremented when minor bugs were fixed).

6.1 Effectiveness for Detecting Architectural Tactics

Overall, using the 36 deltas generated from the 37 analyzed versions we detected 103 occurrences of tactics' applications and 33 tactics' cancellations. To compute the precision and recall of our results, we used the output of MADMatch to manually identify all the changes that correspond to true tactics applications or cancellations. Regarding the occurrences of tactics applications, we were able to confirm that 85 of these occurrences were true positives resulting in a precision of 82.52 %. We also identified 3 occurrences of tactics applications that our tool did not detect, resulting in a recall of 96.59 %. Interestingly, only 19 among the 33 occurrences of tactics cancellations were true positives, giving a precision of 57.57 % while manual analysis of MADMatch's output did not reveal any false negatives, resulting in a recall of 100 %.

These results suggest that our operational representations are effective in detecting the application of architectural tactics but may not be enough to automatically infer cancellations. Indeed, our simple technique for inferring the opposite evolution pattern from an operational representation of a tactic is not enough to precisely define the tactic's cancellation. The opposite evolution pattern may lead to a high number of negatives identified as positives (high recall and low precision) or to a misinterpretation of the appropriate tactic that was cancelled. For instance, during the transition from version 0.7.0 to version 0.7.1, the Separate Responsibility tactic was applied by moving a number of classes from the package com.jrefinery.chart into a new package com.jrefinery.chart.combination. However, during the transition from version 0.8.1 to version 0.9.0, the package com.jrefinery.chart.combination was deleted and its classes were moved back into two different packages (com.jrefinery.chart and com.jrefinery.data). This was recognized by our detection process as a cancellation of the Abstract Common Services tactic. Indeed, the SR tactic that was detected the first time was in fact part of the application of an ACS that was incrementally introduced through several transitions from versions 0.7.0 to 0.8.1 and then cancelled later in version 0.9.0. Future work is needed to define the relationships between operational representations so that we can aggregate and correctly interpret a number of successive applications of some tactics and thus define and appropriately trace cancellations to tactics.

To identify the factors that influence the effectiveness of our operational representations, we examined in detail the false results (i.e., false positives and false negatives) returned by our detection process. We uncovered that all these errors were due to the external tools MADMatch (85 %) for the deltas and PtiDej (15 %) for the reverse engineering of the project binaries. MADMatch sometimes returns incorrect matching in its deltas in part because its default parameters, which we used, promote recall over precision. We decided to leave these parameters unchanged in order to get more data for our manual analysis and thus a better approximation of the recall. Experimentation with different parameters is planned for future work.

6.2 Detecting Architectural Evolution Trends

Regarding our second research question, we investigated the applications and cancellations of tactics that were manually confirmed. Table 3 displays the distribution of both tactics applications and cancellations per deltas (i.e., the table displays true positives). To reduce the size of the table, we have omitted the deltas that do not have any occurrences. In purely quantitative terms, if we consider the total numbers of the tactics that were applied (85) and those cancelled (19) through all the analyzed versions, cancellations represent 22 % of applications. We further investigated the observed cancellations to understand the causes of such a high percentage.

Our analysis revealed that out of the 19 cancellations of tactics, 11 cancellations were related to tactics already present in the first available release 0.5.6 while 8 cancellations are related to tactics that were introduced during the subsequent versions. For instance, in the revision from versions 0.9.16 to 0.9.17, the class org.jfree.chart.renderer.AbstractSeriesRenderer was introduced as a superclass for two other existing sub-classes but was deleted two revisions later (i.e., in 0.9.19). We also observed an interesting evolution pattern which involves the introduction, through different versions, of a number of super-classes that centralize a number of common constants and the deletion of these classes later in other versions. For instance, from 0.8.1 to 0.9.0, the classes CategoryPlotConstants and ChartPanelConstants (both in the package com. jrefinery.chart) were created to centralize a number of constants. CategoryPlotConstants was deleted later in the revision from 0.9.9 to 0.9.10 and its content was moved back to the class com.jrefinery.chart.CategoryPlot. Likewise ChartPanelConstants was deleted later in the transition from 0.9.20 to 1.0.0 and its content was moved to org. jfree.chart.ChartPanel. This tendency to apply and cancel tactics raises some questions about the consistency of the evolution of the system in general and its conformance to architectural decisions in particular. In fact, this could be construed as a motivational case for the importance of detecting architectural tactics and reminding them to developers (especially in open-source and collaborative settings) in order to prevent seemingly erratic modifications.

We also compared the results of our detection process when applied to the deltas from two successive minor (respectively major) releases versus those generated by the intermediate revisions between these minor (respectively major) versions. We presume that if the developer consistently evolves the system through the intermediate revisions between two successive minor (respectively major) versions, the aggregated results of our detection process through these revisions would lead to the same result than the one generated using the two minor (respectively major) versions. Table 4 displays the number of occurrences of both applications and cancellations of tactics generated from successive minor or major revisions. Similar to Tables 3 and 4 displays true positives and it omits minor and major releases for which no occurrences were found (e.g., from 0.6.0 to 0.7.0) and successive minor releases for which there was no intermediate revisions (e.g., from 0.5.6 to 0.6.0).

From 0.7.0 to 0.8.0, the only tactic occurrence (out of 7) that was detected in the delta between these two minor versions but not in the revisions between them, is an incremental application of the User Encapsulation (UE) tactic; i.e., a class (SignalsDataset) was created in 0.7.1 and an inheritance relationship was added later in 0.7.2 between this class and an existing subclass (SubSeriesDataset). As for the detected tactics applications and cancellations from 0.8.0 and 0.9.0 (i.e., 9 occurrences), they match the aggregated results of the detection when applied to the revisions from 0.8.0 to 0.8.1 and from 0.8.1 to 0.9.0. Finally, we found 34 occurrences of applications and cancellations of tactics from 0.9.0 to 1.0.0 which is a major revision.

Table 3. Number of tactics applied or cancelled per deltas generated from successive versions

Delta	Application of tactics				Cancellation of tactics			
	SR	UE	ACS	IC	SR	UE	ACS	IC
v0.5.6_v0.6.0	1	2	1					
v0.7.0_v0.7.1	1							
v0.7.3_v0.7.4	1	2						
v0.7.4_v0.8.0		1						
v0.8.0_v0.8.1		1						
v0.8.1_v0.9.0		3	1	1	1	1	1	
v0.9.1_v0.9.2			1					
v0.9.2_v0.9.3		1						
v0.9.4_v0.9.5	3	5	2			1		
v0.9.6_v0.9.7	1	4		1				
v0.9.8_v0.9.9	1	1		1		6		
v0.9.9_v0.9.10		1	1			1		
v0.9.11_v0.9.12	1	1	1	2				
v0.9.12_v0.9.13	1	2						
v0.9.13_v0.9.14			2			1		
v0.9.14_v0.9.15	1	1						
v0.9.15_v0.9.16	1						1	
v0.9.16_v0.9.17		2		5				
v0.9.18_v0.9.19		3	2			2	1	
v0.9.19_v0.9.20		1						
v0.9.20_v1.0.0	9	3	2	4		2	1	
v1.0.2_v1.0.3			1					
v1.0.4_v1.0.5		1						
v1.0.5_v1.0.6		1						

Table 4. Number of tactics applied or cancelled per deltas generated from successive minor or major versions

Delta	Application of tactics				Cancellation of tactics				Total
	SR	UE	ACS	IC	SR	UE	ACS	IC	
v0.7.0_v0.8.0	2	5							7
v0.8.0_v0.9.0		4	1	1	1	1	1		9
v0.9.0_v1.0.0	10	5	14	1		4			34

However, the aggregation of the results from all the intermediate revisions between 0.9.0 and 1.0.0 yields 85 occurrences. We identified three main reasons for this discrepancy some of which were already discussed above. First, some tactics were applied through one or several revisions but all the entities involved in these tactics appear as added in the major revision (i.e., the evolution pattern is visible through revisions but not at the major versions level). For example, the UE tactic was incrementally applied by adding a set of classes (e.g., ObjectList) in the revision from 0.9.9 to 0.9.10 and their superclass (AbstractObjectList) in the revision from 0.9.11 to 0.9.12. This whole evolution pattern is not detectable when we analyze the delta from 0.9.0 to 1.0.0; the entire inheritance hierarchy appears to be newly created at the same time. Second, some tactics were applied in an incremental way through changes spread over several revisions starting from the revision 0.9.0. These occurrences are only detectable when we analyze the delta from 0.9.0 to 1.0.0. Finally, as discussed before, several tactics were applied and then cancelled through the revisions; these tactics are not present at major versions level.

6.3   Threats to Validity

External validity: Our case study was carried out on a subset of the modifiability tactics that we were able to detect through static analysis of different releases of a software system. This is possible for most of the modifiability tactics and some other tactics such as exception handling (for availability) and creating additional threads or reducing the number of iterations (for performance). However, other tactics may require a dynamic analysis of the code or are even not present in the source code (e.g., increasing computational efficiency or maintaining multiple copies of data). Thus, our approach is limited to those tactics that have an observable impact on the source code. As future work, we plan to extend our work to other tactics and identify precisely the type of tactics to which our approach may be applied.

Internal validity: Some tactics (e.g., ACS) may be composed of several other more elementary tactics (e.g., SR). Since we did not implement yet a mechanism that enables to relate and aggregate detected tactics through a number of releases, we tend to interpret each detected tactic locally and individually. This may have an impact on our interpretation of the overall architectural evolution trend. Thus, as discussed in Sect. 6.1, future work is needed to define the relationships between operational representations and exploit these relationships to correctly aggregate and interpret a number of successive applications of related tactics. Finally, our results are dependent on the effectiveness of the other tools used, notably MADMatch that was used to compute the deltas. We selected MADMatch because it is a recent tool which compared favorably to other techniques [16] but other tools may provide different (better or worse) results. Future work is planned for experimentation with different parameters of MADMatch and different tools.

7   Conclusion and Future Work

In this paper, we present a first iteration of a tool-supported approach that allows the definition and detection of architectural tactics or more general evolution patterns using basic changes extractable from the differencing of software versions. Once these architectural tactics or patterns are defined, our technique automatically generates algorithms able to parse the differencing data in order to detect occurrences of the application or cancellation of these tactics. A case study conducted on a well-studied open source system (JFreeChart) suggest that the technique is effective at detecting the occurrences of the application of defined tactics but is not as successful at detecting their cancellation. While few occurrences of these tactics are missed by our technique, there is some noise (lack of precision), especially for the detection of cancellations. Many of these errors are related to the parameterizing of the external tool selected to provide differencing data. Nevertheless, the study revealed many instances of cancellations of tactics that may be ill-advised and could have been prevented if the developers had access to the history and present of tactics involving the code they are working on or plan to work on.

The conclusions of this study are still preliminary and future work with case studies involving different parameters, tools and systems is needed to confirm our findings. Additionally, we intend to experiment with more evolution patterns and eventually discover desirable or harmful patterns through analyses of the change and defect proneness of the components they involve.

References

1. Negara, S., Vakilian, M., Chen, N., Johnson, R.E., Dig, D.: Is it dangerous to use version control histories to study source code evolution? In: Noble, J. (ed.) ECOOP 2012. LNCS, vol. 7313, pp. 79–103. Springer, Heidelberg (2012). doi:10.1007/978-3-642-31057-7_5
2. Garlan, D., Barnes, J.M., Schmerl, B.R., Celiku, O.: Evolution styles: foundations and tool support for software architecture evolution. In: WICSA/ECSA, pp. 131–140 (2009)
3. Garlan, D., Schmerl, B.: Ævol: a tool for defining and planning architecture evolution. In: the 31st International Conference on Software Engineering, pp. 591–594 (2009)
4. Tonu, S.A, Ashkan, A, Tahvildari, L.: Evaluating architectural stability using a metric-based approach. In: CSMR 2006, 22–24 March 2006, p. 10, 270 (2006)
5. McNair, A., German, D.M., Weber-Jahnke, J.: Visualizing software architecture evolution using change-sets. In: WCRE 2007, 28–31 October 2007, pp. 130–139 (2007)
6. Abi-Antoun, M., Aldrich, J., Nahas, N., Schmerl, B., Garlan, D.: Differencing and merging of architectural views. ASE 15(1), 35–74 (2008)
7. Breivold, H.P., Crnkovic, I., Larsson, M.: A systematic review of software architecture evolution research. IST 54(1), 16–40 (2012)
8. Le, D.M., Behnamghader, P., Garcia, J., Link, D., Shahbazian, A., Medvidovic, N.: An empirical study of architectural change in open-source software systems. In: IEEE/ACM 12th Working Conference on Mining Software Repositories, Florence, pp. 235–245 (2015)
9. Eden, A.H., Kazman, R.: Architecture design implementation. In: 25th International Conference on Software Engineering, pp. 149–159 (2003)
10. Fairbanks, G.: Just Enough Software Architecture: A Risk-Driven Approach. Marshall & Brainerd, Boulder (2010)
11. Bass, L., Clements, P., Kazman, R.: Software Architecture in Practice. Addison-Wesley, Boston (2003)
12. Bachmann, et al.: Modifiability tactics, CMU Software Engineering Institute Technical Report CMU/SEI-2007-TR-002

13. D'Ambros, M., Gall, H., Lanza, M., Pinzger, M.: Analysing software repositories to understand software evolution. In: D'Ambros, M., Gall, H., Lanza, M., Pinzger, M. (eds.) Software Evolution, pp. 37–67. Springer, Heidelberg (2008)
14. Kim, M., Gee, M., Loh, A., Rachatasumrit, N.: Ref-Finder: a refactoring reconstruction tool based on logic query templates. In: FSE 2010, Santa Fe, New Mexico, USA, pp. 371–372 (2010)
15. Fowler, M.: Refactoring: Improving the Design of Existing Code. Addison-Wesley, Boston (1999)
16. Kpodjedo, S., et al.: Madmatch: many-to-many approximate diagram matching for design comparison. IEEE Trans. Softw. Eng. 39(8), 1090–1111 (2013)
17. Aldrich, J., Sazawal, V., Chambers, C., Notkin, D.: Language support for connector abstractions. In: Cardelli, L. (ed.) ECOOP 2003. LNCS, vol. 2743, pp. 74–102. Springer, Heidelberg (2003). doi:10.1007/978-3-540-45070-2_5
18. Gueheneuc, Y.G., Antoniol, G.: DeMIMA: a multilayered approach for design pattern identification. IEEE Trans. Softw. Eng. 34(5), 667–684 (2008)
19. Gamma, E., Helm, R., Johnson, R., Vlissides, J.: Design Patterns: Elements of Reusable Object-Oriented Software. Addison-Wesley, Reading (1995)
20. Barnes, J.M., Garlan, D.: Challenges in developing a software architecture evolution tool as a plug-in. In: 3rd International Workshop on Developing Tools as Plug-ins (TOPI), San Francisco, CA, pp. 13–18 (2013)

Evolution Style: Framework for Dynamic Evolution of Real-Time Software Architecture

Adel Hassan[1]([✉]), Audrey Queudet[2], and Mourad Oussalah[1]

[1] University of Nantes, LINA CNRS UMR 6241, Nantes, France
{adel.hassan,audrey.queudet}@univ-nantes.fr
[2] University of Nantes, IRCCyN UMR CNRS 6597, Nantes, France
Mourad.Oussalah@univ-nantes.fr

Abstract. Software systems need to be continuously maintained and evolved in order to cope with ever-changing requirements and environments. Introducing these changes without stopping the system is a critical requirement for many software systems. This is especially so when the stop may result in serious damage or monetary losses, hence a mechanism for system change at runtime is needed. With the increase in size and complexity of software systems, software architecture has become the cornerstone in the lifecycle of a software system and constitutes the model that drives the engineering process. Therefore, the evolution of software architecture has been a key issue of software evolution research. Architects have few techniques to help them plan and perform the dynamic evolution of software architecture for real-time systems. Thus, our approach endeavors to capture the essential concepts for modeling dynamic evolution of software architectures, in order to equip the architects with a framework to model this process.

1 Introduction

With daily changes in technologies and business environments, software systems must evolve in order to adopt to the new requirements of these changes. Generally, the software evolution is a complex process that requires a great deal of knowledge and skills. This is due to the fact that all artifacts produced and used in the software development life-cycle are subject to changes. Since software systems change fairly frequently, it is essential that their architectures must be restructured. With the increase in size and complexity of software systems, the computing community acknowledges the importance of software architecture as a central artifact in the lifecycle of a software system. In this respect, the architecture is specified early in the software lifecycle, and constitutes the model that drives the engineering process [10]. In the evolution process, architecture can elucidate the reason behind design decisions that guided the building of the system. Moreover, it can permit planning and system restructuring at a high level of modeling, where business goals and quality requirements can be ensured and where an alternative scenario of evolution can be explored. Modeling architecture evolution process can support architects in representing reusable practices

© Springer International Publishing AG 2016
B. Tekinerdogan et al. (Eds.): ECSA 2016, LNCS 9839, pp. 166–174, 2016.
DOI: 10.1007/978-3-319-48992-6_12

in a domain-specific architecture evolution. Accordingly, the term *evolution style* has been introduced (Oussalah et al. [2]) as an approach, the aim of which is to capture the main characteristics of a set of activities performed for evolving software architecture. It defines the set vocabulary of concepts necessary in order to model the potential scenarios for evolving a domain-specific software architecture. These scenarios can be grouped together as a library of evolution styles. Both the analysis and comparison of scenarios will assist architects in choosing an evolution scenario for a future evolution [1].

Software evolution is a complex and multifaceted process that requires a number of techniques and skills. This is particularly so when it is required to introduce these changes without halting the system. Some critical issues like synchronous task handling, schedulability analysis, consistency and integrity for dynamic evolution of a real-time system deserve further exploration.

In our previous work [1], we presented the Meta-Evolution Style MES for modeling software architecture evolution (static evolution style), but we did not delve into the dynamic aspects of this process. Therefore, in this paper, we endeavor to probe more deeply into the issues and rules which must be considered when handling dynamic evolution of software architecture in order to extract the needed information, which will be annotated with MES to fulfill the dynamic evolution style. The research ultimately intends to establish a foundational step of a generic process framework for dynamic evolution of software architecture that could provide a means to facilitate analysis and to formally model software architectures and their dynamic evolution processes. Likewise, this framework should provide reusable concepts that could express the way(s) to dynamically evolve software architecture and provide the means to compare these different trajectories.

The rest of the paper is organized as follows. Section 2 briefly reviews related works. Section 3 discusses the real-world issues in integrating architecture changes at run-time [3]. Section 4 extends the meta-evolution style to embrace the concepts of dynamic evolution. Finally, the paper contributions are summarized in Sect. 5.

2   Related Work

The necessity of introducing change at runtime has resulted in different architecture centric approaches for dynamic evolution. Dowling and Cahill [17] present the K-Component model as a reflective framework for building self-adaptive systems. K-Components are components with an architecture meta-model and adaptation contracts to support their dynamic reconfiguration. Cuesta et al. [16] present a reflective Architecture Description Language (ADL) named PiLar which provides a framework to describe the dynamic change in software architecture. It consists of a structural part and a dynamic part, which defines patterns of change. Costa-Soria et al. [12] define a reflective approach for supporting dynamic evolution of architectural types in a decentralized and independent way. Their approach is applied to ADL, in particular to the PRISMA meta-model, in order to develop an evolveable component type that is provided with an infrastructure to support its evolution at run-time. Romero in his PhD thesis [13], develops a component-based framework support safety replacing the real-time components. The approach implementation is integrated in the OSGi platform in order to exploit the OSGi capabilities like load and unload of code at runtime, and enhances the framework with all the required elements to provide a safe component replacement for real-time characteristics by supporting on-line schedulability analysis. Richardson [9] presents an extension of the OSGi Framework in order to be able to perform dynamic reconfiguration of real-time systems. He proposes an RT-OSGi that can be used to develop real-time systems which are dynamically reconfigurable: by integrating the OSGi Framework with the Real-Time Specification for Java (RTSJ). Unlike these approaches, our work attempts to develop a framework to model such activities and techniques in dynamic evolution of software architecture. This can support architects in analyzing and better understanding the process of introducing changes at run-time.

3   Issues in Dynamic Software Architecture Evolution

Irrespective of the mechanism of an evolution model that is used to perform the dynamic architecture evolution, some issues [3] should be addressed by any approach in order to efficiently handle the dynamic evolution process. This section presents these issues in order to annotate MES with the required information, which will be extracted from these issues to fulfill the requirements of dynamic evolution modeling.

3.1   Safe Stopping of Running Artifacts

One of the main issues that must be considered when handling dynamic evolution is to leave systems in a consistent state after a change is performed. Evolving an artifact at runtime without considering its thread may disrupt or suspend its service for an arbitrarily long time, which can lead real-time tasks to miss some deadlines. Detecting when it is safe to actually evolve the artifacts is a crucial key to guarantee that the system will not encounter an inconsistent state. Therefore, various strategies have been defined in order to tackle this issue, namely Quiescence [4] and Tranquility [5]. They differentiate the passive state from the active state of software artifact and assume that an affected artifact should be placed into a passive state before performing the evolution operation.

Generally, a real-time system consists mainly of a set of elements which provide or/and create real-time services (threads). These real-time tasks can be periodic, aperiodic or sporadic [15], depending on how their corresponding jobs are activated. The passive elements in a real-time system are those that do not have any execution thread, but typically provide services for other elements. The quiescence and tranquility techniques can fit the dynamic evolution of these passive elements. On the contrary, the active elements are those that have active real-time threads; these techniques [4,5] require that elements should be shifted into a passive state in order to be modified. This means that the real-time threads in the element would need to be suspended, thus potentially resulting in deadline misses for the threads of the element being under evolution. This behavior is, of course, undesirable for hard real-time systems. Therefore, the evolution operation should respect the timing constraints of the active element that is subject to change. In this respect, the evolution operation execution time is part of the timing constraints of the real-time system itself. Therefore, it must not exceed the safe state time of this element, i.e. the maximum duration of the evolution operation should be less than the minimum separation between two consecutive jobs of this element's task.

3.2 Transferring State

Another crucial issue of system consistency that should be considered when addressing a dynamic evolution is that of handling stateful elements (components that may have internal information, or connectors that may have buffers full of messages [6]). In the case of replacing elements, information integrity requires that the state of the old element must be transferred, or possibly transformed (in the case the data structure is different), to the new element. Meanwhile, this step is not required for the replacement of stateless elements. This activity can be more complex if the internal structure of the two elements is different, which requires identifying and extracting the relevant data from the old element. These date will be modified to fit the new element.

Practically, it is difficult to develop a generic abstract that can fit the internal data structure for all the system elements, in order to store the state of any element during its evolution. Therefore, preserving and transferring or transforming the internal state of elements is a specific step. Thus, if a transfer state is required, this process should be specifically remedied with each operation.

3.3 Change Management

Another issue in dynamic evolution is relevant to the mechanism to preform this process and how the changes are driven (activeness of change), how evolution events can be detected, then how the suitable reactions can be effected. More accurately, it relates to how this process can be managed.

Generally, the software system can be reactive (changes are driven externally), or proactive (drives changes to itself) [7]. Thus, either the system is instrumented with change management, or with an interface to allow an external agent to dynamically introduce the changes. In dynamic evolution, management can be represented as an evoluter (Role) who is responsible for dynamically performing the evolution. This can be formulated as a controlling system that monitors a controlled system in order to detect and analyse an evolution event when it occurs on the controlled system or its environment to select or synthesize the appropriate action or scenario of evolution. The dynamic MES should provide a modeling concept to express both the controlling techniques for proactive and reactive system.

3.4 Dynamic Evolution Scheduling

The issue of the timing constraints is more important when we handle a dynamic evolution of a hard real-time system, which needs to maintain high levels of application availability. In fact, whatever the change management system be used, the dynamic evolution operation is considered as a real-time task, and once this unscheduled task occurs, it should not affect the timing constraints of system's tasks.

System tasks are scheduled and executed according to their dynamic priorities. Indeed, whatever the system tasks are, the evolution operation should interact/behave without compromising the system tasks' completion. Generally, tasks in a hard real-time system have higher priority than the evolution operation, which is usually handled as a background task (with lower priority). In this aspect, if a background priority task is used to evolve an element, this evolution task can be preempted by any higher priority task (including a task from the element under evolution), which can lead to an unsafe state or loss of the internal state of the element. Therefore, an evolution task should directly derive its priority from the element that undergoes its change. Thus, the management change should be able to safely handle the evolution tasks while still guaranteeing the timing constraints of the system, e.g. it should dynamically prioritize this unexpected event (evolution operation) within the system threads.

Furthermore, in the replacement and addition operations, it is necessary to guarantee that the new element threads have taken over the role of the old element threads without deadline violation, which also requires a dynamic rescheduling in order to integrate the new element threads with the rest of the system's threads in the scheduler.

4 Dynamic Meta Evolution Style

MES consists in defining foundational meta-concepts for describing a software architecture evolution. These essential concepts were used in modeling and analyzing static evolution styles [1]. MES can be refined to any other kind of architecture evolution. In this sense, the intent is not to define a new meta style for modeling dynamic evolution of real-time and embedded systems, but to annotate MES with information required to analyze and model this process. Hence, this work focuses on integrating the concepts of dynamic interaction and schedulability analysis into evolution styles. Figure 1 illustrates our proposition to extend MES with the necessary information to fulfill the requirement for modeling the dynamic evolution styles (gray boxes refer to MES elements; white boxes refer to proposed additional elements). Actually, dynamic evolution of a real-time system requires introducing changes in bounded time. Managing and performing this process without violating the timing constraints is more complex. This requires a fast, interactive Role (intelligent change management) which minimizes or eliminates the human intervention Role and shifts it from operational to strategic. Thus, the Role in dynamic MES should support the concept of an automatic Role either as an internal instrument or an external agent. That satisfies the change management requirement for dynamic evolution.

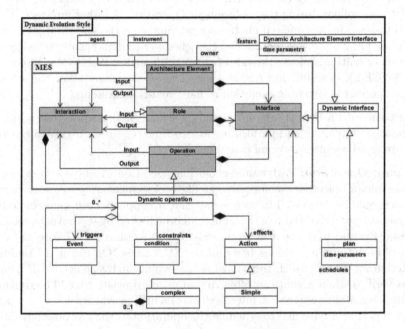

Fig. 1. Dynamic-evolution style

Indeed, the needs of an architectural element to change are required when an evolution event has occurred. Therefore, the unexpected evolution events must be assigned with their potential scenarios of reactions (evolution paths). A strategy to synthesize the suitable reactions is defined such that all the affected elements complete within their deadlines. In this sense, each evolution path consists of a series of evolution operations and represents one choice to evolve the architecture from the current state to the target state. Therefore, each simple evolution operation must have a dynamic interface which provides the necessary parameters (priority, time execution) in order to be safely handled and not cause timing misbehavior. Several scheduling methods for the handling of unexpected events in real-time systems have been proposed in the literature in order to service aperiodic requests, where a set of hard aperiodic tasks is scheduled using the Earliest Deadline First (EDF) algorithm [8]. Among them, the Total Bandwidth Server (TBS) [14] and Earliest Deadline as Late as possible server (EDL) [11] both provide an efficient aperiodic service under EDF. In TBS, worst-case execution time of aperiodic requests must be known in advance (which is not the case of care evolution operation). That is why we will turn to EDL to dynamically schedule this unexpected event jointly with the system threads. Thus, the Operation should provide the necessary parameters that are needed by a dynamic scheduling algorithm in order to be scheduled.

The architectural element that can be changed at its active state must also have the suitable (dynamic) interfaces to provide the required parameters in order to be dynamically evolved. An interface is needed to handle the internal state of the element during the replacement Operation. Another interface is also needed to provide the time parameters for guaranteeing the safe stopping. These scheduling parameters are required by the scheduler to dynamically schedule the evolution operation and the threads of the new elements: Worst Case Execution Time (WCET), deadline and release time. These parameters allow the schedulability analysis of dynamic evolution of hard real-time systems.

Role: Generally, a Role is responsible for the evolution operation that performs the changes. Managing and performing at run-time requires a highly interactive Role (external agent or internal instrument).

Dynamic Operation: A dynamic evolution operation can be a simple evolution like add or delete, or a composite one like replacement. A dynamic evolution process should be expressed in such a way that it supports both kinds of activeness, namely proactive and reactive. This can be achieved by separating evolution requests (Events) from the evolution mechanisms (Actions). Therefore, the construct of evolution operation is based of the ECA rules "On Event If Condition Do Action At Time" which means: when an evolution Event occurs, if Condition is verified, then execute suitable Action at appropriate time. The dynamic operation must offer a dynamic interface (plan) which provides relevant run-time parameters that are needed to schedule the operation as soon as possible within the system tasks.

Dynamic Architecture Elements: An architecture element must be evolutionary open, which means it has an interface with the necessary parameters that enables it to dynamically react to evolution operation. An element should be able to provide its scheduling parameters to allow the Role to dynamically effect the changes without breaking the timing constraints of the system.

Interaction: In fact, the dynamic evolution is a real-time task, so the interaction element must guarantee that evolution Operations are subject to the timing constraints. The interaction element ensures the availability of required interfaces and parameters among elements (Operation, Architecture Element, Role) in the process.

Dynamic Interface: A dynamic element should have appropriate interface which provides the required parameters to efficiently interact at run-time. Such an interface is required, for example, to allow the Instrument (the Role in self-managing system) to observe an architecture element in order to detect any evolution event or to determine the appropriate time to effect the changes.

Process: Represents the dynamic configuration of the evolution elements which transfers a software architecture from its current architecture style to a target style. This configuration provides the temporal and topological organizing of evolution operations while respecting the consistency and integrity of the architecture elements.

5   Conclusions

In this paper, we propose a dynamic evolution style for specifying the dynamic evolution for software architecture. Our intent is to provide a style sufficiently rich to model the dynamic changes in software architecture of a real-time system and to be able to represent the potential ways of performing these changes. To better realize this intent, we integrate the behavior concepts of dynamic changes into the MES so we can have a sound understanding of dynamic evolution issues and constraints, which is a prerequisite to developing a modeling environment that supports dynamic evolution styles. Our ongoing work is devoted to developing this environment.

References

1. Hassan, A., Oussalah, M.: Meta-evolution style for software architecture evolution. In: Freivalds, R.M., Engels, G., Catania, B. (eds.) SOFSEM 2016. LNCS, vol. 9587, pp. 478–489. Springer, Heidelberg (2016). doi:10.1007/978-3-662-49192-8_39
2. Oussalah, M., Tamzalit, D., Le Goaer, O., Seriai, A.: Updating styles challenge updating needs within component-based software architectures. In: SEKE (2006)
3. Oreizy, P.: Issues in modeling and analyzing dynamic software architectures. In: Proceedings of the International Workshop on the Role of Software Architecture in Testing and Analysis (1998)
4. Kramer, J., Magee, J.: The evolving philosophers problem: dynamic change management. IEEE TSE 16(11), 1293–1306 (1990)
5. Vandewoude, Y., Ebraert, P., Berbers, Y., D'Hondt, T.: Tranquility: a low disruptive alternative to quiescence for ensuring safe dynamic updates. IEEE Trans. Softw. Eng. 33(12), 856–868 (2007)
6. Oreizy, P., Medvidovic, N., Taylor, R.N.: Runtime software adaptation: framework, approaches, and styles. In: Companion of the 30th International Conference on Software Engineering, pp. 899–910. ACM (2008)
7. Buckley, J., Mens, T., Zenger, M., Rashid, A., Kniesel, G.: Towards a taxonomy of software change. J. Softw. Maint. Evol. Res. Pract. 17(5), 309–332 (2005)
8. Liu, C.L., Layland, J.W.: Scheduling algorithms for multiprogramming in a hard-real-time environment. J. ACM (JACM) 20(1), 46–61 (1973)
9. Richardson, T.: Developing dynamically reconfigurable real-time systems with real-time OSGi (RT-OSGi). Ph.D. dissertation, University of York (2011)
10. Garlan, D., Perry, D.E.: Introduction to the special issue on software architecture. IEEE Trans. Softw. Eng. 21(4), 269–274 (1995)
11. Chetto, H., Chetto, M.: Some results of the earliest deadline scheduling algorithm. IEEE Trans. Softw. Eng. 15(10), 1261–1269 (1989)
12. Costa-Soria, C. Hervás-Muñoz, D., Pérez, J., Carsí, J.Á: A reflective approach for supporting the dynamic evolution of component types. In: 14th IEEE International Conference, pp. 301–310 (2009)
13. Romero, C., J.Á: Contributions to the safe execution of dynamic component-based real-time systems. Ph.D. dissertation, Carlos III University of Madrid (2012)
14. Spuri, M., Buttazzo, G.: Scheduling aperiodic tasks in dynamic priority systems. Real-Time Syst. 10(2), 179–210 (1996)
15. Li, Q., Yao, C.: Real-Time Concepts for Embedded Systems. CRC Press, Boca Raton (2003)

16. Cuesta, C.E., de la Fuente, P., Barrio-Solórzano, M., Beato, E.: Coordination in a reflective architecture description language. In: Arbab, F., Talcott, C. (eds.) COORDINATION 2002. LNCS, vol. 2315, pp. 141–148. Springer, Heidelberg (2002). doi:10.1007/3-540-46000-4_15

17. Dowling, J., Cahill, V.: The K-component architecture meta-model for self-adaptive software. In: Yonezawa, A., Matsuoka, S. (eds.) Reflection 2001. LNCS, vol. 2192, pp. 81–88. Springer, Heidelberg (2001). doi:10.1007/3-540-45429-2_6

Retrofitting Controlled Dynamic Reconfiguration into the Architecture Description Language MontiArcAutomaton

Robert Heim[1], Oliver Kautz[1(✉)], Jan Oliver Ringert[2], Bernhard Rumpe[1,3], and Andreas Wortmann[1]

[1] Software Engineering, RWTH Aachen University, Aachen, Germany
{heim,kautz,rumpe,wortmann}@se-rwth.de
[2] School of Computer Science, Tel Aviv University, Tel Aviv, Israel
[3] Fraunhofer FIT, Aachen, Germany

Abstract. Component & connector architecture description languages (C&C ADLs) provide hierarchical decomposition of system functionality into components and their interaction. Most ADLs fix interaction configurations at design time while some express dynamic reconfiguration of components to adapt to runtime changes. Implementing dynamic reconfiguration in a static C&C ADL by encoding it into component behavior creates implicit dependencies between components and forfeits the abstraction of behavior paramount to C&C models. We developed a mechanism for retrofitting dynamic reconfiguration into the static C&C ADL MontiArcAutomaton. This mechanism lifts reconfiguration to an architecture concern and allows to preserve encapsulation and abstraction of C&C ADLs. Our approach enables efficient retrofitting by a smooth integration of reconfiguration semantics and encapsulation. The new dynamic C&C ADL is fully backwards compatible and well-formedness of configurations can be statically checked at design time. Our work provides dynamic reconfiguration for the C&C ADL MontiArcAutomaton.

1 Introduction

Component & connector (C&C) architecture description languages (ADLs) [1,2] combine the benefits of component-based software engineering with model-driven engineering (MDE) to abstract from the accidental complexities [3] and notational noise [4] of general-purpose programming languages (GPLs). They employ abstract component models to describe software architectures as hierarchies of connected components. This allows to abstract from ADL implementation details to a conceptual level applicable to multiple C&C ADLs.

In many ADLs, including MontiArcAutomaton [5], the configuration of C&C architectures is fixed at design time. The environment or the current goal of the system might however change during runtime and require dynamic adaptation of the system [6] to a new configuration that only includes a subset of already

© Springer International Publishing AG 2016
B. Tekinerdogan et al. (Eds.): ECSA 2016, LNCS 9839, pp. 175–182, 2016.
DOI: 10.1007/978-3-319-48992-6_13

existing components and their interconnections as well as introduces new components and connectors. To support dynamic adaptation, a C&C architecture either has to adapt its configuration at runtime or it must encode adaptation in the behaviors of the related components. This encoding introduces implicit dependencies between components and forfeits the abstraction of behavior paramount to C&C models. It imposes co-evolution requirements on different levels of abstraction and across components. Dynamic reconfiguration mechanisms and their formulation in ADLs help to mitigate these problems by formalizing adaptation as structural reconfiguration. This ensures that components keep encapsulating abstractions over functionality.

We develop a concept for retrofitting controlled dynamic adaptation into the static C&C ADL MontiArcAutomaton. The concept lifts reconfiguration to the conceptual level of components and connectors to preserve the fundamental abstraction and encapsulation mechanisms of C&C ADLs. It is *controlled* in the sense that it enables a restricted dynamism to benefit from greater run-time flexibility without loosing the validation properties of static configurations and their testability. Our concept enables efficient retrofitting by a smooth integration of reconfiguration semantics and encapsulation. It is implemented in the C&C ADL MontiArcAutomaton and its code generation framework. Our design for retrofitting reconfiguration kept changes to the language and code generation local and the resulting dynamic C&C ADL is fully backwards compatible.

Section 2 gives an example to demonstrate benefits of dynamic reconfiguration. Afterwards, Sect. 3 introduces our concept of controlled dynamic reconfiguration for MontiArcAutomaton and describes its implementation. Section 4 discusses our approach and compares it to related work and Sect. 5 concludes.

2   Example

Automatic transmission is a commonly used type of vehicle transmission, which can automatically change gear ratios as a vehicle moves. The driver may choose from different transmission operating modes (TOMs) such as Park, Reverse, Neutral, Drive, Sport, or Manual while driving. Depending on the chosen TOM, a transmission control system decides when to shift gears.

A C&C architecture might provide one component for each different shifting behavior. If the architecture is static, components must exchange control information at runtime to decide whether they take over the shifting behavior. The architect then has to define and implement inter-component protocols for switching between different behaviors. Dynamic reconfiguration enables to model structural flexibility in composed software components explicitly. Here, the transmission control system's architecture uses only components related to the selected transmission operating mode by reconfiguring connections between components as well as by dynamic component activation and instantiation.

Figure 1 (top) depicts a C&C model showing the composed component ShiftController. It contains the three subcomponents manual, auto, and sport for the execution of different gear shifting behaviors and the subcomponent scs for providing sensor data comprising the current revolutions per

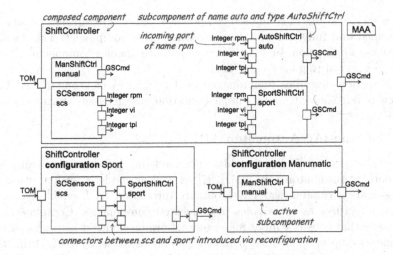

Fig. 1. Three configurations of the ShiftController component. Top: initial configuration. Middle: configuration for shifting gears during the transmission operating mode Sport. Bottom: configuration for shifting gears during the transmission operating mode Manumatic.

minute (rpm), the vehicle inclination (vi), and the throttle pedal inclination (tpi) encoded as integers. The component ShiftController has an interface of type TOM to receive the currently selected TOM and one interface of type GSCmd to emit commands for shifting gears. Immediately after engine start up all subcomponents are neither active nor connected (top configuration). Once the currently selected TOM is known to component ShiftController, it changes its configuration accordingly and starts the contributing subcomponents (bottom configurations). While the currently selected TOM is Sport (bottom left configuration), only subcomponents scs and sport are active to emit sensor data and commands for shifting gears, whereas only subcomponent manual is active when the currently selected TOM is Manumatic (bottom right configuration). Making the active components and connectors explicit increases comprehensibility of the architecture. The deactivation of components at runtime has further practical benefits, such as saving computation time and power consumption.

3   Retrofitting Controlled C&C Reconfiguration

We present a concept for retrofitting dynamic reconfiguration into the MontiArcAutomaton ADL [5]. All possible component configurations and their transitions are defined at design time, which allows static analysis to prevent malformed configurations from being deployed. At runtime, the reconfiguration is applied when pre-defined conditions for reconfiguration are met. No configuration validity changes are required at runtime. The reconfiguration mechanism is self-directed and pre-defined: Initiation and application of dynamic reconfiguration can only be applied by a component itself. This allows independent and reusable specifications of composed components. All reconfiguration possibilities are specified and fully available in the reconfiguring component. This facilities analysis and application. In addition, our approach enables component instantiation and removal to gain greater flexibility.

This section describes preliminaries on the MontiArcAutomaton ADL, an overview of our concept, and its implementation within MontiArcAutomaton.

3.1   The MontiArcAutomaton ADL

MontiArcAutomaton [5] is an architecture modeling infrastructure comprising the MontiArcAutomaton C&C ADL [7] as well as model transformation and code generation capabilities. The MontiArcAutomaton ADL enables to model C&C architectures as hierarchies of connected components. Components are black-boxes that consume input messages and produce output messages. Atomic components employ embedded behavior models or attached GPL artifacts to perform computations. The behavior of composed components emerges from the interaction of their subcomponents. These interact via unidirectional connectors between the typed ports of their interfaces. Components and connectors cannot be instantiated, nor removed at runtime. The data types of ports are defined in terms of class diagrams. The MontiArcAutomaton ADL distinguishes component types from instances, supports component configuration, and components with generic type parameters. Its infrastructure supports transformation of platform-independent architecture models into platform-specific models and composition of code generators to reuse generation capabilities for different aspects.

3.2   Overview: Component Modes for Dynamic Reconfiguration

Our approach for modeling dynamic reconfiguration relies on explicit modes, which fully define possible configurations. A mode is a configuration of a composed component and components can only switch between their pre-defined modes. In modes, we distinguish subcomponent instantiation and activation: the lifecycle of instantiated subcomponents ends with any mode switch, while deactivated subcomponents retain their state between modes. Components switch between their modes via mode transitions, which are again fixed at design time. Each mode transition consists of a source mode, a target mode, and a guard expression (e.g., over ports of the composed component and its direct subcomponents). Intuitively, when the source mode equals the current mode of a corresponding component instance, and the guard is satisfied, reconfiguration to the target mode takes place. The mode transitions of a component define a state machine over the state space of component modes with input of data messages observable within the component.

MontiArcAutomaton distinguishes component types and instances. Modes and mode transitions are defined on the component type level of MontiArc-Automaton. However, at runtime each component instance reconfigures itself independently based on its current mode and observable messages. Thus there is no synchronization overhead induced by component types.

```
                                                      ┌─────────────────────────┐
                                                      │   MontiArcAutomaton     │
   ┌──────────────────────────────────────────────────┘                         │
 1 │ component ShiftController {
 2 │   port in TOM tom, out GSCmd cmd;
 3 │
 4 │   component ManShiftCtrl manual;
 5 │   component AutoShiftCtrl auto;
 6 │   component SCSensors scs;
 7 │
 8 │   mode Idle {}   mode Manumatic { /* ... */ }   mode Auto { /* ... */ }
 9 │
10 │   mode Sport, Kickdown {
11 │     activate scs;
12 │     component SportShiftCtrl sport;
13 │     connect scs.rpm -> sport.rpm; connect scs.vi -> sport.vi;
14 │     connect scs.tpi - sport.tpi; connect sport.cmd -> cmd;
15 │   }
16 │
17 │   modetransitions {
18 │     initial Idle;
19 │     Idle -> Auto [tom == DRIVE];
20 │     Auto -> Kickdown [scs.tpi > 90 && tom == DRIVE];
21 │     Kickdown -> Auto [scs.tpi < 90 && tom == DRIVE]; // further transitions
22 │   }
23 │ }
```

Listing 1. Excerpt of the `ShiftController` component type definition with five modes (ll. 8–15) and a mode transition automaton (ll. 17–22).

3.3 Defining Component Modes

The C&C core concepts identified in [1] and implemented in MontiArc-Automaton consist of components with interfaces, connectors, and architectural configurations (i.e., topologies of subcomponents). In MontiArcAutomaton, architectural configurations are defined locally within composed components. For dynamic reconfiguration we extend the existing single component configuration with multiple modes, where each mode expresses one configuration. We continue the `ShiftController` example depicted in Fig. 1 in MontiArcAutomaton syntax with support for modes shown in Listing 1.

Subcomponents with instances shared between multiple modes are defined in the body of the composed component and can be activated or deactivated in modes. As an example, the subcomponent `scs` of type `SCSensors` is defined in Listing 1, l. 6 and activated in modes `Sport` and `Kickdown` in l. 11. Subcomponents are deactivated by default, e.g., subcomponents `manual` and `auto`, ll. 4–5 are deactivated in mode `Sport`, ll. 10–15. In addition, subcomponents can be instantiated when entering a mode and destroyed when switching to another mode. As an example, instances of subcomponent `sport` of type `SportShiftCtrl` as defined in l. 12 are unique to modes `Sport` and `Kickdown`. Connectors between components are defined for each mode.

For each mode we can determine at design time whether the expressed configuration is a valid MontiArcAutomaton component configuration. In addition some well-formedness rules need to be checked: (1) Each mode of each composed component type has a unique name. (2) Each subcomponent instantiated in a mode has a unique name in the context of the component containing the mode. (3) Each subcomponent instance referenced in a mode exists.

3.4   Defining Mode Transitions

Composed components with multiple modes change their configuration based on observable messages. The messages observable by a component are messages on its own ports and messages on ports of its subcomponent instances.

All mode transitions are defined locally within the composed component. An example is shown in Listing 1, ll. 17–22. Following the keyword modetransitions, the mode automaton contains a single initial mode declaration (l. 18) and multiple transitions (ll. 19–21). These describe mode switches and their conditions in guard expressions. Guard expression are written in a language resembling expressions in an object-oriented GPL (e.g., it uses dot-notation to reference messages on ports of components).

The following well-formedness rules apply for the definition of mode transitions: (4) Each composed component type has exactly one initial mode. (5) The subcomponent interface elements referenced in guards exist. (6) Modes referenced in transitions exist in the containing component.

3.5   Implementation Details of Retrofitting

We now highlight some implementation details of retrofitting dynamic reconfiguration into the MontiArcAutomaton infrastructure.

On the language level, modes reuse existing modeling elements for subcomponents, ports, and connectors. Mode transitions reuse the automata modeling elements presented in [7], which allowed us to reuse existing well-formedness rules of the MontiArcAutomaton ADL to describe the static semantics of dynamic reconfiguration. We added the well-formedness rules described above.

We extended the existing code generators [5] to enable integration of dynamic reconfiguration with the dynamic semantics of MontiArcAutomaton. Due to localizing the impact of reconfiguration in composed components only, retrofitting into code generation was straightforward. The extended MontiArc-Automaton ADL and the generated code are backwards compatible because we could transfer the encapsulation of reconfiguration from the model level to the code level.

4   Discussion and Related Work

The importance of dynamic reconfiguration has long been recognized [8] and is implemented for multiple ADLs [9–17]. Nonetheless, many ADLs focus on other aspects and support static architectures only (e.g., DiaSpec [18], Palladio [19], xADL [20]). Also, there is no consensus on how architectural models describe dynamic reconfiguration. Usually, specific modeling elements exist [10–13,15–17].

Similar to our concept, some ADLs (e.g., AADL [15], AutoFocus [16,17]) enable dynamic reconfiguration in a controlled fashion. Here, composed components change between configurations (called "modes") predefined at design time only. Specific transitions control when components may change their configuration. While this restricts arbitrary reconfiguration (cf. π-ADL [11], ArchJava [10]), it increases comprehensibility and guarantees static analyzability.

Dynamic reconfiguration can be *programmed* or *ad-hoc* [21]. In programmed reconfiguration (e.g., ACME/Plastik [13], AADL [15], ArchJava [10]), conditions and effects specified at design time are applied at runtime. Ad-hoc reconfiguration (e.g., C2 SADL [9], Fractal [14], ACME/Plastik [13]) does not necessarily have to be specified at design time and takes place at runtime, e.g., invoked by reconfiguration scripts. It introduces greater flexibility, but component models do not reflect the reconfiguration options. This enables simulating unforeseen changes to test an architecture's robustness, but it complicates analysis and evolution. For the latter reason MontiArcAutomaton's concept solely includes programmed reconfiguration.

Besides modeling dynamic removal and establishment of connectors, MontiArcAutomaton supports dynamic instantiation and removal of components. In ACME/Plastik [13], so-called actions can remove and create connectors and components. ArchJava [10] embeds architectural elements in Java and, hence, enables instantiating corresponding component classes as Java objects. C2 SADL [9] supports ad-hoc instantiation and removal of components. Fractal [14] provides similar concepts in its aspect-oriented Java implementation. π-ADL's [11] language constructs enable instantiation, removal, and movement of components.

5 Conclusion

We have developed and presented a concept for retrofitting controlled dynamic reconfiguration into the static ADL MontiArcAutomaton. Our concept maintains important abstraction and encapsulation mechanisms. Dynamic reconfigurable components have modes and mode automata to switch between configurations declaratively programmed at design time. The state of components during runtime can be either retained between different configurations or components can be instantiated and removed. We implemented our concept within the MontiArcAutomaton architecture modeling infrastructure. The implementation includes an extended syntax, analysis tools, and a code generator realizing semantics of dynamic reconfigurable components with synchronous communication. Interesting future work could investigate the applicability of our concept for retrofitting dynamic reconfiguration into further ADLs.

References

1. Medvidovic, N., Taylor, R.: A classification and comparison framework for software architecture description languages. IEEE Trans. Softw. Eng. **26**, 70–93 (2000)
2. Malavolta, I., Lago, P., Muccini, H., Pelliccione, P., Tang, A.: What industry needs from architectural languages: a survey. IEEE Trans. Softw. Eng. **39**, 869–891 (2013)
3. France, R., Rumpe, B.: Model-driven development of complex software: a research roadmap. In: 2007 Future of Software Engineering. ICSE (2007)

4. Wile, D.S.: Supporting the DSL spectrum. Comput. Inf. Technol. **9**, 263–287 (2001)
5. Ringert, J.O., Roth, A., Rumpe, B., Wortmann, A.: Language and code generator composition for model-driven engineering of robotics component & connector systems. J. Softw. Eng. Robot. (JOSER) **6**, 33–57 (2015)
6. Salehie, M., Tahvildari, L.: Self-adaptive software: landscape and research challenges. ACM Trans. Auton. Adapt. Syst. (TAAS) **4**, 14–15 (2009)
7. Ringert, J.O., Rumpe, B., Wortmann, A.: Architecture and behavior modeling of cyber-physical systems with MontiArcAutomaton. Shaker Verlag (2014)
8. Lim, W.Y.P.: PADL-a packet architecture description language. Massachusetts Institute of Technology, Laboratory for Computer Science (1982)
9. Medvidovic, N.: ADLs and dynamic architecture changes. In: Joint Proceedings of the Second International Software Architecture Workshop (ISAW-2) and International Workshop on Multiple Perspectives in Software Development (Viewpoints 1996) on SIGSOFT 1996 Workshops (1996)
10. Aldrich, J., Chambers, C., Notkin, D.: ArchJava: connecting software architecture to implementation. In: Proceedings of the 24th International Conference on Software Engineering (ICSE) (2002)
11. Oquendo, F.: π-ADL: an architecture description language based on the higher-order typed π-calculus for specifying dynamic and mobile software architectures. ACM SIGSOFT Softw. Eng. Notes **29**, 1–14 (2004)
12. Cuesta, C.E., de la Fuente, P., Barrio-Solórzano, M., Beato, M.E.G.: An "abstract process" approach to algebraic dynamic architecture description. J. Log. Algebr. Program. **63**, 177–214 (2005)
13. Joolia, A., Batista, T., Coulson, G., Gomes, A.T.: Mapping ADL specifications to an efficient and reconfigurable runtime component platform. In: 5th Working IEEE/IFIP Conference on Software Architecture, WICSA 2005 (2005)
14. Bruneton, E., Coupaye, T., Leclercq, M., Quéma, V., Stefani, J.: The fractal component model and its support in Java. Softw. Pract. Exp. **36**, 1257–1284 (2006)
15. Feiler, P.H., Gluch, D.P.: Model-Based Engineering with AADL: An Introduction to the SAE Architecture Analysis & Design Language. Addison-Wesley, Upper Saddle River (2012)
16. AutoFocus 3 Website. http://af3.fortiss.org/. Accessed: 18 Jan 2016
17. Aravantinos, V., Voss, S., Teufl, S., Hölzl, F., Schätz, B.: AutoFOCUS 3: tooling concepts for seamless, model-based development of embedded systems. In: Joint Proceedings of ACES-MB 2015 – Model-Based Architecting of Cyber-physical and Embedded Systems and WUCOR 2015 – UML Consistency Rules (2015)
18. Cassou, D., Koch, P., Stinckwich, S.: Using the DiaSpec design language and compiler to develop robotics systems. In: Proceedings of the Second International Workshop on Domain-Specific Languages and Models for Robotic Systems (DSLRob) (2011)
19. Becker, S., Koziolek, H., Reussner, R.: Model-based performance prediction with the palladio component model. In: Proceedings of the 6th International Workshop on Software and Performance (2007)
20. Khare, R., Guntersdorfer, M., Oreizy, P., Medvidovic, N., Taylor, R.N.: xADL: enabling architecture-centric tool integration with XML. In: Proceedings of the 34th Annual Hawaii International Conference on System Sciences (2001)
21. Bradbury, J.S.: Organizing definitions and formalisms for dynamic software architectures. Technical report, School of Computing, Queen's University (2004)

Verification and Consistency Management

Statistical Model Checking of Dynamic Software Architectures

Everton Cavalcante[1,2]($\boxtimes$), Jean Quilbeuf[2,3], Louis-Marie Traonouez[3],
Flavio Oquendo[2], Thais Batista[1], and Axel Legay[3]

[1] DIMAp, Federal University of Rio Grande do Norte, Natal, Brazil
`everton@dimap.ufrn.br, thais@ufrnet.br`
[2] IRISA-UMR CNRS/Université Bretagne Sud, Vannes, France
`{jean.quilbeuf,flavio.oquendo}@irisa.fr`
[3] INRIA Rennes Bretagne Atlantique, Rennes, France
`{louis-marie.traonouez,axel.legay}@inria.fr`

Abstract. The critical nature of many complex software-intensive systems calls for formal, rigorous architecture descriptions as means of supporting automated verification and enforcement of architectural properties and constraints. Model checking has been one of the most used techniques to automatically verify software architectures with respect to the satisfaction of architectural properties. However, such a technique leads to an exhaustive exploration of all possible states of the system, a problem that becomes more severe when verifying dynamic software systems due to their typical non-deterministic runtime behavior and unpredictable operation conditions. To tackle these issues, we propose using statistical model checking (SMC) to support the verification of dynamic software architectures while aiming at reducing computational resources and time required for this task. In this paper, we introduce a novel notation to formally express architectural properties as well as an SMC-based toolchain for verifying dynamic software architectures described in π-ADL, a formal architecture description language. We use a flood monitoring system to show how to express relevant properties to be verified. We also report the results of some computational experiments performed to assess the efficiency of our approach.

Keywords: Dynamic software architecture · Architecture description language · Formal verification · Statistical model checking

1 Introduction

One of the major challenges in software engineering is to ensure correctness of software-intensive systems, especially as they have become increasingly complex and used in many critical domains. Ensuring these concerns becomes more important mainly when evolving these systems since such a verification needs to be performed before, during, and after evolution. Software architectures play an essential role in this context since they represent an early blueprint for the system construction, deployment, execution, and evolution.

© Springer International Publishing AG 2016
B. Tekinerdogan et al. (Eds.): ECSA 2016, LNCS 9839, pp. 185–200, 2016.
DOI: 10.1007/978-3-319-48992-6_14

The critical nature of many complex software systems calls for rigorous architectural models (such as formal architecture descriptions) as means of supporting the automated verification and enforcement of architectural properties. However, architecture descriptions should not cover only structure and behavior of a software architecture, but also the required and desired architectural properties, in particular the ones related to consistency and correctness [15]. For instance, after describing a software architecture, a software architect might want to verify if it is complete, consistent, and correct with respect to architectural properties.

In order to foster the automated verification of architectural properties based on architecture descriptions, they need to be formally specified. Despite the inherent difficulty of pursuing formal methods, the advantage of a formal verification is to precisely determine if a software system can satisfy properties related to user requirements. Additionally, automated verification provides an efficient method to check the correctness of architectural design. As reported by Zhang et al. [19], one of the most popular formal methods for analyzing software architectures is *model checking*, an exhaustive, automatic verification technique whose general goal is to verify if an architectural specification satisfies architectural properties [8]. It takes as inputs a representation of the system (e.g., an architecture description) and a set of property specifications expressed in some notation. The model checker returns true if the properties are satisfied, or false with the case in which a given property is violated.

Despite its wide and successful use, model checking faces a critical challenge with respect to scalability. Holzmann [10] remarks that no currently available traditional model checking approach is exempted from the *state space explosion problem*, that is, the exponential growth of the state space. This problem is exacerbated in the contemporary dynamic software systems for two main reasons, namely (i) the non-determinism of their behavior caused by concurrency and (ii) the unpredictable environmental conditions in which they operate. In spite of the existence of a number of techniques aimed at reducing the state space, such a problem remains intractable for some software systems, thereby making the use of traditional model checking techniques a prohibitive choice in terms of execution time and computational resources. As a consequence, software architects have to trade-off the risks of possibly undiscovered problems related to the violation of architectural properties against the practical limitations of applying a model checking technique on a very large architectural model.

In order to tackle the aforementioned issues, this paper proposes the use of *statistical model checking* (SMC) to support the formal verification of dynamic software architectures while striving to reduce computational resources and time for performing this task. SMC is a probabilistic, simulation-based technique intended to verify, at a given confidence level, if a certain property is satisfied during the execution of a system [13]. Unlike model checking, SMC does not analyze the internal logic of the target system, thereby not suffering from the state space explosion problem [12]. Furthermore, an SMC-based approach promotes better scalability and less consumption of computational resources, important factors to be considered when analyzing software architectures for complex critical systems. An architect wishing to verify the correctness of a software architecture with SMC has to build an executable model of the system, a task that is much easier than building a model of the system that is abstract enough to be used by a model checker and still detailed enough to detect meaningful errors.

The main contribution presented in this paper is an SMC-based toolchain for verifying dynamic software architectures described in π-ADL, a formal language for describing dynamic software architectures [5,16]. π-ADL does not natively allow for a probabilistic execution, but rather provides a non-deterministic specification of a dynamic architecture. Therefore, we obtain a probabilistic model by resolving non-determinism by probabilities, enforced by a stochastic scheduler. We also make use of DynBLTL [18], a new logic to express properties about dynamic systems. Using a real-world flood monitoring system, we herein show how to express relevant properties to be verified and we report the results of some computational experiments performed to assess the efficiency of our approach.

The remainder of this paper is organized as follows. Section 2 briefly presents the SMC technique. Section 3 details how to stochastically execute π-ADL architecture descriptions. Section 4 introduces our notation to formally express properties of dynamic software architectures. Section 5 presents the developed toolchain to verify dynamic software architectures. Section 6 uses the flood monitoring system as case study to show how to express properties with DynBLTL, as well as it reports the results of experiments on the computational effort to verify these properties. Finally, Sect. 7 contains concluding remarks.

2   Statistical Model Checking

The SMC approach consists of building a statistical model of finite executions of the system under verification and deducing the probability of satisfying a given property within confidence bounds. This technique provides a number of advantages in comparison to traditional model checking techniques. First (and perhaps the most important one), it does not suffer from the state space explosion problem since it does not analyze the internal logic of the system under verification, neither requires the entire representation of the state space, thus making it a promising approach for verifying complex large-scale and critical software systems [12]. Second, SMC requires only the system be able to be simulated, so that it can be applied to larger classes of systems, including black-box and infinite-state systems. Third, the proliferation of parallel computer architectures makes the production of multiple independent simulation runs relatively easier. Fourth, despite SMC can provide approximate results (as opposed to exact results provided by traditional model checking), it is compensated by a better scalability and less consumption of computational resources. In some cases, knowing the result with less than 100 % of confidence is quite acceptable or even the unique available option. Therefore, SMC allows trading-off between verification accuracy and computational time by selecting appropriate precision parameter values.

Figure 1 illustrates a general schema on how the SMC technique works. A statistical model checker basically consists of a simulator for running the system under verification, a model checker for verifying properties, and a statistical analyzer responsible for calculating probabilities and performing statistical tests. It receives three inputs: (i) an *executable stochastic model* of the target system M; (ii) a formula φ expressing a *bounded property* to be verified, i.e., a property that can be decided over a finite execution of M; and (iii) user-defined *precision parameters* determining the accuracy of the probability estimation. The model M is stochastic in the sense that the next state is probabilistically chosen among the states that are reachable from the current one. Depending on the probabilistic choices made during the executions of M, some executions will satisfy φ and others will not. The simulator executes M and generates an *execution trace* σ_i composed of a sequence of *states*. Next, the model checker determines if σ_i satisfies φ and sends the result (either success or failure) to the statistical analyzer, which in turn estimates the probability p for M to satisfy φ. The simulator repeatedly generates other execution traces σ_{i+1} until the analyzer determines that enough traces have been analyzed to produce an estimation of p satisfying the precision parameters. A higher accuracy of the answer provided by the model checker requires generating more execution traces through simulations.

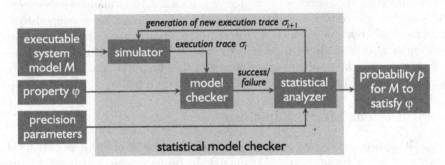

Fig. 1. Working schema of the SMC technique.

3   Stochastic Execution of π-ADL Models

In this section, we briefly recall how the π-ADL language allows describing dynamic software architectures. As SMC is a stochastic technique, the executable model representing the system needs to be stochastic, a feature that π-ADL does not possess. For this reason, we have provided a way of producing a stochastic executable model from π-ADL architecture descriptions, thus allowing for property verification using SMC. Finally, we show how to extract execution traces from a stochastic execution.

3.1   Modeling Dynamic Architectures in π-ADL

π-ADL [16] is a formal, well-founded theoretically language intended to describe software architectures under both structural and behavioral viewpoints. In order to cope with dynamicity concerns, π-ADL is endowed with architectural-level primitives for specifying programmed reconfiguration operations, i.e., foreseen, pre-planned changes described at design time and triggered at runtime by the system itself under a given condition or event [5]. Additionally, code source in the Go programming language [1] is automatically generated from π-ADL architecture descriptions, thereby allowing for their execution [6].

From the structural viewpoint, a software architecture is described in π-ADL in terms of *components, connectors,* and their composition to form the system, i.e., an *architecture* as a configuration of components and connectors. From the behavioral viewpoint, both components and connectors comprise a *behavior*, which expresses the interaction of an architectural element and its internal computation and uses *connections* to send and receive values between architectural elements. The attachment of a component to a connector (and vice-versa) is made by *unifying* their connections. Therefore, the transmission of a value from an architectural element to another is possible only if (i) the output connection of the sender is unified to the input connection of the receiver, (ii) the sender is ready to send a value through that output connection, and (iii) the receiver is ready to receive a value on that input connection.

In π-ADL, dynamic reconfiguration is obtained by *decomposing* architectures [5]. The decomposition action removes all unifications defined in the original architecture, but it does not terminate its elements. The decomposition of a given architecture A is typically called from another coexisting architecture B, which results from a reconfiguration applied over A. After calling the decomposition of A, B can access and modify the elements originally instantiated in A.

3.2   Resolving Non-determinism in π-ADL

In π-ADL, non-determinism occurs in two different ways. First, whenever several actions are possible, any one of them can be executed as the next action, i.e., the choice of the next action to execute is non-deterministic. Second, some functions and behaviors can declared as *unobservable*, thus meaning that its internal operations are concealed at the architectural level. In this case, the value returned by the function is also non-deterministic because it is not defined in the model. As performing SMC requires a stochastic process, we resolve the non-determinism of π-ADL models by using probabilities. In the following, we describe how to proceed in the aforementioned cases.

Resolving Non-determinism in the Choice of the Next Action. The Go code from a π-ADL architecture description encodes architectural element (component or connector) as a concurrent goroutine, a lightweight process similar to a thread. The communication between architectural elements takes place via a channel, another Go construct. If several communications are possible, the Go runtime chooses one of them to execute according to a FIFO policy, which is not suitable for SMC since it is necessary to specify how the next action is chosen.

To support the stochastic scheduling of actions, we have implemented a scheduler as a goroutine controlling all non-local actions, i.e., composition, decomposition, and communication. Whenever an architectural element needs to perform a non-local action, it informs the scheduler and blocks until the scheduler responds. The scheduler responds with the action executed (if the component has submitted a choice between several actions) and a return value, corresponding either to the receiving side of a communication or a decomposed architecture.

Figure 2 depicts the behavior of the scheduler. The scheduler waits until all components and connectors have indicated their possible actions. At this step, the scheduler builds a list of possible rendezvous by checking which declared unifications have both sender and receiver ready to communicate. For this purpose, the scheduler maintains a list of the active architectures and the corresponding unifications. The possible communications are added to the list of possible actions and the scheduler chooses one of them according to a probabilistic choice function. The scheduler then executes the action and outputs its effect to the statistical model checker. Finally, the scheduler notifies the components and connectors involved in the action.

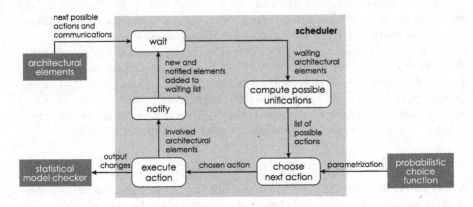

Fig. 2. Scheduler to support the stochastic simulation of a π-ADL model.

Resolving Non-determinism in Unobservable Functions Functions declared as unobservable require an implementation to allow simulating the model. In practice, this implementation is provided in form of a Go function whose return value can be determined by a probability distribution. Such an implementation relies on the Go libraries implementing usual probability distributions. In particular, such functions can model inputs of the systems that have a known probabilistic value, i.e., input to a component, time to the next failure of a component, etc.

3.3   Trace of a Stochastic Execution

In order to verifying dynamic software architectures with SMC, we abstract away the internal structure of architectural elements and represent a state of the system as a directed graph $g = (V, E)$ in which V is a finite set of nodes and E is a finite set of edges. Each node $v \in V$ represents an architectural element (component or connector) whereas each direct edge $e \in E$ represents a communication channel between two architectural elements.

The SMC technique relies on checking multiple execution traces resulted from simulations of the system under verification against the specified properties. Therefore, as a simulation ω results in a trace σ composed of a finite sequence of states, σ can be defined as a sequence of state graphs g_i ($i \in \mathbb{N}$), i.e., $\sigma = (g_0, g_1, \ldots, g_n)$. Aiming at obtaining an execution trace from an architecture description in π-ADL, the simulation emits explicit messages recording a set of actions on the state graph.

4   A Novel Notation for Expressing Properties in Dynamic Software Architectures

Most architectural properties to be verified by using model checking techniques are temporal [19], i.e., they are qualified and can be reasoned upon a sequence of system states along the time. In the literature, linear temporal logic (LTL) [17] has been often used as underlying formalism for specifying temporal architectural properties and verifying them through model checking. LTL extends classical Boolean logic with *temporal operators* that allow reasoning on the temporal dimension of the execution of the system. In this perspective, LTL can be used to encode formulas about the future of execution paths (sequences of states), e.g., a condition that will be eventually true, a condition that will be true until another fact becomes true, etc.

Besides using standard propositional logic operators, LTL defines four temporal operators, namely: (i) *next*, which means that a formula φ will be true in the next step; (ii) *finally* or *eventually*, which indicates that a formula φ will be true at least once in the time interval; (iii) *globally* or *always*, which means that a formula φ will be true at all times in the time interval; and (iv) *until*, which indicates that either a formula φ is initially true or another previous formula ψ is true until φ become true at the current or a future time. SMC techniques verify *bounded properties*, i.e., where temporal operators are parameterized by a time bound. While LTL-based formulas aim at specifying the infinite behavior of the system, a time-bounded form of LTL called BLTL considers properties that can be decided on finite sequences of execution states.

Temporal logics such as LTL and BLTL are expressed over atomic predicates that evaluate properties to a Boolean value at every point of execution. However, a key characteristic of dynamic software systems is the impossibility of foreseeing the exact set of architectural elements deployed at a given point of execution. Such traditional formalisms do not allow reasoning about elements that may appear, disappear, be connected or be disconnected during the execution of the system for two main reasons. First, specifying a predicate for each property of each element is not possible as the set of architectural elements may be unknown a priori. Second, there is no canonical way of assigning a truth value to a property about an element that does not exist at the considered point of execution. In addition, existing approaches to tackle such issues typically focus on behavioral properties, but they do not address architectural properties [7]. On the other hand, some approaches assume that the architectures are static [3]. These limitations have led us to propose DynBLTL, an extension of BLTL to formally express properties in dynamic software architectures [18].

DynBLTL was designed to handle the absence of an architectural element in a given formula expressing a property. In practice, this means that a Boolean expression can take three values, namely *true, false* or *undefined*. The undefined value refers to the fact that an expression may not be evaluated depending on the current runtime configuration of the system. This is necessary for situations in which it is not possible to evaluate an expression in the considered point of execution, e.g., a statement about an architectural element that does not exist at that moment. Some operators interpret the undefined value as true or false, depending on the context. Furthermore, DynBLTL allows expressing properties using (i) arithmetic, logical, and comparison operations on values, (ii) existential and universal quantifications, traditionally used in predicate logic, and (iii) some predefined functions that can be used to explore the architectural configuration. Four temporal operators are available, namely *in, eventually before, always during,* and *until,* which are similar to the ones defined in both LTL and BLTL. Some examples of DynBLTL properties are presented in Sect. 6.2.

5   A Toolchain to Simulate and Verify Dynamic Software Architectures

SMC techniques rely on the simulation of an executable model of the system under verification against a set of formulas expressing bounded properties to be verified (see Sect. 2). These elements are provided as inputs to a statistical model checker, which consists of (i) a simulator to run the executable model of the system, (ii) a model checker to verify properties, and (iii) a statistical analyzer responsible for calculating probabilities and performing statistical tests.

Among the SMC tools available in the literature, PLASMA [2] is a compact, flexible platform that enables users to create custom SMC plug-ins atop it. For instance, users who have developed their own model description language can use it with PLASMA by providing a simulator plug-in. Similarly, users can add custom languages for specifying properties and use the available SMC algorithms through a checker plug-in. Besides its efficiency and good performance results [4, 11, 14], such a flexibility was one of the main reasons motivating the choice of PLASMA to serve as basis to develop the toolchain for specifying and verifying properties of dynamic software architectures.

Figure 3 provides an overview of our toolchain. The inputs for the process are (i) an architecture description in π-ADL and (ii) a set of properties specified in DynBLTL. By following the process proposed in our previous work [5, 6], the architecture description in π-ADL is translated towards generating source code in Go. As π-ADL architectural models do not have a stochastic execution, they are linked to a stochastic scheduler parameterized by a probability distribution for drawing the next action, as described in Sect. 3. Furthermore, we use existing probability distribution Go libraries to model inputs of system models as user functions. The program resulting from the compilation of the generated Go source code emits messages referring to transitions from a given state to another in case of addition, attachment, detachment, and value exchanges of architectural elements.

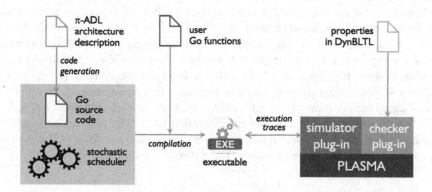

Fig. 3. Overview of the toolchain to verify properties of dynamic software architectures.

We have developed two plug-ins atop the PLASMA platform, namely (i) a simulator plug-in that interprets execution traces produced by the generated Go program and (ii) a checker plug-in that implements DynBLTL. With this toolchain, a software architect is able to evaluate the probability of a π-ADL architectural model to satisfy a given property specified in DynBLTL. The developed tools are publicly available at http://plasma4pi-adl.gforge.inria.fr.

6 Case Study

In this section, we apply our approach to a real-world flood monitoring system used as a case study. Section 6.1 presents an overview of the system and Sect. 6.2 describes some relevant properties to be verified in the context of this system. At last, Sect. 6.3 reports some computational experiments performed to assess the efficiency of our approach with the developed toolchain.

6.1 Description

A flood monitoring system can support monitoring urban rivers and create alert messages to notify authorities and citizens about the risks of an imminent flood, thereby fostering effective predictions and improving warning times. This system is typically based on a wireless sensor network composed of sensors that measure the water level in flood-prone areas near the river. In addition, a gateway station analyzes data measured by motes, makes such data available, and can trigger alerts when a flood condition is detected. The communication among these elements takes place by using wireless network connections, such as WiFi, ZigBee, GPRS, Bluetooth, etc.

Figure 4 shows the main architecture of the system. Sensor components communicate with each other through ZigBee connectors and a gateway component receives all measurements to evaluate the current risk. Each measure from a sensor is propagated its neighbors via ZigBee connectors until reaching the gateway. The environment is modeled through the *Env* component and the *SensorEnv* and *Budget* connectors. *Env* is responsible for synchronizing the model by defining cycles corresponding to the frequency at which measures are taken by sensors. A cycle consists of: (i) signaling *Budget* that a new cycle has started; (ii) updating the river status; (iii) registering deployed sensors; (iv) signaling each *SensorEnv* connector to deliver a new measure; and (v) waiting for each *SensorEnv* connector to confirm that a new measure has been delivered. The *Sensor*, *SensorEnv*, and *ZigBee* elements can added and removed during the execution of the system through reconfigurations triggered by the gateway component.

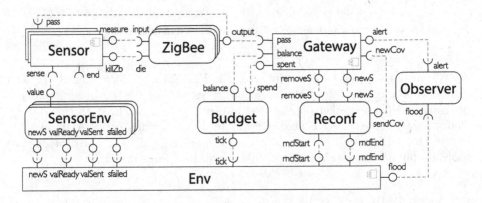

Fig. 4. Overview of the main architecture for the flood monitoring system.

Figure 5 shows an excerpt of the π-ADL description for the sensor component. The behavior of this components comprises choosing between two alternatives, either obtaining a new measure (i) from the environment via the *sense* input connection or (ii) from a neighbor sensor via the *pass* input connection. After receiving the gathered value, it is transmitted through the *measure* output connection. Reading a negative value indicates a failure of the sensor, so that it becomes a *FailingSensor*, which simply ignores all incoming messages.

We have modeled two reconfigurations, namely adding and removing a sensor, as depicted in Fig. 6. The gateway component decides to add a sensor if the coverage of the river is not optimal and the budget is sufficient to deploy a new sensor. This operation is triggered by sending a message to *Reconf* via the *newS* connection, with the desired location for the new sensor. The new sensor is connected to other sensors in range via a ZigBee connector, as shown in Fig. 6(a).

```
component Sensor is abstraction() {
  connection sense is in(MV)
  connection measure is out(CmH2O)
  connection pass is in(CmH2O)
  behavior is {
    choose {
        via sense receive m : MV
        via measure send CmH2O(tuple[self, m])
        if m < 0.0 then {
          become(FailingSensor())
        }

        or
        via pass receive other_measure : CmH2O
        via measure send other_measure
    }
  }
}
```

Fig. 5. Partial π-ADL description of the sensor component.

During this operation, *Reconf* decomposes the main architecture to include the new elements and unifications before recomposing it. The reconfiguration uses the position of each sensor to determine which links have to be created. After triggering the reconfiguration, the gateway indicates to the *Budget* connector that it has spent the price of a sensor.

Fig. 6. Reconfigurations in the flood monitoring system: adding sensor s_3, which requires connecting it to existing sensors s_1 and s_2 through new ZigBee connectors (left), and removal of sensor s_5 (right).

The gateway removes a sensor when it receives a message indicating that it is in failure. This operation is triggered by sending a message to *Reconf* via the *removeS* connection, with the name of the sensor to remove. Removing a sensor may isolate other sensors that are further away from the gateway as it in shown in Fig. 6(b). In this case, sensors that were sending their measures via the removed sensor (such as s_4) are instead connected to a sink connector, which loses all messages. This new connection prevents deadlocks that occur when the last element of the isolated chain cannot propagate its message. When a sensor is removed, the connected *ZigBee* and *SensorEnv* are composed in a separated architecture. This architecture connects the *killZb* connection of the sensor to the *die* connections of the ZigBee connectors, which allows an other branch of the behavior to properly terminate these components.

6.2   Requirements

As previously mentioned, a DynBLTL formula requires bounds on temporal operators to ensure that it can be decided in a finite number of steps. We have two possibilities to express bounds, namely using steps or using time units. Usually, the number of steps executed during a time unit depends on the number of components in the system. In the case of our flood monitoring system, the number of steps executed during a cycle mainly depends on the number of sensors deployed since each sensor reads one value at each cycle. Therefore, a time unit correspond to a cycle, thus allowing us to specify bounds independently from the number of components in the system.

First, we want to evaluate the correctness of our model with respect to its main goal, i.e., warning about imminent flooding. In this context, a false negative occurs when the system fails to predict a flood.

```
eventually before X time units {                        // FalseNegative(X,Y)
  (gw.alert = "low")
  and (eventually before Y time units env.flood)
}
```

This property characterizes a false negative: the gateway predicts a low risk and a flood occurs in the next Y time units. The parameters of this formula are X, the time during which the system is monitored, and Y, the time during which the prediction of the gateway should hold.

Similarly, a false positive occurs when the system predicts a flood that does not actually occur:

```
eventually before X time units {                        // FalsePositive(X,Y)
  gw.alert = "flood detected"
  and always during Y time units not env.flood
}
```

The system is correct if there is no false negatives nor false positives for the expected prediction anticipation (parameter Y).

These two formulas are actually BLTL formulas as they involve simple predicates on the state. However, DynBLTL allows expressing properties about the dynamic architecture of the system. For example, suppose that one wants to check that if a sensor sends a message indicating that it is failing, then it must be removed from the system in a reasonable amount of time. This disconnection is needed because the sensor in failure will not pass incoming messages. We characterize the removal of a sensor by a link on the *end* connection, corresponding to the initiation of the sensor termination (not detailed here).

In our dynamic system, sensors may appear and disappear during execution. Therefore, the temporal pattern needs to be dynamically instantiated at each step for each existing sensor:

```
always during X time units {                        // RemoveSensor(X,Y)
   forall  s:allOfType(Sensor) {
      (isTrue s.measure <  0) implies {
         eventually before Y time units {
            exists st:allOfType(StartTerminate)
               areLinked(st.start ,s.end)
         }
      }
   }
}
```

This property cannot be stated in BLTL since it does not have a construct such as forall for instantiating a variable number of temporal sub-formulas depending on the current state.

Another property of interest consists in checking if a sensor is available, i.e., at least one sensor is connected to the gateway. More precisely, there must be a ZigBee connector between the gateway and a sensor. If not, we require that such a sensor appear in less than Y time units:

```
always  during X time units {                        // SensorAvailable(X,Y)
   (not (exists zb:allOfType(ZigBee) areLinked(zb.output ,gw.pass)
   and (exists s:allOfType(Sensor)   areLinked(s.measure ,zb.input))))
   implies (eventually before Y time units {
      exists zb:allOfType(ZigBee) areLinked(zb.output ,gw.pass)
      and (exists s:allOfType(Sensor) areLinked(s.measure ,zb.input))
   }
}
```

6.3   Experimental Results

In this section, we report some experiments aiming to quantitatively evaluate the efficiency of our approach. Considering that the literature already reports that PLASMA and its SMC algorithms outperform other existing approaches (c.f. [4,11,14]), we are hereby interested in assessing how efficient is our approach and toolchain to verify properties in dynamic software architectures. In the experiments, we have chosen computational effort in terms of execution time and RAM consumption as metrics, which were used to observe the performance of our toolchain when varying the precision of the verification. As PLASMA is executed upon a Java Virtual Machine, 20 runs were performed for each precision value in order to ensure a proper statistical significance for the results. The experiments were conducted under GNU/Linux on a computer with a quad-core 3 GHz processor and 16 GB of RAM. Time and RAM consumption measures were obtained by using the *time* utility from Linux.

The toolchain was evaluated with the FalsePositive, SensorAvailable, and RemoveSensor properties described in Sect. 6.2. These properties were evaluated using the Chernoff algorithm [9] from PLASMA, which requires a precision and a confidence degree as parameters and returns an approximation of the probability with an error below the precision parameter, with the given confidence.

A confidence of 95 % was chosen and the precision has ranged on 0.02, 0.03, 0.04, 0.05, and 0.1, respectively requiring 4612, 2050, 1153, 738, and 185 simulations.

Figure 7(a) how the average analysis time (in seconds) increases when the precision increases, i.e., the error decreases. As highlighted in Sect. 2, a higher accuracy of the answer provided by the statistical model checker requires generating more execution traces through simulations, thereby increasing the analysis time. The property regarding the sensor availability evaluated over a window of 50 time units requires less time than the other properties evaluated over a window of 100 time units because the analysis of each trace is faster. In Fig. 7(b), it is possible to observe that the increase of the average amount of RAM (in megabytes) required to perform the analyses is nearly constant, thus meaning that the precision has no strong influence on the RAM consumption. This can be explained by the fact that SMC only analyzes one trace at a time. Therefore, we can conclude that our SMC approach and toolchain can be regarded as efficient with respect to both execution time and RAM consumption.

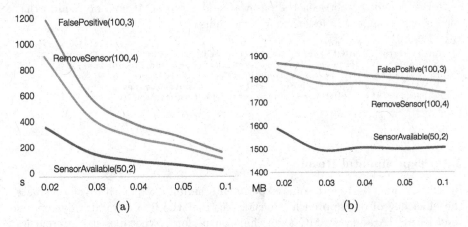

Fig. 7. Effects of the variation in the precision in the analysis of three properties upon analysis time (a) and RAM consumption (b).

We rely on the Chernoff bound to compute the number of required simulations, which increases quadratically with respect to the precision. In case of rare events, i.e., properties that have a very low probability to happen, a better convergence can be obtained by using dedicated methods [11]. Regarding size, our current model contains about 30 processes in total.

7   Conclusion

In this paper, we have presented our approach on the use of statistical model checking (SMC) to verify properties in dynamic software architectures. Our main contribution is an SMC-based toolchain for specifying and verifying such properties atop the PLASMA platform. The inputs for this process are a probabilistic version of an architecture description in the π-ADL language and a set of properties expressed in DynBLTL. We have used a real-world flood monitoring system to show how to specify properties in a dynamic software architectures, as well as it was used in some computational experiments aimed to demonstrate that our approach and toolchain are efficient and hence feasible to be applied on the verification task. To the best of our knowledge, this is the first work on the application of SMC to verify properties in dynamic software architectures.

As future work, we need to assess the expressiveness and usability of DynBLTL for expressing properties in dynamic software architectures. We also intend to integrate our approach into a framework aimed to support software architects in activities such as architectural representation and formal verification of architectural properties.

Acknowledgments. This work was partially supported by the Brazilian National Agency of Petroleum, Natural Gas and Biofuels through the PRH-22/ANP/MCTI Program (for Everton Cavalcante) and by CNPq under grant 308725/2013-1 (for Thais Batista).

References

1. The Go programming language. https://golang.org/
2. PLASMA-Lab. https://project.inria.fr/plasma-lab/
3. Arnold, A., Boyer, B., Legay, A.: Contracts and behavioral patterns for SoS: the EU IP DANSE approach. In: Larsen, K.G., Legay, A., Nyman, U. (eds.) Proceedings of the 1st Workshop on Advances in Systems of Systems, EPTCS, vol. 133, pp. 47–60 (2013)
4. Boyer, B., Corre, K., Legay, A., Sedwards, S.: PLASMA-lab: a flexible, distributable statistical model checking library. In: Joshi, K., Siegle, M., Stoelinga, M., D'Argenio, P.R. (eds.) QEST 2013. LNCS, vol. 8054, pp. 160–164. Springer, Heidelberg (2013). doi:10.1007/978-3-642-40196-1_12
5. Cavalcante, E., Batista, T., Oquendo, F.: Supporting dynamic software architectures: from architectural description to implementation. In: Proceedings of the 12th Working IEEE/IFIP Conference on Software Architecture, pp. 31–40. IEEE Computer Society, USA (2015)
6. Cavalcante, E., Oquendo, F., Batista, T.: Architecture-based code generation: from π-ADL descriptions to implementations in the Go language. In: Avgeriou, P., Zdun, U. (eds.) ECSA 2014. LNCS, vol. 8627, pp. 130–145. Springer, Switzerland (2014). doi:10.1007/978-3-319-09970-5_13
7. Cho, S.M., Kim, H.H., Cha, S.D., Bae, D.H.: Specification and validation of dynamic systems using temporal logic. IEE Proc. Softw. **148**(4), 135–140 (2001)
8. Clarke, E.M., Grumberg, O., Peled, D.A.: Model Checking. The MIT Press, Cambridge (1999)
9. Hérault, T., Lassaigne, R., Magniette, F., Peyronnet, S.: Approximate probabilistic model checking. In: Steffen, B., Levi, G. (eds.) VMCAI 2004. LNCS, vol. 2937, pp. 73–84. Springer, Heidelberg (2004). doi:10.1007/978-3-540-24622-0_8
10. Holzmann, G.J.: The logic of bugs. In: 10th ACM SIGSOFT Symposium on Foundations of Software Engineering, pp. 81–87. ACM, New York (2002)

11. Jegourel, C., Legay, A., Sedwards, S.: A platform for high performance statistical model checking - PLASMA. In: Flanagan, C., König, B. (eds.) TACAS 2012. LNCS, vol. 7214, pp. 498–503. Springer, Heidelberg (2012). doi:10.1007/978-3-642-28756-5_37

12. Kim, Y., Choi, O., Kim, M., Baik, J., Kim, T.H.: Validating software reliability early through statistical model checking. IEEE Softw. **30**(3), 35–41 (2013)

13. Legay, A., Delahaye, B., Bensalem, S.: Statistical model checking: an overview. In: Barringer, H., et al. (eds.) RV 2010. LNCS, vol. 6418, pp. 122–135. Springer, Heidelberg (2010). doi:10.1007/978-3-642-16612-9_11

14. Legay, A., Sedwards, S.: On statistical model checking with PLASMA. In: Proceedings of the 2014 Theoretical Aspects of Software Engineering Conference, pp. 139–145. IEEE Computer Society, Washington, DC (2014)

15. Mateescu, R., Oquendo, F.: π-AAL: an architecture analysis language for formally specifying and verifying structural and behavioural properties of software architectures. ACM SIGSOFT Softw. Eng. Notes **31**(2), 1–19 (2006)

16. Oquendo, F.: π-ADL: an architecture description language based on the higher-order typed π-calculus for specifying dynamic and mobile software architectures. ACM SIGSOFT Softw. Eng. Notes **29**(3), 1–14 (2004)

17. Pnueli, A.: The temporal logics of programs. In: Proceedings of the 18th Annual Symposium on Foundations of Computer Science, pp. 46–57. IEEE Computer Society, Washington, DC (1977)

18. Quilbeuf, J., Cavalcante, E., Traonouez, L.M., Oquendo, F., Batista, T., Legay, A.: A logic for statistical model checking of dynamic software architectures. In: Margaria, T., Steffen, B. (eds.) ISoLA 2016. LNCS, vol. 9952, pp. 806–820. Springer, Heidelberg (2016). doi:10.1007/978-3-319-47166-2_56

19. Zhang, P., Muccini, H., Li, B.: A classification and comparison of model checking software architecture techniques. J. Syst. Softw. **83**(5), 723–744 (2010)

Consistent Inconsistency Management:
A Concern-Driven Approach

Jasper Schenkhuizen[1], Jan Martijn E.M. van der Werf[1(✉)], Slinger Jansen[1],
and Lambert Caljouw[2]

[1] Department of Information and Computing Science,
Utrecht University, P.O. Box 80.089, 3508 TB Utrecht, The Netherlands
{j.schenkhuizen,j.m.e.m.vanderwerf,slinger.jansen}@uu.nl
[2] Unit4, Papendorpseweg 100, 3528 BJ Utrecht, The Netherlands
lcaljouw@unit4.com

Abstract. During the development of a software system, architects deal with a large number of stakeholders, each with differing concerns. This inevitably leads to inconsistency: goals, concerns, design decisions, and models are interrelated and overlapping. Existing approaches to support inconsistency management are limited in their applicability and usefulness in day to day practice due to the presence of incomplete, informal and heterogeneous models in software architecture. This paper presents a novel process in the form of a lightweight generic method, the Concern-Driven Inconsistency Management (CDIM) method, that is designed to address limitations of different related approaches. It aims to aid architects with management of intangible inconsistency in software architecture.

1 Introduction

Inconsistency is prevalent in software development and software architecture (SA) [7]. Although inconsistency in software architecture is not necessarily a bad thing [18], undiscovered inconsistency leads to all kinds of problems [17,20]. Inconsistency is present if two or more statements made about a system or its architecture are not jointly satisfiable [9], mutually incompatible, or conflicting [3]. Examples of inconsistency are: failure of a syntactic equivalence test, non-conformance to a standard or constraint [9], or two developers implementing a non-relational and a relational database technology for the same database, to name a few.

In SA, inconsistency has a wide range of dimensions, such as inconsistency in code, inconsistent requirements, or model inconsistency. We refer to these types of inconsistency as 'tangible' inconsistency. On the contrary, an 'intangible' inconsistency is often denominated as a *conflict*, still being undocumented or unspecified: inconsistent design decisions or concerns. In architecture, a conflict between concerns occurs if their associated design decisions are mutually incompatible, or negatively affect each other. That is, a conflict (intangible inconsistency) can potentially manifest itself as a tangible inconsistency. Thus, if design

B. Tekinerdogan et al. (Eds.): ECSA 2016, LNCS 9839, pp. 201–209, 2016.
DOI: 10.1007/978-3-319-48992-6_15

decisions are *conflicting* (intangible inconsistency), they are mutually incompatible [3], and càn lead to tangible inconsistency. This corresponds with the view to see architectural design decisions as first-class entities [14]. Adopting the definition that a software system's architecture is the set of principal design decisions about the system [3], we see that inconsistency in SA – even though it may be intangible (undocumented) at early stages – already emerges if design decisions are inconsistent or contradictory. At early stages in the architecting process, architects deal with coarse-grained models and high-level design decisions, which are usually recorded and documented using more informal notations [3]. As a result, related formal and model-checking approaches for inconsistency management (IM) are less applicable.

Traditional approaches are based on logic or model-checking. The former uses formal inference techniques to detect model inconsistency, which makes them difficult to scale. The latter disposes model-verification algorithms that are sufficiently suited to detect specific inconsistencies, but do not fit well to other kinds of inconsistency [2]. Currently, no appropriate infrastructure is available that is capable of managing a broad class of inconsistency [9].

To address the limitations of related approaches and to support the architect in the difficult process of IM, this paper proposes a simple, lightweight method, enabling the architect to systematically manage inconsistency: the Concern-Driven Inconsistency Management (CDIM) method. CDIM identifies important concerns of different stakeholders, as these are a source of inconsistency [19], and utilizes a matrix to discuss overlapping concerns to find and manage diverse types of inconsistency. CDIM consists of a 7-step cyclic process, based on the Plan Do Check Act (PDCA) cycle [11], work of Nuseibeh [20], Spanoudakis [24], and related architecture evaluation methods. The reader is referred to [23] for a detailed overview of the construction of the CDIM and its design decisions.

The remainder of this paper is structured as follows: Sect. 2 provides a short overview of inconsistency management in practice. The CDIM method is briefly demonstrated in Sect. 3, followed by a conclusion and directions for future work in Sect. 4.

2   Inconsistency Management in SA

An important task of the software architect is inconsistency management (IM): identifying inconsistency, preserving it when acceptable, and deferring or solving it when required [5,20]. Spanoudakis and Zisman [24] propose a framework for IM, based upon [6] and [20], consisting of six activities: (1) *detection of overlaps*, (2) *detection of inconsistencies*, (3) *diagnosis of inconsistencies*, (4) *handling of inconsistencies*, (5) *tracking of findings*, and (6) *specification of an IM policy*. A critical component in IM is identifying overlap, as it is a precondition for inconsistency [6]. Concerns have overlap when associated design decisions influence each other. Overlap emerges due to different views, assumptions, and concerns all being interrelated because they are related to the same system [17]. The presence of such interrelations introduces the potential for inconsistency [24]. Techniques that focus on *detection of overlaps* do this based on for example representation conventions, shared ontologies, or similarity analysis [24]. Techniques for *detection of inconsistencies* are logic-based approaches, model-checking approaches, specialized model analyses, and human-centered collaborative approaches [24]. *Inconsistency diagnosis* is concerned with the identification of the source, cause and impact of an inconsistency [24]. *Handling inconsistency* is concerned with the identification and execution of the possible actions for dealing with an inconsistency. *Tracking* refers to recording important information of the inconsistency in a certain knowledge base [24].

Applicable approaches in the context of informal models are stakeholder-centric methods for inconsistency management. These involve human inspection of overlap, and human-based collaborative exploration [24] (e.g. Synoptic [4] or DealScribe [21]). These techniques assume that detection of inconsistency is the result of a collaborative inspection of several models by stakeholders [24]. Approaches like Synoptic [4] and DealScribe [21] solely focus on model inconsistency, and therefore, cannot be used for other types of inconsistency, such as inconsistent design decisions. Synoptic requires stakeholders to specify conflicts in so-called 'conflict forms' to describe conflicts that exist in models. In DealScribe, stakeholders look for 'root-requirements' in their models. Root requirements are identified for concepts present in the models, and pairwise analysis of possible interactions between root requirements results in a list of conflicting requirements. A limitation of this approach is that pairwise sequential comparison is time-consuming and labour-intensive.

Inconsistency arises inevitably due to the fact that SA is concerned with heterogeneous, multi-actor, multi-view and multi-model activities [19]. Consequently, this heterogeneity and the diverse context of software architecture causes IM to be inherently difficult [20]. In addition, a lot of architectural knowledge is contained in the heads of involved architects and developers [13]. Though IM is needed, the possibilities for managing inconsistency in software architecture are limited [17], and architects thus benefit from methods that aid in management of inconsistency.

3 Concern-Driven Inconsistency Management

As a means to address several limitations of related approaches this paper presents the CDIM method, to systematically identify and keep track of intangible inconsistency, based on concerns and perspectives. CDIM is developed using the Method Association Approach (MAA) [16] together with input from experts through semi-structured interviews. MAA takes existing methods into account to methodically assemble a new method for use in new situations [16]. IM is a part of the process of verification and validation [9]. Verification and validation of an architecture is done with the use of architectural evaluation methods (AE) methods, which is why several AE methods are used as a basis for CDIM. Many different AE methods have been developed over the past decade, and many of them have proved to be mature [1]. Due to space limitations, we refer the reader to e.g. [1] for

Phase:	Activity:	Roles:
Plan	**Initiate:** set goal, discuss situational factors, determine scope, prepare and involve stakeholders, decide on definitions	SA
Plan	**Construct:** choose perspectives, gather, define and prioritize, specify concerns, select concerns, populate matrix	SA
Do	**Identify:** workshop: identify overlaps, identify and discuss possible conflicts	SA + involved stakeholders
Do	**Discover:** use the results of previous activities to discover inconsistency in the architecture	SA
Check	**Diagnose:** diagnose inconsistency type and cause, classify inconsistency	SA + involved stakeholders
Act	**Execute:** define action plan, execute actions	SA
Act	**Follow up:** monitor impact, add results to knowledge base, follow up, plan	SA

SA = software architect

Fig. 1. This figure describes the 4 phases of the CDIM, with the 7 corresponding activities. The activities are performed in cyclic manner. Each of the activities consists of different sub steps.

a discussion on and comparison of various AE methods, and to [23] for a technical report documenting the design and development of the CDIM method.

The method is based on the inconsistency management process as introduced by Spanoudakis [24] and Nuseibeh [20], combining several AE methods and IM techniques with the traditional iterative phases *Plan, Do, Check,* and *Act* (PCDA) cycle [11]. Figure 1 depicts these 4 phases. They are divided in 7 activities: each of the activities contains multiple steps. Concerns form the drivers of the CDIM. The following section motivates the use of concerns as central elements, and the subsequent section briefly describes the four phases of the CDIM.

3.1 Concerns and Concern-Cards

It is cost-effective to discover inconsistency early in the process [9]. One of the first elements that an architect needs to consider, are *concerns* [10]. Furthermore, concerns are the driving force of building an architecture and designing the system [14]. Concerns express the aspects that should be relevant to a software system in the eyes of a software architect [14]. According to [22] *a concern about an architecture is a requirement, an objective, an intention, or an aspiration a stakeholder has for that architecture"*. Software architects benefit from inconsistency discovery and management at an early stage, as principal decisions are often hard to reverse. Conflicts in these decisions can lead to tangible inconsistency, which emphasizes the value of focusing on concerns and design decisions.

The use of templates to capture information makes methods more consistent across evaluators [12]. To ease IM, we propose the use of concern-cards, a template that enables reasoning about a concern. Such a template makes methods more consistent across evaluators [12]. Additionally, the use of cards in software development is not unusual (such as planning poker [8] used by many SCRUM teams [15]). Concern-cards are collected and kept in a concern-card desk. A concern card consists of:

1. a unique identifier,
2. a short, concise name,
3. a comprehensive definition and explanation of the concern,
4. the concern's priority,
5. related stakeholders that have an interest in the concern,
6. the perspective or category to which the concern belongs, and
7. possible associated architectural requirements, which can be used during discussion.

During the execution of the CDIM, concern-cards are used to assist the architect in collecting and understanding the different concerns, by making these explicit.

3.2   Plan Phase

The Plan phase consists of two activities *initiate* and *construct*. During *initiate* the architect develops an action plan containing the goal of the CDIM cycle, the scope of the architecture under analysis, the organization's situational factors, and which stakeholders are needed during the CDIM cycle. During *construct*, the architect selects perspectives and collects concerns from stakeholders. A perspective enables the architect to categorize the concerns gathered and to analyze the architecture from a certain angle. For each perspective, the architect collects important and relevant concerns, and documents these as concern cards. The Plan phase results in an action plan, a concern-card desk, and a prioritized matrix of concerns.

3.3   Do Phase

The Do phase consists of two activities: *identify* and *discover*. In *identify* the architect tries to identify possible conflicts through a workshop with the relevant stakeholders. Input of the workshop is the previously constructed matrix. The principal idea behind the cells of the matrix is that these provide the hotspots: areas in the architecture where concerns could possibly overlap or conflict. Multiple overlaps or conflicts may be contained in each cell, as visualized in Fig. 2. The "hotspots" are discussed by the architect and stakeholders. Their role is to aid the evaluator with deciding on how conflicts affect the architecture or possibly could affect the architecture, and which conflicts could be problematic. The outcome is a completed matrix, presenting the architect the important areas where inconsistencies may arise.

In *discover*, the architects go through the existing architecture to discover whether these are actual inconsistencies, possibly together with relevant stakeholders. The architect uses a combination of his expertise and knowledge of the system, to systematically search for important inconsistencies, using the conflicts identified in the matrix. Given the deliberate simplicity of CDIM, and the complexity of a software architecture context, the steps in this phase are inevitably one of judgment rather than quantifiable assessment. The drawback is that this approach is less explicit and more based on subjective factors as intuition and experience. The advantage is that this is easier and more flexible. The main outcome of this activity is a list of important inconsistencies in the architecture.

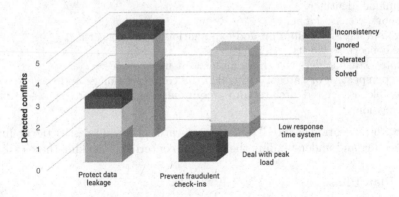

Fig. 2. A tool can be beneficial to the extent that the architect can use an overview of the amount of inconsistencies that are still open (red), that are carefully ignored (bright yellow), tolerated (cream yellow), or that have been solved (green) to indicate what needs to be done. (Color figure online)

3.4   Check Phase

Once the matrix is completed, and possible inconsistencies in the architecture have been discovered, the architect determines the type and cause of the inconsistency, and subsequently classifies the inconsistency. Classification is done on the basis of four aspects: *impact, business value, engineering effort,* and the individual *characteristics* of the inconsistency (such as the type and cause). *Impact* refers to an inconsistency's consequences, *business value* to whether the inconsistency is perceived as critical by the business, *engineering effort* addresses the effort of solving an inconsistency and the availability of design alternatives, and *characteristics* addresses factors related to the inconsistency itself such as the type or cause of the inconsistency. These factors are context-specific but should be considered as well [20]. The output is a *classification* in terms of these factors. Despite being still conceptual, results from the matrix could be visualized as presented in Fig. 2.

3.5   Act Phase

In the final phase of CDIM, the architect creates and executes handling actions for each inconsistency if needed (*execute*), and determines how to proceed (*follow up*). In *execute*, the architect handles discovered inconsistency based on five actions for settling inconsistencies: 'resolve', 'ignore', 'postpone', 'bypass', and 'improve'. It is important to note that handling an inconsistency is always context-specific and requires human insight. 'Resolving' the inconsistency is recommended if the impact is high, the business value is high, regardless of the engineering effort. Solving an inconsistency could be relatively simple (adding or deleting information from a description or view). However, in some cases resolving the inconsistency relies on making important design decisions (e.g. the introduction of a complete new database management technology) [6,20]. 'Ignoring' the inconsistency is recommended if the potential impact is low, the business value is low, and the engineering effort is high. 'Postponing' the decision is recommended when both impact and business value are relatively low, and engineering effort is relatively high. Postponing provides the architect with more time to elicit further information [20]. 'Bypassing' is a strategy in which the inconsistency is circumvented by adapting the architecture in such a way that the inconsistency itself still exists, but not touched upon. It is recommended when the current impact is low and the business value and engineering effort are relatively high, in which case continuity is important. 'Improving' on an inconsistency might be cost-effective in other situations, in which time pressure is high, and the risk is low. To improve on an inconsistency, inconsistent models can be annotated with explanations, in order to alleviate possible negative consequences of the inconsistent specification. The main outcome are the actions referring to how and when to settle the inconsistency, possibly with requests for change on the architecture, code or any other specifications that are important.

In *follow up*, the architect assesses the impact of the chosen actions, and adds gained knowledge to a knowledge base and determines how to proceed. The architect checks (a) whether a handling action intervenes with other actions; (b) whether a handling action affects existing concerns; and (c) whether a handling action results in new concerns. The architect decides whether a new cycle is needed, or iteration to previous steps is needed.

4   Conclusions and Future Work

Managing inconsistencies in software architecture consistently and systematically is a difficult task. This paper presents CDIM, an inconsistency management method that aims to support software architects in managing and detecting intangible inconsistencies and conflicts in software architecture. Through concern cards, the architect can discover and document relevant concerns. Using the CDIM matrix, overlapping and conflicting concerns, and thus (undocumented) inconsistent design decisions can be detected as well as it helps architects to search for inconsistency in informal models. The method still needs careful and thorough evaluation. Initial results show that the method is simple to use, and offers the desired flexibility in combination with fast, practical results. As the method yields design solutions and concrete suggestions for architectural design, we envision the use of CDIM as a tool for communication and documenting design rationale as well. As the proof of the pudding is in the eating, we plan to build tool support to aid the architect, and evaluate the method in large case studies.

References

1. Babar, M.A., Zhu, L., Jeffery, R.: A framework for classifying and comparing software architecture evaluation methods. In: 15th Australian Software Engineering Conference, pp. 309–319. IEEE Computer Society (2004)
2. Blanc, X., Mounier, I., Mougenot, A., Mens, T.: Detecting model inconsistency through operation-based model construction. In: 30th International Conference on Software Engineering, pp. 511–520. ACM (2008)
3. Dashofy, E.M., Taylor, R.N.: Supporting stakeholder-driven, multi-view software architecture modeling. Ph.D. thesis, University of California, Irvine (2007)
4. Easterbrook, S.: Handling conflict between domain descriptions with computer-supported negotiation. Knowl. Acquis. **3**(3), 255–289 (1991)
5. Finkelstein, A.: A foolish consistency: technical challenges in consistency management. In: Ibrahim, M., Küng, J., Revell, N. (eds.) DEXA 2000. LNCS, vol. 1873, pp. 1–5. Springer, Heidelberg (2000). doi:10.1007/3-540-44469-6_1
6. Finkelstein, A., Spanoudakis, G., Till, D.: Managing interference. In: 2nd International Software Architecture Workshop (ISAW-2) and International Workshop on Multiple Perspectives in Software Development, pp. 172–174 (1996)
7. Ghezzi, C., Nuseibeh, B.: Guest editorial: introduction to the special section - managing inconsistency in software development. IEEE Trans. Softw. Eng. **25**(6), 782–783 (1999)
8. Grenning, J.: Planning Poker or How to Avoid Analysis Paralysis While Release Planning, vol. 3. Renaissance Software Consulting, Hawthorn Woods (2002)
9. Herzig, S.J.I., Paredis, C.J.J.: A conceptual basis for inconsistency management in model-based systems engineering. Procedia CIRP **21**, 52–57 (2014)
10. Hilliard, R.: Lessons from the unity of architecting. In: Software Engineering in the Systems, Context, pp. 225–250 (2015)
11. Johnson, C.N.N.: The benefits of PDCA. Qual. Prog. **35**(3), 120 (2002)
12. Kazman, R., Bass, L., Klein, M.: The essential components of software architecture design and analysis. J. Syst. Softw. **79**(8), 1207–1216 (2006)
13. Kruchten, P., Lago, P., Vliet, H.: Building up and reasoning about architectural knowledge. In: Hofmeister, C., Crnkovic, I., Reussner, R. (eds.) QoSA 2006. LNCS, vol. 4214, pp. 43–58. Springer, Heidelberg (2006). doi:10.1007/11921998_8
14. Lago, P., Avgeriou, P., Hilliard, R.: Guest editors' introduction: software architecture: framing stakeholders' concerns. IEEE Softw. **27**(6), 20–24 (2010)
15. Lucassen, G., Dalpiaz, F., van der Werf, J.M.E.M., Brinkkemper, S.: The use and effectiveness of user stories in practice. In: Daneva, M., Pastor, O. (eds.) REFSQ 2016. LNCS, vol. 9619, pp. 205–222. Springer, Heidelberg (2016). doi:10.1007/978-3-319-30282-9_14
16. Luinenburg, L., Jansen, S., Souer, J., van de Weerd, I., Brinkkemper, S.: Designing web content management systems using the method association approach. In: 4th International Workshop on Model-Driven Web Engineering, pp. 106–120 (2008)
17. Muskens, J., Bril, R.J., Chaudron, M.R.V., Generalizing consistency checking between software views. In: 5th Working IEEE/IFIP Conference on Software Architecture, pp. 169–180. IEEE Computer Society (2005)
18. Nentwich, C., Capra, L., Emmerich, W., Finkelstein, A.: xlinkit: a consistency checking and smart link generation service. ACM Trans. Internet Technol. **2**(2), 151–185 (2002)
19. Nuseibeh, B.: To be, not to be: on managing inconsistency in software development. In: 8th International Workshop on Software Specification and Design, p. 164. IEEE Computer Society (1996)

20. Nuseibeh, B., Easterbrook, S.M., Russo, A.: Making inconsistency respectable in software development. J. Syst. Softw. **58**(2), 171–180 (2001)
21. Robinson, W.N., Pawlowski, S.D.: Managing requirements inconsistency with development goal monitors. IEEE Trans. Softw. Eng. **25**(6), 816–835 (1999)
22. Rozanski, N., Woods, E.: Software Systems Architecture: Working with Stakeholders Using Viewpoints and Perspectives. Addison-Wesley, Reading (2012)
23. Schenkhuizen, J.: Consistent inconsistency management: a concern-driven approach. Technical report, Utrecht University (2016). http://dspace.library.uu.nl/bitstream/handle/1874/334223/thesisv1_digitaal.pdf
24. Spanoudakis, G., Zisman, A.: Inconsistency management in software engineering: survey and open research issues. Handb. Softw. Eng. Knowl. Eng. **1**, 329–380 (2001)

Formal Verification of Software-Intensive Systems Architectures Described with Piping and Instrumentation Diagrams

Soraya Mesli-Kesraoui[1,2,4](✉), Djamal Kesraoui[1], Flavio Oquendo[2],
Alain Bignon[1], Armand Toguyeni[3], and Pascal Berruet[4]

[1] SEGULA Technologies, Lanester, France
{soraya.kesraoui,djamal.kesraoui,alain.bignon}@segula.fr
[2] IRISA - Université Bretagne-Sud, Vannes, France
flavio.oquendo@irisa.fr
[3] CRIStAL - Ecole Centrale de Lille, Villeneuve-d'Ascq, France
armand.toguyeni@ec-lille.fr
[4] Lab-STICC - Université Bretagne-Sud, Lorient, France
pascal.berruet@univ-ubs.fr

Abstract. Socio-technical systems are increasingly becoming software-intensive. The challenge now is to design the architecture of such software-intensive systems for guaranteeing not only its correctness, but also the correctness of its implementation. In social-technical systems, the architecture (including software and physical elements) is described in terms of Piping and Instrumentation Diagrams (P&ID). The design of these P&ID is still considered an art for which no rigorous design support exists. In order to detect and eliminate architectural design flaws, this paper proposes a formal-based automated approach for the verification of the essential architecture "total correctness" properties, i.e. compatibility, completeness, consistency, and correctness. This approach is based on the definition of an architectural style for P&ID design in Alloy. We use MDE to automatically generate Alloy models from a P&ID and check their compatibility with the style and its completeness, consistency, and correctness properties. Our approach is presented through an industrial case study: the system of storage and production of freshwater for a ship.

Keywords: System architectures · Software-intensive systems · Architectural style · Formal verification · Alloy · P&ID

1   Introduction

Socio-technical systems are complex software-intensive systems. The design of these systems involves designers from different technical fields. This diversity may lead to misinterpretation of the specifications by the designers, which lead to errors in the system architecture. A previous exploratory study showed that different designs of socio-technical systems are based on an abstract technical

B. Tekinerdogan et al. (Eds.): ECSA 2016, LNCS 9839, pp. 210–226, 2016.
DOI: 10.1007/978-3-319-48992-6_16

diagram describing the architecture of the system porting the system in its entire cycle of development [3]. Piping and Instrumentation Diagrams (P&IDs) are technical diagrams widely used in the process industry.

P&ID is a detailed graphic description of the architecture in terms of process flows showing all the pipes, the devices, and the instrumentation associated with a given system [16]. The P&ID is the standard diagram that maps all the components and connections of an industrial process. Each component is represented by a symbol defined in ANSI/ISA 5.1 [9]. These components are connected by physical connectors such as pipes and cables, or software links [3]. The exchanged data (instrumentation) between the physical system and the control programs are also represented in this diagram.

Currently, designers of socio-technical systems describe manually and informally the system architectures, which leads to several errors that are detected in the testing phases. Verification steps must be integrated into the design process in order to prevent errors and minimize costs. Despite the standardization efforts of P&ID by ANSI/ISA-5.1 [9], there is currently no formal definition of these diagrams enabling analysis. By verifying the P&ID already in the architectural phase, can significantly reduce costs and errors [17]. We propose in this paper a three-step formal approach to verify the "total correctness" in terms of completeness, consistency, compatibility, and correctness of P&ID. In the first step, we propose to formalize the P&ID as an architectural style with Alloy. This architectural style provides a common representation vocabulary and rules for architectures described in terms of P&ID [22]. In the second step, in order to verify the architectural models in P&ID, we generate from these diagrams (by using MDE) a formal model in Alloy. In the third step, we verify the compatibility of the generated models with the style defined in the first step, its completeness, consistency, and correctness using the Alloy Analyzer.

The remaining of this paper is organized as follows: in Sect. 2, we present the state of the art on the formal verification of P&ID, including modeling and analysis techniques applied to software architectures, and introduce the Alloy language. In Sect. 3, we present our approach for the formal verification of P&ID. We present our formalization of the P&ID architectural style with Alloy in Sect. 4. The automated generation of Alloy models from the P&ID is shown in Sect. 5. In Sect. 6, we illustrate our approach through an industrial case study. In the final section, we present our conclusion and perspectives for future research.

2   State of the Art

Few studies have focused on the formal verification of the P&ID. Yang [25] proposes a semi-automatic approach to build SMV models from plants CDEP and P&ID. These models are used to verify safety properties written in CTL by model checking (SMV). Krause et al. [15] propose a method to extract, from the P&ID, the data related to the safety and reliability of systems. These data are extracted in two graphs: Netgraph and a reliability graph. NetGraph represents all the information related to devices and connections (structure). The reliability graph includes information about the reliability of these components. These graphs are then used to analyze the reliability of the systems.

The studies cited above assume that the architectural structure is correct, before initiating the reliability and safety formal verification. Our work is placed upstream of these studies. We treat the formal verification of P&ID at a structural level, drawing on the literature regarding the formal modeling and verification of software architectures in the field of software engineering.

2.1 Software Architecture

A software architecture is generally specified as a **configuration** (topology) of a set of **components** and **connectors**. Components represent the computational or data storage units in the system. Connectors represent each element (e.g., function calls, communication protocol) allowing the interaction between components. Both components and connectors are characterized by a type, a set of interfaces for their communication, a semantics (behavior), a set of constraints, and non-functional properties [17]. The architecture can be described from several viewpoints: structural, behavioral, physical, etc. [20]. From the structural point of view, the architecture is described by the structural arrangement of the various components and connectors constituting the system in terms of a topology. From the behavioral point of view, the architecture is described by the behavior of connectors and components expressing how they interact, the actions that the system performs, and the relations between these actions [20]. The physical point of view captures the physical components and their interactions through the physical connectors.

Several formal or semi-formal languages, called ADLs (Architecture Description Languages), have been proposed to describe software architectures. Wright [2] for example, is an ADL based on the CSP process algebra. π-ADL [20] is based on the π-calculus and involves the description of mobile architectures. ACME [7] is core ADL supporting exchange of architecture descriptions. These languages are domain-independent. In complement of these ADLs, some others target specific domains, such as, EAST-ADL [5] for embedded automotive systems.

In this sense, ANSI/ISA-5.1 [9] for describing P&IDs is a domain specific ADL for socio-technical systems in the process industry. However, P&ID with ANSI/ISA lacks a formal definition, as EAST-ADL. For enabling the formal verification of the P&ID, we chose to use the Alloy language [10].

2.2 Alloy

Alloy is a formal declarative language based on relations and first-order logic [10]. The idea behind Alloy is to enable system modeling with an abstract model representing the important functionalities of the system (micro model).

Alloy logic is based on the concepts of atoms and relations. The atom represents all the basic elementary entities characterized by a type. The relation is a set of tuples linking atoms. These relations are combined with operators to form expressions. There are three types of Alloy operators: *set operators* such as union (+), difference (−), intersection (&), inclusion (*in*) and equality (=); *relational operators* such as product (->), joint (.), transposed (∼), transitive closure (∧) and reflexive transitive closure (∗); *logical operators* such as negation (!), conjunction (&&), disjunction (||), implication (→) and bi-implication (↔). Quantified constraints have the form: $Q\,x : e\,|\,F$, with F a constraint on the set x, e an expression on the elements of the type x and Q a quantifier that can take one of the values: **all** (each element in x), **some** (at least one element), **no** (no element), **lone** (at most one element) and **one** (exactly one element). For example, **all** $x : e\,|\,F$ is true if all elements in x satisfy F. Declarations, in Alloy, are in the form: *relation: expression*, with *expression* a constraint bounding the relation elements. For example, $r : An \rightarrow mB$ with $n, m \in \{$**set** (set of elements), **one**, **lone**, **some**$\}$ and A, B a sets of atoms. The relation r defines that each element of the set A is mapped to m elements of the set B, and that each element in the set B is mapped to n elements of the set A.

An Alloy model, organized in *modules*, consists of a set of signatures, constraints and command. A signature, declared by **sig**, introduces a set of atoms and defines the basic types, through a set of attributes and relations with other signatures. It matches the notion of class in object-oriented modeling in that it can be abstract and inherits other signatures [11]. Constraints, organized in facts (**fact**), predicates (**pred**), functions (**fun**), and assertions (**assert**) [11], restrict the space of model instances. The fact is a Boolean expression that each instance of the model must satisfy. A pred is a reusable constraint that returns Boolean values (true, false) when it is invoked. A fun is a reusable expression that can be invoked in the model. It may have parameters and returns Boolean or relational values. An assert is a theorem that has no arguments and that requires verification. Commands describe the purpose of the verification. The Alloy Analyzer [1] can be used as a simulator, with the **run** command, to obtain a solution (instance) that satisfies all the constraints, or as a checker, with the **check** command, for searching a counterexample that violates an assertion [11]. The model is transformed by the parser into Boolean expressions that can be verified by different SAT (kodkod, SAT4J ...). A scope is necessary to limit (bound) the search space.

The Alloy language has been used to specify architectural styles [14,24] and to model and verify model architectures [4,13]. The atoms and relations are used to model the design vocabulary (components and connectors). The constraints (fact, pred, fun, assert) are used to manage style invariants (rules) that describe the allowable configurations from its design vocabulary. In the next sections, we present our formal approach to verify the P&ID.

3 Proposed Approach

In our previous study, we defined a standard library for performing a P&ID for a fluid management system [3]. We used Microsoft Visio tool to capture the structure of different P&ID components and connectors. Figure 1 shows an extract of

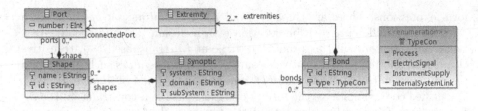

Fig. 1. An extract of P&ID metamodel [3]

the P&ID metamodel. The P&ID is an assembly of shapes and bonds. Each shape represents a component of the standard ANSI/ISA-5.1 [9]. It is characterized by a *name* and *id* that correspond respectively to the component type and component identifier. The shape contains a set of ports that represent its interaction points. The bonds types can be: process (Process, in the enumeration TypeCon), electrical (ElectricalSignal), instrument (InstrumentSupply), and software links (InternalSystemLink). The Bonds ensure the interaction between components and comprises at least two extremities and each extremity is connected to one port.

As the P&ID is an architectural diagram, it must be complete, consistent, compatible with an architectural style, and correct with the system requirements [22]. To this end, we propose a three-step approach to formally verify the P&ID. In the first step, we defined an architectural style in Alloy, based on ANSI/ISA-5.1 [9] standard, to describe the different constraints that the P&ID must satisfy. In the second step, we used the concepts of MDE to generate a configuration in Alloy from the P&ID. The Alloy analyzer was used, in the third step, to verify the completeness, consistency, compatibility of the P&ID to the style and its correctness with system requirements.

Two modules were used for checking the P&ID. The first module, called library, represents the architectural style and its invariants. The second module, automatically generated from a P&ID, describes a configuration of a fluid management system. We show bellow the P&ID architectural style formalization and the automatic transformation of P&ID into Alloy.

4   P&ID Architectural Style

To formally model the P&ID architectural style, we especially based on the work of Kim and Garlan [14] who used the Alloy language for modeling and analyzing the basic architectural styles. We adapted their basic formalization of component, connector, role, port, and configuration to our needs. Then, we extended the task by formalizing the specific components and connectors of the P&ID and its style invariants.

4.1 Component

We model the components by the `Component` and `Port` signatures (Listing 1). The component is an abstract signature (`abstract sig`) that contains a set of ports, described by the relation `ports: set Port`, and a set of actions. Actions, modeled by the relation `actions: Port set -> set Port`, represent the component's actions on the fluid through its ports, i.e. the routing of the fluid, in the component, from port A to port B. The constraint `actions.Port in ports` means that the join between the sets of `actions` and `Port` is included in the set of component ports. In other words, the component actions concern just its ports. The `Port` signature describes a port related to one and only one component, modeled by the relation `component: one Component`.

Listing 1

```
abstract sig Component {
ports: set Port,
actions: Port set -> set Port
}{this = ports.component
actions.Port in ports
actions[Port] in ports}


abstract sig Port {
component: one Component
}{this in component.ports}


abstract sig Process extends
Component{}


abstract sig Instrument
extends Component{}
```

```
abstract sig PP extends Port{}
abstract sig IP extends Port{}
abstract sig EP extends Port{}
abstract sig SP extends Port{}


abstract sig V3VM extends Process{
p1: lone PP, p2: lone PP,
p3: lone PP, p4: lone EP
}{p1 + p2 + p3 + p4 = ports
actions = (p1->p2) + (p2->p1) +
 (p1->p3) + (p3->p1)
lone ports & p1
lone ports & p2
lone ports & p3
lone ports & p4}
```

There are two types of components in ANSI/ISA-5.1 [9]: Process (`abstract sig Process`) and Instrument (`abstract sig Instrument`) that inherit the component signature (`extends Component`, Listing 1). Process components represent components that have a behavior involving a change of energy, state, or other properties in the system [9]. In the system of fluid management, these components (e.g., pumps, valve) have an action on the routing of fluid. On the other hand, instrument components (e.g., indicators, transmitters) are used directly or indirectly to measure and/or control a variable [9]. Each component has several types of ports describing the kind of its interactions. We model these types by the signatures: PP (Process Port), IP (Instrument Port), EP (Electrical Port) and SP (Software Port), which extend the port signature (Listing 1). For example, a component with a PP can interact with other `Process` components through this port.

The motorized three-way valve (V3VM) is a process component (`extends Process`) with 3 PP (p1, p2, p3) and an EP (p4) (Listing 1). The valve is used to route the fluid from p1 to p2 (p1->p2) and vice-versa (p2->p1). It also allows routing of the fluid from p1 to p3 and vice-versa. However, it does not route the fluid between p2 and p3. The constraint (`lone ports & p1`) means

that the valve contains at most one port of the type p1. In the same way, we
modeled 30 other components.

4.2   Connector

The connectors are described by two abstract signatures: Connector and Role
(Listing 2). A connector (abstract sig Connector) is a set of roles. Each role
(abstract sig Role) is related to a single connector. The relation connected:
one Port describes the fact that each role is connected to a single port. The
different connectors in the P&ID are: process link (PL, in Listing 2), instrument
link (IL), electrical link (EL), or software link (SL).

Listing 2

```
abstract sig Connector {
roles : set Role
}{this = roles.connector}

abstract sig PL extends Connector{}
```

```
abstract sig Role{
connector : one Connector,
connected : one Port
}{this in connector.roles}
```

4.3   Configuration

The configuration (Listing 3) is composed of a set of components (components:
set Component) and a set of connectors (connectors: set Connector). Hence,
it is an instance of all signatures that respect the style invariants described in
the next subsection.

Listing 3

```
abstract sig Configuration{
components : set Component,
connectors : set Connector
}{connectors.roles.connected in components.ports
 components.ports.~connected in connectors.roles}
```

4.4   Style Invariants

To model the style invariants, derived from the ANSI/ISA-5.1 [9] standard, we
use the expressions presented in Listing 4. The pred isTyped returns true if
an element e1 is e2 typed, else, it returns false. The pred Attached returns
true if a role r is attached to port p by the relation connected. Finally, the
pred isCompatible determines if a connector c is compatible with the attached
port p.

Different style invariants are modeled as a fact (each element of the Alloy
model must satisfy it) named StyleInvariants (Listing 4); these invariants
concern:

1. Compatibility Connector/Port: each connector extremities are attached to a port and are compatible with the attached ports. For example, a port of type EP should be attached with an EL (Electrical Link). This invariant is modeled in Listing 4, with the number (1).
2. Connected relation: it is Irreflexive, namely, the extremities of each connector should not be attached to ports of the same component (the component is not connected to itself), see Listing 4, number (2).
3. Component: each component must be connected. This invariant is codded in Alloy at Listing 4, number (3).
4. Double connection: it does not exist, namely, there are no two connectors between the same ports (Listing 4, number (4)).

Listing 4

```
pred isTyped[e1:univ,e2:univ]{e1 in e2}
pred Attached[r:Role,p:Port]{r->p in connected}
pred isCompatible[c:Connector, p:Port]{isTyped[c,PL]
 => isTyped[p,PP] else (isTyped[c,IL] => isTyped[p,IP]
 else (isTyped[c,EL] => isTyped[p,EP] else (isTyped[c,SL]
 => isTyped[p,SP])))}

fact StyleInvariants{
 (1) all r:Role|some p:Port|Attached[r,p] &&
  isCompatible[r.connector,p]
 (2) all disj r1, r2:Role | (r1.connector= r2.connector )
 => (r1.connected.component != r2.connected.component)
 (3) all c:Component|!(c.ports.~connected = none)
 (4) all disj c1,c2:Connector|
 no (c1.roles.connected & c2.roles.connected)}

pred show {#St>=1 #V2VM>=1 #Interface>=1}

run show for 8
```

4.5 Style Consistency

The style is said to be consistent if and only if there is no contradiction between the style invariants [2]. This means that there is one configuration that meets the style structure and its invariants [14]. To check the consistency of our architectural style, we simulate it with the Alloy Analyzer: if an instance (configuration) is found, the style is consistent. When we execute the command **run show for 8** (Listing 4), we obtain an instance shown in Fig. 2(a). The corresponding P&ID is illustrated in Fig. 2(b). This configuration satisfies all the style invariants, which means that the style is consistent.

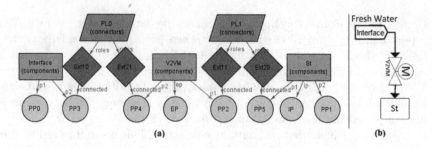

Fig. 2. Style consistency checking: (a) alloy instance; (b) corresponding diagram

5   Translation of P&ID into Alloy

Transformation models have been developed in ATL language of the Eclipse Modeling Project [12], to transform P&ID into an Alloy module. For this, we used the Alloy metamodel described in [6] and the P&ID metamodel of Fig. 1. The Alloy metamodel (module) is composed of one header, a set of imports, and a set of paragraphs. Paragraphs consist of signature, fact, pred, fun, assert, check, and run. In our case, the generated module (configuration) imports the library module where the style is modeled. The rest of the module consists of a set of sig, fact, run, and check paragraphs, representing the configuration. The set of rules used to transform P&ID into Alloy are described below.

SynopticToModule. The root of the diagram (the Synoptic node) is transformed into a module in Alloy. This module is composed of one signature named Eds (Listing 5), corresponding to the subsystem in the synoptic metamodel. This signature inherits from the Configuration signature (Listing 3). The field components, in the configuration, corresponds to the union of all the shapes transformed into signatures (Listing 5). The connectors field involves on the union of all connectors, derived from synoptic bonds.

ShapeToSignature. Each shape corresponds to a component which inherits from the signature defined in the style. The *name* in the shape defines the type of the component. The *id* attribute is used for naming the signature. The predefined ports in each component (example p1, p2, p3, p4 in V3VM) are assigned to the signature generated automatically from each port. In Listing 5, we show an instance of the V3VM component. This instance named V3VM1 inherits from V3VM and the V3VM1_P1, generated from a port, corresponds to the port p1.

PortToSignature. Each port, in the synoptic model, is transformed into a signature that inherits from the corresponding port type. In Listing 5, we can see that the V3VM1_P1 inherits from the signature PP because it is a process. The disconnected ports (such as p4 in V3VM1) are not generated.

BondToSignature. Each bond is transformed into a signature that inherits from the corresponding connector types. For example, the *Process* bond in Fig. 1 is transformed into the signature inheriting from the signature PL (Listing 2). The roles field in the signature corresponds to the union of its extremities, transformed into the `Role`. For example, in Listing 5, the process link connector `PL_3` is composed of the roles: `PL_3_1` and `PL_3_2`.

ExtremityToSignature. Each extremity is transformed into a role (`exten-ds Role`). It is composed of two fields: `connector` and `connected` (Listing 5). The `connector` field defines the containing connector. The `connected` field determines the port to which the role is connected. In Listing 5, for example, the role `PL_3_1` is connected to the port `p1` of the component `V3VM1`.

Listing 5

```
one sig EdS extends Configuration{}
{components = V3VM1 +...
connectors = PL_3 +... }


one sig PL_3 extends PL{}{
PL_3_1 + PL_3_2 = roles}


one sig V3VM1_P1 extends PP{}{
component = V3VM1}
```

```
one sig V3VM1 extends V3VM{}
{p1 = V3VM1_P1
p2 = V3VM1_P2
p3 = V3VM1_P3}


one sig PL_3_1 extends Role{}
{connector = PL_3
connected = V3VM1.p1}
```

6   Case Study

Our work is in the maritime field. Specifically, we examine the system of production, storage, and distribution of fresh water called EdS (standing for *Eau douce Sanitaire* in French, or sanitary freshwater in English). An extract of the P&ID of this system is illustrated in Fig. 3. This diagram must meet the architectural style defined above and several requirements that come from the specifications, standards, business rules, etc. We followed the protocol described by Wohlin et al. [23] for performing an exploratory study of the case study to extract the requirements that this system must meet.

6.1   Requirements Elicitation

In order to retrieve and categorize the different requirements, we combined several data extraction methods (independents and directs). First, we recovered the project technical documentation (e.g., specifications, guidelines, patterns). After analyzing the documentation, we realized that the system must also meet the standards defined in the specifications. We recovered these standards to extract and expand the set of requirements. Then we noticed that the designers applied business rules in the design of the P&ID. To capture the designers' knowledge, we developed semi-structured interviews (direct methods) with five experts (engineers) who all had a significant experience (on average ten years) in the design of the P&ID.

The interviews questions were written and then validated by a specialist. The interviews, lasting between 1h30 and 1h45, were recorded in audio form and then transcribed for data extraction. A Ph.D. student performed the data extraction,

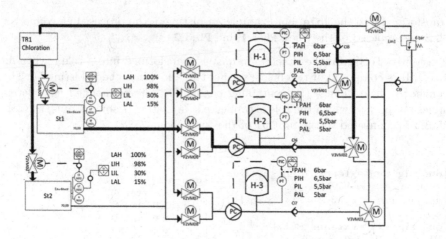

Fig. 3. An extract of P&ID of EdS system

and each step was validated by three professors and two industry experts. We used an Excel document to identify and categorize requirements.

The information collected by the methods listed above is qualitative. The different requirements are categorized and classified in the following sections.

6.2   Requirements Definition

According to INCOSE [8], the system requirements are: functional, non-functional, architectural constraints, and performance. Functional requirements are the constraints related to the functions of the system. They represent *what the system should do*. The non-functional requirements, called "ilities", consist of constraints describing the operational quality that the system must address [8]. Architectural constraints are all constraints related to the architecture or design. Performance requirement is a quantitative measure characterizing the system functionality. In this study, we consider just the functional, non-functional, and architectural constraints requirements.

Architectural Constraints. They include the related standards, physical requirements, constraints of cost, programming language, and time. For example, in our case, these requirements involve the compatibility of the P&ID with the architectural style, and the presence of some instruments on specific components according to different standards.

Functional Requirements. The EdS system must ensure seven functions: transfer, treatment, embedded distribution, distribution from quay, production, loading, and unloading.

The transfer function, for example, must ensure the transfer of a volume V of water from a tank A to another tank B, necessary passing by through one of the pumps (H1, H2, H3). This functional requirement is shown in the P&ID (Fig. 3) by a path (in bold) between the tank St1 and the tank St2 through the pump H2. To achieve this, the designer sequenced the following components: the tank St1, the pump H2, the chlorination unit TR1 used to treat water by chlorine, and finally the tank St2. These components are isolated by motorized two-way valves (V2VM02, V2VM05) and a motorized three-way valve (V3VM02) to facilitate routing and maintenance. Check valves return (Cl6, Cl8) are also used to prevent the fluid to circulate in opposite way of the flow.

To check that this diagram ensures the different functions, we used the funs and preds in Listing 6. The function `ComponentConnected` returns the tuples of components that communicate through the same connector. The `pred` `ExistPath` returns true if a component destination `dest` can be reached from a source `sc` component, passing by `pas` components. The `pred` `isTransfer` determines if a path exists from a tank (St) source to a tank destination, passing by the pump (HP).

Listing 6

```
fun ComponentConnected : Component−>Component{
  {s1 ,s2 :  Component |( disj [s1 ,s2] && not ((s1.ports).(s1.actions).
  ~(connected).RoleConnected.(connected).(s2.actions) = none)}}

fun RoleConnected : Role−>Role{
  {disj r1 ,r2 :  Role | connector[r1] = connector[r2]}}

pred ExistPath [sc :Component ,pas :set Component ,dest :Component]{
  (pas in sc.~(ComponentConnected)) &&
  (dest in pas.~(ComponentConnected))}

pred isTransfer [sc :Component ,pas :set Component ,dest :Component]{
  ExistPath [sc , pas , dest] && (sc in St) &&
  (dest in St) && (pas in HP)}
```

Non-functional Requirements. We present below examples of these requirements as applied to the EdS system. They represent the qualities of the offered functions such as:

- Overall efficiency: for example, the flow in the pipe should not exceed 6 bars or the production of $30\,\mathrm{m}^3$ of freshwater.
- Dependability: these requirements determine the necessary material redundancies (3 pumps) and the operating time of components.
- Maintainability: each component must be preceded and followed by an isolating element (a valve) to facilitate maintenance.
- Safety: these requirements include the presence of the check valves to prevent the traffic flow in opposite directions (leading to a collision of flows). It must never be a check valve upstream of a pump.

– Usability: as the presence of instruments to manage alarms in the machine
rooms of industrial monitoring interfaces.
– Scalability: ease of expansion by other components.

In Listing 7, we modeled the invariants of maintainability (pred Isolated-
Component). Each of the type TR or St or HP (TR + St + HP) must be preceded
(IsolatedComponentDown) and followed (IsolatedComponentUp) by a valve
(V2VM + V3VM).

Listing 7

```
pred IsolatedComponent {
  let valves = V2VM+V3VM | all s:TR+St+HP |
  some (IsolatedComponentUp[s] & valves) &&
  some (IsolatedComponentDown[s] & valves)}

fun IsolatedComponentDown [s:Component]: Component{
{c: V2VM+V3VM| some cl:Cl | c in s.ComponentConnected ||
((cl in s.ComponentConnected) && (c in cl.ComponentConnected))}}

fun IsolatedComponentUp [s: Component]: Component{
{c: V2VM+V3VM | some cl:Cl | s in c.ComponentConnected ||
((s in cl.ComponentConnected) && (cl in c.ComponentConnected))}}
```

6.3   Completeness, Consistency, Compatibility, Correctness

There are four goals to an architectural analysis, namely completeness, consistency, compatibility, and correctness [22]. Completeness means that there is
sufficient information to pretend to an analysis [2], i.e. that the system always
knows what to do. Consistency ensures that there are no contradictions between
model elements. Compatibility ensures that the architecture model conforms to
the architectural style and its invariants. Finally, correctness ensures that the
architecture model meets the system specifications.

Completeness. Completeness in the EdS system entails naming of the different elements, i.e. components and connectors must be named. This property is
verified automatically by the Alloy Editor. When the name of the generated signature is null, the Alloy Editor detects it as a syntactic error. Another external
completeness property in the P&ID is the instrumentation. The absence of this
information does not affect the architecture model. However, this information
is required during refinement (e.g. the automatic generation of the supervision
interface from the P&ID). This requirement is not verified in this study.

Consistency. Consistency dimensions include names, interface, behavior, interaction, and refinement [22]. In this paper, we deal with just the name and interface consistency. The name consistency means that the names of components and

connectors must be unique to avoid confusion. This property is verified automatically by the Alloy Editor as a syntactic error. The interface consistency involves the Connector/Port consistency, which means that the connector type must be consistent with the port type to which it is connected. This property is among the invariants of style (invariant 1, Listing 4). If the diagram is compatible with the style, then it meets this property.

Compatibility. The EdS P&ID (Fig. 3) must be compatible with the style defined in Sect. 4. To check the P&ID compatibility, we used the Alloy Analyzer as simulator. If the simulator finds a solution for the generated model including the library module (style formalization), this means there is diagram compatibility.

Correctness. The EdS system (Fig. 3) must meet its functional and non-functional properties. We modeled these requirements as assertion (Listing 8) and we checked the existence of a counterexample by the command `check Correctness_Analysis for 1`. The assertion (`Correctness_Analysis`) checks that each component is isolated (`IsolatedComponent`) by the valves and that the diagram ensures a transfer function (`isTransfer[St2,HP,St1]`) between tanks St1 and St2.

Listing 8

```
assert Correctness_Analysis {
  IsolatedComponent && isTransfer [St1,HP,St2]}

check Correctness_Analysis for 1
```

6.4 Formal Verification Analysis

The verification was performed on 2.7 GHz i5 CPU and 8 GB of memory. We executed the analysis using Alloy Analyzer version 4.2_20150222 with SAT4J as SAT Solver. The library module is composed of 46 signatures, 7 preds, 6 functions and 1 fact. The EdS module, corresponding to the case study of Fig. 3 and representing the half of a complex and large size auxiliary system in a ship [3], is composed of 176 signatures, 1 assertion and 1 check command. This number is due to the industrial nature of our case study (238 paragraphs in total). The results show that the P&ID of Fig. 3 is complete, consistent and compatible with the style. When we checked the correctness of the model, we executed Listing 8. The verification took 1.13 min and did not return a counterexample. This result means that the model meets its requirements.

6.5 Threats to Validity

To discuss threats to validity, we used the classification scheme proposed in [21].

Construct validity reflects the fact that the completed study must address the problems identified. In this study, this threat may concern the interpretation of the questions by subjects and researchers. To reduce this threat, we worked with the technical terminology experts who had participated in the interviews.

Internal validity concerns the examination of causal relations in studies [21]. This study is explorative, hence less susceptible to this type of threat. Another potential threat involves the small number of experts (five). To counter this threat, we used semi-structured interviews to extract the maximum of data and complemented them by archival data consisting of project documentation and standards.

External validity refers to the generalization of the study findings to other cases. We proposed an architectural style based on the ANSI/ISA-5.1 [9] standard. Hence, it can be used for all P&ID based on this standard. Another potential threat is that the interviews and the extraction data were performed by the same researchers. To reduce the risk of bias, the interview questions were reviewed and corrected by an independent expert. The data transcription and extraction were also reviewed by this independent expert.

Reliability addresses the possibility that other researchers can replicate the study. To facilitate this replication, we transcribed the interviews and placed the complete project documentation on the company network.

7   Conclusion

In this paper, we proposed three contributions for the formal verification of the physical architecture of an industrial process. This architecture is modeled by P&ID, which captures the physical components and connectors constituting the system. First, we proposed the formalization, with Alloy language, of an architectural style for the ANSI/ISA-5.1 [9] standard. Second, to facilitate the use of formal methods in industry, we presented the MDE-based approach to generate formal models, in Alloy, from the P&ID. The third contribution of this paper includes the formal verification of the generated models. We verified the compatibility of these models with the defined architectural style. We also checked their completeness, consistency, and correctness with regard to the system requirements. These contributions are illustrated through an industrial case study: a system of production, storage, and distribution of freshwater on a ship. For this case study, we carried out a survey with five experts to determine the requirements to check. Then, we analyzed the P&ID of the EdS system.

In the near future, we intend to display the counterexample, returned by the Alloy Analyzer, on the P&ID to facilitate the interpretation of errors by the engineers. In complement of the presented work, we formalized the behavior of the architectural elements [18,19] and we are now studying compositional frameworks for verifying system behavioral properties driven by the formalized architecture.

References

1. The alloy analyzer. http://alloy.mit.edu/
2. Allen, R.: A formal approach to software architecture. Ph.D. thesis, Carnegie Mellon, School of Computer Science (1997)
3. Bignon, A., Rossi, A., Berruet, P.: An integrated design flow for the joint generation of control and interfaces from a business model. Comput. Ind. **64**(6), 634–649 (2013)
4. Brunel, J., Rioux, L., Paul, S., Faucogney, A., Vallée, F.: Formal safety and security assessment of an avionic architecture with alloy. In: Proceedings 3rd International Workshop on Engineering Safety and Security Systems, ESSS 2014, pp. 8–19 (2014)
5. Debruyne, V., Simonot-Lion, F., Trinquet, Y.: EAST-ADL an architecture description language. In: Michel, P., Vernadat, F. (eds.) WADL 2005. IFIP, vol. 176, pp. 181–195. Springer, Boston (2005)
6. Garis, A., Paiva, A.C.R., Cunha, A., Riesco, D.: Specifying UML protocol state machines in alloy. In: Derrick, J., Gnesi, S., Latella, D., Treharne, H. (eds.) IFM 2012. LNCS, vol. 7321, pp. 312–326. Springer, Heidelberg (2012). doi:10.1007/978-3-642-30729-4_22
7. Garlan, D., Monroe, R., Wile, D.: ACME: an architecture description interchange language. In: CASCON First Decade High Impact Papers, pp. 159–173. IBM Corp. (2010)
8. Haskins, C.: INCOSE Systems Engineering Handbook v. 3.2. International Council on Systems Engineering, San Diego (2010)
9. ISA: 5.1 instrumentation symbols and identification (1992)
10. Jackson, D.: Alloy: a lightweight object modelling notation. ACM Trans. Softw. Eng. Methodol. (TOSEM) **11**(2), 256–290 (2002)
11. Jackson, D.: Software Abstractions: Logic, Language, and Analysis. MIT Press, Cambridge (2012)
12. Jouault, F., Allilaire, F., Bézivin, J., Kurtev, I., Valduriez, P.: ATL: a QVT-like transformation language. In: Companion to 21st ACM SIGPLAN Symposium on Object-oriented Programming Systems, Languages, and Applications, OOPSLA 2006, pp. 719–720. ACM (2006)
13. Khoury, J., Abdallah, C.T., Heileman, G.L.: Towards formalizing network architectural descriptions. In: Frappier, M., Glässer, U., Khurshid, S., Laleau, R., Reeves, S. (eds.) ABZ 2010. LNCS, vol. 5977, pp. 132–145. Springer, Heidelberg (2010). doi:10.1007/978-3-642-11811-1_11
14. Kim, J.S., Garlan, D.: Analyzing architectural styles. J. Syst. Softw. **83**(7), 1216–1235 (2010)
15. Krause, A., Obst, M., Urbas, L.: Extraction of safety relevant functions from CAE data for evaluating the reliability of communications systems. In: Proceedings of 2012 IEEE 17th International Conference on Emerging Technologies Factory Automation (ETFA 2012), pp. 1–7 (2012)
16. McAvinew, T., Mulley, R.: Control System Documentation: Applying Symbols and Identification. ISA-The Instrumentation, Systems, and Automation Society (2004)
17. Medvidovic, N., Taylor, R.N.: A classification and comparison framework for software architecture description languages. IEEE Trans. Softw. Eng. **26**(1), 70–93 (2000)
18. Mesli-Kesraoui, S., Bignon, A., Kesraoui, D., Toguyeni, A., Oquendo, F., Pascal, B.: Vérification formelle de chaînes de contrôle-commande d'éléments de conception standardisés. In: MOSIM 2016, 11ème Conférence Francophone de Modélisation, Optimisation et Simulation (2016)

19. Mesli-Kesraoui, S., Toguyeni, A., Bignon, A., Oquendo, F., Kesraoui, D., Berruet, P.: Formal and joint verification of control programs and supervision interfaces for socio-technical systems components. In: IFAC HMS, pp. 1–6 (2016)
20. Oquendo, F.: π-ADL: an architecture description language based on the higher-order typed π-calculus for specifying dynamic and mobile software architectures. ACM SIGSOFT Softw. Eng. Notes **29**, 1–14 (2004)
21. Runeson, P., Höst, M.: Guidelines for conducting and reporting case study research in software engineering. Empirical Softw. Eng. **14**(2), 131–164 (2009)
22. Taylor, R.N., Medvidovic, N., Dashofy, E.M.: Software Architecture: Foundations, Theory, and Practice. Wiley, Hoboken (2009)
23. Wohlin, C., Runeson, P., Höst, M., Ohlsson, M.C., Regnell, B., Wesslén, A.: Experimentation in Software Engineering. Springer Science & Business Media, Berlin (2012)
24. Wong, S., Sun, J., Warren, I., Sun, J.: A scalable approach to multi-style architectural modeling and verification. In: 13th IEEE International Conference on Engineering of Complex Computer Systems, ICECCS 2008, pp. 25–34 (2008)
25. Yang, S., Stursberg, O., Chung, P., Kowalewski, S.: Automatic safety analysis of computer-controlled plants. Comput. Chem. Eng. **25**(46), 913–922 (2001)

The Software Architect's Role and Concerns

Architects in Scrum: What Challenges Do They Face?

Samuil Angelov[1]([⊠]), Marcel Meesters[1], and Matthias Galster[2]

[1] Software Engineering, Fontys University of Applied Sciences, Eindhoven,
The Netherlands
{s.angelov,m.meesters}@fontys.nl
[2] Department of Computer Science and Software Engineering,
University of Canterbury, Christchurch, New Zealand
mgalster@ieee.org

Abstract. Context: Even though Scrum (the most popular agile software development approach) does not consider architecting an explicit activity, research and professional literature provide insights into how to approach architecting in agile development projects. However, challenges faced by architects in Scrum when performing tasks relevant to the architects' role are still unexplored. Objective: We aim at identifying challenges that architects face in Scrum and how they tackle them. Method: We conducted a case study involving interviews with architects from six Dutch companies. Results: Challenges faced by architects are mostly related to the autonomy of development teams and expected competences of Product Owners. Conclusions: The results presented in this paper help architects understand potential pitfalls that might occur in Scrum and what they can do to mitigate or to avoid them.

Keywords: Software architect · Architecture · Agile development · Scrum

1 Introduction

Agile software development has gained substantial popularity in recent years [1]. Even though software architecture is considered crucial for software project success [2], architecting activities and the role of software architects are not explicitly considered in agile development methods [3]. Numerous publications have discussed the role of the architecture in agile projects, and how software architecting could be approached in agile projects [4]. However, there is currently little attention on the *role* of architects. Few publications discuss the types of architects (e.g., generic types such as solution and implementation architects [5], enterprise/domain and application architects [6]), and their responsibilities and tasks in agile projects (e.g., [5, 7]).

In a development context where software architecting is not explicit, architects may face particular challenges. However, few publications discuss such challenges. Faber describes on a high level experiences from architecting and the role of architects in agile projects at a specific company [7]: Architects should actively guide (but not dominate) developers and be open to suggestions from the developers to deviate from originally proposed design solutions. Woods reports that "difficulties frequently arise

© Springer International Publishing AG 2016
B. Tekinerdogan et al. (Eds.): ECSA 2016, LNCS 9839, pp. 229–237, 2016.
DOI: 10.1007/978-3-319-48992-6_17

when agile development teams and software architects work together" and proposes general architecture practices (e.g., work in teams) that encourage collaborative architecture work in agile development [8], but does not describe challenges faced by architects. Martini et al. note that architecting in large agile projects is challenging and propose a number of architectural roles to improve architecting practices [9].

In this paper, we identify challenges that architects face in Scrum when they perform their tasks and how they address these challenges. Our study provides insights for architects on how to improve their work in agile projects (e.g., by focusing their attention on particular pitfalls) and will better prepare less experienced (or novice) architects for challenges in agile projects. We focus on Scrum projects as Scrum is the most often used agile development framework [1].

2 Background

The main roles in Scrum are the Scrum Master (SM), the team (including testers and developers) and the Product Owner (PO). In Scrum, there is no explicit architect role [10] and an architecture may emerge during a project rather than being designed upfront. However, in many organizations that follow Scrum, architects create architecture designs and communicate their decisions to development teams [10]. The setup in which architects are involved in agile projects (and Scrum) can differ [11]:

- In a "Team architect" setup, the architect is part of the development team [12]. If there is no dedicated architecture expert, the role of the architect can be taken by the whole team [13].
- In an "External architect" setup, the architect is not part of the agile team. He/she might work with multiple agile teams and partner with other architects (for example, as a project architecting team or as a member of an architecture board) [7].
- In a "Two architects" setup, there is an external and an internal architect. Abrahamsson et al. define the types of architects as: architects who focus on big decision, facing requirements and acting as external coordinators, and architects who focus on internal team communications, mentoring, troubleshooting and code [3].

3 Research Method

As we want to study architecture-related challenges in Scrum in practice which cannot be studied in isolation from its context, we follow an "in the wild" approach and apply case study research [14]. Also, we have little control over all variables (e.g., people, organizational structures). The research process followed the guidelines described by Runeson and Hoest [14] and is outlined in the following.

Case Study Design: To empirically investigate challenges that architects face in Scrum projects, we defined the following research questions: **RQ1:** *What are challenges that architects face in Scrum projects?* **RQ2:** *How do architects handle the challenges related to their role in Scrum projects?* Our study is a multiple-case study with six cases. Our research is exploratory as we are looking into an unexplored phenomenon [15]. Our unit of analysis is the architecting process in Scrum projects. Our sampling method is quota sampling (because we included two cases for each of the three setups described in Sect. 2) augmented with convenience sampling (because we selected cases based on their accessibility) [16]. We selected representative projects from six organizations from the Netherlands with established software development practices.

Preparation for Data Collection: Data for each case was collected via semi-structured interviews on-site and follow-up phone calls and e-mails. To avoid terminology conflicts, we have selected interviewees based on their involvement in architecting activities instead of solely focusing on the job title of individuals. We asked questions about tasks which architects perform using tasks-descriptions in [17, 18] and questions based on the potential challenges that may occur in the setups as described in Sect. 2. For each task, we asked if it was performed, if challenges/problems were observed when performing it, and what was done to address the challenge. The interview guideline can be found online[1].

Analysis of Collected Data: The transcripts and the recordings were analysed and information was clustered using open coding [19]. After initial coding, we looked at groups of code phrases and merged them into concepts and related them to the research questions. Codes and concepts emerged during the analysis. Since our data is context sensitive, we performed iterative content analysis to make inferences from collected data in its context [20]. Data were analysed by all authors.

4 Study Results

In Table 1, we provide an overview of the six cases. Next, we introduce the cases and present the main challenges that we identified and their resolutions.

Table 1. Overview of the cases studied

Case	Domain	Company Size	Architect setup	Interviewees
Case 1	E-commerce solutions	Medium	Team architect	Lead developer
Case 2	Software solutions	Small	Team architect	Lead developer
Case 3	Navigation systems	Large	Two architects	Senior software architect, Software architect
Case 4	Appliances	Large	Two architects	Design Owner
Case 5	Finance	Large	External architect	Enterprise architect,
Case 6	Software consultancy	Large	External architect	Senior security architect

---

[1] https://sites.google.com/site/samuilangelov/InterviewQuestions.docx.

4.1   Cases

- **Case 1:** In the organization of case 1, there is no explicit architect role in the company and discussions and decisions about the architecture involve the whole Scrum team. The lead developer is the most senior technical person in the team and has the final say in an architectural decision.
- **Case 2:** In the organization of case 2, a project is usually done by one team. Each team has a lead developer who is responsible for the architecting activities but the whole team works on the architecture.
- **Case 3:** In the organization of case 3, a senior software architect and a software architect are involved in Scrum projects as external and internal to the Scrum team, respectively. Scrum teams can be distributed geographically.
- **Case 4:** In this case, an architecture team maintains a reference architecture which Scrum teams apply. The architecture team provides to the Scrum team the reference architecture and a prototype implementation at a start of a project. A system architect residing outside the team maintains a requirements specification documentation focusing on legal and regulatory aspects of the software. A team has a "design owner" who streamlines the architecting activities in the team.
- **Case 5:** In the organization of case 5, an enterprise architect residing outside the Scrum team elaborates a high-level architecture, explains it to the team leader (who fulfils the role of the SM and also is the most experienced software designer), and provides support during the project. The PO is also a product manager.
- **Case 6:** Case 6 is a consultancy company offering specialized architects to clients. Architects reside outside the Scrum teams.

4.2   Challenges Between Architect(S) and PO(S)

Challenge 1: _PO lacks architecting/technology competence_ (reported in cases 1, 2, 4, 5, 6): POs are business-oriented with little technical/architectural knowledge. They do not realize the importance of architecting and do not consider it in their activities. They cannot provide architectural information and engage in architecting discussions.

Resolution in case 1: Architectural decisions and activities are presented by the team to the PO in a simplified form. For gathering and providing architecting information, the team communicates directly with external stakeholders. The PO accepts this "loss of control" over communication and accepts architecting activities and decisions without understanding them.
Resolution in cases 2, 4, 5, 6: The PO is not involved in the architectural discussions. The architect (team) talks to other project stakeholders on architectural issues.

Challenge 2: _PO lacks Scrum skills_ (reported in case 2): Insufficient competence of POs on their responsibilities leads to incomplete information from stakeholders and the PO then provides incomplete information to the team.

Resolution in case 2: Some external stakeholders approach the team directly, circumventing the PO. The team architect also approaches external stakeholders (including end users) and discusses functional and non-functional requirements with them. Some POs are against architects to approach end users and the architect has to justify talking directly to end users.

Challenge 3: *Unavailability of PO* (reported in cases 2, 3, 4, 5): The PO is sometimes unavailable and the architect cannot obtain and provide information from/to the PO.

Resolution in case 2, 4: The team discusses the problem of not being available with the PO. If this does not help, the problem is escalated to higher management.
Resolution in case 3: The external architect is empowered to remove user stories from the sprint backlog which the PO did not elaborate on in sufficient detail.
Resolution in case 5: To compensate for the POs unavailability, the architect communicates with other stakeholders for providing and getting relevant information.

4.3   Challenges Between External Architect(s) and External Stakeholders

Challenge 1: *External architect(s) get/provide insufficient input from/to external stakeholders* (reported in cases 3, 4): There is no (or only one-directional) communication between external architects and external stakeholders as external stakeholders are architecturally unsavvy.

Resolution in case 3: Realising drawbacks of not talking to external stakeholders, the external architect communicates with them on issues and in a way that external stakeholders can understand.
Resolution in case 4: Not resolved.

Challenge 2: *External stakeholders do not understand the value of architecting* (reported in cases 3 and 5).

Resolution in case 3: The external architect communicates with external stakeholders on issues and in a way that external stakeholders can understand.
Resolution in case 5: The external architect is trying to educate the external stakeholders who are not architecturally knowledgeable.

4.4   Challenges Between External Architect(s) and Team

Challenge 1: *External architect(s) and team cannot agree* (reported in cases 3, 5, and 6): Architects face challenges in conveying their ideas to the team. Sometimes, the team and architect disagree.

Resolution in case 3: The external and team architects discuss and agree on the architectural decisions. Then, the external architect explains the reasoning behind architectural decisions to the team at the beginning of each sprint. During demos he reviews whether architectural directions are followed.

Resolution in case 5: The architect offers an architecture to the team leader. The architect and team leader together introduce the architecture to the team. If the architect and team disagree, the dispute is escalated to external managers.

Resolution in case 6: The architect tries to explain his choices to the team in a courteous way. The architect would try to use the already convinced team members to influence the rest of the team. In cases where still parts of the team would disagree, the architect has to escalate the problem to external managers. On one occasion the architect disagreed with the manager's decision and left the project.

Challenge 2: *External architect(s) cannot easily reach team members* (reported in case 3): Reaching all team members is difficult for the external architect, as the team members are spread across multiple locations around the world.

Resolution in case 3: The external architect still tries to meet them physically 1–2 times a year. This results in additional effort (e.g., travelling) and time required.

Challenge 3: *External architect(s) provide insufficient input to the team* (reported in cases 4 and 5): The team has to align its decisions with the external architect(s) but does not receive enough input or guidance during the project.

Resolution in case 4: A developer from the architectural team joins the Scrum team during the first months of a project.

Resolution in case 5: The external architect talks to the team leader as a first point of communication about architectural issues. He is "trying to make the team leader a sort of architect in the team".

Challenge 4: *Teams struggle to provide documentation to external architect(s)* (reported in case 4): The architect expects from the team documentation. This often conflicts with the team's perception of agile practices.

Resolution in case 4: A separate task-board is created to make documentation more efficient while still being conformant to regulatory requirements.

4.5   Challenges Between Architect(s) in Team and External Stakeholders

Challenge 1: *Higher-level management interferes with team* (reported in cases 1, 4): Managers outside the team tend to pressure the team (e.g., to make certain architectural choices, to deliver faster, to prioritize architecting activities low).

Resolution in case 1: The team tries to resist external influences.

Resolution in case 4: Since this results in architectural debt, dedicated architectural projects are started, which are not hindered by too strong business deadlines.

Challenge 2: *Team architect(s) cannot easily reach external stakeholders* (reported in case 2): Reaching external stakeholders requires travelling.

Resolution case 2: The architect uses telephone or VoIP applications or visits a stakeholder (preferred, especially in the case of new stakeholders).

Challenge 3: *Team architects do not communicate with each other* (reported in case 3): Team architects do not communicate with each other and do not align their decisions, making suboptimal choices within their teams.

Resolution in case 3: The team architects are encouraged to communicate between each other on architectural decisions that span across teams and impact multiple teams.

4.6 Discussion

In all cases, the POs were reported to lack certain competences. In cases 1, 2, 4, 5, 6 they lack technical and architecting knowledge. POs performed their core activities insufficiently in four of the cases: insufficient communication with external stakeholders in case 2 and insufficient time for the team in cases 2, 3, 4, 5. Resolving these challenges causes overhead (time, effort) for architects in reaching external stakeholders and excluding the PO from architectural decisions in cases 2, 4, 5, 6.

In cases 1, 3, 4, 5, and 6, architects face conflicting situations with respect to architectural decisions. Cases 3, 5, and 6 report disagreements between external architects and teams. In cases 1 and 4 disagreements between management and teams occurred. Resolutions to disagreements between external and team architects are about getting buy-in from teams and team leaders or escalating to managers. To mitigate problems caused by interfering management in case 4, an isolated (from management) architecture prototyping project is started prior to the actual project. Challenges related to architectural decisions were not reported only in case 2. This could be because the organization of case 2 follows strictly Scrum practices (advocating team autonomy and team architecting).

External architects fail to provide sufficient information to external stakeholders about architectural decisions made (cases 3, 4) and to teams (cases 4, 5). This is unexpected as this is one of the reasons for establishing an external architect. A possible explanation can be their high and diverse workloads (reported in case 5), geographical distance between a team and external architect (reported in case 3), or lack of understanding for the value of architecting at external stakeholders (cases 3 and 5).

4.7 Threats to Validity

With regards to *construct validity*, our study is limited since we gathered data only from a limited number of sources. However, we obtained insights from different organizations and projects. We included control questions and checked the accuracy of data with the organizations. With regards to *external validity* (extent to which findings are of interest outside the investigated cases), we acknowledge that we focus on an analytical generalization (i.e., our results are generalizable to other organizations that have similar characteristics as the cases in our case study and use Scrum). The list of challenges is based on six cases is insufficient for drawing major conclusions. However, the presented study is a first of its kind. With regards to *reliability*, we recorded interviews and interview data, and reviewed data collection and analysis procedures before conducting the study. Our study does not make any claims about causal relationships and therefore *internal validity* is not a concern.

5 Conclusions

We studied six cases involving companies that apply Scrum practices to identify challenges that architects face in Scrum projects and what architects do about these challenges. The cases were chosen to cover different setups of how architects can be involved in Scrum. Main challenges found in the cases are (a) busy and incompetent POs, (b) conflicts between architects and teams, and architects and management, (c) failure of architects outside the Scrum teams to provide sufficient information to stakeholders. The challenges reported in this paper increase architects' awareness and can be used to proactively address potential problems. As further research, we plan to extend the number of cases and provide more general conclusions.

References

1. VersionOne: 9th Annual State of Agile Survey (2015)
2. Bass, L., Clements, P., Kazman, R.: Software Architecture in Practice. Addison-Wesley Professional, Boston (2012)
3. Abrahamsson, P., Babar, M.A., Kruchten, P.: Agility and architecture: can they coexist? IEEE Softw. **27**, 16–22 (2010)
4. Yang, C., Liang, P., Avgeriou, P.: A systematic mapping study on the combination of software architecture and agile development. J. Syst. Softw. **111**, 157–184 (2016)
5. Babar, M.A.: An exploratory study of architectural practices and challenges in using agile software development approaches. In: Joint Working IEEE/IFIP Conference on Software Architecture, 2009 and European Conference on Software Architecture, WICSA/ECSA 2009, pp. 81–90 (2009)
6. van der Ven, J.S., Bosch, J.: Architecture decisions: who, how, and when? In: Babar, M.A., Brown, A.W., Mistrik, I. (eds.) Agile Software Architecture, chap. 5, pp. 113–136. Morgan Kaufmann, Boston (2014)
7. Faber, R.: Architects as service providers. IEEE Softw. **27**, 33–40 (2010)
8. Woods, E.: Aligning architecture work with agile teams. IEEE Softw. **32**, 24–26 (2015)
9. Martini, A., Pareto, L., Bosch, J.: Towards introducing agile architecting in large companies: the CAFFEA framework. In: Lassenius, C., Dingsøyr, T., Paasivaara, M. (eds.) XP 2015. LNBIP, vol. 212, pp. 218–223. Springer, Heidelberg (2015). doi:10.1007/978-3-319-18612-2_20
10. Eloranta, V.-P., Koskimies, K.: Lightweight architecture knowledge management for agile software development. In: Babar, M.A., Brown, A.W., Mistrik, I. (eds.) Agile Software Architecture, chap. 8, pp. 189–213. Morgan Kaufmann, Boston (2014)

11. Rost, D., Weitzel, B., Naab, M., Lenhart, T., Schmitt, H.: Distilling best practices for agile development from architecture methodology. In: Weyns, D., Mirandola, R., Crnkovic, I. (eds.) ECSA 2015. LNCS, vol. 9278, pp. 259–267. Springer, Heidelberg (2015). doi:10. 1007/978-3-319-23727-5_21
12. Schwaber, K., Beedle, M.: Agile Software Development with Scrum. Prentice Hall, Upper Saddle River (2002)
13. Beck, K.: Extreme Programming Explained (1999)
14. Fowler, M.: Who needs an architect? IEEE Softw. **20**, 11–13 (2003)
15. Runeson, P., Höst, M.: Guidelines for conducting and reporting case study research in software engineering. Empirical Softw. Eng. **14**, 131–164 (2008)
16. Wohlin, C., Runeson, P., Höst, M., Ohlsson, M.C., Regnell, B., Wesslén, A.: Experimentation in Software Engineering. Springer, Heidelberg (2012)
17. Kitchenham, B., Pfleeger, S.L.: Principles of survey research: part 5: populations and samples. SIGSOFT Softw. Eng. Notes **27**, 17–20 (2002)
18. Kruchten, P.: What do software architects really do? J. Syst. Softw. **81**(12), 2413–2416 (2008)
19. Miles, M., Huberman, M., Saldana, J.: Qualitative Data Analysis. Sage Publications, Thousand Oaks (2014)
20. Krippendorff, K.: Content Analysis: An Introduction to its Methodology. Sage Publications, Thousand Oaks (2003)

An Empirical Study on Collaborative Architecture Decision Making in Software Teams

Sandun Dasanayake[✉], Jouni Markkula, Sanja Aaramaa,
and Markku Oivo

M3S, Faculty of Information Technology and Electrical Engineering,
University of Oulu, Oulu, Finland
{sandun.dasanayake,jouni.markkula,sanja.aaramaa,
markku.oivo}@oulu.fi

Abstract. Architecture decision making is considered one of the most challenging cognitive tasks in software development. The objective of this study is to explore the state of the practice of architecture decision making in software teams, including the role of the architect and the associated challenges. An exploratory case study was conducted in a large software company in Europe and fifteen software architects were interviewed as the primary method of data collection. The results reveal that the majority of software teams make architecture decisions collaboratively. Especially, the consultative decision-making style is preferred as it helps to make decisions efficiently while taking the opinions of the team members into consideration. It is observed that most of the software architects maintain a close relationship with the software teams. Several organisational, process and human related challenges and their impact on architecture decision-making are also identified.

Keywords: Software architecture · Group decision making · Software teams

1 Introduction

Software architecture serves as the intellectual centrepiece that not only governs software development and evolution but also determines the overall characteristics of the resulting software system [1]. It provides support for various aspects of software system development by facilitating functions such as enabling the main quality attributes of the system, managing changes, enhancing communication among the system stakeholders and improving cost and schedule estimates [2]. Architecture decisions stand out from the rest because they dictate all downstream design choices; thus, they have far-reaching consequences and are hard to change [3]. Making the right architecture decisions, understanding their rationale and interpreting them correctly during software system development are essential to building a system that satisfies stakeholder expectations. As the system evolves, making new architecture decisions and removing obsolete ones to satisfy changing requirements while maintaining harmony with the existing decisions are crucial to keeping the system on course [4].

B. Tekinerdogan et al. (Eds.): ECSA 2016, LNCS 9839, pp. 238–246, 2016.
DOI: 10.1007/978-3-319-48992-6_18

A new perspective on software architecture and making architecture decisions has emerged with the popularity of lean and agile development practices [5]. The discussion regarding the big upfront design and continuous design, challenges to find the right balance of initial architecture design and its evolution during the software system life cycle [6]. At the same time, the emphasis on collaboration and agility causes architects to rethink making decisions from their ivory towers [7]. In most cases, architects are now part of the software team, and the important architecture decisions are made by the team rather than an individual architect [8]. With this change of perspective, software architecture decision making is now mostly considered a group decision-making (GDM) activity [9, 10].

2 Background

Although the importance of architecture decisions has long been recognised, they only began to gain prominence in software architecture about a decade ago [4]. Since then, architecture decisions and the rationale behind them have been considered first-class entities. Reasons such as dependencies between decisions, considerable business impact, possible negative consequences and a large amount of effort required for analysing alternatives are also recognised as factors contributing to the difficulty of architectural decisions [8]. Due to the importance and complexity of architecture decision making, the research community has given considerable attention to the topic, and a number of techniques, tools and processes have been proposed to assist in different phases of the architecture decision-making process [2]. Even though some attempts have been made to develop GDM solutions for architecture decision making, most of the solutions, including the most widely used ones, are not developed from a GDM perspective [11].

The groups can choose different decision-making methods such as consensus decision making, majority rule, decisions by an internal expert and decisions by an external expert, to reach a decision [12]. Based on the interaction between the team leader and the team, the decision styles in teams can also be classified into many different categories [13–15]. GDM has advantages such as increased acceptance, a large amount of collective knowledge, multiple approaches provided by the different perspectives and better comprehension of the problem and the solution [16]. At the same time, there are also some weaknesses that undermine the use of GDM in certain situations. Liabilities such as being time-consuming and resource heavy, vulnerability to social pressure, possible individual domination and the pursuit of conflicting secondary goals can result in low-quality compromised solutions [16]. One of the major weaknesses of GDM is *groupthink* [17], where the group makes faulty decisions without exploring the solutions objectively because of the social pressure to reach a consensus and maintain the group solidarity.

3 Case Study

In this research, the case study approach was selected for two main reasons. First, the case study is recommended for the investigation of a phenomenon when the current perspectives seem inadequate because they have little empirical evidence [18].

Although generic GDM is a well-researched area, few empirical studies have been made about GDM in software architecture. Second, in the case of decision making, the context in which the decision is made is essential to understanding the decision fully [19]. Since the case study allows us to study a phenomenon in its natural setting, the case study makes it possible to gather insights about the phenomenon itself as well as its interactions with its surroundings.

3.1 Case Study Design

This exploratory case study was designed to seek new insights into architecture decision making in software teams. A European software company was selected as the case company and the software teams in the company were used as the unit of analysis of the study. The case company specialises in providing software products and services to the consumer market, enterprise customers and third-party service providers. It has around a thousand employees and has a strong global customer base as well as offices and partners around the world. The company's product development activities are carried out in development centres located in multiple countries. At the time of the study, the company had three parallel business units: independent profit centres (BU1, BU2 and BU3) that focused on different product and service offerings, and market segments. In addition, there was a horizontal unit (BU4) that provided common solutions such as backend services for the other thee business lines. Finally, there was a centralised technical decision-making body, the tech committee (TC), which made company-wide technical policy decisions.

Two research questions (RQs) were derived based on the objectives of the study. While the questions are correlated to each other, each question is designed to find answers to a different aspect of the problem.

RQ1. *How do software teams make architecture decisions?* The aim of this question is to understand the state of the practice of architecture decision making in the case company, including the processes, tools and techniques, together with the contextual information. Answers to this question will help in understanding the overall architecture decision-making approach of the company as well as the architecture decision-making approaches of individual software teams.

RQ2. *What are the challenges in architecture decision making in software teams?* Identifying various challenges faced by the software teams during architecture decision making is the main goal of this research question. Answers to this question will also reveal the underlying sources of those challenges and their impact on architecture decision making.

3.2 Data Collection

Fifteen software architects from the different teams of the case company were selected to represents their respective teams (ST1–ST15). As shown in Table 1, they represent all the business and technical units of the company. Despite the variation in the job

Table 1. Interviewee information

Unit	Team ID	Site	Interviewee title	Team size
BU1	ST1	DC1	Domain architect	5
	ST2	HQ	Lead software engineer	7
	ST3	HQ	Lead software engineer	4
BU2	ST4	DC1	Domain architect	4–6
	ST5	DC1	Software architect	5
	ST6	HQ	Lead architect	8
	ST7	HQ	Program lead	5–7
	ST8	HQ	Senior software engineer	6
BU3	ST9	HQ	Senior software engineer	8
	ST10	DC2	Domain architect	4–7
	ST11	HQ	Software engineer	4
	ST12	DC2	Senior software engineer	5
BU4	ST13	HQ	Senior software engineer	7
	ST14	HQ	Senior software engineer	8
TC	ST15	HQ	Chief architect	N/A

titles, all of them perform duties as software architects in their respective teams. The software architects are located in three different sites: the headquarters (HQ) and two development centres (DC1 and DC2).

A set of questions divided into different themes was used to guide the interviews. The interview begins with questions related to the context and then gradually focuses on software architecture and architecture decision making. The interview questions later discuss the challenges that are faced and the possible solutions to these challenges. The interviews were conducted by two researchers. Most of the interviews were carried out face to face on site. Skype was used for three interviews due to travelling and scheduling issues. Each interview lasted about 1.5 h. All interviews were recorded with the consent of the interviewees.

3.3 Data Analysis

A set of decision-making styles derived from the research literature [13–15] was adapted to the software architecture decision-making context to analyse the decision making in the software teams in the case company. Each of these decision-making styles has different characteristics in terms of the decision maker, the origin of the solution and participation in the decision-making process, as shown in Table 2.

Based on the degree of involvement of each party, these decision styles can be placed on a continuum and grouped into three categories: architect driven (authoritative, persuasive), team driven (delegative) and collaborative (consultative, consensus). In addition to using the above classification to capture the decision-making styles, the identified challenges are categorized into three different groups as organizational, process and human, based on the origin of the challenge.

Table 2. Software architecture decision-making styles

Decision style	Decision maker	Solution origin	Participation	
			SW team	Architect
Authoritative	Architect	Architect	Passive	Active
Persuasive	Architect	Architect	Active	Active
Consultative	Architect	Shared	Active	Active
Consensus	Shared	Shared	Active	Active
Delegative	SW team	SW team	Active	Passive

4 Architecture Decision Making in the Case Company

It is clear that most of the software teams in the company follow GDM to make architecture decisions. The decision-making process appears to be informal. However, each team have some form of structured decision-making practice as all the interviewees were able to describe it during the interviews. The software architecture decision-making process in the case company is mainly a two-fold process composed of team level and organisational level decision making. In addition to that, there is also individual level decision-making, as each decision-maker makes individual decisions while participating team level or organizational level decision-making sessions. Even though software teams have freedom to make architecture decisions regarding their own software components, architecture steering groups and the TC are involved in making high-impact decisions that can affect the other teams or the company's business performances.

Architecture decision-making styles in each software team are based on the preferences of the software architect and the team members. However, all the interviewees made it clear that they selected the decision-making style based on the context, since there is no "one size fits all" kind of solution. Meanwhile, the decisions related to tasks that have an impact beyond the scope of the team are escalated to the architecture steering groups or the TC. Figure 1 shows the most commonly used architecture decision-making style of each team. According to that, consultative decision-making is the most commonly used decision-making style; 8 teams (53 %) claimed to use that as their primary decision-making style. One notable fact that is brought up during the interviews was the majority of the consultative decision-making style followers are willing to reach consensus during the consultation process if possible. However, they keep consultative decision-making as the primary decision-making approach as it allows them to avoid deadlocks and make timely decisions as the projects demand.

The interviewees provided arguments for choosing and not choosing each decision-making style. The arguments in favour of collaborative decision-making styles are that they increase team motivation, promote continuous knowledge sharing and identify team members who have expertise in the problem domain. The main arguments against these styles are that they are time-consuming and that it is difficult for team members to come to an agreement. Clarity of responsibility and saving time and money were given as reasons for using architect-driven decision-making styles. Others claimed that architecture decision making is too complex to be handled by one person. It can

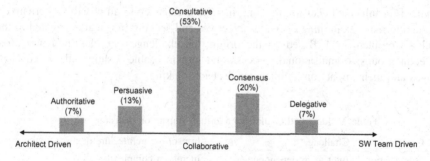

Fig. 1. Primary decision making style in software teams

limit the creativity of the solutions and introduce bias into the decisions since all the interviewees use personal characteristics such as experience and intuition for individual level decision-making. The only reason given for opting for delegative decision-making style is that the architect's unwillingness to take the responsibility of the design process.

The consultative decision-making style, which is preferred by the majority, brings the right balance into the decision-making process as it allows the software teams to makes decisions promptly while taking the opinion of the team members into consideration. This style makes it easier to attribute a certain decision to the decision-maker, hence maintaining the design rationale to some extent. The consultation process also helps to share information and spread the knowledge within the team. Since the majority of those who use consultative decision-making are open to reach consensus during the consultation, there is a possibility of making collective decisions when there are no demanding constrains. Eleven out of fifteen software teams use either consultative or consensus decision-making styles, thus it is possible to claim that collaborative way of decision-making has a strong presence in the case company.

Despite the availability of various architecture decision-making techniques, none of the teams use any standard technique to make architecture decisions. Although a few teams use software tools to create diagrams that can be used for decision making and communication, the whiteboard is the standard tool for architecture decision making in the case company. Despite being an external entity, the majority of interviewees view architecture steering groups as useful bodies that support them in decision making. One of the main reasons given for this view is that these groups support the teams by reducing the complexity of the decision problem. Most of the time, software teams or their representatives take the initiative to consult the steering group. That can also have an impact on the teams' view on steering groups, as consulting the steering group is voluntary rather than forced upon the team.

5 Identified Architecture Decision-Making Challenges

The interviewees mentioned several challenges associated with architecture decision making. Multiple interviewees provided evidence of the presence of *groupthink*, which leads groups to make inadequate decisions because it prevents them from taking actions required for informed decision making, including considering all possible alternatives, evaluating risks, examining decision objectives and seeking information related to the decision problem [17]. Based on the origin, the challenges are classified into three different groups: organisational, process and human. Table 3 shows identified challenges and their impact on architecture decision-making.

Table 3. Identified challenges and their impact on decision making

Category	Challenge	Impact on architecture decision making
Organisational	Inter team dependencies	Increased complexity
	Change of personnel	Loss of architecture knowledge
	Imposed technical constraints	Limit potential solutions
	Globally distributed teams	Lack of involvement
	Lack of a common tool chain	Difficult to collaborate
Process	Inadequate preparation time	Low quality decisions
	Dynamic requirements	Short term decisions
	Requirement ambiguity	Unclear decision goals
	Improper documentation	Missing design rationale
Human	Clash of personalities	Lengthy decision sessions/deadlocks
	Passive participation	Limited view points

Revisiting the design rationale appears to be a significant problem due to improper documentation and organisational changes. Most of the interviewees admitted that they experience several issues related to the design documents, particularly regarding their quality and maintenance. The majority opinion is that the documentation practices in the company are minimal or, in some cases, non-existent. Multiple interviewees stated that differing opinions and personality traits are among the major challenges faced during architecture decision making. Several reasons such as non-flexibility, personal ego and loyalty towards a preferred technology prevent the team from reaching an agreement. Some team members constantly try to force their way of doing things on others rather than objectively participating in the discussion. On the other hand, some of the members prefer to just attend decision meetings but never express their opinions.

6 Conclusion

The study revealed that the majority of software teams in the company use a consultative decision-making approach to make architecture decisions. We were able to identify the challenges related from three different aspects: organisational, process and human, and their impact on architecture decision making. While discussing the overall results, we also uncovered the existence *groupthink* that is known to influence group decision making activities. The next logical step is to identify the relationship between the type of architecture decisions and the decision-making style followed. Identifying decision-making patterns that should be applied in different contexts will help software architects and teams select the best possible course of action to make their decisions.

We are currently planning to cross analyse our previous case study findings [20] with the findings of this study to assess the generalisability.

Acknowledgements. This research is funded by ITEA2 and Tekes, the Finnish Funding Agency for Innovation, via the MERgE project, which we gratefully acknowledge. We would also like to thank all the interviewees and the management of the case company.

References

1. Taylor, R.N., Medvidovic, N., Dashofy, E.M.: Software Architecture: Foundations, Theory, and Practice. Wiley, Hoboken (2010)
2. Bass, L., Clements, P., Kazman, R.: Software Architecture in Practice. Addison-Wesley Professional, Reading (2012)
3. Clements, P.: A survey of architecture description languages. In: Proceedings of 8th International Workshop on Software Specification and Design, pp. 16–25 (1996)
4. Jansen, A., Bosch, J.: Software architecture as a set of architectural design decisions. In: 5th Working IEEE/IFIP Conference on Software Architecture (WICSA 2005). pp. 109–120 (2005)
5. Kruchten, P.: Software architecture and agile software development: a clash of two cultures? In: 2010 ACM/IEEE 32nd International Conference Software Engineering, vol. 2, pp. 497–498 (2010)
6. Shore, J.: Continuous design. IEEE Softw. **21**, 20–22 (2004)
7. Abrahamsson, P., Ali Babar, M., Kruchten, P.: Agility and architecture: can they coexist? IEEE Softw. **27**, 16–22 (2010)
8. Tofan, D., Galster, M., Avgeriou, P.: Difficulty of architectural decisions – a survey with professional architects. In: Drira, K. (ed.) ECSA 2013. LNCS, vol. 7957, pp. 192–199. Springer, Heidelberg (2013)
9. Rekhav, V.S., Muccini, H.: A study on group decision-making in software architecture. In: 2014 IEEE/IFIP Conference on Software Architecture, pp. 185–194 (2014)
10. Tofan, D., Galster, M., Lytra, I., Avgeriou, P., Zdun, U., Fouche, M.-A., de Boer, R., Solms, F.: Empirical evaluation of a process to increase consensus in group architectural decision making. Inf. Softw. Technol. **72**, 31–47 (2016)
11. Rekha V.S., Muccini, H.: Suitability of software architecture decision making methods for group decisions. In: Avgeriou, P., Zdun, U. (eds.) ECSA 2014. LNCS, vol. 8627, pp. 17–32. Springer, Heidelberg (2014)
12. Beebe, S.A., Masterson, J.T.: Communication in Small Groups: Principles and Practice. Pearson Education Inc., New York (2009)
13. Hersey, P., Blanchard, K.H., Johnson, D.E.: Management of Organizational Behavior. Pearson, New York (2012)
14. Tannenbaum, R., Schmidt, W.H.: How to choose a leadership pattern. Harv. Bus. Rev. **36**, 95–101 (1958)
15. Stewart, L.P., Gudykunst, W.B., Ting-Toomey, S., Nishida, T.: The effects of decision-making style on openness and satisfaction within Japanese organizations. Commun. Monogr. **53**, 236–251 (1986)
16. Schachter, S., Singer, J.E.: Assets and liabilities in group problem solving: the need for an integrative function. Psychol. Rev. **74**, 239–249 (1967)

17. Janis, I.L.: Groupthink: Psychological Studies of Policy Decisions and Fiascoes. Cengage Learning, Boston (1982)
18. Eisenhardt, K.M.: Building theories from case study research. Acad. Manag. Rev. **14**, 532–550 (1989)
19. Fantino, E., Stolarz-Fantino, S.: Decision-making: context matters. Behav. Process. **69**, 165–171 (2005)
20. Dasanayake, S., Markkula, J., Aaramaa, S., Oivo, M.: Software architecture decision-making practices and challenges: an industrial case study. In: Proceedings of 24th Australasian Software Engineering Conference (2015)

Architecture Enforcement Concerns and Activities - An Expert Study

Sandra Schröder[✉], Matthias Riebisch, and Mohamed Soliman

Department of Informatics, University of Hamburg,
Vogt-Koelln-Strasse 30, 22527 Hamburg, Germany
{schroeder,riebisch,soliman}@informatik.uni-hamburg.de

Abstract. Software architecture provides the high-level design of software systems with the most critical decisions. The source code of a system has to conform to the architectural decisions to guarantee the systems' success in terms of quality properties. Therefore, architects have to continuously ensure that architecture decisions are implemented correctly to prevent architecture erosion. This is the main goal of Architecture Enforcement. For an effective enforcement, architects have to be aware of the most important enforcement concerns and activities. Unfortunately, current state of the art does not provide a concrete structure on how the process of architecture enforcement is actually applied in industry. Therefore, we conducted an empirical study in order to gain insight in the industrial practice of architecture enforcement. For this, we interviewed 12 experienced software architects from different companies. As a result, we identified the most important concerns that software architects care about during architecture enforcement. Additionally, we investigated which activities architects usually apply in order to enforce those concerns.

Keywords: Software architecture · Architecture enforcement · Software architecture in industry · Empirical study

1 Introduction

Software architecture [1] builds the basis for the high-level design for a software system and provides the basis for its implementation. It defines the fundamental rules and guidelines that developers have to follow to ensure achieving quality attributes such as performance or security.

In software engineering literature and community, the role of the architect is widely discussed, especially in the context of agile development processes. For example, McBride [14] defined the role of the architect as being *"responsible for the design and technological decisions in the software development process"*. However, the software architect role [7,12] is not only limited to making architecture design decisions [10]. Additionally, the software architect is also responsible for *"sharing the results of the decision making with the stakeholders and the project team, and getting them accepted"* [23]. This task is called *Architecture Enforcement*.

© Springer International Publishing AG 2016
B. Tekinerdogan et al. (Eds.): ECSA 2016, LNCS 9839, pp. 247–262, 2016.
DOI: 10.1007/978-3-319-48992-6_19

During implementation or maintenance activities, developers could intentionally or accidentally deviate from the prescribed architecture. This may result in the degradation of architectural quality. Consequently, the architect needs to proactively care about the adherence of the implementation to the chosen architecture decisions as a necessary part of the architecture enforcement task. For this, he needs to detect implementation decisions made by developers that indicate *architectural violations*, i.e. low-level decisions that do not follow the prescribed architectural constraints. The accumulation of architectural violations results in a phenomenon called *architecture erosion* [17,20].

Architecture enforcement faces several challenges such as the high effort required to assess the adherence of the implementation to architecture decisions, as well as the social and technical complexities in dealing with the development team. Facing these challenges requires methods and tools to support the architect during the architecture enforcement activities. To the best of our knowledge there is no detailed study about what are the necessary responsibilities and concerns related with architecture enforcement and about how architects actually monitor an implementation of architecture decisions.

As a starting point to achieve this goal, we conducted an empirical study with the purpose of understanding the process of architecture enforcement in industry. We interviewed 12 experienced architects from various companies. Based on their answers, we elaborated the most important concerns that are targeted by software architects during architecture enforcement, together with the related architects' activities and Best Practices. By defining the most important concerns, we provide the basis for focusing architecture enforcement on the essential aspects.

The following two research questions guided the empirical study:

- **RQ1: What are the concerns which architects consider during the enforcement process?** With this question we investigate which categories of concerns software architects usually consider important. This will give us further directions for our research activities in terms of detection and prioritization of architectural violations concerning decisions that are especially important for software practitioners.
- **RQ2: What are the activities performed by the architects in order to enforce and validate those concerns?** The answer to this question gives us a basis for developing appropriate approaches that best integrate with methods that are currently used in practice in order to gain acceptance by practitioners for new approaches.

2   Background and Related Work

In this section we present topics that are related with our study. We first present related work concerning architecture decision enforcement. After that we present related studies that investigate the concerns and activities of software architects and discuss to which degree those studies consider architecture enforcement.

2.1 Architecture Decision Enforcement

Zimmermann et al. propose a model-driven approach called *decision injection* in order to enforce the correct implementation of decisions in the source code [23]. Jansen et al. implemented a tool that allows the management of architectural decisions [11]. Among other things Jansen et al. emphasize that the tool should provide appropriate support for checking the implementation against architectural decisions. The tool implemented by the authors warns the architect or the developer if the team ignores a specific decision or introduces a violation against a decision. However, it is not clear what type of decision violations are detected with this tool. In order to control erosion of architecture decisions, traceability approaches as proposed by Mirakhorli and Cleland-Huang [15] can be applied. Their approach allows tracing architectural tactics to architecture-relevant pieces of code and warns the developer if he/she changes code of this significant part.

Software architecture conformance checking is another enforcement method. It allows the enforcement of the modular structure and dependencies of the software system. Well-known approaches encompass reflexion modeling [16], dependency structure matrices [18], design tests [2], or domain specific languages [3,21] - to name a few. However, static conformance checking methods are restricted to the modular structure and are not able to enforce arbitrary types of decisions, e.g. for checking constraints of architectural styles or the adherence to the separation of concerns principle.

2.2 Architects' Concerns and Activities During Enforcement

In [5] the authors conducted an empirical study about the architects' concerns. They present some interesting findings. For example they found that "People quality is as important as structure quality". This is also confirmed by our study, but we investigate in a more detailed fashion which are the actual dimensions of "people quality". Additionally, the authors' understanding about "architects' concerns" is a bit more general than ours. While they actually regard all the phases (i.e. architecture analysis, evaluation, architecture design, realization etc.) during the software engineering process as architects' concerns, we especially focus on the concerns that architects have corresponding to the architecture enforcement process.

The study of Caracciolo et al. [4] is similar to ours. They investigated how quality attributes are specified and validated by software architects and therefore also investigated what are important concerns for architects in terms of quality attributes. They also conducted expert interviews as part of their study. They identified several quality attributes that are important to software architects. Nevertheless, they solely concentrate on quality attributes and they do not especially focus on architectural enforcement and by which activities it is achieved.

3   Study Design

In our study we followed a qualitative research approach by applying a process with two main phases: Practitioners Interviews, and Literature Categories' Integration. The main purpose of the first phase is to explore the important aspects in the current state of the practice regarding architecture enforcement, while the second phase complements and relates the interviews' findings with existing concepts from the current state of the art. The two phases will be explained in the following sub-sections.

3.1   Phase 1: Practitioners Interviews

In order to collect data, we used expert interviews with open questions. Those interviews are an integral part of this type of research and are commonly used in order to generate new knowledge about a specific topic. An interview guide helped us to focus on the research questions, but also let the participants speak freely about their experiences. In this way, we could get as many examples as possible about architects' concerns and architectural rules and the methods architects use in the context of architecture enforcement. We followed the interviews with an inductive content analysis for the interview transcripts, from which we were able to derive our concepts.

Selection of Interview Participants. As participants of the study, we targeted experienced software architects from industry. Those architects come from different companies from Germany and Switzerland. All study participants had at least a master's degree or a similar qualification in computer science or related fields, e.g. electrical engineering or physics. In total, we interviewed 12 architects from 11 different companies. The interview participants are listed in Table 1. The

Table 1. List of study participants, their domain and their years of experience.

#	Domain	Role(s)	Exp. (years)
A	Enterprise (application, integration)	Software architect	>15
B	Enterprise	Software architect consulting	10–15
C	Enterprise	Software architect	>20
D	Logistic/enterprise	Software architect agile test engineer	10
E	Accounting/enterprise (migration)	Software architect section manager	10–15
F	Enterprise	Software architect lead developer	10–15
G	Enterprise/embedded	Software architect coach	10–15
H	Insurance/enterprise	Software architect project manager	5–10
I	Medical	Software architect software developer	5–10
J	Government/enterprise (application)	Software architect consulting	10
K	Logistic/enterprise	Software architect	5–10
L	Banking, control systems, enterprise	Software architect project manager	>20

professional experience of the participants ranged from 5 to over 20 years, with an average of 13 years. They worked in teams of size varying between 2 and 200 developers (team size not shown in the table). All of them work as a software architect or made significant practical experience in architectural design. Other participants are also responsible for project management tasks. The main criteria of choosing participants for this study was that architects should be closely involved with the implementation of the software architecture, for example in code reviews, and that they consider the maintenance of architectures with a long-term perspective. That means that architects should not solely participate in the modeling phase, but also in the implementation and maintenance phase. We did not focus on any specific domains, since we believe that architecture enforcement problem is a relevant and well-known problem in almost every domain.

Interview Guide Design and Conduction of the Interviews. The interview guide was designed for a semi-structured interview containing open questions that were chosen according to the research questions. The method helps to gain a possibly comprehensive overview of the state of the practice [9]. As we wanted to collect as much new knowledge as possible, we let the participants talk freely about their experiences concerning architectural enforcement.

The interview guide contains three parts. In the first part, we wanted to classify the experiences and background of the participants such as the domain in which they are working, years of experience, the team size and the development process (agile, waterfall etc.). The second part is related to the first research question. In this interview part we let the experts talk freely about their experiences concerning violations against decisions and important concerns. In the third part, we wanted to discover methods that are used by the architects in order to enforce architecture. The detailed interview guide is given in the supplementary and can be accessed via the paper's website[1]. When presenting our study results in the next sections, we are going to present some of the questions from the guide and the corresponding responses of the participants.

The interviews were conducted personally or via Skype by the same person and were recorded on agreements using a Dictaphone on the interviewers laptop or a call recorder for Skype conversations. The twelve interviews took between 40 and 90 min and 56 min on average. The interview guide directed the interviews, so that no important questions were missed concerning the research goals.

Data Analysis Phase. For further analyses, all interviews were transcribed word-by-word. After transcribing the interviews and checking them for correctness and completeness, we followed an inductive method for data analysis. Instead of defining codes before analyzing the interviews, we let the categories directly emerge from the data. For this, we first adapted Open Coding [19]. In this step phenomena in the data are identified and labeled using a code that

---

[1] http://swk-www.informatik.uni-hamburg.de/~schroeder/ECSA2016/.

summarizes the meaning of the data. During this process, emerging codes are compared with earlier ones in order to find similarities and maybe to merge similar codes. Then we compared codes with each other and aggregated them where possible to a higher level category. We used $AtlasTi^2$ in order to support the codification process.

3.2   Phase 2: Literature Categories' Integration

In this phase, we integrate our findings from Phase 1 with existing categories in the current state of the art. We analyzed existing related work (see Sect. 2), and identified categories related to architecture enforcement. The analysis has been done independently of the concepts derived from the interviews. We combined deductively the results of inductive content analysis (Phase 1) with the identified categories from existing literature. We used Mind Mapping in order to visualize the categories. By comparing the categories derived from both phases, we found that some of the categories derived by the literature review act as high level categories for inductively derived categories. On the other hand, some of the inductive categories could not be related to existing categories from the literature review. Section 4 presents our identified categories.

4   Results

Because of space limitations we discuss only the most interesting aspects in more detail. The complete discussion with the data used is provided as supplementary material and can be accessed through the paper's website (see footnote 1).

4.1   Enforcement Concerns

As Enforcement Concerns (Fig. 1) we summarized all aspects that have to be assessed by architects to ensure the correct implementation of decisions. Figure 1 gives an overview over the identified concerns from the interviews.

Macro and Micro Architecture Decisions. When talking about software architecture, it was interesting that experts differentiate basically between decisions in two different views, namely macro architecture and micro architecture [22]. Other terms like strategic or global (i.e. macro) and tactical or local (i.e. micro) views were used. The architect can decide which decisions are located in the macro architecture, and which decisions are left open for the development team. In this way the architect can decide how much freedom he gives teams in designing the micro architecture. The macro architecture represents the general idea (or "philosophy", the "spirit", the "big picture" or metaphor) of the system and its fundamental and most critical architectural decisions, e.g. on structures, components, data stores, communication style or architectural styles: "... it is

---

^{2} http://atlasti.com/.

important how you regard it. For me there do exist basically two views about how software is built. First you have the global view [...] There I decide how I design my software, for example using Domain Oriented Design or SOA." (code: two different views of architecture, Participant D) and another participant reported: *"...then we have the micro architecture, this is the architecture within each team. A team can decide for its own component for which it is responsible which libraries it wants to use."* (code: two different views of architecture, macro architecture, micro architecture; Participant K). Those two views define what architects basically consider as important for architecture enforcement in different ways. The architects report to be concerned with macro architecture issues and consider the micro architecture as developers' responsibility, except the coding style because of its relevance for maintainability: *"...architecture is also present in a single code statement. Code styles belong to it. Or simple things like how do I define an interface..."* (code: micro architecture, Participant J).

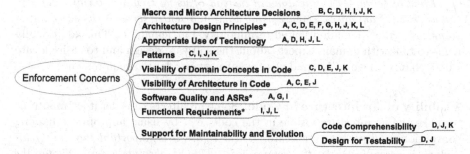

Fig. 1. Overview of the identified categories of Enforcement Concerns from the interviews and the corresponding participant. Concerns marked with an asterisk are not explained in detail in this paper but are available in the supplementary on the paper's website (see footnote 1).

Appropriate Use of Technology. Technology was also mentioned as an important concern. The architect may not check technologies used within a single component, but may for example enforce the technology for the communication style between several components. Since technologies like frameworks or libraries offer a lot of complex functionality, software architects also monitor the way how those technologies are used by developers. One architect stated that developers can easily violate important architecture rules due to this complexity. Some architects reported that developers often tend to use a lot of tools and technologies that are not necessary: *"...aim for technologies is the biggest problem. And if you like to use those frameworks because they are providing gross things, but those gross things cannot be controlled..."* (code: aim for technologies, Participant J). They stated that software architecture is likely to erode where too much technology is used, because this part of code is hard too understand (see also "Support for Evolution and Maintenance"). This is why some experts emphasized it is important to control what kind of technologies are used.

Patterns. The architect may want to ensure that patterns are implemented accordingly. Patterns related with the macro architecture view have to be enforced and validated, patterns on the micro level are mostly considered as a developers' concern. But sometimes, pattern implementations are also checked by architects on the micro architecture level, e.g. in order to discover what types of design and architecture patterns are implemented and if they fit in the specific context: *"which patterns are used and in which context. Are they only used just because I have seen it in a book or because I wanted to try it or is it really reasonable at this place..."* (code: pattern suitability, Participant C).

Visibility of Domain Concepts in Code. Some experts emphasize a clear representation of domain concepts in the architecture, e.g. by expressing a mapping between them. For this, some architect strive to use a domain oriented terminology, that means using terms and names adapted from the business domain: *"...I like to be guided by the domain instead of using technical terms [...] both can work, but from my experience using domain oriented terms is easier to understand..."* (code: domain oriented terminology, Participant J). This additionally helps to talk with domain experts about the software design and to easier locate where changes have to be made in case of new or adapted requirements.

Visibility of Architecture in Code. Some architects consider it as important to make the architecture visible in the code, e.g. by using appropriate naming conventions and package structure: *"...therefore it is important that the architecture is recognizable in the source code. This is absolutely essential for the structure of the project."* (code: making architecture visible in the code, Participant J). This is helpful for tools like Sonargraph[3] that for example use naming conventions in order to highlight layers. It was also mentioned to be useful during code inspections in order to easily locate architecture decisions in code. This concern is similar to the idea using an architecturally-evident coding style suggested by Fairbanks [6].

Support for Evolution and Maintenance. A challenge in constructing long-lived system is to make decisions that support the software system's ability to easily be adapted to future changes, that is, we need support for evolution and maintenance during the entire software lifecycle.

- **Code Comprehensibility** was explicitly mentioned as a concern, on the basis that comprehensibility helps preventing architectural violations: *"if you strictly follow this approach then you have very readable code and normally readable Code - from my experience - tends to be stable that is conform concerning architecture and does not have any [architecture] violations..."* (code: code comprehensibility, code comprehensibility supports architecture conformance; Participant J).

---

[3] https://www.hello2morrow.com/products/sonargraph.

– **Design for Testability.** Another interesting aspect that might be surprising was that architects are strongly concerned with tests. Systems that cannot be properly tested, cannot be changed successfully since software modifications during maintenance and implementation activities may lead to errors. That is why testability is an important concern especially in the context of evolution and maintenance. Participants aim a high test coverage in order to avoid architectural violations: *"... in case there exist only a few tests, then it is likely people do not build it correctly. This leads to incomprehensible code and consequently to architectural violations."* (test coverage supports architecture conformance, Participant J). Tests are therefore an important concern for enforcement.

4.2   Architects' Activities for Enforcement

During the interview we asked all participants the question: *"How do you ensure that your architecture and your concerns are implemented as intended? Do you follow any strategies?"*. The result of this question is a categorization of activities that architects apply in order to enforce and validate their architecture decisions. Figure 2 shows the identified categories. In the following we describe the two categories Coaching and Supporting, and Assessing the Decisions' Implementation in more detail. Moreover we discovered several dimensions that are important for those activities. The complete mindmap with a mapping of codes and interview statements is provided in the supplementary (see footnote 1).

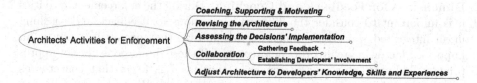

Fig. 2. Identified categories of enforcement activities.

We discovered the need for a distinction between situations with more or less equal architectural skills among the development team, as typical for agile processes, and situations with a leading role of the architect, frequently referred to as "architecture-first" approach. The latter is for example driven by limited skills of developers, or by stronger constraints and higher risks of the project. The first situation was mentioned by participant **B**, and the second one by participant **H**. In both situations, enforcement is necessary with different priorities, affecting the balance between the different dimensions of coaching and supporting (see below) on the one side, and assessment on the other side.

(1) Coaching and Supporting. It is important that architects provide guidance during the implementation phase in order to support developers in their programming activities. Coaching was mentioned to be highly important, both for explanation and motivation. Both is crucial to provide a clear picture and a shared understanding for architecture solutions, the corresponding design decisions, together with its goals, motivation and benefits: *"I have to explain [the developers] the term "architecture" and they have to internalize and understand what are the goals of architectural design and what has to be supported by the architecture..."* (code: architect as a coach, Participant **B**) or *"...as an architect you are committed to teach the developers and explain them what it [the architecture] is about..."* (code: architect as a coach, Participant **G**). A combination of coaching and supporting can be done in several ways. For example, the architect can provide **architectural templates and prototypes** in order to guide how a specific decision has to be implemented or a specific technology has to be used, and he provides support by pre-fabricated building blocks. Architectural prototyping is another effective technique that combines support for developers with early identification and solution of high-risk aspects during early stages of the development process. Those templates can also be used to provide a reference during the implementation for the developers, that is for coaching and guiding purposes: *"...you build something as an example and present it to the developers..."* (code: architectural templates, Participant **A**). It was emphasized by participant **A**, that those templates should be built precisely and carefully according to architectural decisions and state-of-the-art best practices. Otherwise developers could violate the underlying decisions without knowing it because the architect did not show it correctly.

Dimensions for Feedback and Coaching. During the enforcement activities it is important to consider the different dimensions for feedback and coaching in an integrated way. Both dimensions emphasize that personal quality is an important factor in architecture enforcement. If those dimensions are not appropriately addressed during enforcement activities, it is likely that concerns as presented in the previous sections cannot be satisfied. We found the following dimensions during the analysis:

– **Skills, Experiences, Programming Habits.** Every developer has a different set of skills and experiences, e.g. from previous projects and from his education. Those qualities and together with personal programming habits influence greatly how developers make low-level decisions and how they implement architectural decisions. The low-level decisions could violate important architecture decisions: *"...and if I leave it to the developers then it does not work since every developer has a different background and experiences. When I tell them that they should start with programming, then this leads to chaos..."* (code: programming habits and experience of developers).
– **Architecture acceptance.** We define architecture acceptance as the degree to which a programmer is willing to implement the prescribed architecture. The architect should always be *"...anxious for getting the architecture accepted by the developers and that they [the developers] want to implement it*

this way." (codes: encourage acceptance of developers for architecture, willingness; Participant B). The architects have to encourage developers to achieve the architecture's acceptance, otherwise it is likely that architecture rules are not followed and consequently violated.

- **Architecture awareness.** Describes the consciousness of developers regarding the prescribed architecture, its rationale and its goals that have to be achieved with it: *"skilled people do automatically know how they ensure architecture, because they know, why it should be like that. Then - without help - developers have the architecture in their mind and recognize if architectural goals are ensured or not."* (codes: architecture awareness, personal quality; Participant B). If developers are not aware of architecture goals it might happen that they unintentionally violate the architecture. The architect is responsible for achieving and encouraging architecture awareness appropriately; coaching and supporting are activities to address this dimension.
- **Shared understanding.** There must be a coherence of concepts between the members of a team about how an architecture looks like. Mostly, an architecture is constructed in the mind of the developers and the architects – either supported by models, diagrams or by speech – and it is important that all of them have the same imagination about the architecture in their mind: *"a common picture - keyword modeling - is very important here, to have a starting point and to have it started in the same direction"* (code: common understanding of architecture, using models for comprehension, Participant B). If a shared understanding about the architecture is achieved it is more likely that architectural rules are ensured and followed by the developers.

(2) Assessing the Decisions' Implementation. During the interviews we asked all participants the following question: *"What are the specific steps when you inspect the source code in order to assess the implementation of the architecture decisions?"* We developed the following categories of activities that are strongly interwoven.

- **Code Review.** We found that code review is a consent activity for assessing the decisions' implementation. One architect stated that this activity *"is similar to the comprehension process of a developer who is new in the team and tries to understand how the software systems works. But developers and architects have each different goals during this process. The developer mainly wants to implement new features, while the architect wants to check architecture conformance"* (participant **C**). Architects form a mental model of a software system and its relation to implementation based on architectural decisions. By doing this they have specific imagination about what they expect in the code: *"... a picture about if the components are appropriate, if the modules are implemented according to how it was intended..."* (Code: expectation about intended design, Participant C). In this process, software architects often ask questions about the observed software systems that entail exploration and navigation, such as who implemented this component and where is a specific feature, architectural pattern, design pattern, technology implemented or used. It is then evaluated informally if an implementation roughly represents this mental model. During this process, code analysis tools can be used as a source of information: *"... what you can do is, you run a code analysis tool and then you are looking at the spots that are interesting..."* (code: finding hot spots, results from code analysis tools as first impression, Participant **K**).

– **Repository Mining.** One expert uses review systems in order to review the implementation concerning architecture issues. In this way it is possible to investigate *what type of changes* were applied on a set of classes and especially *who* did the change. Moreover they can trace back how an architecture violation was introduced. They reproduce the steps of implementation and try to understand rationale and code-level decisions behind past changes. If an architect knows about the individual skills in a team, he can focus source code inspections on changes by developers with less skills, inexperienced, or new to a project. In this way he can raise his overall productivity as well as reducing the risks: *"... you know basically who works on which parts, this means if I know from experience that I have to have a closer look on what he or she has created then it is possible that I have to inspect each class [...] because he or she can create an unusual solution on the most unobtrusive parts"* (code: focused inspection based on individual skills of developer, Participant **C**).

– **Model-Code-Comparison.** We asked the participants how and if the architecture documentation and models are used in assessments. Some experts (**B, I, J, L**) use documented diagrams and models for conformance validation between implemented software system and architecture. For this, they use UML class diagrams, sequence diagrams or component diagrams and compare them with models extracted from the underlying implementation. The comparison is performed manually. For example they check if a message exchange between components complies to the prescribed behavior by comparing UML sequence diagrams extracted from source code with prescribed sequence diagrams.

– **Automatic Validation of Architectural Constraints.** We also asked architects to which degree they formalize architectural aspects in order to allow a formal validation of a software architecture. We found that architects seem not to formalize to a great extent. Some experts formalize and evaluate the adherence to the layer pattern or general module dependency rules automatically by using tools such as Sonargraph. Additionally software architects define rules concerning such as naming conventions, thresholds for complexity metrics or other low-level rules that can be performed automatically by tools like Sonarqube or Checkstyle. Other aspects of software architectures, for example other architectural patterns, are not formalized.

5   Discussion

In this section we discuss the results of the study and additionally important implications of these results for future approaches concerning architecture enforcement.

Social Dimensions of Architecture Enforcement. Based on our findings we can summarize that experienced practitioners understand enforcement as a supportive process for developers, instead of an authoritative, dictating or leadership-like process. They actively want to involve developers, and gather feedback on the architectural solutions. They strive a shared understanding about the software architecture. While motivating, encouraging and supporting developers in implementing the architecture, architects are open for revisions of their architecture solutions to minimize the risks of malfunction, misunderstandings or failures. Moreover, architects need to be anxious for encouraging acceptance and architecture awareness of the developers to decrease the probability of intentional and unintentional architecture violations. We propose that future approaches and tools should also respect the social dimension.

Developers' Flexibility and Responsibility. As stated in the introduction, an architecture violation can result from a piece of code that contradicts the rules defined by the software architecture. Nevertheless, software architecture is described on a higher level of abstraction, whereas developers are working on a lower level. Consequently, violations may occur that cannot be avoided due to this abstraction gap. That is why architects need to define the degree of flexibility and when developers are allowed to violate certain aspects of the architecture. It needs to be further investigated which criteria are needed to define this flexibility, e.g. based on the qualification of the developers.

Appropriate Formalization Support. Formalization in context of software engineering and especially software architecture is still not widely accepted, due to the expected extra effort as well as the lack of usability and appropriate tool support [13]. This can be also implied from the findings of our study. For example, we found that static dependencies are often used as a main criteria to define architectural constraints. Constraints concerning layer dependencies are validated regularly, whereas other types of architectural solutions, e.g. Model-View-Controller-Pattern, architectural tactics or communication styles, are not validated. One reason for this could be that there is a manifold and well-established tool support for static conformance checking, e.g. by Sonargraph or Structure101[4]. Therefore we can conclude that the availability of easy-to-use tool support strongly influences the acceptance of formalization approaches. A consequence might be that research should provide easy-to-use verification including tool support for other architectural aspects as well.

Guidance for Software Architects in Violation Detection and Prioritization. Based on the statements we can conclude that architects evaluate the severity of architectural violations rather intuitively. As we can imply from the results of our survey, architects often use metrics for example on static package dependencies in order to find hot spots that could give hints for crucial

---

[4] http://structure101.com/.

architectural violations. We suggest that a better guidance is needed for software architects in order to evaluate architecture violations and their severity. For this, a catalog could be developed that lists common and well-known architecture violations, similar to a pattern catalog. The catalog maps decisions to possible violations. Furthermore, corresponding detection and repair strategies can be recorded in the catalog. Architects can use the catalog during code reviews to focus on the implementation of the most important decisions. Moreover, appropriate guidance in metrics analysis and interpretation is still missing. We think that research does not necessarily needs to invent new metrics, but needs to investigate how those metrics can be appropriately used during the analysis of implemented architectures.

5.1 Limitations

Gasson et al. proposed the criteria confirmability, dependability, internal consistency, and transferability [8] in order to evaluate qualitative studies. As we described and captured the background of all the study participants we address transferability. Confirmability is addressed by repeatedly discussing and restructuring the categories in an iterative process. In order to address dependability we followed a research process (Sect. 3) and described all the steps that were conducted. In terms of internal consistency the statements and the corresponding codes were cross-checked by another researcher. As similar to other qualitative studies we have a limited number of participants. However since we wanted to generate new knowledge and not to evaluate or confirm existing knowledge we find that this limited number is acceptable.

Another limitation might be that we did not consider specific dimensions that could influence the experts' view on enforcement concerns. For example, skills and tasks of a software architect could influence his view about what are important concerns and activities in context of architecture enforcement. The domain a software application is developed for could also influence the importance of specific concern or even add further concerns to the list presented in this study. As we tried to get a general overview about architecture enforcement concerns, this was not the focus of our study and creating the correlation between specific dimensions and enforcement concerns is left for future work.

6 Conclusion and Future Work

An expert study with the goal of understanding architecture enforcement process in practice has been presented. To reach this goal, we gathered data by interviewing experienced software architects from several companies. Our contribution in this paper is the determination of the most important concerns, which are considered by architects, as well as the activities performed by them during the architecture enforcement process. In addition, our results show the important role of architects during system implementation, and the importance of the relationship between software architect and development team, in order to properly implement software architecture decisions. The findings of this paper contribute towards methods for systematic and goal-oriented architecture enforcement. Thus, we are willing to extend our study to additionally explore some of the architecture enforcement concerns and activities in detail, and to determine which methods and tool support is required for each. Furthermore, we intend to merge our findings on essential enforcement concerns with architecture modeling approaches for agile development processes.

References

1. Bass, L., Clements, P., Kazman, R.: Software Architecture in Practice, 3rd edn. Addison-Wesley Professional, Boston (2012)
2. Brunet, J., Serey, D., Figueiredo, J.: Structural conformance checking with design tests: an evaluation of usability and scalability. In: 27th IEEE International Conference on Software Maintenance (ICSM), pp. 143–152. IEEE Computer Society, Washington, DC, September 2011
3. Caracciolo, A., Lungu, M.F., Nierstrasz, O.: A unified approach to architecture conformance checking. In: 12th Working IEEE/IFIP Conference on Software Architecture (WICSA), pp. 41–50. IEEE Computer Society, Washington, DC, May 2015
4. Caracciolo, A., Lungu, M.F., Nierstrasz, O.: How do software architects specify and validate quality requirements? In: Avgeriou, P., Zdun, U. (eds.) ECSA 2014. LNCS, vol. 8627, pp. 374–389. Springer, Switzerland (2014). doi:10.1007/978-3-319-09970-5_32
5. Christensen, H.B., Hansen, K.M., Schougaard, K.R.: An empirical study of software architects' concerns. In: 16th Asia-Pacific Software Engineering Conference, pp. 111–118. IEEE Computer Society, Washington, DC, December 2009
6. Fairbanks, G.: Just Enough Software Architecture: A Risk-Driven Approach. Marshall & Brainerd, Boulder (2010)
7. Fowler, M.: Who needs an architect? IEEE Softw. 20(5), 11–13 (2003)
8. Gasson, S.: Rigor in grounded theory research: an interpretive perspective on generating theory from qualitative field studies. In: The Handbook of Information Systems Research, pp. 79–102 (2004)
9. Hove, S.E., Anda, B.: Experiences from conducting semi-structured interviews in empirical software engineering research. In: 11th IEEE International Software Metrics Symposium (METRICS 2005), pp. 10–23, September 2005
10. Jansen, A., Bosch, J.: Software architecture as a set of architectural design decisions. In: 5th Working IEEE/IFIP Conference on Software Architecture, WICSA 2005, pp. 109–120. IEEE Computer Society, Washington, DC (2005)
11. Jansen, A., van der Ven, J., Avgeriou, P., Hammer, D.K.: Tool support for architectural decisions. In: Sixth Working IEEE/IFIP Conference on Software Architecture, WICSA 2007, p. 4. IEEE Computer Society, Washington, DC (2007)
12. Kruchten, P.: What do software architects really do? J. Syst. Softw. 81(12), 2413–2416 (2008)
13. Malavolta, I., Lago, P., Muccini, H., Pelliccione, P., Tang, A.: What industry needs from architectural languages: a survey. IEEE Trans. Softw. Eng. 39(6), 869–891 (2013)
14. McBride, M.R.: The software architect. Commun. ACM 50(5), 75–81 (2007)

15. Mirakhorli, M., Cleland-Huang, J.: Detecting, tracing, and monitoring architectural tactics in code. IEEE Trans. Softw. Eng. **42**(3), 205–220 (2016)
16. Murphy, G.C., Notkin, D., Sullivan, K.: Software reflexion models: bridging the gap between source and high-level models. In: Proceedings of the 3rd ACM SIGSOFT Symposium on Foundations of Software Engineering, SIGSOFT 1995, pp. 18–28. ACM, New York (1995)
17. Perry, D.E., Wolf, A.L.: Foundations for the study of software architecture. SIGSOFT Softw. Eng. Notes **17**(4), 40–52 (1992)
18. Sangal, N., Jordan, E., Sinha, V., Jackson, D.: Using dependency models to manage complex software architecture. In: Proceedings of the 20th Annual ACM SIGPLAN Conference on Object-Oriented Programming, Systems, Languages, and Applications, pp. 167–176. ACM, New York (2005)
19. Strauss, A., Corbin, J., et al.: Basics of Qualitative Research, vol. 15. Sage, Newbury Park (1990)
20. Taylor, R.N., Medvidovic, N., Dashofy, E.M.: Software Architecture: Foundations, Theory, and Practice. Wiley Publishing, Chichester (2009)
21. Terra, R., Valente, M.T.: A dependency constraint language to manage object-oriented software architectures. Softw. Pract. Exper. **39**(12), 1073–1094 (2009)
22. Vogel, O., Arnold, I., Chughtai, A., Kehrer, T.: Software Architecture: A Comprehensive Framework and Guide for Practitioners. Springer, Heidelberg (2011)
23. Zimmermann, O., Gschwind, T., Küster, J., Leymann, F., Schuster, N.: Reusable architectural decision models for enterprise application development. In: Overhage, S., Szyperski, C.A., Reussner, R., Stafford, J.A. (eds.) QoSA 2007. LNCS, vol. 4880, pp. 15–32. Springer, Heidelberg (2007). doi:10.1007/978-3-540-77619-2_2

Software Architectures for Web and Mobile Systems

The Disappearance of Technical Specifications in Web and Mobile Applications
A Survey Among Professionals

Theo Theunissen[✉] and Uwe van Heesch

HAN University of Applied Sciences, Arnhem, The Netherlands
theo.theunissen@gmail.com, uwe@vanheesch.net

Abstract. In recent years, we have been observing a paradigm shift in design and documentation practices for web and mobile applications. There is a trend towards fewer up-front design specification and more code and configuration-centric documentation. In this paper we present the results of a survey, conducted with professional software engineers who build web and mobile applications. Our focus was on understanding the role of software architecture in these applications, i.e. what is designed up-front and how; which parts of the architecture are reused from previous projects and what is the average lifetime of such applications. Among other things, the results indicate that free-text design specification is favored over the use of modeling languages like UML; architectural knowledge is primarily preserved through verbal communication between team members, and the average lifetime of web and mobile applications is between one and five years.

1 Introduction

In recent years, we have been observing a paradigm shift in the software engineering community. Professional software development projects traditionally relied on upfront planning and design, distinct software phases and often a clear separation of roles and responsibilities within project teams. Ever growing time-to-market constraints, however, leads to high innovation pressure, which brought forth methods and techniques like agile project management, continuous delivery, and DevOps, which break with the traditional way of approaching software projects. Apart from this, primarily for web and mobile application development, developers now need to deal with an increasingly heterogeneous tool and language stack. In that domain in particular, software is often designed ad-hoc, or at best by drawing informal sketches on a white board while discussing with peers. The reasons for this are multifold: where applications must be developed and rolled out quickly, designers do not seem to see the value of spending much time on modeling and documenting solutions. A second reason is that software engineering has no guidelines for efficient modeling of heterogeneous multi-paradigm applications. This is partly due to the fact that software engineering curricula at universities are still heavily focused on traditional object-oriented analysis and design using UML, which is not a good fit for applications that are not

© Springer International Publishing AG 2016
B. Tekinerdogan et al. (Eds.): ECSA 2016, LNCS 9839, pp. 265–273, 2016.
DOI: 10.1007/978-3-319-48992-6_20

purely object-oriented. In this paper, we describe a questionnaire-based survey, conducted to understand current design and documentation practices that companies use for developing web and mobile applications. Our investigation leads to the conclusion that in the design phase, "experimentation" with *proof of concepts* has the highest score, and "free-text documentation" is more used than technical documentation (UML, ERD). The continuity of knowledge is primarily achieved using free-text documentation and verbal communication.

The study is part of a larger research project, in which we develop an architecture framework that is streamlined for modern web and mobile applications. In the framework, we plan to provide just-enough architecture and design specification for supporting agile web and mobile application development, while preserving core decisions and design for re-use in subsequent projects.

The rest of this paper is organized as follows. Section 2 describes the research questions and presents and motivates the study design. Section 3 presents the results of the questionnaire and our interpretations with respect to the research questions. The next section presents potential threats to validity. Finally, we conclude and present directions for future work.

2   Study Design

In this section, we present our research questions and the study design.

2.1   Research Questions

As described in the introduction, the goal of our research project is to develop an architecture framework that optimally supports software engineers in building and maintaining web and mobile applications. The study presented was conducted to settle the baseline process and to get a better understanding of current design and documentation processes, as well as developers' concerns in the industry. In particular, we address the following research questions:

RQ1. How are web and mobile applications designed and how is design knowledge preserved in the industry?

RQ2. Which parts of the software architecture are re-used across web and mobile applications within a development team?

RQ3. What is the average life expectancy of web and mobile applications?

The first question aims at finding out how web and mobile applications are designed, i.e. which modeling languages, or more generically: which approaches, are used to support the design process. By design, we refer to activities conducted prior to technical implementation. The second objective of RQ1[1] is to find out how architectural knowledge about these applications is maintained. This includes decisions made during the architecting process, as well as information about the problem and solution space.

---

[1] Because of space limitations, in this paper, we bundled two of our original research questions into one.

RQ2 originates from the conjecture that development teams partially reuse architectural design from previous projects. Architectural reuse improves development efficiency, which contributes to fast time-to-market of features. Furthermore, reuse is a means for risk mitigation [1]. Here, we want to find out which parts of an architecture are typically re-used.

The third question concerns the timespan, developers expect their applications to reside on the market before they are discarded or subject to a major re-engineering. This is relevant because the cost-effectiveness of documentation effort is proportional to the expected lifetime of an application.

2.2 Methodology

A survey was conducted to collect data for our research questions. We chose to use a web-based questionnaire over individual interviews, because we wanted to reach a sufficiently large subject population. Questionnaire-based surveys additionally exhibit a higher degree of external validity than interviews [2]. When used with closed-ended questions and fixed response options, data gathered with questionnaires can easily be processed automatically. This is in contrast to interviews, which have high costs in terms of time per interview, traveling and processing the results. On the other hand, interviews provide greater flexibility and allow for more in-depth exploration of the respondents' answers. As described in Sect. 5, we plan to conduct interviews with a small number of the subjects at a later stage to get more in-depth insight in the phenomena we observe through the questionnaire.

We conducted a pilot study with three members from the target population to improve the wording, order and answering options of the questions.

2.3 Participants and Sampling

The target population of this study is professional software engineers who develop web and/or mobile applications. We used snowball sampling, i.e. the questionnaire was sent out to members from our professional network using e-mail. We asked the receivers to forward the questionnaire to colleagues and peers from their own network, which is a means to achieve a more randomized sample [3]. The questionnaire was spread in form of an online form.

3 Data Analysis and Interpretation

This section presents the data analysis and interpretation. We primarily use descriptive statistics to analyze the collected data. The section is divided according to the three research questions. Table 1 maps the research questions to the questions from the questionnaire.

A total of 73 subjects responded to the questionnaire. From these respondents, 39.7 % completed the questionnaire and answered all questions. For reasons of space limitations, we only report on the most interesting findings of our

Table 1. Mapping of questions and research questions

No	Question	RQ1	RQ2	RQ3
A1	What is the number of employees working in your organization?	✓		
A2	How many employees are working on software development in your organization?	✓		
A3	How many employees are working on your currently running project?	✓		
A4	Which of the following activities do you perform within your organization?	✓		
B1	What is the average number of users per day as anticipated at design time?	✓		
B2	What is the peak number of concurrent users during operations?	✓		
B3	Which of the following components are used in your web application?		✓	
B4	Which of these aforementioned components are obtained from a cloud service?	✓	✓	✓
B5	Suppose you start a new project or a major re-engineering of an existing application, which of these aforementioned components will you use again for Web applications that have been rebuild or evolved?		✓	
B6	What is the average lifetime of your application in number of years?			✓
B7	Within your organization how many applications share the same overall architectural design?		✓	
B8	How often do you release new features?			✓
C1	Which of the following activities are typical for software projects you have worked on?	✓	✓	
C2	Which of the following process methods are used in your projects?	✓		
C3	What types of tools do you use during your design process?	✓	✓	
C5	How do you ensure that knowledge about features, implementations, design decisions etc. is maintained?	✓		
D1	What are your three top priorities in software development?	✓	✓	✓
D2	What are your three top priorities in software development when you need to successfully maintain software in the long term?	✓	✓	✓

study. Our study database, which contains the questionnaire and all responses, can be found on http://2question.com/q1q3/.

The questionnaire has four sections. The first section (A) includes questions about the organization, role of the respondent and previous experience. The second section (B) concerns the applications developed. The third section (C) addresses the design, development and maintenance. The last section (D) concerns priorities regarding software development and software maintenance.

In the remainder of this section, we present the results and most relevant answers for every research question. Additionally we discuss results of supporting questions and control questions. This section ends with an interpretation of the results, discussion and expected and remarkable outcomes.

3.1 Analysis RQ1: How are Web and Mobile Applications Designed and How is Design Knowledge About These Applications Preserved in the Industry?

The questions most relevant to RQ1 are "What types of tools do you use during your design process?" (C3) and "How do you ensure that knowledge about features, implementations, design decisions etc. is maintained?" (C5).

In question C3, we asked participants to specify the tools[2] used for design, the time they spend on each of these tools (as a percentage of the total time spent on design activities), and the quantity of results (number of occurrences or number of produced deliverables). The design approaches, where participants spend most time on are "Experimenting, building proofs of concept" (26%), "Documented concepts in written language like Word documents" (22%) and "Sketches like annotated block/line diagrams" (19%). With 11% of total design time, technical documentation (e.g. UML, SysML, ERD, Database models) received the lowest score. In terms of quantity, the top three answers were "Verbal communication" (14), "Sketches like annotated block/line diagrams" (6) and "Experimenting, building proofs of concept" (3).

For knowledge preservation (question C5), the top three methods used in terms of spent time (percentage of overall time spent on knowledge preservation) are "Documented concepts in written language like Word documents" (26%), "Documented code (with tools like JavaDoc, JSDoc or no tools)" (26%) and "Verbal communication" (17%).

Additionally, we asked participants about their top three priorities during software development (question D1) and software maintenance (D2). During *development time*, the top three priorities are "Quality" (7,2%), "(Functional) requirements" and "time-to-market" (both 6,6%), and "Maintainability" (4,8%). During *maintenance*, the top three priorities are "Documentation" (18%), "Code quality" (17%) and both "Architecture" and "Maintainability" (6,8%).

---

[2] The term *tool* is used in a wide sense here, covering among others UML, free-text, but also conversations and informal whiteboard sketches.

3.2   Questions Related to RQ2: Which Parts of the Software Architecture are Re-used Across Modern Web Applications?

The most relevant question that relates to this research question is B5: "Suppose you start a new project or a major re-engineering of an existing application, which of these aforementioned components will you use again for Web applications that have been rebuilt or evolved?"

The top three reuslts from C5 are "Webservice API (eg. RESTful, SOAP)" (86 %), "SQL Database(s)" (83 %) and "Server side web frameworks" (79 %)

A supporting question is B7: "Within your organization how many applications share the same overall architectural design?" 76 % of the applications share between 21 % and 80 % of the overall architectural design. This is equally distributed over the three categories. 21 % are from applications that share almost all components. The rest (1 %) does not share any component. Another supporting question is B3 where participants where asked about the types of software components they typically use in applications. The components mentioned most prominently (53 %) are: *Build Tools*, *Test tools*, *Server Side Frameworks*, and *Web Services*.

3.3   Questions Related to RQ3: What is the Average Life Expectancy of Modern Web Applications?

The most relevant question related to this research question is B6: "What is the average lifetime of your application in number of years?".

62 % of the applications have a lifetime between 1 and 5 years. 14 % of the applications have a lifetime of more than 10 years. The lifetime of an application determines the selection of components. For start-up companies, the initial application architecture will be sufficient for the first period. When growing in number of customers, transactions, and processes, we expect that the initial application has to be replaced with a scaleable architecture and infrastructure.

3.4   Interpretation RQ1-RQ3

In this section, we discuss the results regarding all three research questions.

In many software engineering curricula, students are taught to use (semi-) formal modeling languages like UML for designing software before coding. In contrast to this, we found that technical documents are not intensively used for design purposes in the software engineering industry. Instead, at least for mobile and web applications, the design process is primarily driven by verbal communication and informal sketches. This is in line with Sonnenburg, who describes software design as a collaborative creative activity [4], which benefits from approaches that are not constrained by fixed notations and formalisms.

On the other hand, we found that projects create more output in the shape of technical documentation than in other forms. This may be surprising at first, as less time is spent on technical documentation. On the other hand, there may be a causal relationship between those two aspects, i.e. software engineers spend less time on technical documentation, because they are reluctant to spend time on non-engineering activities, i.e. activities that are no integral part of the built process.

In question C5, we assume a typical division between development and maintenance, in which developers in a project are not responsible for deployment and maintenance of applications. In this scenario, documentation is crucial for deployment and maintenance, as well as for managing responsibilities [5]. However, most participants chose "Verbal communication" as the primary method for handing over the code to other team members. In discussions with software engineers in the pilot group and remarks from participants, we found that engineers rather rely on proven practices in their teams, rather than formal methods, to design, develop and maintain applications. One of these proven practices is the use of verbal communication in weekly team meetings to discuss code and design. These discussions aim at improving the quality of the code by reviewing the contributions for that week and sharing the concepts and implementations.

In line with [6–8], we did not expect that webservice API's (SOAP, RESTful) would be the most re-used architectural assets (question B5). We had rather expected that data would have a higher value both for business and for software engineers and thus would be more often re-used that services.

With B6, we expected that the average life time of an application will be within 3 to 5 years (as in [9]). This is related to IT expenditures that are typically budgeted from capital expenditures. Capital expenditures have a typical amortization of 5 years. Nowadays, companies do not have to invest in costly server infrastructure anymore (capital expenditure). Instead, web and mobile applications are typically deployed in cloud environments, in which infrastructure is payed for as-a-service and is thus operational expenditure [10]. Furthermore, software engineers typically change their employer or job-role between 2 years [11] and 4.6 years [12]. Finally, software engineers typically favor building from scratch over brown-field applications that have been patched over the years. In the latter cases, the technical debt exceeds the cost of re-building from scratch.

4   Threats to Validity

In this section, we discuss possible threats to the internal and external validity of our findings. A common threat to internal validity in questionnaire-based surveys stems from poorly understood questions and a low coverage of constructs under study. The former threat was mitigated to a large extent by piloting the questionnaire with three participants form the target population. We asked these participants to fill in the questionnaire. Afterwards, they were asked to describe their interpretations of the questions and their answers. We used this input in multiple iterations to revise the questions and answering options. We addressed construct validity by explicitly mapping the questions of our questionnaire to the research questions (see Table 1) and by making sure that each research question is covered by multiple questions in the questionnaire.

External validity is concerned with the degree, to which the study results can be generalized for a larger subject population [13]. We used statistical methods to analyze whether our results are significant. Mason et al. postulate that, as a rule of thumb, questionnaires require between 30 and 150 responses in order to yield valid responses [14].

We had a total of 73 respondents; 39.7 % of whom answered all questions. Thus, we suppose that the number of respondents is sufficient.

Two remarkable outcomes from the questionnaire (questions C3 and C5) are (1) that technical documentation is less popular than plain text documentation and (2) that continuity of knowledge is achieved primarily through verbal communication. We calculated the variance and standard deviation of our responses. For C3 the variance is 0.2 and thus very low; for C5 the calculated mean is 423, the standard deviation is 193 and the weighted value for verbal communication is 425. The actual weighted value deviates by 2 points only. Thus, the results with respect to our most surprising outcomes are statistically significant.

5   Conclusions and Future Work

In this paper, we investigated how web and mobile applications are designed and documented. We found that verbal communication and informal sketches are clearly preferred over modeling languages. To preserve and transfer application-specific knowledge, companies deem code documentation equally important as technical documentation. Furthermore, for many companies, verbal communication is the primary approach for transferring knowledge within teams. This may be surprising at first as it bears the risk that knowledge gets lost, because of key employees leaving the company or a lack of communication in teams. However, web and mobile applications are primarily developed in small teams using agile development processes. Such development approaches rely heavily on verbal communication, and practices like daily stand ups in Scrum achieve that knowledge is widely spread within the development team.

Another remarkable outcome is the very high degree of architectural re-use across projects. In particular, we found that web-service APIs, SQL databases and server-side frameworks are re-used across projects in more than 80 % of the cases. This is certainly impacted by the focus of our research on web and mobile applications. Teams build up knowledge and expertise in certain technologies and exploit this knowledge to a large degree for reasons of efficiency.

Regarding the average expected life-time of web and mobile applications, we found that most applications ($\sim$ 60 %) are built for being rather short-lived (1–5 years). Further investigation is required to understand the reasons for this phenomenon.

As explained in the introduction, we will use these results for creating an architecture framework streamlined for web and mobile applications. The framework will anticipate the reluctance to produce (semi-)formal documentation and the high degree of technological re-use. We will conduct further research to understand the impact of the short life-times of such applications on the effort found reasonable for producing written documentation.

We started this research with a questionnaire to obtain quantitative data. The next phase in our research plan is to conduct interviews to collect qualitative and more in-depth data.

References

1. van Heesch, U., Avgeriou, P.: Mature architecting - a survey about the reasoning process of professional architects. In Proceedings of the Ninth Working IEEE/IFIP Conference on Software Architecture, pp. 260–269. IEEE Computer Society (2011)
2. Ciolkowski, M., Laitenberger, O., Vegas, S., Biffl, S.: Practical experiences in the design and conduct of surveys in empirical software engineering. In: Conradi, R., Wang, A.I. (eds.) Empirical Methods and Studies in Software Engineering. LNCS, vol. 2765, pp. 104–128. Springer, Heidelberg (2003). doi:10.1007/978-3-540-45143-3_7
3. Teddlie, C., Fen, Y.: Mixed methods sampling a typology with examples. J. Mixed Methods Res. **1**(1), 77–100 (2007)
4. Sonnenburg, S.: Creativity in communication: a theoretical framework for collaborative product creation. Creativity Innov. Manage. **13**(4), 254–262 (2004)
5. Carzaniga, A., Fuggetta, A., Hall, R.S., Heimbigner, D., van der Hoek, A., Wolf, A.L.: A Characterization Framework for Software Deployment Technologies. Colorado State Univ Fort Collins Dept of Computer Science (1998)
6. Teece, D.J.: Capturing value from knowledge assets: the new economy, markets for know-how, and intangible assets. Calif. Manage. Rev. **40**(3), 55–79 (1998)
7. Rayport, J.F., Sviokla, J.J.: Exploiting the virtual value chain. Harvard Bus. Rev. **73**(6), 75 (1995)
8. Howard, R.A.: Information value theory. IEEE Trans. Syst. Sci. Cybern. **2**(1), 22–26 (1966)
9. Tamai, T., Torimitsu, Y.: Software lifetime and its evolution process over generations. In: Proceedings, Conference on Software Maintenance, pp. 63–69. IEEE (1992)
10. Armbrust, M., Fox, A., Griffith, R., Joseph, A.D., Katz, R., Konwinski, A., Lee, G., Patterson, D., Rabkin, A., Stoica, I., et al.: A view of cloud computing. Commun. ACM **53**(4), 50–58 (2010)
11. Eriksson, T., Ortega, J.: The adoption of job rotation: testing the theories. Ind. Labor Relat. Rev. **59**(4), 653–666 (2006)
12. U.S. Bureau of Labor Statistics. Employee tenure summary, September 2014. http://www.bls.gov/news.release/tenure.nr0.htm. Accessed 28 Mar 2016
13. Kitchenham, B.A., Pfleeger, S.L., Pickard, L.M., Jones, P.W., Hoaglin, D.C., El Emam, K., Rosenberg, J.: Preliminary guidelines for empirical research in software engineering. IEEE Trans. Softw. Eng. **28**(8), 721–734 (2002)
14. Mason, M.: Sample size and saturation in PhD studies using qualitative interviews. Forum Qual. Sozialforschung/Forum: Qual. Soc. Res. **11**(3), Art. 8 (2010). http://nbn-resolving.de/urn:nbn:de:0114-fqs100387

Architecture Modeling and Analysis of Security in Android Systems

Bradley Schmerl[1]([✉]), Jeff Gennari[1], Alireza Sadeghi[2], Hamid Bagheri[3],
Sam Malek[2], Javier Cámara[1], and David Garlan[1]

[1] Institute for Software Research, Carnegie Mellon University, Pittsburgh, PA, USA
schmerl@cs.cmu.edu
[2] School of Information and Computer Sciences,
University of California, Irvine, CA, USA
[3] Department of Computer Science and Engineering,
University of Nebraska, Lincoln, NE, USA

Abstract. Software architecture modeling is important for analyzing system quality attributes, particularly security. However, such analyses often assume that the architecture is completely known in advance. In many modern domains, especially those that use plugin-based frameworks, it is not possible to have such a complete model because the software system continuously changes. The Android mobile operating system is one such framework, where users can install and uninstall apps at run time. We need ways to model and analyze such architectures that strike a balance between supporting the dynamism of the underlying platforms and enabling analysis, particularly throughout a system's lifetime. In this paper, we describe a formal architecture style that captures the modifiable architectures of Android systems, and that supports security analysis as a system evolves. We illustrate the use of the style with two security analyses: a predicate-based approach defined over architectural structure that can detect some common security vulnerabilities, and inter-app permission leakage determined by model checking. We also show how the evolving architecture of an Android device can be obtained by analysis of the apps on a device, and provide some performance evaluation that indicates that the architecture can be amenable for use throughout the system's lifetime.

1 Introduction

Software architecture modeling is an important tool for early analysis of quality attributes [22]. Architecture analysis of run-time quality attributes such as performance, availability, and reliability can increase confidence at design time that quality goals will be met during implementation. Component-and-connector view architectures are especially important to reason about the desired run-time qualities of the system. Static analysis at the architectural level can support identification of possible issues and focus dynamic analysis efforts. When evaluating security, the combined use of static and dynamic analysis provides a

© Springer International Publishing AG 2016
B. Tekinerdogan et al. (Eds.): ECSA 2016, LNCS 9839, pp. 274–290, 2016.
DOI: 10.1007/978-3-319-48992-6_21

comprehensive evaluation approach, where static analysis identifies possible vulnerabilities (e.g. static code and information flow paths) and dynamic analysis detects and mitigates active exploitation. A combined approach that includes static and dynamic analysis leads to more efficient, effective, and comprehensive security evaluation.

Architecture analysis of security involves understanding the information flow through an architecture to uncover security related issues such as information leakage, privilege escalation, and spoofing [1]. Many of these analyses assume the existence of complete architectures of the system being analyzed, and in the case of security analysis, knowledge of the entire information flow of the system.

However, in many modern systems, architectures can evolve and change at run time, and so new paths of communication, and thus new vulnerabilities, can be introduced into these systems. A critical example of this is software frameworks, which are used in many software projects in many domains. Frameworks offer a means for achieving composition and reuse at scale — frameworks can be extended with plugins during use. Examples of such frameworks include mobile device software, web browser extensions, and programming environments. The mobile device arena, in particular the Android framework, is an interesting case. The Android framework provides flexible communication between apps (plugins that use the framework) that allows other apps to provide alternative core functionality (such as browsing, SMS, or email) or to tailor other parts of the user experience. However, this flexibility can also be exploited by malicious apps for nefarious purposes [10]. We need ways to analyze the architectures of these systems, in particular for security properties.

Like many of these frameworks, the architectures of the software of Android devices exhibit a number of challenges when it comes to modeling and analysis of security properties: (1) the system architectures evolve as new apps are installed, activated, and used together; (2) the architectures of each app, while conforming to a structural style, are constructed by independent parties, with differing motivations and tradeoffs, (3) there are no common goals for a particular device.

This means that security needs to be reanalyzed as the system changes [6]. In particular, we need to be able to do analysis over a good model that is abstract enough for analysis to be computationally feasible, yet detailed enough for analysis to produce meaningful and accurate results. And so there is a question of how to specify the new evolved architecture, and at what level of abstraction. Moreover, to support the way that these systems evolve over time, the architecture model of the system needs to be derived from the system itself, so that all communication pathways throughout deployment can be analyzed as the system changes.

In this paper, we describe an architecture style for Android that supports analysis of security. We show how instances of this style can be derived from Android apps to specify an up-to-date architecture of the entire software on an Android device as apps are installed and removed. We also give examples of two kinds of security analysis that is supported for this style — constraint-based analysis that detects the presence of a category of threats commonly known as STRIDE [23], and a model-checking approach that determines potentially vulnerable communication pathways among apps that may result in leakage of information and permissions.

This paper is organized as follows: In Sect. 2 we introduce Android, and discuss work on architecture modeling of Android and architecture-based security analysis. Building on this, we define the requirements for an architecture style for Android security analysis in Sect. 3 and then describe the Acme architecture style in Sect. 4. We describe a tool to automatically derive instances of this style from Android apps in Sect. 5. Section 6 describes two security analyses using this architectural abstraction. In Sect. 7, we show how long it takes to discover the architecture of a number of differently sized apps available in the play store. We conclude with discussion and future work in Sect. 8.

2   Background and Related Work

In this section, we first provide an overview of Android to help the reader follow the discussions that ensue. We then provide an overview of the prior work in architectural modeling and analysis, particularly with respect to the security of Android.

2.1   Introduction to Android

Android is a popular operating system for mobile devices, like phones, tablets, etc. It is deployed on a diverse set of hardware, and can be customized by companies to provide additional features. Android is designed to allow programs, known as apps, to be installed on the device by end users. From an operating systems perspective, Android provides apps with communication mechanisms and access to underlying device hardware and services, such as telephony features.[1] Furthermore, it allows end-user extension in the form of installing additional apps that are provided by third parties. The provision of explicit communication channels between apps allows for rich app ecosystems to emerge. Apps can use standard apps for activities such as web browsing, mapping, telephony, messaging, etc., or they can be flexible and allow third party apps to handle these activities. Because security is a concern in Android, apps are sandboxed from each other (using the Unix account access control where every app has its own account), and can only communicate through mechanisms provided by Android.

An app in Android specifies in a manifest file what activities and other components comprise it. In this manifest, activities further specify the patterns of messages that they can process. Apps specify the permissions that they require that need to be granted by users when they install the apps.[2] Activities in an app communicate by sending and receiving messages, called *intents*. These intents

---

[1] https://developer.android.com/.

[2] The most recent version of Android, Marshmallow, has a more dynamic form of permission granting, which allows permissions to be granted as they are needed dynamically by the app. This paper discusses the Lollipop version of Android.

can be sent either to other activities within the app, or to activities that belong to other apps. There are two forms of intent: *explicit* and *implicit*. Senders of explicit intents specify the intended recipients, which can be in the same or another app. For implicit intents, a recipient is not specified. Instead, Android conducts intent resolution that matches the intent with intent patterns specified by activities. So, for example, an activity can request that a web page be displayed, but can allow that web page to be displayed by third party browsing apps that may be unknown at the time the requesting app is developed.

While intents provide a great deal of flexibility, they are also the source of a number of security vulnerabilities such as intent spoofing, privilege escalation, and unauthorized intent receipt [10]. To some degree, these vulnerabilities can be uncovered by analyzing apps and performing static analysis to see how intents are used, what checks are made on senders and receivers of intents, and so on [21]. However, Android is an extendable platform that allows users to dynamically download, update, and delete apps that makes a full static analysis impossible.

2.2 Security Architecture Modeling and Analysis

As mentioned, many security vulnerabilities in Android result from unexpected interactions between components. Many of the communication pathways of interest are specified at the component level within the manifest definition of the app, or can be extracted by analyzing calls in its bytecode (described in Sect. 5). Therefore, analysis for security can be focused at the architecture level - analyzing at the level of components and interactions.

Specialized ADLs geared towards security analysis exist. These tend to focus on specific security properties, such as access control [12,20]. In [2] UML OCL-type constraints are used to specify constraints that uncover threats defined by the Common Attack Pattern Enumeration and Classification (CAPEC)[3] and tool support is described for security risk analysis during the system design phase using system architecture and design models.

The key point of these architectural security analyses is that the communication pathways need to be represented at the architecture level, along with the security relevant properties needed for analysis. However, all of this work relates to security design, and so there is an assumption that a complete architecture is available for analysis. Furthermore, the approaches discussed rely on developers to implement the systems according to the architecture. To enable these kinds of analysis on Android requires being able to extract the properties relevant to security from Android apps.

In [3], the authors study the extent to which Android apps employ architectural concepts in practice. This study provides a characterization of architectural principles found in the Android ecosystem, supported with mining the reverse-engineered architecture of hundreds of Android apps in several app repositories. We build on this work to provide automated architectural extraction from Android devices.

---

[3] http://capec.mitre.org.

SEPAR [7] provides an automatic scheme for formal synthesis of Android inter-component security policies, allowing end-users to safeguard the apps installed on their device from inter-component vulnerabilities. It relies on a constraint solver to synthesize possible security exploits, from which fine-grained security policies are derived. Such fine-grained, yet system-specific, policies can then be enforced at run time to protect a given device.

Bagheri et al. conduct a bounded verification of the Android permission protocol modeled in terms of architectural-level operations [4,5]. The results of this study reveal a number of flaws in the permission protocol that cause serious security defects, in some cases allowing the attacker to entirely bypass the Android permission checks.

SECORIA [1] provides security analysis for architectures and conformance for systems with an underlying object-oriented implementation. Through static analysis, a data flow architecture of a system is constructed as an instance of a data flow architecture style defined in Acme [18]. Components are assigned a trust level and data read and write permissions are specified on data stores. Security constraints particular to a software systems (such as that "Access to the key vault [...] should be granted to only security officers and the cryptographic engine") are captured as Acme rules. In [16], this dataflow style is extended with constraints for analyzing a subset of the STRIDE vulnerabilities. We show in Sect. 6.2 how this latter approach can be applied to analyze vulnerabilities in Android.

3   Modeling Requirements for Android

To evaluate the security of Android apps, the core Android architectural structures need to be represented in an architecture style that is expressive enough to capture security properties. Android app component types, such as activities, services, and content providers form the building blocks of all apps. Each Android component type possesses properties that are critical for security assessment. For example, activities can be designated as "exported" if they can be referenced outside of the app to which they belong. Exported activities are a common source of security vulnerabilities, thus a security-focused architectural model must include information about whether an activity is exported. Android apps are distinct, yet they share many commonalities necessary for app creation and interaction. A major consequence of this design is that boundaries between apps are loosely defined and enforced. To identify and evaluate potential security issues that emerge from app interaction on a device, all apps and their connections deployed on the device must be made explicit in the architecture. Furthermore, because apps can be updated, installed, and removed during the lifetime of the device, the architecture model must be flexible and easy to modify.

Since a significant number of Android security issues arise from unexpected interactions between apps, modeling communication pathways between apps on a device is perhaps the most critical requirement for security analysis. At the device level, each individual app is essentially a subsystem that operates in the context of a larger, device-wide ensemble. Apps are often designed to rely on other apps, many of which may not be known at design time. For instance, if an app needs a mapping service, it does not necessarily know which specific mapping service will be available at run time. An app can be reasonably secure in isolation, but when evaluated in the presence of other apps, it may contribute to critical security vulnerabilities.

Android's intent passing system provides a common communication mechanism to simplify inter-app communication. Android supports many intent passing modes, such as asynchronous and synchronous delivery. However, Android's intent passing system includes additional semantics that can have different security implications; for example, whether an intent is delivered to one specific component or broadcast to all components. Differences in intent passing semantics need to be made explicit in an Android architecture style to enable analysis of common security issues that rely on certain types of communication, such as intent or activity spoofing. Android app components and connectors are organized in apps by configuring them via a "manifest" file. The boundaries set in the manifest creates an important trust boundary and must be explicit to evaluate data flowing in to, or out of, an app. To be complete, the architecture style must support component-to-component interaction and inter-app communication.

Android permissions are another core mechanism used to prevent security-related issues. Given the pervasive intent-based communication system, it is left to permissions to control access and information flow between components. Android supports a wide array of core permissions and provides ways to add new permissions. Due in part to the nature of Android permission management, many security issues result from components with insufficient privileges gaining access to privileged components and system resources. The architecture modeling language must support Android privileges. Identifying security vulnerabilities often involves determining whether permissions can be subverted. Thus, permissions must be attached to various resources in a way that allows them to be analyzed.

4   An Android Architecture Style

Based on the requirements above, we define a formal architectural model of the Android framework in order to have a basis for modeling the structures and constraints in Android, and to permit analysis of security vulnerabilities and exploits. To do this, we have developed an architecture style in Acme [18], that represents intent interactions and permissions in Android. We chose Acme as the modeling language because of its flexibility in defining architecture styles, and its ability to specify formal first-order predicate logic rules to evaluate the correctness of instances of these styles.

All components types specify a property that indicates the class that implements them and the permissions needed to access them, as well as whether they are exported (or public) to other applications. The types of components are:

AcvtivityT: This component type specifies an activity within an app. Activities represent components in an app that have a user interface.

Communicating with that activity involves instantiating this user interface. Specified with the activity are the intent patterns that it understands and can process, the kinds of intent that it sends, in addition to the services and resources that it accesses. These latter communications are all represented by distinct port types, as described below.

ServiceT: This component type specifies a service within an app. According to the standard Android description, "a Service is an application component that can perform long-running operations in the background and does not provide a user interface. Another application component can start a service and it will continue to run in the background even if the user switches to another application. Additionally, a component can bind to a service to interact with it and even perform interprocess communication (IPC). For example, a service might handle network transactions, play music, perform file I/O, or interact with a content provider, all from the background."[4] Services have ports that specify the interfaces they provide and the services they use.

ContentProviderT: Content providers encapsulate and manage data. They provide mechanisms, such as read and write permissions, to manage security. Architecturally, we distinguish read and write permissions on the data provided by these components.

BroadcastReceiverT: Broadcast receivers are components that receive system level events, like PHONE BOOT COMPLETED or BATTERY LOW. We model broadcast receivers as distinct from activities because they can only receive a subset of intent types called standard broadcast actions.

Figure 1 gives an example of an instance of the style showing two apps: K9-Email (at the top) and PhotoStream. Each of the component types described above is represented by a rectangle or hockey puck shape with a solid line. We describe the connectors and how we represent apps below.

Component type definitions for the style are relatively straightforward to derive, and are consistent with other work on modeling Android. However, port and connector modeling, in addition to modeling apps themselves, presents some challenges.

4.1 Modeling Apps as Groups

So far we have discussed how we have modeled elements of an app, but not the app itself. Because most vulnerabilities involve inter-app communication, and apps themselves specify additional information (e.g., which activities are exported), we need a way to explicitly represent them. One way to do this would be via hierarchy: make each app a separate component with a subsystem that is composed of the activities, services, etc. This would mean that we could represent a device as a collection of App components, where the structure is hidden in the hierarchy. However, this complicates security checking, because it involves analyzing communication that is directly between activities and services

---

[4] http://developer.android.com/guide/components/services.html

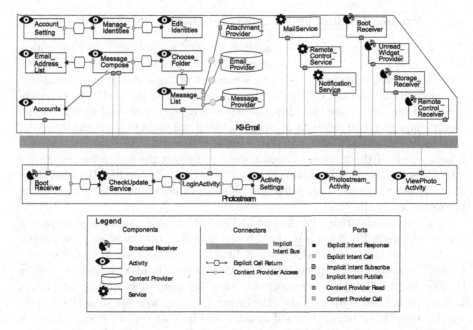

Fig. 1. An architecture instance in Android that captures two apps on a device.

(and not apps); in such cases, any analysis would inevitably need to traverse the hierarchy, complicating rules and pathways that are directly between constituent components.

Alternatively, Acme has a notion of *groups*, which are architectural elements that contain components and connectors as members. Like other architectural elements, groups can be typed and can define properties and rules. So, we use groups to model apps. The **AppGroupT** group type defines the permissions that an Android app has as a property. It then specifies its members as instances of the component types described above. Rules check that member elements do not require permissions that are not required by the app itself, providing some consistency checking about permission usage in the app. Groups naturally capture Android apps as collections of activities, services, content providers, etc., as well as the case where communication easily crosses app boundaries by referring directly to activities that may be external to the app. Groups are shown in Fig. 1 as dashed lines around the set of components that are provided by the app. Furthermore, for security analysis, groups form natural trust boundaries – communication within the app can be trusted because permissions are specified at the app level; communication outside the app should be analyzed because information flows to apps that may have different permissions. Therefore we also capture the permissions that are specified by apps as properties of the group. An application (group) specifies the set of permissions that an app is granted; activities specify the permissions that are required for them to be used.

4.2   Modeling Implicit and Explicit Intent Communication

One of the key requirements for enabling security analysis with formal models is being able to explicitly capture inter-app communication. All intents use the same underlying mechanism, but the *semantics* of implicit and explicit intents are markedly different. Explicit intents require the caller to specify the target of the intent, and hence are more like peer-to-peer communication. Implicit intents require apps that can process the intent to specify their interest via subscription. Senders of the intent do not name a receiver, and instead Android (or the user) selects which of the interested apps should process it through a process called intent resolution. This communication is like publish subscribe. Because these different semantics are susceptible to different vulnerabilities, they need to be distinguished in the style.

Explicit intents are modeled as point-to-point connectors (pairwise rectangular connectors in Fig. 1), where there is one source of the intent and one target. On the other hand, we model implicit intent communication via publish subscribe. We model one implicit intent bus per device. Implicit intents sent from components in all apps are connected to this bus; publishers specify the kind of intent that is being published (i.e., the intent's action), whereas subscribers specify the intent filter being matched against. In Fig. 1 we can see one device-wide implicit intent bus as the filled-in long rectangle in the middle of the figure. Elements from all apps connect to this bus (the intent type and intent subscriptions are specified as properties on the ports of connected components).

Different connector types for each intent-messaging type allows for more nuanced and in-depth reasoning about security properties than if they were modeled using the same type. For example, identifying unintended recipients of implicit intents is easier if implicit intents are first-order connectors.

Android also has a notion of broadcasts (intents sent to broadcast receivers in apps). We did not define a separate connector for broadcasts because, for the purposes of security analysis, broadcast communication is done by sending intents (though via different APIs). Subscribing to broadcasts is also done by registering an intent filter, making both the sending and receiving for broadcasts the same as for intents.

5   Architecture Discovery

For security analysis to be work for an extendable system such as Android, we need to be able to derive the architecture from the system. Being able to do this means that a tool can be provided to construct Android architectures incrementally, and is needed because the architecture is unique for each device. Figure 2 depicts an overview of our approach for recovering the architecture of an Android system. Given a set of Android application packages (also known as APKs), our architecture discovery method is able to recover the architecture of an entire phone system. For this purpose, we leverage three components: *Model Extractor*, *Template Engine*, and *Acme Studio*.

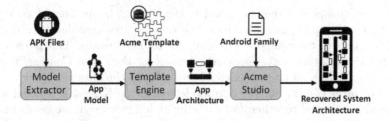

Fig. 2. Overview of Android system architecture discovery

The model extractor relies on the Soot [24] static analysis framework to capture an abstract model of each individual app. The captured model encodes the high-level, static structure of each app, as well as possible intra- or inter-app communications. To obtain an app model, the model extractor first extracts information from the manifest, including an app's components and their types, permissions that the app requires, and permissions enforced by each component to interact with other components. It also extracts public interfaces exposed by each app, which are entry points defined in the manifest file through Intent Filters of components. Furthermore, the model extractor obtains complementary information latent in the application bytecode using static code analysis [6]. This additional information, such as intent creation and transmission, or database queries, are necessary for further security analysis.

Once the generic model of an app (*App Model* in Fig. 2) is obtained, the template engine translates it to an Acme architecture. In fact, the input and output of this phase are models extracted from apps APK files in an XML format and their corresponding architecture descriptions in the Acme language, respectively. Our template engine, which is based on the FreeMarker framework,[5] needs a template (i.e., *Acme Template* in Fig. 2) that specifies the mapping between an app's extracted entities and the elements of the Acme's architectural style for Android (c.f. Sect. 4).

The model transformation process consists of multiple iterations over three elements of apps (i.e., components, intents, and database queries) extracted by the model extractor. It first iterates over the components of an app, and generates a **component** element whose type corresponds to one of the four component types of Android. The properties of the generated components are further set based on the extracted information from the manifest (e.g., component name, permissions, etc.). If the type of a component is *ContentProvider*, a provider *port* is added to the component. Moreover, if a component has defined any public interface through IntentFilters, a receiver port is added and connected to the Implicit Intent Bus. Afterwards, it iterates over intents of the given app model. For explicit intents, two ports are added to the sender and receiver components of the intent, and a Explicit Intent connector is generated to connect those ports. For implicit intents, however, only one port is added to the component sending

---

[5] http://freemarker.org/.

the message; this port is then attached to the Implicit Intent bus. Moreover, to capture data sharing communications, the tool iterates over database queries, and adds a port to the components calling a *ContentProvider*. This port is then connected to the other port, previously defined for the called *ContentProvider*, which is resolved based on the specified authority in the database query.

Finally, after translating the app models of all APK files, generated architectures are combined together and with the architecture style we developed for the Android framework (*Android Family*), which are then fed as a whole into AcmeStudio as the architecture of the entire system. This recovered architecture is further analyzed to identify flaws and vulnerabilities that could lead to security breaches in the system.

6   Architecture Analysis of Android

We now describe how the Android-specific architecture models specified in Acme can be analyzed using both inherent analysis capabilities of Acme, as well as external analysis capabilities that require an architecture model of the system as input. To that end, we first describe two types of analyses supported directly by Acme: the ability to evaluate the conformance of architecture models to constraints imposed by the Android framework, and the ability to evaluate the architecture models against a predefined set of security threats. We then describe an integration of Acme with an external toolset, called COVERT [6], that given an architectural representation of software is able to employ model-checking techniques to detect security vulnerabilities.

6.1   Conformance Analysis Using Acme

In Sect. 4 we described the characteristics of the style, which are derived from the constraints imposed by the Android framework on the structure and behavior of apps. Given the properties associated with permissions, exports, and intent filters, it is possible to describe well-formed architectures in this style using first-order predicate logic rules. For example,

- Permission use within apps is consistent, meaning that any component of an app that has a permission must be declared also at the app level. This constraint is defined for each application group.

    invariant **forall** m :! AppElement in **self**.MEMBERS |
       (hasValue(m.permission) −> contains (m.permission, usesPermissions));

- Explicit intent connectors should reference valid targets.

    heuristic **forall** p in /**self**/components/ports:!ExplicitIntentCallPortT |
       exists c:!AppElement in **self**.components |
          c.class == p.componentReference;

- All implicit intents are attached to the global implicit intent bus.

    invariant **forall** c1 :! IntentFilteringApplicationElementT in **self**.components |
       size (c1.intentFilters) > 0 −> connected (ImplicitIntentBus, c1);

- Activities and services that are not exported by an app are not connected to other apps.

```
invariant forall g1 :! AndroidApplicationGroupT in self.groups |
  forall g2 :! AndroidApplicationGroupT in self.groups |
    forall a1 :! IntentFilteringApplicationElementT in g1.members |
      forall a2 :! AppElement in g2.members |
        ((a1 != a2 and connected(a1, a2) and !a1.exported) -> g1 == g2);
```

Using these rules, Acme is able to check the architecture of individual apps, as well as a set of apps deployed together on an Android device. In Acme, *invariants* are used to specify rules that must be satsified, whereas *heuristics* represent rules-of-thumb that should be followed. When used in a forward engineering setting, where a model of an app is constructed prior to its implementation, the analysis can find flaws early in the development cycle. When used in a reverse engineering setting, where a model of an app is recovered using the techniques described in Sect. 2, the rules can be applied to identify flaws latent in the implemented software or introduced as the system evolves.

6.2 Acme Security Analysis

A certain class of threats facing a system can be classified using STRIDE [23], which captures five different kinds of threat categories: Spoofing, Tampering, Repudiation, Denial of Service, and Elevation of Privilege. According to STRIDE, a system faces security threats when it has information or computing elements that may be of value to a stakeholder. Such components or information are termed the *assets* of the system. Furthermore, most threats occur when there is a mismatch of trust between entities producing and those consuming the data. This approach conforms to the security level approach mismatch idea proposed in [13,14] and used by others since then (e.g., [8,15]).

STRIDE is often applied in the context of a larger threat modeling activity where the system is represented as a dataflow diagram. This representation is particularly useful for evaluating Android security issues that emerge from unintended intent passing. Viewing apps and the data they access as assets in terms of data flow exposes situations when possibly sensitive data passes between apps in an insecure way. For each data path between apps on a device, careful analysis can be performed to identify vulnerabilities, such as *spoofing* and *elevation of privilege* issues. Intent spoofing is a known classes of threat common in Android systems that occurs when a malicious activity is able to forge an intent to achieve an otherwise unexpected behavior. In one scenario the targeted app contains exported activities capable of receiving the spoofed intent. Once processed by the victim app it can be leveraged to elevate the privileges of the malicious app by possibly providing access to protected resources.

Acme provides a framework for reasoning about app security. The properties needed to reason about these threats are present in terms of Android structures and data flow concerns. For example, Acme handles inter-app communication and exposes security properties about apps, such as whether they are exported and what permissions they possess. With this information in the model, automatically detecting app arrangements that may allow intent spoofing, information disclosure, and elevation of privilege can be written as first order predicate rules over the style. Consider Listing 1 which shows how information disclosure vulnerabilities are detected. Each application group is assigned a trust level, based on the category of the app - for example, banking and finance apps would be more trusted than game apps; apps from certain providers like Google would have higher trust. The rule specifies that if a source application sends an implicit intent to a target application then the source applications trust level must be lower than or equal to the recipient. These rules for STRIDE are consistent with the approach taken in [16] for general data-flow architectures.

```
rule noInfoDisclosure = heuristic
     forall a1 :! ApplicationGroupT in self.GROUPS |
       forall a2 :! ApplicationGroupT in self.GROUPS |
        ((a1 != a2) −>
         (forall src :! ImplicitIntentBroadcastAnnouncerPortT in
               /a1/members:!ApplicationElementT/ports:!ImplicitIntentBroadcastAnnouncerPortT |
           forall activity :! ApplicationElementT in a2.members |
             forall tgt :! ImplicitIntentBroadcastReceiverPortT in activity.ports |
              (connected (src, tgt) and contains(src.action, tgt.intentFilters)) −>
                a1.trustLevel <= a2.trustLevel));
```

Listing 1. Acme Rule for Information Disclosure

This rule (and others that are being checked) highlight potential pathways of concern and may generate false positives. This is one reason why in the style we specify the rule as a heuristic, rather than as an invariant. These pathways would need to be more closely monitored at run time than other pathways that do not fail the heuristic, to determine whether the information should be transmitted.

6.3   Integrating with COVERT Security Analysis

In this section, we demonstrate how we can leverage the architectural models developed in Acme, together with external analysis toolsets that require such a model, to evaluate the security posture of an Android system. One such external toolset employed in our research is COVERT [6], which provides the ability to automatically check inter-app vulnerabilities, i.e., whether it is safe for a combination of applications – holding certain permissions and potentially interacting with each other – to be installed simultaneously.

COVERT assumes that system architectural specifications are realized in a first-order relational logic [19]. Such specifications are amenable to fully automated yet bounded analysis. Specifically, the set of architectural models recovered by parsing individual apps installed on the device (c.f. Sect. 4) are first automatically transformed into Alloy [19], a specification language based on relational logic, with an analysis engine that performs bounded verification of models.

In addition to extracted app specifications, the COVERT analyzer relies on two other kinds of specifications: a formal architectural model of the Android framework and the axiomatized inter-app vulnerability signatures. Recall from

Sect. 4, the architectural style for the Android framework represents the foundation upon which Android apps are constructed. Our formalization of these concepts includes a set of rules to lay this foundation (e.g., application, component, messages, etc.), how they behave, and how they interact with each other. We regard vulnerability signatures as a set of assertions used to reify security vulnerabilities in Android, such as privilege escalation. All the specifications are uniformly captured in the Alloy language. As a concrete example, we illustrate the semantics of one of these vulnerabilities in the following. The others are evaluated similarly.

```
assert privilegeEscalation{
  no disj src, dst: Component, i:Intent|
    (src in i.sender) &&
    (dst in src.^transitiveIPC) &&
    (some p: dst.app.usesPermissions |
      not (p in src.app.usesPermissions) &&
      not ((p in dst.permissions) ||(p in dst.app.appPermissions)))
}
```

Listing 2. Specification of the privilegeEscalation assertion in Alloy, adopted from [6].

Listing 2 presents an excerpt from an Alloy assertion that specifies the elements involved in and the semantics of the privilege escalation vulnerability. In essence, the assertion states that the victim component (dst) has access to a permission (usesPermission) that is missing in the src component (malicious), and that permission is not being enforced in the source code of the victim component, nor by the application embodying the victim component. As a consequence, an application with less permissions (a non-privileged caller) is not restricted to access components of a more privileged application (a privileged callee) [11].

The analysis is conducted by exhaustive enumeration over a bounded scope of model instances. Here, the exact scope of each element, such as Application and Component, required to instantiate each vulnerability type is automatically derived from the system architectural model. If an assertion does not hold, the analyzer reports it as a counterexample, along with the information helpful in locating the root cause of the violation. A counterexample is a certain model instance that makes the assertion false, and encompasses an exact scenario (states of all elements, such as components and intents) leading to the violation.

7   Performance Analysis

To evaluate the performance of our approach, we randomly selected and downloaded 15 popular Android apps of different categories from the Google Play repository, and ran the experiments on a computer with 2.2 GHz Intel Core i7 processor and 16 GB DDR3 RAM. We repeated our experiments 33 times, the minimum number of repetitions needed to accurately measure the average execution time overhead at 95 % confidence level. Table 1 summarizes the performance measurements for the architecture discovery process described in Sect. 5, divided into the time of model extraction and architecture generation.

Table 1. Performance of architecture extraction

Apps	Kilo # of Instructions	# of Components				# of Explicit Connectors	total # of Components Connectors &	Average Extraction Time (Sec)	
		Activity	Service	Receiver	Provider			Model	ADL
Amwell	1516	64	2	1	0	51	118	59.16	0.69
Audible's audiobooks	2016	48	8	13	1	24	94	77.78	0.71
Baby tracker	2163	79	30	46	4	90	249	84.76	0.73
BetterBatteryStats	388	9	3	6	0	23	41	18.43	0.66
Book catalogue	119	21	0	0	1	21	43	31.93	0.65
K-9 Mail	835	28	7	5	3	38	81	33.48	0.63
LINE	2575	217	13	6	2	21	259	103.52	0.89
Mileage	128	50	2	2	1	18	73	9.54	0.62
MS Office mobile	601	29	4	2	1	11	47	29.72	0.65
OctoDroid	447	53	0	0	0	31	84	21.88	0.64
Photo grid	1771	54	5	3	1	32	95	73.42	0.74
SwiftKey	1159	35	13	19	0	16	83	49.28	0.68
Tango	1859	73	10	10	1	6	100	67.6	0.82
TextNow	1957	42	9	11	2	14	78	99.94	0.72
TouchPal	1538	88	6	16	0	81	191	66.19	0.78

The first column shows the number of instructions in the Smali assembly code[6] of the apps under analysis, representing their size in lieu of their corresponding line of code due to unavailability of their source code. Moreover, as an architectural metric, the number of components, categorized by their types (i.e., Activity, Service, Broadcast Receiver, Content Provider), and explicit connectors, are provided in the table.

As shown in Table 1, there is a relationship between size (number of instructions) of the apps and model extraction time – apps with more instructions require more time to capture their model. On the other hand, the performance of the second part of the process, i.e., translating the extracted model to an Acme architecture, depends on the total number of components and connector, as the translator iterates over each of them.

8   Discussion and Future Work

In this paper, we have described an architecture style for Android that can be used to do various kinds of analysis to uncover, in particular, vulnerabilities related to inter-app intent communication. One of the challenges of doing such analysis in this domain is the evolving nature of Android, and the need to understand all the related information flows. This paper describes an approach in which the architecture (and information flows) of the system can be derived from analysis of the code and can then be used to analyze potential vulnerabilities on a per-device basis.

The static analysis described in this paper identifies possible places where vulnerabilities may exist, but not actual exploits that may happen at run time. This requires a combination of static analysis and run-time analysis to capture and prevent actual exploits. Hence, static analysis can inform the run-time analysis of parts of the system that need monitoring and deeper analysis, for example to examine the contents of intents, in order to determine if an exploit exists.

---

[6] http://baksmali.com.

Our approach can be used to facilitate this combination of static and dynamic analysis. We are in the process of connecting our tool-suite to the Rainbow self-adaptive framework [9,17], where the vulnerabilities found statically can be used to choose adaptation strategies to change communication behavior in Android. We are in the process of addressing some of the challenges in integrating these two approaches, including disconnected operation and prevention of behaviors rather than reaction to behaviors.

For the modeling aspect, we have concentrated on understanding the architecture of the applications on the device, and the communication pathways. However, many apps are part of a large ecosystem with diverse back ends that are not on the device. Many of these apps may have information flows that affect security. How we model this, and how much, is an area of future work. Furthermore, security aspects are context-sensitive in the domain of mobile devices, where the degree of analysis required might change depending on whether devices are, for example, being used in a public coffee bar, or at home. We focused on analyzing Android and extensions to it. In future work we plan to apply this type of reasoning to other plugin frameworks, and assess how we might inform the design of new frameworks for which security is a concern.

Acknowledgments. This work is supported in part by awards H98230-14-C-0140 from the National Security Agency, CCF-1252644 from the National Science Foundation, FA95501610030 from the Air Force Office of Scientific Research, and HSHQDC-14-C-B0040 from the Department of Homeland Security. The views and conclusions contained herein are those of the authors and should not be interpreted as representing the official policies, either expressed or implied, of the National Security Agency or the U.S. government.

References

1. Abi-Antoun, M., Barnes, J.M.: Analyzing security architectures. In: Proceedings of the IEEE/ACM International Conference on Automated Software Engineering, ASE 2010, pp. 3–12. ACM, New York (2010)
2. Almorsy, M., Grundy, J., Ibrahim, A.S.: Automated software architecture security risk analysis using formalized signatures. In: 2013 35th International Conference on Software Engineering (ICSE), pp. 662–671, May 2013
3. Bagheri, H., Garcia, J., Sadeghi, A., Malek, S., Medvidovic, N.: Software architectural principles in contemporary mobile software: from conception to practice. J. Syst. Softw. **119**, 31–44 (2016)
4. Bagheri, H., Kang, E., Malek, S., Jackson, D.: Detection of design flaws in the Android permission protocol through bounded verification. In: Bjørner, N., de Boer, F. (eds.) FM 2015. LNCS, vol. 9109, pp. 73–89. Springer, Heidelberg (2015). doi:10.1007/978-3-319-19249-9_6
5. Bagheri, H., Kang, E., Malek, S., Jackson, D.: A formal approach for detection of security flaws in the Android permission system. Formal Aspects Comput. (2016)
6. Bagheri, H., Sadeghi, A., Garcia, J., Malek, S.: COVERT: compositional analysis of Android inter-app permission leakage. IEEE Trans. Software Eng. **41**(9), 866–886 (2015)

7. Bagheri, H., Sadeghi, A., Jabbarvand, R., Malek, S.: Practical, formal synthesis and automatic enforcement of security policies for Android. In: Proceedings of the 46th IEEE/IFIP International Conference on Dependable Systems and Networks (DSN), pp. 514–525 (2016)

8. Bodei, C., Degano, P., Nielson, F., Nelson, H.R.: Security analysis using flow logics. In: Current Trends in Theoretical Computer Science, pp. 525–542. World Scientific (2000)

9. Cheng, S.-W.: Rainbow: cost-effective software architecture-based self-aaptation. PhD thesis, Carnegie Mellon University, Institute for Software Research Technical Report CMU-ISR-08-113, May 2008

10. Chin, E., Felt, A.P., Greenwood, K., Wagner, D.: Analyzing inter-application communication in Android. In: Proceedings of the 9th International Conference on Mobile Systems, Applications, and Services, MobiSys 2011, pp. 239–252. ACM, New York (2011)

11. Davi, L., Dmitrienko, A., Sadeghi, A.-R., Winandy, M.: Privilege escalation attacks on Android. In: Proceedings of the 13th International Conference on Information Security (ISC) (2010)

12. Deng, Y., Wang, J., Tsai, J.J.P., Beznosov, K.: An approach for modeling, analysis of security system architectures. IEEE Trans. Knowl., Data Eng. **15**(5), 1099–1119 (2003)

13. Denning, D.E.: A lattice model of secure information flow. Commun. ACM **19**(5), 236–243 (1976)

14. Denning, D.E., Denning, P.J.: Certification of programs for secure information flow. Commun. ACM **20**(7), 504–513 (1977)

15. Fernandez, E.B., Larrondo-Petrie, M.M., Sorgente, T., Vannhist, M.: A methodology to develop secure systems using patterns. In: Integrating Security and Software Engineering: Advances and Future Visions. Idea Group Inc. (2007)

16. Garg, K., Garlan, D., Schmerl, B.: Architecture based information flow analysis for software security (2008). http://acme.able.cs.cmu.edu/pubs/uploads/pdf/ArchSTRIDE08.pdf

17. Garlan, D., Cheng, S.-W., Huang, A.-C., Schmerl, B., Steenkiste, P.: Rainbow: Architecture-based self adaptation with reusable infrastructure. IEEE Comput. **37**(10), 46–54 (2004)

18. Garlan, D., Monroe, R.T., Wile, D.: Acme: architectural description of component-based systems. In: Foundations of Component-Based Systems, pp. 47–67. Cambridge University Press, New York (2000)

19. Jackson, D., Abstractions, S.: Logic, Language, and Analysis, 2nd edn. MIT Press, London (2012)

20. Ren, J., Taylor, R.: A secure software architecture description language. In: Workshop on Software Security Assurance Tools, Techniques, and Metrics, pp. 82–89 (2005)

21. Sadeghi, A., Bagheri, H., Malek, S.: Analysis of Android inter-app security vulnerabilities using COVERT. In: Proceedings of the 37th International Conference on Software Engineering, ICSE 2015, vol. 2, pp. 725–728. IEEE Press, Piscataway (2015)

22. Shaw, M., Garlan, D.: Software Architecture: Perspectives on and Emerging Discipline. Prentice Hall, Englewood Cliffs, NJ (1996)

23. Swiderski, F., Snyder, W.: Threat Modeling. Microsoft Press, Redmond (2004)

24. Vallée-Rai, R., Co, P., Gagnon, E., Hendren, L., Lam, P., Sundaresan, V.: Soot-a Java bytecode optimization framework. In: Proceedings of the Conference of the Centre for Advanced Studies on Collaborative Research, p. 13. IBM Press (1999)

Towards a Framework for Building SaaS Applications Operating in Diverse and Dynamic Environments

Ashish Agrawal[✉] and T.V. Prabhakar

Department of Computer Science and Engineering,
Indian Institute of Technology Kanpur, Kanpur, UP 208016, India
{agrawala,tvp}@cse.iitk.ac.in

Abstract. Enterprises have increasingly adopted the Software-as-a-service (SaaS) model to facilitate on-demand delivery of software applications. A SaaS customer - tenant - may operate in diverse environments and may demand a different level of qualities from the application. A tenant may also operate in a dynamic environment where expectations from the application may change at run-time. To be able to operate in such environments, SaaS application requires support at both the architecture and implementation levels. This paper highlights the issues in building a SaaS that can accommodate such diverse and dynamic environments. We propose a methodological framework called *Chameleonic-SaaS* that abstracts out the responsibilities involved and provides guidelines to realize it. Our framework introduces variability in the architecture to manipulate the architecture-level decisions, especially tactics. Feasibility of the framework is demonstrated by an example of a MOOC application.

Keywords: Software as a service · Variability · Adaptive SaaS · Dynamic quality attributes

1 Introduction

Software-as-a-Service (SaaS) - a delivery model for software applications - attracts customers by presenting features such as no up-front cost, on-demand provisioning at an application-level of granularity and free from maintenance [3,12]. In SaaS model, the service provider is responsible for managing all service components (software and hardware) and ensuring application-level quality attributes desired by a customer. These SaaS customers - "tenants" - may operate in diverse environments and may demand different levels of qualities (e.g., low or high availability) from the application [4,15]. For example, considering an ERP SaaS, a small organization may need low availability (95 %) and an enterprise may demand high availability (99.99 %). Similarly, a tenant may also operate in a dynamic environment where expectations from the application may change at run-time to accommodate changes in the environment. In our scenario, the small organization may desire to have high availability for a time

© Springer International Publishing AG 2016
B. Tekinerdogan et al. (Eds.): ECSA 2016, LNCS 9839, pp. 291–306, 2016.
DOI: 10.1007/978-3-319-48992-6_22

period such as peak load and business events. The motivation behind the need for such dynamic quality requirements is the fact that some quality attributes have an impact on the operational cost of the application, and the application may not require high values of these quality attributes all the time. For example, if an application achieves high availability by replicating to a redundant server, this additional server will increase the operational cost. Figure 1 depicts a case of quality expectations of tenants of a SaaS.

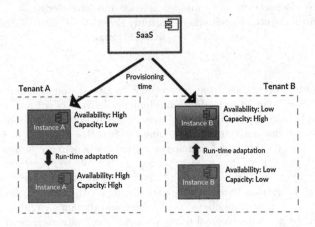

Fig. 1. An example showing diverse and dynamic quality expectations from a SaaS

To make the offering attractive to the tenants, a SaaS should have the ability to address diverse and dynamic quality requirements. From an architectural perspective, two most common patterns [4,14] for building a SaaS are; (1) *Multi-tenant* where all tenants share a common instance along with the code components, and (2) *Multi-instance* where every tenant has a dedicated instance allocated to it.

For building a SaaS operating in diverse and dynamic environments, *Multi-tenancy* would be beneficial in terms of operational cost and maintenance. However, this pattern requires designing tenant-aware components that can increase development cost and time to market. Although the development cost would be high, it might be compensated by lower operational cost [6]. Contrary to this, benefits of *Multi-instance* are; less time to market, lower design cost, and flexibility for customization. However, *Multi-instance* pattern may have high operational cost and high maintenance if there are a large number of tenants. A service provider can select a pattern by analyzing these parameters in the context of its business goals and policies. One can also use a combination of these patterns where a group of tenants shares a common instance.

One thing to note here is that addressing diversity issues of the tenants in *Multi-tenancy* may create a very complex architecture and design that can create issues for maintaining the service. In some scenarios, it may be easy to maintain multiple simple instances than a single complex instance. In this paper, we focus on using the *Multi-instance* pattern for implementing a SaaS as it provides more flexibility to handle diverse and dynamic environments.

One way to accommodate diversity and dynamism is to identify the set of possible quality requirements and build different versions of the application separately for every member of such a set. However, in this case, development and maintenance cost would be very high. As the quality requirements are also dynamic in nature, migrating between members of the set might not be possible. Another approach could be to provide maximum values of quality attributes to all tenants at all time. However, this may not be cost-effective from the provider's perspective. Diversity and dynamism can also be handled by customizing the size of an instance (e.g., CPU, RAM, etc.) according to a tenant's requirements. However, only a few quality attributes (e.g., performance, capacity, etc.) can be changed using this approach. Also, variations in quality values will be limited.

Our idea for solving these issues is to model quality attributes as scriptable resources. That means that the application exposes a programmable interface to the tenants for requesting quality attributes. To handle diversity, a tenant can specify its quality requirements at the time of requesting a new instance i.e. provisioning-time. To accommodate dynamic environments, a tenant can change the quality attributes of its instance dynamically at run-time on demand basis. To handle such requests from a tenant, application modifies the architecture-level decisions of its instance such as tactics. To facilitate such features and to manage all running instances, the application should be designed with the ability to dynamically modify its architecture.

To realize our approach, we identify the suitable tactics and introduce variability in the architecture by modeling these tactics as variation points. To be able to change the quality attributes dynamically, we model the service as an adaptive system using the concepts of MAPE-K loop architecture [10]. Findings of our investigation are formulated as a methodological framework called *Chameleonic-SaaS*. Main contributions of this paper are:

- An idea to model quality attributes as scriptable resources.
- A methodological framework called *Chameleonic-SaaS* for building SaaS operating in diverse and dynamic environments. The framework abstracts out the responsibilities involved and provides guidelines for the same.

The rest of the paper is organized as follows. Section 2 describes the problem statement and our approach. Section 3 explains the *Chameleonic-SaaS* framework in detail. Section 4 presents an example by building a MOOC application. Section 5 provides a brief summary of existing work related to this paper. Section 6 discusses benefits and limitations of our approach. Section 7 concludes the paper with scope of future work.

2   Problem Statement and Approach

This section defines the problem statement and describes our approach.

2.1 Problem Statement

This work aims to investigate the issues in building a SaaS operating in diverse and dynamic environments. Requirements from such a SaaS are:

- Service should have the ability to address diverse quality requirements of different tenants at provisioning-time.
- Service should have the ability to change quality attributes for a particular tenant dynamically at run-time.
- It should be easy to maintain the service.

2.2 Approach

Our idea is to expose quality attributes as scriptable resources to the tenants of a SaaS. Using such resources, a tenant can customize the set of quality attribute values provided by an application instance. Such customization can occur either at provisioning-time or dynamically at run-time on demand basis. Here, customizations in the quality attribute values are achieved by modifying architecture-level decisions of the application.

This leads to the question of what architectural decisions need to be changed in the architecture. Such architectural decisions should only impact quality attributes of the application. We use the architectural tactics as the architectural decisions that can be modified at run-time. A tactic is an architectural tool that can be used to improve a particular quality attribute of an application [2]. For example, *Ping & Echo* [2] is a tactic to improve the availability of an application by detecting failures such as network failure. Thus, to modify quality attributes of a tenant's instance, SaaS can add or remove tactics in its architecture. The approach mentioned above leads to a natural question:

- **RQ1**: How to externally add a tactic to an application instance deployed on a virtual machine?

In architecture, realization of a tactic can be seen as a set of operations (add, remove or modify) on architectural elements – components, connectors, and links. We categorize the architectural elements into three groups; (1) *pure application elements* incorporating application logic, (2) *pure tactic elements* which are tactic elements that are independent of application logic, and (3) *application-specific tactic elements* which are tactic elements that requires knowledge of application logic. For example, *Ping & Echo* tactic can be implemented using three pure tactic components; *PingSender* sends ping requests periodically, *PingReceiver* sends an echo for a received ping, and *Monitor* notifies the occurrence of a failure.

One of the ways to achieve *Ping & Echo* tactic at a virtual machine level is as follows. Deploy *PingReceiver* on the virtual machine that host the application and deploy rest of the tactic components on a separate virtual machine. As there are no links between the tactic components and the application components, we can add this tactic without any modification to the application components.

Some tactics may include application-specific components. For example, implementation of the *Passive Redundancy* tactic requires a *StateManager* component to fetch and update the application state. The *StateManager* being an application-specific component, has to be a part of the application architecture. If the application exposes an interface for the *StateManager* with dynamic binding then the *Passive Redundancy* tactic can be added to the application.

To be able to add a tactic, application architecture should provide support by exposing application-specific tactic elements. This decision to implement such elements in the application is based on the trade-off between customization enabled by the tactic and its impact on the development cost. By examining such support, we can decide whether it is feasible to use a tactic in the present context. An application-specific tactic component may also enable multiple tactics. For example, *StateManager* may enable both *Passive Redundancy* and *Rollback*. These components have a higher impact on the ability to customize in comparison with the development cost.

Not all tactics can be added using this approach. For example, tactics related to quality attributes not discernible at run-time cannot be used here. Similarly, if the application architecture does not provide support by exposing application-specific tactic components and the ability to run-time binding, it may not be possible to add such tactics. The capability of our approach to change quality attributes depends on the number of tactics supported by the application architecture for dynamic addition.

These tactic-specific components may have an adverse effect on other quality attributes. In the case of a large number of such components, they should be incorporated in only the instances whose tenants demand variations in the respective qualities. Some tactic components may also have an exclusive relationship with other tactic components. Thus, to maintain the system easily and dynamically select the tactics components, we introduce variability in the application architecture where tactic components are modeled as variation points.

3   Chameleonic-SaaS Framework

Findings of our investigation on building SaaS applications for diverse and dynamic environments are formulated as a methodological framework called *Chameleonic-SaaS*. Applications built using this framework can provision instances with different quality attributes to address diverse quality requirements of SaaS-users. Quality attributes of such instances can also be changed dynamically at run-time, to accommodate dynamic operating environments. This framework abstracts out the responsibilities involved and provides architectural guidelines for building such SaaS applications. Steps of the framework (depicted in Fig. 2) are explained in the following sections.

3.1   Identify QA Scenarios

The first step is to identify the quality requirements of the application that can vary either at provisioning time or run-time. This task has to be done manually

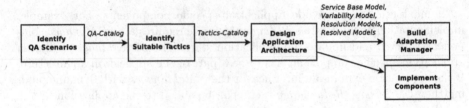

Fig. 2. Steps of the Chameleonic-SaaS framework

by analyzing the application requirements (using requirement specification or user stories) and separate out such quality concerns. By this analysis, we identify a list of quality attributes that can differ in multiple instances of the application or can vary at run-time in a particular instance. For example, in a SaaS application, availability requirements may vary with tenants from highly available to moderate available. Similarly, a tenant having moderate availability initially, may require high availability on an environmental change (e.g., peak load, business event, etc.). The output of this step is a *QA-Catalog* that includes; (1) Quality attributes identified by the analysis along with desired range of their values, and (2) Scenarios for run-time variation in the quality attributes documented as *Quality Attribute Scenarios (QASs)* [2].

3.2 Identify Suitable Tactics

In this step, we identify the architectural tactics that can be used to achieve the desired quality requirements specified in the *QA-Catalog*. This task is done by analyzing the tactics repositories [2,16] along with the application architecture using the methodology specified in Sect. 2.2. Tactics may also have dependencies with each other. For example, *Active Redundancy* and *Passive Redundancy* tactics have an exclusive relationship with each other and cannot be applied together in a system. Similarly, a tactic for one quality attribute may also have an impact on other quality attributes. For example, *Active Redundancy* tactic of availability can have an adverse impact on performance. This step aims to identify a set of feasible tactics for every QAS specified in the *QA-Catalog* by analyzing the architectural tactics, their relationships with each other and their impact on the quality attributes. The output of this step is an artifact called *Tactics-Catalog* that consists a list of mappings between a quality value and a set of tactics that can be used to achieve that quality.

3.3 Design Application Architecture

In the previous step, we identified a set of tactics that can be incorporated into the architecture to handle the desired QASs. These tactics need to be incorporated in the architecture design in a way such that their existence can vary with tenants as well as with time for a particular tenant. Instead of designing multiple architectures of the application, our approach is to introduce variability in the architecture for quality concerns. To model variability, we follow the *Orthogonal Variability Modeling (OVM)* [13] approach and model the quality concerns separately from the application base architecture. Following the OVM approach, we use the *Common Variability Language (CVL)* [8] to describe the variability. CVL is a domain independent language for specifying variability models and has an execution engine to generate the *resolved models* i.e. instance architectures. In this step, we prepare the following models as depicted in Fig. 3. Examples of these models in our context are presented in the Sect. 4.

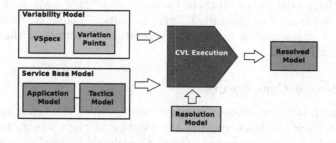

Fig. 3. Models in the CVL approach

1. **Application Model**: This model captures the architectural elements that are common to all tenants. Our approach is to capture quality related concerns in a separate model and this model only includes the support required to handle those concerns. This approach gives us the ability to re-use such quality related concerns and manage them independently from the application components. Thus, the *Application Model* includes *pure application elements* and *application-specific tactics elements* (defined in Sect. 2.2). The model can be described using any domain specific language such as UML.
2. **Tactics Model**: This model includes *pure tactic elements* that are agnostic to the application logic.
3. **Service Base Model**: In order to describe variability, this model is prepared by combining the *Application Model* and the *Tactics Model*. Apart from the elements of these two models, this model also includes elements that establish links between them. This model is considered as a base model to describe variability.
4. **Variability Specification (VSpecs)**: This model specifies the variability at an abstract level i.e. irrespective of its mapping to the *Service Base Model*. We incorporate the quality attributes and the tactics as first-class concepts in this model. This approach provides us the ability to choose variations at the granularity of tactics. Thus, the *QA-Catalog* and the *Tactics-Catalog* are used to describe tactics and relationships between tactics. Such relationships can be modeled as *choice multiplicity* or constraints. For example, a tactic for fault recovery requires a tactic from fault detection. These variations are captured as a tree structure of choices.

5. **Variation Points**: This model includes variation points referencing to the *Service Base Model*. Variation points are the modifications applied to the *Service Base Model* to generate an instance architecture. For example, a variation point specifies the existence of a tactic component called *PingSender*. To re-use the variation points related to pure tactics elements, they can be combined and represented as *Configurable Units*. Every variation point has a binding to exactly one VSpec.

6. **Resolution Models**: This model resolves VSpecs. For example, a choice resolution may resolve a choice VSpec. In our case, every QAS is mapped to a resolution model representing the tactics to be selected for that QAS. Thus, *QA-Catalog* is used to generate different resolution models corresponding to each QAS. These models are used to generate architectures of the instances i.e. *Resolved models*.

3.4 Implement Components

In our scenario, tactic components are dynamically added to an existing instance at run-time. Such operation requires modification in the connections between application and tactics components. Thus, they should be implemented in such a way so that their binding can be configured at run-time. Some techniques that can be used for such implementation are:

- *Encapsulate*: Components should provide an explicit interface such as an API.
- *Defer Binding*: Components should defer their binding so that it can be decided or changed at run-time.

3.5 Build Adaptation Manager

This component is responsible for managing the SaaS application (and its instances) for adaptation at provisioning time and at run-time. It exposes an interface to the tenants for two kinds of operations; (1) Provisioning of an instance for a given set of quality requirements, and (2) Provisioning of a quality attribute value to an existing instance. Design of the *Adaptation Manager* is based on the MAPE-K loop [10] of adaptive systems. Figure 4 depicts run-time view of a SaaS application that includes the following components:

- **Event Monitor**: This component is responsible for capturing the events that demands provisioning of instances or quality attributes. Sensors running on an instance to monitor its environment can trigger the *Event Monitor*.
- **Architecture Analyzer**: On an adaptation request from the *Event Monitor*, this component identifies the QAS from *QA-Catalog* and analyzes the current architecture of the concerned instance (stored in *Architectural Knowledge Repository*) to check the feasibility of the requested operation.
- **Adaptation Planner**: On the occurrence of a QAS, *Planner* component identifies the desired tactics from the *Tactic-Catalog* and generate instance architecture using a *Resolution Model*. Using the current architecture of the concerned instance, it plans for changes to be applied to the instance.

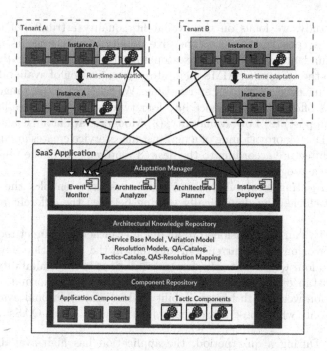

Fig. 4. A run-time scenario of a SaaS application

- **Instance Deployer**: This component executes the changes proposed by the *Planner* component. To deploy the tactics related component, it uses the programmable interfaces of underlying cloud resources.
- **Architectural Knowledge Repository**: This repository contains the architectural knowledge that is used by other components of the *Adaptation Manager* such as *Application Model, Tactic Model, Variability Model, QA-Catalog, Tactics-Catalog* and current architecture of all instances (*Resolution Models*).

4   Example

This section presents an example SaaS called *MOOC Management System (MMS)* built using the methodology specified by the *Chameleonic-SaaS* framework. This service facilitates provisioning of application instances to customers (organizations or individuals) to deliver and manage online courses. Quality attributes desired by a MMS instance such as capacity, availability and performance may vary with the organizations depending on the factors such as the number of students and credit vs. non-credit courses. For a particular organization, quality expectations may also change during run-time on the occurrence of events such as quizzes/exams and real-time hangout sessions. This study aims to check the applicability of our approach by identifying QASs and tactics, designing application architecture and deploying the service.

In this study, we focus on the availability quality attribute of the MMS. Availability is considered as an expensive quality attribute as its realization through redundant resources increases operational cost. To make the offering attractive to the customers, MMS facilitates customization of availability values at provisioning time as well as at run-time. We categorize the range of availability values offered by the service into four types; (1) Default availability (no additional support) (2) Low availability, (3) Moderate availability, and (4) High availability. During provisioning of a new instance, service creates an appropriate instance architecture according to the desired requirements of the tenant. MMS also exposes a programmable interface to change availability of a provisioned instance. Projecting availability as scriptable resources enables the tenant to become cost-efficient by dynamically varying between the different availability offerings.

Availability can be provisioned to an instance either on a direct request from the customer or on the occurrence of an event in the application environment. We identified four QASs that may demand variations in the availability values of a running instance. The basic idea of these QASs is that in normal operations, the application works with low availability values and additional availability is provisioned only when these is a demand for the same. These QASs are:

- **QAS-1**: "During a quiz period, the application has high availability". As quizzes/exams have time duration associated with them, the application is expected to have high availability to avoid or at least reduce any downtime.
- **QAS-2**: "If new course material is released, the application has moderate availability". It has been observed that release of course material (stimulus) results in a large number of students accessing the application. Downtime during such periods should be avoided. However, it is not as critical as quizzes/exams.
- **QAS-3**: "In normal operations, the application has low availability". In the absence of any critical events, the application is expected to have low availability.
- **QAS-4**: "If the course is migrated to read-only (self-paced) mode, the application has default availability". The self-paced mode is a low priority scenario, and the application does not need any additional support for availability (low availability) to have minimum operational cost.

In our example, these requirements are handled by realization of three tactics; *Ping & Echo*, *Cold Spare* and *Passive Redundancy* [2]. Figure 5 depicts mapping of these tactics to their respective quality requirements along with the tactics components used to realize them in the application. Realization of *Cold Spare* and *Passive Redundancy* requires application to expose an application-specific tactic component called *State Manager* to be able to get and set application state.

Figure 6 depicts the *Service Base Model* along with variation points bound to the *VSpecs*. The *Service Base Model* is prepared by integrating the *Application Model* and the *Tactic Model*. In the *VSpecs*, availability is modeled as an optional

QA	QA Requirement	QA Measure	Tactics	Tactics Components	
				Application-specific	Application-agnostic
Availability	Default	-	-	-	-
	Low	Detect fault within 3 minutes	Ping/Echo	-	PingSender, PingReceiver, FaultMonitor
	Moderate	Detect fault within 3 minutes and recover within 2 minutes	Ping/Echo Cold Spare	StateManager	PingSender, PingReceiver, FaultMonitor SpareManager
	High	Detect fault within 3 minutes and recover within 1 minutes	Ping/Echo Passive Redundancy	StateManager	PingSender, PingReceiver, FaultMonitor Proxy, StateSyncManager

Fig. 5. Availability requirements and the corresponding tactics

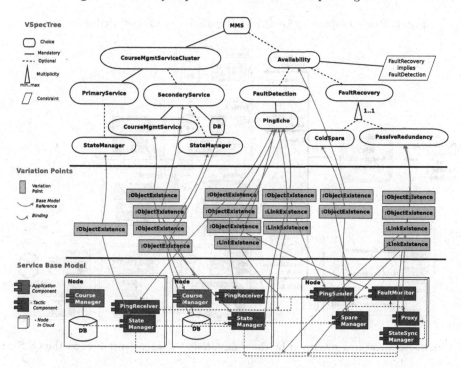

Fig. 6. Service base model with variation points bound to the VSpecs

choice that further has two child choices; *FaultDetection* and *FaultRecovery*. There is also a constraint specifying that *FaultRecovery* requires *FaultDetection* to be present in the instance. *FaultDetection* has *PingEcho* as a child choice that is linked to various *Variation Points* relating to the existence of components (*PingSender, PingReceiver*, etc.) and links. Figure 7 depicts resolution model for QAS-1 where *PassiveRedundancy* choice is *True* but *ColdSpare* is *False*. Figure 8 depicts architectures of the various instances generated by the service depending upon the resolution models.

For variation triggered by the events in the application environment, a sensor to monitor events - course material release, quiz period and self-pace mode - is implemented in the application that triggers the *Event Monitor* component of

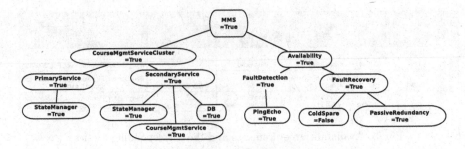

Fig. 7. Resolution model for QAS-1 (PingEcho and PassiveRedundancy)

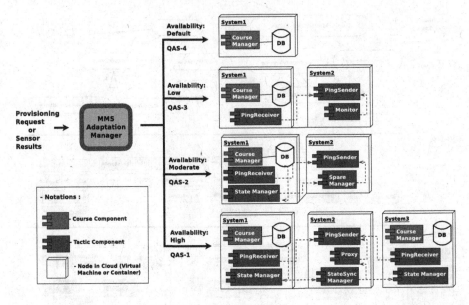

Fig. 8. Architectures generated by the *Adaptation Manager* depending on the QAS

the *Adaptation Manager*. These events are analyzed to check occurrence of any QAS. *Adaptation Manager* also exposes an API through which a customer can directly request for an availability value (default, low, moderate, or high) to an existing instance. Depending upon the current architecture of the instance and the desired QAS, *Adaptation Manager* modifies the instance architecture by adding or removing components.

Figure 9 presents experiments results conducted by dynamically provisioning the availability values to a MMS instance. In our setup, service is offered by creating MMS instance over Linux containers (LXC). LXC containers were setup on a virtual machine (1CPU Core, 2 GB RAM) running Ubuntu operating system. For deployment of tactics components, we used the *Puppet* tool [18]. The results show that adding quality to an existing instance is fast due to quick creation of containers. Also, *Passive Redundancy* has less fault recovery time compared to *Cold Spare* tactic as the later requires creating a new container to recover. These timings directly depend on our execution environment and should not be used as benchmarks.

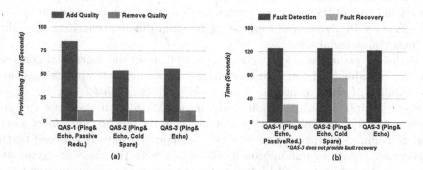

Fig. 9. Experiment results for availability scenarios in MMS (a) Provisioning time in adding or removing the QASs, and (b) Availability benefits in terms of time consumed in fault detection and fault recovery

5   Related Work

The demand for tenant-specific customization of a service has been highlighted by several researchers [1,12,17]. Here, customization is desired in features, workflow, user-interface, etc., and facilitated using the virtualization techniques [4]. In context of SaaS applications, researchers have identified some architectural patterns such as *Multi-tenancy* and *Multi-instance* and discussed their impact on the quality attributes [4,6,14]. Koziolek [11] discussed various quality requirements from a SaaS such as resource sharing, scalability, maintainability, customizability, and usability. The work also includes an architectural style called SPOSAD based on multi-tier style. Software engineering issues with developing SaaS applications have also been discussed [5].

Variability has been presented as a quality attribute of architecture [2] and has been extensively used in Product Line Engineering (PLE). However, variability in quality attributes (performance variability, availability variability, etc.) has not been much used and requires more explorations [7].

Several researchers have proposed techniques to design a SaaS as a *Product Line Architecture* by introducing variability in the architecture [1,15,17]. Matar et al. [1] discussed different kinds of variability for a SaaS such as application variability, business process variability and provisioning variability. However, most of these works are focused only on the variations in the feature models. These approaches are also not able to handle the environmental changes demanding variations only in quality attributes. Horcas et al. [9] presented a technique to inject functional quality attributes (that results in functional components) in an application. In our work, our focus is on varying only the quality attributes of a SaaS instance, by changing architectural decisions at a tactic level granularity.

6   Discussion

Quality attributes exposed as scriptable resources enable variation in their values for a running instance. As run-time quality attributes have an impact on the operational cost of the instance, a tenant can exploit such resources to achieve cost-efficiency by dynamically migrating between different offerings of quality attributes on demand basis.

Modeling quality related concerns separately from the functional concerns provides reusability of the quality concerns across multiple applications, and modifiability of these concerns. For example, *Tactics Model* can be shared between multiple applications. Similarly, in our MMS application, we can add a new tactic such as *Rollback* without modifying the *Application Model* as the support required by this new tactic (*StateManager*) is already exposed by the *Application Model*. In our approach, all instances of the SaaS are generated using a single architecture which makes the maintenance easier compared to the approach where every instance is designed and build separately.

In our framework, tactics are modeled as first-class concepts in the *Variability Model*. As tactics are standard validated tools to improve quality attributes, such modeling helps in evaluating the variations in an instance architecture in terms of their impact on the quality attributes.

The framework only considers variations in the architectural decisions of an instance, and does not cover other decisions such as deployment-level decisions (e.g., sizing of hardware resources, etc.), implementation-level details (e.g., code, logging, etc.), or application functionality. We do not aim to replace the other techniques but to augment their capability to reach more diverse levels of quality attributes. In a holistic approach, variability at different levels (architecture, deployment, implementation, features) can be combined.

Another limitation of our work is that we presented a methodological framework where several steps of the framework like *Identify Tactics*, merging the *Application Model* with the *Tactic Model*, etc. are not automated. In this paper, we explored adding tactics at the top level of application architecture. However, variations may be desired at a lower level architecture element such as a microservice. Our framework can be further extended to handle such scenarios.

Not all quality attributes can be modeled as scriptable resources. For example, quality attributes not discernible at run-time such as modifiability cannot be changed using our approach. The capability of our approach to change quality attributes depends on the number of tactics supported by the application architecture for dynamic addition (in terms of application-specific tactic components exposed by the application). Our approach has an impact on design and development cost of the application. Re-using the tactics related concerns can help in reducing such overhead.

7   Conclusion and Future Work

In this paper, we presented an approach to offer quality attributes of a SaaS application as scriptable resources. To build such an application, we need to identify the suitable tactic-level architectural decisions, introduce variability in the architecture and incorporate the ability to change an instance architecture dynamically at run-time. In our methodological framework, tactics are modeled as first-class concepts in the application architecture. This enables to articulate the impact of architectural variations on the quality attributes. Our example MOOC application facilitates a tenant to vary its availability values between default, low, moderate, and high. The current version of the *Chameleonic-SaaS* framework is applicable only for a multi-instance SaaS. To build a multi-tenant SaaS with the ability to dynamically change quality attributes of tenants can be further explored. To transform an existing application to a SaaS would also be an interesting problem especially in the scenarios when the application does not provide any direct support for adding the tactics externally.

Acknowledgment. The authors gratefully acknowledge the financial support from Tata Consultancy Services and MHRD, Govt. of India for this work.

References

1. Abu Matar, M., Mizouni, R., Alzahmi, S.: Towards software product lines based cloud architectures. In: 2014 IEEE International Conference on Cloud Engineering (IC2E), pp. 117–126, March 2014
2. Bass, L., Clements, P., Kazman, R.: Software Architecture in Practice, 3rd edn. Addison-Wesley Professional, Boston (2012)
3. Benlian, A., Hess, T.: Opportunities and risks of software-as-a-service: Findings from a survey of IT executives. Decis. Support Syst. **52**(1), 232–246 (2011)
4. Bezemer, C.P., Zaidman, A.: Multi-tenant SaaS applications: maintenance dream or nightmare? In: Proceedings of the Joint ERCIM Workshop on Software Evolution (EVOL) and International Workshop on Principles of Software Evolution (IWPSE), IWPSE-EVOL 2010, pp. 88–92. ACM, New York (2010)
5. Cai, H., Wang, N., Zhou, M.J.: A transparent approach of enabling saas multi-tenancy in the cloud. In: 2010 6th World Congress on Services (SERVICES-1), pp. 40–47, July 2010
6. Frederick Chong, G.C., Wolter, R.: Multi-tenant data architecture, June 2006. http://msdn.microsoft.com/en-us/library/aa479086.aspx
7. Galster, M.: Architecting for variability in quality attributes of software systems. In: Proceedings of the 2015 European Conference on Software Architecture Workshops, ECSAW 2015, pp. 23:1–23:4. ACM, New York (2015)
8. Haugen, O., et al.: Common variability language (CVL). OMG Submission (2012)
9. Horcas, J.M., Pinto, M., Fuentes, L.: Injecting quality attributes into software architectures with the common variability language. In: Proceedings of the 17th International ACM Sigsoft Symposium on Component-based Software Engineering, CBSE 2014, pp. 35–44. ACM, New York (2014)
10. Jacob, B., Lanyon-Hogg, R., Nadgir, D.K., Yassin, A.F.: A practical guide to the to the IBM autonomic computing toolkit, April 2004. http://www.redbooks.ibm.com/redbooks/pdfs/sg246635.pdf
11. Koziolek, H.: The sposad architectural style for multi-tenant software applications. In: 2011 9th Working IEEE/IFIP Conference on Software Architecture (WICSA), pp. 320–327, June 2011

12. La, H.J., Kim, S.D.: A systematic process for developing high quality SaaS cloud services. In: Jaatun, M.G., Zhao, G., Rong, C. (eds.) CloudCom 2009. LNCS, vol. 5931, pp. 278–289. Springer, Heidelberg (2009). doi:10.1007/978-3-642-10665-1_25

13. Metzger, A., Pohl, K.: Software product line engineering and variability management: achievements and challenges. In: Proceedings of the on Future of Software Engineering, FOSE 2014, pp. 70–84. ACM, New York (2014)

14. Mietzner, R., Unger, T., Titze, R., Leymann, F.: Combining different multi-tenancy patterns in service-oriented applications. In: Proceedings of the 13th IEEE International Conference on Enterprise Distributed Object Computing, EDOC 2009, pp. 108–117. IEEE Press, Piscataway (2009)

15. Ruehl, S.T., Andelfinger, U.: Applying software product lines to create customizable software-as-a-service applications. In: Proceedings of the 15th International Software Product Line Conference, SPLC 2011, vol. 2, pp. 16:1–16:4. ACM, New York (2011)

16. Scott, J., Kazman, R.: Realizing and refining architectural tactics: availability, Technical report, CMU/SEI-2009-TR-006 ESC-TR-2009-006 (2009)

17. Tekinerdogan, B., Ozturk, K., Dogru, A.: Modeling and reasoning about design alternatives of software as a service architectures. In: 2011 9th Working IEEE/IFIP Conference on Software Architecture (WICSA), pp. 312–319, June 2011

18. Tool, P.: Puppet tool (retrieved, April 2016). http://puppetlabs.com/

Software Architecture Reconstruction

Materializing Architecture Recovered from Object-Oriented Source Code in Component-Based Languages

Zakarea Alshara[✉], Abdelhak-Djamel Seriai, Chouki Tibermacine, Hinde Lilia Bouziane, Christophe Dony, and Anas Shatnawi

UMR CNRS 5506, LIRMM, University of Montpellier, Montpellier, France
{alshara,seriai,tibermacin,bouziane,dony,shatnawi}@lirmm.fr

Abstract. In the literature of software engineering, many approaches have been proposed for the recovery of software architectures. These approaches propose to group classes into highly-cohesive and loosely-coupled clusters considered as architectural components. The recovered architecture plays mainly a documentation role, as high-level design views that enhance software understandability. In addition, architecture recovery can be considered as an intermediate step for migration to component-based platforms. This migration allows to fully benefit from all advantages brought by software component concept. For that, the recovered clusters should not be considered as simple packaging and deployment units. They should be treated as real components: true structural and behavior units that are instantiable from component descriptors and connected together to materialize the architecture of the software. In this paper, we propose an approach for revealing component descriptors, component instances and component-based architecture to materialize the recovered architecture of an object-oriented software in component-based languages. We applied our solution onto two well known component-based languages, OSGi and SOFA.

1 Introduction

Component Based Software Development (CBSD) has been recognized as a competitive principle methodology for developing modular software systems [4]. It enforces the dependencies between components to be explicit through provided and required interfaces. Moreover, it provides coarse grained high-level architecture views for component-based (CB) applications. These views facilitate the communication between software architects and programmers during development, maintenance and evolution phases [11].

Otherwise, object-oriented (OO) have fine-grained entities with complex and numerous implicit dependencies [7]. Usually, they do not have explicit architectures or even have "drifted" ones. These adversely affect the software comprehension and makes these software systems hard to maintain and reuse [6]. Thus migrating OO software to CB one should contribute to gain the benefits of CBSD [9].

© Springer International Publishing AG 2016
B. Tekinerdogan et al. (Eds.): ECSA 2016, LNCS 9839, pp. 309–325, 2016.
DOI: 10.1007/978-3-319-48992-6_23

The process of migrating OO applications to CB ones involves two major steps: architecture recovery and code transformation [13]. The first step consists of identifying reusable components from legacy OO systems. A component is represented by a cluster of classes where its provided and required interfaces are represented by a set of provided and required methods respectively. The main challenge of this step is to find the best clusters compared to the component definitions which reflect the right software architecture. The second step aims at creating programming level components by transforming and generating a component code based on the OO one. The main problem of this step is to obtain a code which conforms to component principles: encapsulation, interface-based interaction, component instantiation, etc. [25].

Architecture recovery has been largely treated in the literature. Many approaches have been proposed to recover software architectures from legacy OO source code [3,5,16–18]. In contrast, only few approaches have been proposed for really transforming OO code into CB one [7,14,24]. In addition, these approaches have only partially address the code transformation step (c.f. Sect. 6).

In this paper, we propose an approach for transforming OO code to CB one guided by the recovered architecture of the corresponding OO software. This approach allows to reveal component descriptors, component instances and component-based architecture to materialize the recovered architecture. To validate this approach, we applied it to transform Java code to two well known component-based languages; OSGi [23] and SOFA [19].

The remainder of this paper is organized as follows. Section 2 discusses the problem statement. Section 3 presents the transformation of OO code to CB one. Section 4 presents how the proposed solution is mapped onto OSGi and SOFA. Section 5 presents the discussion about our solution. Section 6 discusses related work. Finally, Sect. 7 contains some concluding remarks and gives directions to future work.

2   Problem Statement

To better illustrate our approach aiming to transform OO code to CB one, first, we introduce in this section an example of a simple Java application. Second, we present the expected architecture recovered by analyzing this application. Finally, we illustrate the problem of OO code transformation guided by this architecture.

2.1   Running Example

Figure 1 shows an example of a simple Java application that simulates the behavior of an information screen (e.g. a software system which displays on a bus's screen information about stations, time, etc.). *ContentProvider* class implements methods which send text messages (instances of *Message*), and time information obtained through *Clock* instances based on the data returned by *TimeZone* instances. The *DisplayManager* is responsible for viewing the provided information through a *Screen*.

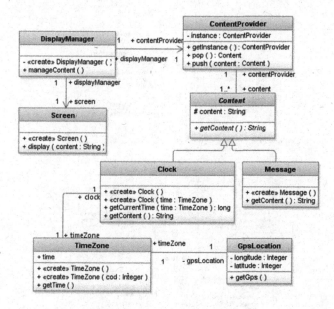

Fig. 1. *Information-screen* class diagram

2.2 Component-Based Architecture Recovery

Architecture recovery approaches consider a component as a cluster of classes [3, 5, 16–18]. In our previous work [16, 18], we have proposed an approach which aims to recover component-based architectures from OO source code. Figure 2 shows the object-component mapping model used in this approach. In this model a cluster is composed of two types of classes: internal classes and boundary classes. The internal classes are those that do not have dependencies with other classes placed into other clusters. In contrast, the boundary classes are those that have dependencies with classes placed into other clusters.

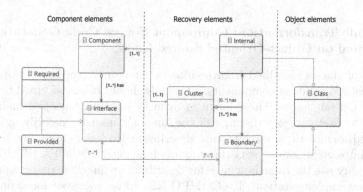

Fig. 2. Object-to-component mapping model

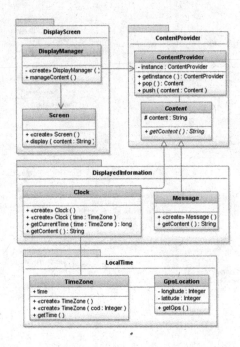

Fig. 3. *Information-screen* architecture recovery

Figure 3 shows the result of architecture recovery step applied on our example. The recovery step identifies four clusters (components), where each cluster may contain one or several classes. We consider a component-based architecture as a set of components connected via interfaces, where interfaces are identified from boundary classes. For example, the component *DisplayedInformation* connected to *ContentProvider* component through two interfaces. The first interface declares *getCurrentTime* method which is placed in class *Clock* and *getContent* method from class *Clock*. The second one declares *getContent* method from class *Message*.

2.3   Code Transformation: Component Source Code Generation Based on Object-Oriented Source Code

Clusters of classes identified from architecture recovery represent the primary implementation code of components. This code should be transformed to match targeted CB languages. These languages can be classified into two main categories. The first category distinguish the language used for describing components and architectures (architecture description language) from the language used to implement components (programing language) like SOFA [19]. The second category use the same language for describing architecture descriptions and component implementations like COMPO [12]. In our work we focus on transforming OO code to one written using CB language of the first category. This

Table 1. Object-based component model specifications [8]

Component models	Language of implementation	Interfacs type	Component descriptor	Component instance
EJB [2]	Java	Operation-based	Yes	Single Object
Fractal citefractal	Java, C#, .Net	Operation-based	Yes	Single Object
JavaBeans [21]	Java	Operation-based	Yes	Single Object
COM [1]	OO languages	Operation-based	Yes	Single Object
OpenCOM [10]	OO languages	Operation-based	Yes	Single Object
OSGi [23]	Java	Operation-based	No	Many Objects
SOFA 2.0 [19]	Java	Operation-based	Yes	Single Object
CCM [22]	Language independent with OO implementation	Operation-based & Port-based	Yes	Single Object
COMPO [12]	COMPO	Operation-based & Port-based	Yes	Single Object
Palladio [15]	Java	Operation-based	Yes	Single Object
PECOS [26]	OO languages	Port-based	Yes	Single Object

transformation allows to reuse classes of recovered clusters as the implementation of the target components. Table 1 summarizes the main structural elements of languages of this category. These consist of:

1. Structural elements that define component descriptions:
   (a) Component interfaces: the component descriptor need to define provided and required interfaces. All interactions between components must be done through these interfaces.
   (b) Implementation reference: the component descriptor need to define references of its component implementation source code.
   (c) Component instantiation: the component descriptor need to define how its component can be instantiated.
2. Architecture description: it describes the structure of component-based systems in terms of component instances and component assembly. It ignores components implementation details and interactions.

Our approach aims at generating structural elements composing component descriptors and architecture description starting from source code of recovered clusters. In our previous work [20], we have proposed an approach that transforms dependencies between clusters to be interface-based ones. This approach presented component interfaces structural elements. In this paper we complete the transformation by addressing the remaining structural elements of component descriptors; implementation references and component instantiation. This leads to revival of the CB architecture.

3   Transforming Object-Oriented Code to Component-Based One

3.1   Generating Component Descriptor and Reference of its Implementation

Our approach uses the concept of class used in OO to express component descriptors. Hence, a class will represent the component descriptor. For example, the descriptor of *DisplayedInformation* component translated by creating a new class *DisplayedInformation*. Where the component descriptor has describe their interfaces, the same concept of interface in OO languages is used to describe component interfaces. Then each provided interface has an OO interface that explicit its services (method signatures). The component descriptor must have the reference of its implementation of all provided interface services. For example, Listing 1.1 shows how the provided interfaces for component *DisplayedInformation* are created. But, what if two interfaces have the same method signature? the descriptor can not implement two services in the same descriptor (this is the case in Java, but in C++ and C# we can implement the same services that have the same signature by referencing the interface name before the implemented methods). For example, component *DisplayedInformation* provides two interfaces and the two interfaces have a method with the same signature(*getContent()*). Consequently, we should provide each interface by a component port.

Listing 1.1. Provided interfaces for *DisplayedInformation* component

```
public interface ITime {
  public String getContent();
  public long getCurrentTime(ITimeZone timeZone);
}
public interface IMessage {
  public String getContent();
}
```

The explicit services provided by a component interface are associated with a port. In our approach, we use the inner-class concept used in OO to represent component ports. Thus, each port is described by an inner-class associated with its interface. For example, in Listing 1.2, the *PortTime* inner-class is created to implement *ITime* interface provided by component *DisplayedInformation*, as same as *PortMessage* inner-class. Moreover, the references of each inner-class (port) are provided by its component (e.g. *portTime* and *portMessage* class-variables) for binding components.

Listing 1.2. Descriptor and ports for *DisplayedInformation* component

```
public class DisplayedInformation{
  public static ITime portTime;
  public static IMessage portMessage;
  private class PortTime implements ITime{
    @Override
    public String getContent() {//TODO: add behaviore implementation }
      @Override
    public long getCurrentTime(ITimeZone timeZone) {//TODO: add behaviore implementation }
  }
  private class PortMessage implements IMessage{
    @Override
    public String getContent() {//TODO: add behaviore implementation }
  }
}
```

3.2 Component Instantiation

Mapping Object Instances to Component Instances. In OO, an instance consists of state and behavior, the state is stored in variables and exposes its behavior through methods. Object hides its internal state where methods operate in an object internal state to provide services through object-to-object communication (encapsulation). However, the recovered component is viewed as a set of one or more cooperating classes. Thus, we infer component instances from a set of class instances belonging to the same component, where the component state is the aggregated state of these instances, and the component behavior is published through the component interfaces. For example, in Fig. 4, we have three object call graphs for a component consisting of five classes (A, B, C, D, E). We can observe that:

(1) The component instance has three different releases (Fig. 4(a), (b) and (c)).
(2) The component instance could have many class instances of the same type. For example, Fig. 4-(c) have two class instances from type E (e1 and e2).
(3) The client needs to have references to the class instances that provide services/methods for them. For example, the classes that implement the provided component services are A and B. Then, the client needs to reference instances of type A and B to get their required services. After that, instances of type A and B are responsible to communicate with other instances to complete its services. And therefore, the classes that have the component provided services are considered as the only entrance to component instance.

Based on our interpretation of the component instance, the set of class instances that constitute a component instance should behave as a single unit. Then, we need to update component descriptor to manage the links between class instances that form a component instance. We propose to delegate provided interface methods in the component descriptors to real ones. For example,

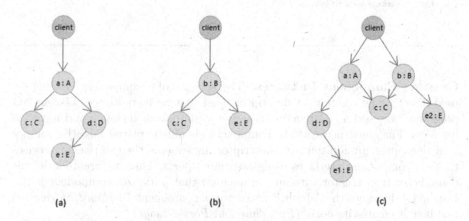

Fig. 4. Different release of the same component instance

316 Z. Alshara et al.

Listing 1.3 describes the update of the descriptor of *DisplayedInformation* component. The descriptor has references of the classes types that are responsible to provide component services *Clock* and *Message*. After that, the delegations of provided services is done through component ports by using the real class instances that have these services. It is worth noting that we used the lazy instantiation of these class instances (delaying the instantiation of class instance until the first time it is needed) for performance reasons.

Listing 1.3. Component descriptor with its behaviors

```
public class DisplayedInformation{
  protected static ITime portTime;
  protected static IMessage portMessage;
  //Boundary Classes
  Clock clock = null;
  Message message = null;
  public DisplayedInformation() {
    //initializing component ports
    portTime = new PortTime();
    portMessage = new PortMessage();
  }
  private class PortTime implements ITime{
    @Override
    public String getContent() {
      if(clock == null){ //lazy instantiation
        clock = new Clock();}
      return clock.getContent();
    }
    @Override
    public long getCurrentTime(ITimeZone timeZone) {
      if(clock == null){ //lazy instantiation
        clock = new Clock();}
      return clock.getCurrentTime(timeZone);
    }
  }
  private class PortMessage implements IMessage{
    @Override
    public String getContent() { //lazy instantiation
      if(message == null){
        message = new Message();}
      return message.getContent();
    }
  }
}
```

Creating Component Instances. The services of a component can not be used directly, the component descriptor must first be instantiated. Like in OO programs, we need a constructor to create a component instance and initialize its state. The constructor of the component should be placed into the component descriptor. In addition, the descriptor implements the component services through component interfaces using associated ports. Thus, we create a default constructor (constructor without parameters) that initializes component ports. Listing 1.4 describes the default constructor of component *DisplayedInformation* and how it creates its ports (*PortTime* and *PortMessage*).

Initializing component state depends on the constructors placed into classes that have provided methods to other components (e.g. *Clock* and *Message* into

DisplayedInformation component). For example, class *Clock* has two constructors, the first one without parameters (default constructor) and the second one with a single parameter of type *ITimeZone*. So there are two possible ways to create an instance of type *Clock*. Therefore, the component descriptor should provide all possible ways to initialize its instances. Consequently, *initialize* methods are created with different parameters to apply component configurations. For example, *DisplayedInformation* component have two classes that can be accessed from outside components (*Clock* and *Message*), and each of them has default constructor while *Clock* class has one more with *ITimeZone* parameter. Therefore, *initialize* methods are created and has *ITimeZone* parameter (see Listing 1.4).

Listing 1.4. Component constructors and initializers

```
public class DisplayedInformation{
...
  public DisplayedInformation() {
    //initializing component ports
    portTime = new PortTime();
    portMessage = new PortMessage();
  }
  public initialize(ITimeZone timeZone) {
    clock.setTimeZone(timeZone);
  }
}
```

Now, we can simply create an instance of the component using its constructor using OO instantiation and then initialize the instance using appropriate initializer. For example, an instance of *DisplayedInformation* component is created by its constructor using *new* keyword. Listing 1.5 differentiates the refactoring resulted from our approach (*ComponentClient*) and the original source code (*ClassClient*).

Listing 1.5. Component instantiation

```
public class ClassClient{
  Clock clock = new Clock(timeZone);
  clock.getCurrentTime();
}
public class ComponentClient{
  DisplayedInformation info = new DisplayedInformation();
  info.initialize(timeZone);
  info.portTime.getCurrentTime();
}
```

3.3   Reveal Component-Based Architecture

An architecture description describes the structure of component-based systems in terms of component instances and binding. Therefore, to reveal a CB architecture, we need to identify its component instances and the binding between these instances. We can identify the component instances by analyzing the instantiation statements of its implementation. We can identify the binding between these instances based on the invocation of its services.

Identify Component Instances. We first statically analyze the source code to check whether to create a new component instance or to use an existing one. The analysis is based on statement scope (i.e. in the same code block) and obliterates state (i.e. the second instantiation statement obliterates the state of the instance resulted from first one). The previous component instance can be replaced by a set of its class instances if these set at the same scope and no one obliterates the state of another one. For example, in Listing 1.6, the IF-BLOCK into class *ClassClient* instantiates an object of type *Clock* and another of type *Message*. However, the proposed approach replaces the two instances with a component instance of type *DisplayedInformation* (*info1*) because they are in the same scope and each one does not obliterate the state of another. An example of the scope condition is obviously shown by defining *info1* and *info2*, where each of them belongs into different scopes. Defining *info2* and *info3* provides an example of obliteration state condition, where *message2* will obliterate the state of *message1* if it translated to one component instance. Listing 1.7 shows the component instances that have been identified from Listing 1.6.

Listing 1.6. Refactoring instantiation from OO code into CB one

```
public class ClassClient{
  if(condition)
  {
    Clock clock = new Clock(timeZone);
    Message message = new Message();
  }else{
    Message message1 = new Message();
    ...
    Message message2 = new Message();
  }
}
public class ComponentClient{
if(condition)
  {
    DisplayedInformation info1 = new DisplayedInformation();
  }else{
    DisplayedInformation info2 = new DisplayedInformation();
    ...
    DisplayedInformation info3 = new DisplayedInformation();
  }
}
```

Listing 1.7. Identified CB instances for architecture discriptor

```
//Darwin ADL
inst
info1 : new DisplayedInformation();
info2 : new DisplayedInformation();
info3 : new DisplayedInformation();
```

Identify Component Binding. Binding between component instances is used to establish interactions between these instances. An instance of component binds to another one to provide or required services through their interfaces. Therefore, we can identify the bindings between components based on service invocations between them where components must firstly bind to provide or

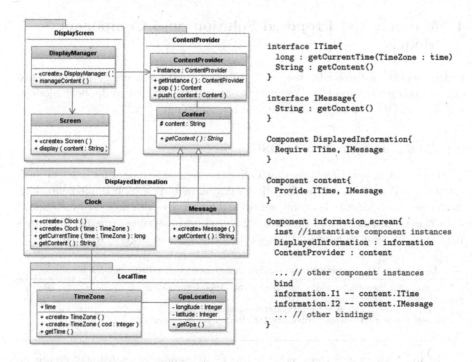

Fig. 5. *Information-screen* architecture recovery and Darwin ADL for *DisplayedInformation* and *ContentProvider*

required services. For example, in Listing 1.8, *ContentProvider* invokes a service *getCurrentTime* from *DisplayedInformation*, so the binding between these two component must be established before. Therefore, we can statically analyze these invocations between components to identify bindings (see Listing 1.9). Figure 5 shows the architecture recovery (c.f. Sect. 2.2) and a snapshot of architecture description for our running example. The architecture description describes component instances and its binding between *DisplayedInformation* and *Content-Provider* component instances.

Listing 1.8. Refactoring instantiation from OO code into CB one

```
public class ContentProvider{
  public void push(DisplayedInformation info1){
    String time = info1.portTime.getCurrentTime();
  }
}
```

Listing 1.9. Refactoring instantiation from OO code into CB one

```
//Darwin ADL
inst
content : new ContentProvider();
information : new DisplayedInformation();
bind
content.I1 -- information.ITime
}
```

4   Mapping the Proposed Solution onto Component Models

In this section we describe how our proposed solution is easily mapped onto existing component models. We have chosen two well known component models, OSGi and SOFA, to explain the ease of the mapping.

4.1   Mapping from Java to OSGi

OSGi is a set of specifications that define a component model for a set of Java classes [23]. It enables component encapsulation by hiding their implementations from other components by using services. The services are defined by standard Java classes and interfaces that are registered into a *service registry*. A component (bundle) can register and use services through the *service registry*.

Listing 1.10. *DisplayedInformation* component describtor and its interface

```
public class DisplayedInformation implements IDisplayedInformation{ /* Contents... */ }
public interface IDisplayedInformation {
  public InterTime portTime = DisplayedInformation.portTime;
  public IMessage portMessage = DisplayedInformation.portMessage;
}
```

To map our transformed code onto OSGi framework, we firstly create an interface (Java interface) to represent the contract of provided component instance. For example, Listing 1.10 shows how we created an interface for *DisplayedInformation* component. Hence we suggest that a component binds through its port associated with a provided interface, then both ports *InterTime* and *IMessage* must be accessed by other components. After that, a metadata for both provided component *DisplayedInformation* and required component *ContentProvider* must be specified. The metadata specified through XML files using the declarative services model. For example, Listing 1.11 describes how *DisplayedInformation* component provides its instances as object interfaces with type *IDisplayedInformation*. And Listing 1.12 describes how *ContentProvider* component uses the provided instances. When both components are activated at runtime, the binding is established between them. Listing 1.13 describes how *ContentProvider* gets an instance of *DisplayedInformation* and call its method *getContent()* through port *portMessage*.

Listing 1.11. DisplayedInformation.xml file to provide the instances of *DisplayedInformation*

```
<?xml version="1.0" encoding="UTF-8"?>
<scr:component xmlns:scr="http://www.osgi.org/xmlns/scr/v1.1.0" name="DisplayedInformation">
   <implementation class="DisplayedInformation"/>
   <service>
      <provide interface="IDisplayedInformation"/>
   </service>
</scr:component>
```

Listing 1.12. ContentProvider.xml to bind the instances of *DisplayedInformation*

```
<?xml version="1.0" encoding="UTF-8"?>
<scr:component xmlns:scr="http://www.osgi.org/xmlns/scr/v1.1.0" name="ContentProvider">
  <implementation class="ContentProvider"/>
  <reference bind="setDisplayedInformation" cardinality="1..n"
       interface="IDisplayedInformation" name="DisplayedInformation" policy="static"
       unbind="setDisplayedInformation"/>
</scr:component>
```

Listing 1.13. Binding between *DisplayedInformation* and *ContentProvider*

```
public class ContentProvider implements Inter_ContentProvider{
  public synchronized void setDisplayedInformation(IDisplayedInformation information) {
    information.portMessage.getContent();
  }
}
```

4.2   Mapping from Java to SOFA 2.0

SOFA is a platform for software components that uses a component model with hierarchically nested components (composite components). It describes a component by its frame (component descriptor) and component architecture. The frame is a black-box view of the component that defines its provided and required interfaces. It provides a metadata (XML files) to describe provided and required services (see Listing 1.14 and Listing 1.15). Components are interconnected via bindings among interfaces using connectors (see Listing 1.16).

Listing 1.14. DisplayedInformation.xml to provide the instances of *DisplayedInformation*

```
<?xml version="1.0"?>
<frame name="DisplayedInformation">
  <provides name="DisplayedInformation" itf-type="sofatype://IDisplayedInformation"/>
</frame>
```

Listing 1.15. ContentProvider.xml to bind the instances of *DisplayedInformation*

```
<?xml version="1.0"?>
<frame name="ContentProvider">
  <requires name="DisplayedInformation" itf-type="sofatype://IDisplayedInformation"/>
</frame>
```

Listing 1.16. Binding between *DisplayedInformation* and *ContentProvider*

```
public class ContentProvider implements SOFALifecycle, Runnable, SOFAClient {
  IDisplayedInformation info = null;
  // Called during initialization of the component.
  public void setRequired(String name, Object iface) {
    if (name.equals("DisplayedInformation")) {
      if (iface instanceof IDisplayedInformation) {
      //get DisplayedInformation instance
        info = (IDisplayedInformation) iface;
        info.portMessage.getContent();
    }}}
}
```

5   Discussion

We can deploy recovered cluster of classes directly onto existing component models without using our approach. Indeed, we can transform each class into a component and then assemble these components that belong to the same cluster using component composition property as a composite component. However, to compare our approach with the composite component approach, we need first to study the component composition types and component models that support these types. Table 2 shows the selected object-based component models and composition supported composition types. Two types of component compositions; the first one is horizontal composition, and the second type is vertical composition. The horizontal composition means that components can be binded through their interfaces to construct component applications. The second type, vertical composition, describes the mechanism of constructing a new component from two or more other components. The new component is then called composite because they are themselves made of more elementary components called internal components. Internal components could be accessible or visible from clients (delegation) or not (aggregation).

We can observe from Table 2 that there are five component models that did not support vertical composition at all (*EJB, JavaBeans, OSGi, CCM* and *Palladio*). Four of them provide vertical aggregation composition and six models support vertical delegation composition. However, vertical delegation composition is not appropriate because clients can access or view the internal components (violates component encapsulation). Consequently, the vertical aggregation composition could be replaced by our approach, but there are just two component models that support it.

Table 2. Composition type in object-based component models

Component models	EJB	Fractal	JavaBeans	COM	OpenCOM	OSGi	SOFA 2.0	CCM	COMPO	Palladio	PECOS
Vertical composition	No	Yes	No	Yes	Yes	No	Yes	No	Yes	No	Yes
Aggregation		✓		✓	✓				✓		
Delegation		✓		✓	✓		✓		✓		✓

6   Related Work

Transforming OO applications to CB ones has two types of related works. The first relates to CB architecture recovery, and the second relates to code transformation from OO applications to Component-oriented ones. Many works have proposed for recovering CB architectures from OO legacy code. A survey on these works is presented in [5,17]. However, only few works have beenproposed a transformation from OO code to CB one.

The approach proposed by [14] applies in transforming Java applications to OSGi. The approach uses OO concepts and patterns to wrap cluster of class to components. However, they did not deal with component instantiation, where they still used instances in terms of OO. Another approach for transforming Java applications into the JavaBeans framework is proposed in [7]. They developed an approach that can generate components from OO programs using a class relations graph. This method did not deal with a component as a set of classes, the authors assume that each class is transformed to a component. Therefore, it can not treat the cluster of classes recovered from architecture recovery methods.

One of the closest works to our approach is proposed by [24]. They used dynamic analysis to define component interfaces and component instances. The idea of their work consists of four steps. The first one is an extraction of object call graphs. The second step is transforming the object call graph into a component call graph. The third step identifies component interfaces based on the connections between component instances. The last step deals with component constructors and its parameters. In contrast to our work, they use dynamic analysis and execution trace, where they supposed the use cases of the recovered applications exist and fully cover all execution cases. Moreover, they suppose that two component instances may have intersected states, where a class instance can be shared between two components which violate the principle of component encapsulation.

7   Conclusion

In this paper, we proposed an approach to transform recovered components from object-oriented applications to be easily mapped to component-based models. We refactored clusters of classes (recovered component) to behave as a single unit of behavior to enable component instantiation. Our approach guarantees component-based principles by resolving component encapsulation and component composition using component instances. The encapsulation of components is guaranteed by transforming the OO dependencies between recovered components which was proposed in our previous work [20]. Moreover, both principles applied by refactoring a recovered component source code to be instantiable, where the provided services are consumed by the component instance through its interfaces (component binding). We have shown that the source code resulted from our approach can be easily projected onto object-based component models. We illustrated the mapping onto two well known component models, OSGi and SOFA. The illustration results show that our approach facilitates the transformation process from OO applications into CB ones. Moreover, it effectively reduces the gap between recovered component architectures and its implementation source code.

References

1. D. Box. Essential com. object technology series (1997)
2. Oracle E.E. Group. Jsr 220: Enterprise javabeanstm, version 3.0 ejb core contracts and requirements version 3.0, final release, May 2006

3. Shatnawi, A., Seriai, A., Sahraoui, H., Al-Shara, Z.: Mining software components from object-oriented APIs. In: Schaefer, I., Stamelos, I. (eds.) ICSR 2015. LNCS, vol. 8919, pp. 330–347. Springer, Heidelberg (2014). doi:10.1007/978-3-319-14130-5_23

4. Bertolino, A., et al.: An architecture-centric approach for producing quality systems. QoSA/SOQUA **3712**, 21–37 (2005)

5. Birkmeier, D., Overhage, S.: On component identification approaches – classification, state of the art, and comparison. In: Lewis, G.A., Poernomo, I., Hofmeister, C. (eds.) CBSE 2009. LNCS, vol. 5582, pp. 1–18. Springer, Heidelberg (2009). doi:10.1007/978-3-642-02414-6_1

6. Constantinou, E., et al.: Extracting reusable components: a semi-automated approach for complex structures. Inf. Process. Lett. **115**(3), 414–417 (2015)

7. Washizaki, H., et al.: A technique for automatic component extraction from object-oriented programs by refactoring. Sci. Comput. Program. **56**(1–2), 99–116 (2005)

8. Crnkovic, I., et al.: A classification framework for software component models. IEEE Trans. Softw. Eng. **37**(5), 593–615 (2011)

9. Lau, K., et al.: Software component models. IEEE Trans. Softw. Eng. **33**(10), 709–724 (2007)

10. Clarke, M., Blair, G.S., Coulson, G., Parlavantzas, N.: An efficient component model for the construction of adaptive middleware. In: Guerraoui, R. (ed.) Middleware 2001. LNCS, vol. 2218, pp. 160–178. Springer, Heidelberg (2001). doi:10.1007/3-540-45518-3_9

11. Shaw, M., et al.: Software Architecture: Perspectives on an Emerging Discipline. Prentice-Hall Inc., Upper Saddle River (1996)

12. Spacek, P., et al.: A component-based meta-level architecture and prototypical implementation of a reflective component-based programming and modeling language. In: Proceedings of the 17th International ACM Sigsoft Symposium on Component-Based Software Engineering, CBSE 2014. ACM (2014)

13. Kazman, R., et al.: Requirements for integrating software architecture, reengineering models: Corum ii. In: Proceedings of Reverse Engineering (1998)

14. Allier, S., et al.: From object-oriented applications to component-oriented applications via component-oriented architecture. In: Software Architecture (WICSA) (2011)

15. Becker, S., et al.: Model-based performance prediction with the palladio component model. In: Proceedings of the 6th International Workshop on Software and Performance, WOSP 2007. ACM (2007)

16. Chardigny, S., et al.: Extraction of component-based architecture from object-oriented systems. In: Software Architecture, WICSA (2008)

17. Ducasse, S., et al.: Software architecture reconstruction: a process-oriented taxonomy. IEEE Trans. Softw. Eng. **35**(4), 573–591 (2009)

18. Kebir, S., et al.: Quality-centric approach for software component identification from object-oriented code. In: Software Architecture (WICSA) and European Conference on Software Architecture (ECSA) (2012)

19. Bures T., et al.: Sofa 2.0: balancing advanced features in a hierarchical component model. In: Software Engineering Research, Management and Applications (2006)

20. Alshara, Z., et al.: Migrating large object-oriented applications into component-based ones: instantiation and inheritance transformation. In: Proceedings of the 2015 ACM SIGPLAN International Conference on Generative Programming: Concepts and Experiences, GPCE 2015. ACM (2015)

21. Sun Microsystems. Javabeans specification (1997)

22. OMG. Omg corba component model v4.0 (2011)
23. Osgi Service Platform. The osgi alliance, release 6 (2015)
24. Seriai, A., Sadou, S., Sahraoui, H.A.: Enactment of components extracted from an object-oriented application. In: Avgeriou, P., Zdun, U. (eds.) ECSA 2014. LNCS, vol. 8627, pp. 234–249. Springer, Heidelberg (2014). doi:10.1007/978-3-319-09970-5_22
25. Szyperski, C.: Component Software: Beyond Object-Oriented Programming, 2nd edn. Addison-Wesley Longman Publishing Co. Inc., Boston (2002)
26. Winter, M.: The pecos software process. In: Workshop on Components-based Software Development Processes, ICSR (2002)

Using Hypergraph Clustering
for Software Architecture Reconstruction
of Data-Tier Software

Ersin Ersoy[1], Kamer Kaya[2], Metin Altınışık[1], and Hasan Sözer[3(✉)]

[1] Turkcell, Istanbul, Turkey
{ersin.ersoy,metin.altinisik}@turkcell.com.tr
[2] Sabanci University, Istanbul, Turkey
kaya@sabanciuniv.edu
[3] Ozyegin University, Istanbul, Turkey
hasan.sozer@ozyegin.edu.tr

Abstract. Software architecture reconstruction techniques aim at recovering software architecture documentation regarding a software system. These techniques mainly analyze coupling/dependencies among the software modules to group them and reason about the high-level structure of the system. Hereby, inter-dependencies among the software modules are mainly represented with design structure matrices or regular directed/undirected graphs. In this paper, we introduce a software architecture reconstruction approach that utilizes hypergraphs for representing inter-module dependencies. We focus on PL/SQL programs that are developed as data access tiers of business software. These programs are mainly composed of procedures that are coupled due to commonly accessed database elements. Hypergraphs are more appropriate for capturing this type of coupling, where an element can relate to more than one procedure. We illustrate the application of the approach with an industrial PL/SQL program from the telecommunications domain. We analyze and represent dependencies among the modules of this program in the form of a hypergraph. Then, we perform modularity clustering on this model and propose a packaging structure to the designer accordingly. We observed promising results in comparison with previous work. The accuracy of the results were also approved by domain experts.

Keywords: Software architecture reconstruction · Reverse engineering · Hypergraph partitioning · Modularity clustering · Industrial case study

1 Introduction

Modularity is one of the key properties for software design [16]. Especially large scale software systems need to have a modular structure. Otherwise, the maintainability and evolvability of the system suffer. A modular structure can be attained by decomposing the system into cohesive units that are loosely coupled. Software architecture design [3,22] defines the gross-level decomposition of

© Springer International Publishing AG 2016
B. Tekinerdogan et al. (Eds.): ECSA 2016, LNCS 9839, pp. 326–333, 2016.
DOI: 10.1007/978-3-319-48992-6_24

a software system. Hence, its documentation is an important asset for coping with evolution [15].

Software architecture documentation might be incorrect/incomplete for old legacy systems due to *architectural drift* [14,17]. Software architecture reconstruction (SAR) techniques [8] have been introduced to recover such documentation. These techniques mainly analyze coupling/dependencies among the software modules to group them and reason about the high-level structure of the system. Hereby, inter-dependencies among the software modules are mainly represented with design structure matrices (DSM) [2] or regular directed/undirected graphs [8]. These models capture direct dependencies between a pair of modules like call relations [13].

In this paper, we focus on PL/SQL programs that are developed as data access tiers of business software. These programs are mainly composed of procedures that are coupled due to commonly accessed database elements [2]. Existing SAR techniques do not consider indirect coupling/dependencies among the software modules based on such persistent data. Several procedures can be coupled due to a commonly accessed element. This type of coupling cannot be directly captured by existing models. Therefore, we introduce a SAR approach that uses a hypergraph model for representing such coupling/dependencies among modules. This model is partitioned to find clusters that maximize modularity. A packaging structure that is aligned with the obtained clusters is proposed to the designer. We illustrate the application of the approach with an industrial PL/SQL program from the telecommunications domain. We observed promising results with this case study in comparison with our previous work [2]. The accuracy of the results were also approved by domain experts.

The paper is organized as follows. In the following section, we provide background information on PL/SQL programs, hypergraphs and modularity clustering. We summarize the related studies in Sect. 3. We present the overall approach in Sect. 4. The approach is evaluated in Sect. 5, in the context of the industrial case study. Finally, in Sect. 6, we conclude the paper.

2   Background

2.1   PL/SQL Programs

PL/SQL (Procedural Language/Structured Query Language) combines procedural language features with the Structural Query Language (SQL) [1]. PL/SQL programs work on Oracle[1] database management system and they constitute significant part of enterprise applications today.

A PL/SQL program includes procedures that can be grouped into packages or remain as standalone procedures [2]. A sample PL/SQL procedure is shown in Listing 1.1. The first part of the procedure (Lines 1–4) declares variables and constants used in the application logic. The second part (Lines 5–19) contains

---

[1] www.oracle.com.

the application logic. This part optionally includes a specification of exception conditions and their handling (Lines 13–18).

Listing 1.1 illustrates the interleaving of imperative code with SQL statements. Procedures are highly coupled with database elements and they are dependent on each other due to commonly accessed elements. In this work, we employ hypergraphs for representing these inter-dependencies. In the following, we shortly introduce the hypergraph formalism and our modeling approach.

Listing 1.1. A sample PL/SQL procedure [2].

```
1  PROCEDURE P(id IN NUMBER) IS
2    sales NUMBER;
3    total NUMBER;
4    ratio NUMBER;
5  BEGIN
6    SELECT x,y INTO sales,total
7     FROM result WHERE result_id = id;
8    ratio := sales/total;
9    IF ratio > 10 THEN
10     INSERT INTO comp VALUES (id,ratio);
11   END IF;
12   COMMIT;
13  EXCEPTION
14    WHEN ZERO_DIVIDE THEN
15     INSERT INTO comp VALUES (id,0);
16     COMMIT;
17    WHEN OTHERS THEN
18     ROLLBACK;
19  END;
```

2.2 Hypergraphs

A hypergraph $\mathcal{H} = (\mathcal{V}, \mathcal{N})$ is defined as a set of vertices $\mathcal{V}$ and a set of nets (hyperedges) $\mathcal{N}$ among those vertices. A net $n \in \mathcal{N}$ is a subset of vertices and the vertices in n are called its *pins*. The number of pins of a net is called the *size* of it, and the *degree* of a vertex is equal to the number of nets it belongs to. We use pins$[n]$ and nets$[v]$ to represent the pin set of a net n, and the set of nets containing a vertex v, respectively. In this work, we assume unit weights for all nets and vertices.

A K-*way partition* of a hypergraph $\mathcal{H}$ is a partition of its vertex set, which is denoted as $\Pi = \{\mathcal{V}_1, \mathcal{V}_2, \ldots, \mathcal{V}_K\}$, where

– parts are pairwise disjoint, i.e., $\mathcal{V}_k \cap \mathcal{V}_\ell = \emptyset$ for all $1 \leq k < \ell \leq K$,
– each $\mathcal{V}_k$ is a nonempty subset of $\mathcal{V}$, i.e., $\mathcal{V}_k \subseteq \mathcal{V}$ and $\mathcal{V}_k \neq \emptyset$ for $1 \leq k \leq K$,
– the union of K parts is equal to $\mathcal{V}$, i.e., $\bigcup_{k=1}^{K} \mathcal{V}_k = \mathcal{V}$.

In our modeling approach, we represent each PL/SQL procedure as a vertex and each database table as a net. A net has several vertices as its pins if the corresponding procedures access the database table represented by the net. We convert this model to a weighted graph model and apply modularity clustering as explained in the following subsection.

2.3 Modularity Clustering

Given a (weighted) graph G, a good clustering of the vertices in G should contain G's edges within the clusters. However, since the number of clusters is not fixed, this objective can be trivially realized by a clustering that consists of a single cluster. Hence, alone, this objective is not a suitable clustering index. By adding a penalty term for larger clusters, we obtain the *modularity* of a clustering $\mathcal{C}$ [6]:

$$Q(\mathcal{C}) = \frac{\sum\limits_{C_i \in \mathcal{C}} \omega(C_i)}{\omega(E)} - \frac{\sum\limits_{C_i \in \mathcal{C}} (2 \times \omega(C_i) + cut(C_i))^2}{\alpha \times \omega(E)^2} \tag{1}$$

where $\omega(E)$ is the total edge weight in the graph, C_i is the ith cluster, $\omega(C_i)$ is the total weight of internal edges in C_i, and $cut(C_i)$ is the total weight of the edges from the vertices in C_i to the vertices not in C_i. Like other clustering indices, modularity captures the inherent trade-off between increasing the number of clusters and keeping the size of the cuts between clusters small. Almost all clustering indices require algorithms to face such a trade-off. Hereby, α is a trade-off parameter, which determines the relative importance of the two trade-off dimensions. The value 4 is commonly assigned for α to establish equal/balanced importance. For this study, we have experimented with a range of α values and obtained the best results when α is equal to 2.8. We observed that the resulting number of clusters is aligned with the number of conceptual entities in the database. Hence, α can be adjusted based on a preprocessing of these entities. However, we left the automated adjustment of α parameter as future work.

3 Related Work

There exist many techniques [8] for SAR. Several of them use DSM for reasoning about architectural dependencies [2,18–20]. Some focus on analyzing the runtime behavior for reconstructing execution scenarios [4] and behavioral views [12]. There are also tools that construct both structural and behavioral views [10,21] which are mainly developed for reverse engineering C/C++ or Java programs. Some tools are language independent; they take abstract inputs like module dependency graphs [13] or execution traces [4]. However, hypergraphs have not been utilized for SAR to the best of our knowledge.

There exist only a few studies [7,11] that focus on reverse engineering PL/SQL programs. They mainly aim at deriving business rules [7] and data flow graphs [11]. Recently, we proposed an approach for clustering PL/SQL procedures [2]. The actual coupling among these procedures can only be revealed based on their dependencies on database elements. In our previous work, we employed DSM [9] for representing these dependencies. In this work, we employ hypergraphs, which can more naturally model such dependencies and lead to more accurate results.

4   Software Reconstruction with Hypergraphs

The overall approach involves 4 steps as shown in Fig. 1. First, the program source code and the database structure (meta-data) is provided to our *Dependency analyzer* tool as input (1). This tool creates a hypergraph model that represents dependencies among the procedures based on database tables that are commonly accessed. Second, the generated model is converted to a weighted graph (2). Then, this graph is recursively bi-partitioned by a clustering tool (3). Finally, the identified partitions are processed by our tool *Partition analyzer* to propose a package structure for the analyzed source code (4).

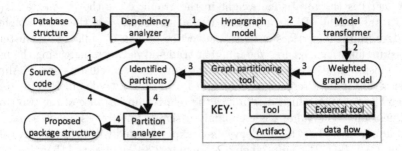

Fig. 1. The overall approach.

Dependency analyzer creates a hypergraph, where the number of vertices is equal to the number of procedures. Then, for each table in the database, it identifies the set of procedures that accesses the table. This set forms the set of pins for the net that represents the table.

To apply the modularity-based clustering, we transform the hypergraph into a weighted graph G as follows: each vertex in the hypergraph is also vertex of G and vice versa. Furthermore, there is an edge between two vertices u and v in the graph if they are connected via at least one net in the hypergraph. The weight of this (u, v) edge is assigned as $|\mathsf{nets}[u] \cap \mathsf{nets}[v]|$. After generating the weighted graph, we used the clustering tool by Çatalyürek et al. [5] to maximize the modularity. Starting with a single cluster G, the tool recursively partitions the clusters into two if the partitioning increases the modularity. We employ PaToH[2] as the inner partitioner in the clustering tool. In the following section, we illustrate the application of the approach in the context of an industrial case study from the telecommunications domain.

5   Industrial Case Study

We have performed a case study for automatically clustering modules of a legacy application implemented with the PL/SQL language. The application is a

---

[2] http://bmi.osu.edu/umit/software.html.

Table 1. A sample list of nets and the set of vertices they interconnect (pins) in the generated hypergraph for the CRM case study.

Net	Vertices
T1	P119, P101, P1, P47, P15, P48
T2	P119, P57, P47, P26, P1
...	...
T11	P27, P26, P7, P1, P117, P119, P115, P111, P110, P109, ...
...	...
T67	P8

Customer Relation Management (CRM) system, which is maintained by Turkcell[3]. Its code comprises around 2 MLOC and the system is operational since 1993, serving more than 10000 users. In this section, we illustrate our approach for this system and discuss the results. We can not share real procedure/table names due to confidentiality; we present abstracted artifacts and results instead.

In our case study, we focused on one of the main schemas of the CRM system, which consists of 157 stored procedures and 690 tables. The same subject system[4] was used for evaluating our previous SAR approach [2]. We filtered out stored procedures that do not use any table. This preprocessing resulted with the final dataset that consists of 67 tables and 120 procedures. Hence, the created hypergraph has 120 vertices and 67 nets. Some of the nets are listed in Table 1 as an example. This hypergraph is processed as explained in Sect. 4 to derive a package structure for the procedures.

Results and Discussion: In total 9 partitions were obtained as listed in Table 2. Hereby, the number of items represent the number of procedures that are placed in the same partition. For instance, *Partition 3* includes 30 procedures. These procedures were not belonging to any package in the original application. They were defined as standalone procedures although they were working on the same database tables. We have validated this result with 4 different domain experts, all of whom agreed that these procedures perform related tasks and they should have been placed in the same package. We also observed that each partition can be mapped to a particular entity such as Customer, Address, Product etc. in the conceptual entity relationship model of the CRM database. The results regarding the partitions 5, 6, 7 and 8 were also validated likewise. The validity of the other partitions 0, 1, 2 and 4 were not confirmed by all the experts and they are also subject to some conflicts with respect to the conceptual entity relationship model. Finally, we compared these results with the results that we obtained using our previous approach [2] based on DSM clustering[5].

---

[3] http://www.turkcell.com.tr.

[4] The number of procedures and tables are slightly different compared to the previous study [2] due to the evolution of the system.

[5] The approach is reevaluated for the new version of the subject system.

Table 2. The set of partitions obtained as a result of clustering.

Partition	# of items	Partition	# of items	Partition	# of items
Partition 0	15	Partition 3	30	Partition 6	9
Partition 1	18	Partition 4	4	Partition 7	17
Partition 2	8	Partition 5	10	Partition 8	9

In total 9 partitions and 120 items

Hypergraph partitioning based approach turned out to be 20% better in terms of the percentage of procedures that are confirmed to be clustered correctly in a package.

There are several validity threats to our evaluation. First, the evaluation is based on subjective expert opinion rather than quantitative measurements. We tried to mitigate this threat by consulting 4 different experts and comparing the results with respect to their consistency with the conceptual entity relationship model. A second threat is regarding the use of a single subject system for the case study. Therefore, we plan to perform more case studies in the future. Although we focused on PL/SQL programs, our approach is relevant and applicable for any type of program that is highly coupled with a database management system.

6   Conclusion and Future Work

We introduced a software architecture reconstruction approach that employs hypergraph partitioning. We showed that hypergraphs can naturally represent dependencies that involve several modules. As a case study, we applied our approach on an industrial PL/SQL program. Procedures of this program are indirectly dependent on each other due to commonly accessed database elements. These dependencies are captured in the form of a hypergraph model. Clustering of this model revealed a packaging structure for the procedures. The accuracy of this structure was evaluated by domain experts. The accuracy was siginificantly higher with respect to the results obtained by clustering design structure matrices that are derived for the same subject system.

Acknowledgements. We thank the software developers and managers at Turkcell for sharing their code base with us and supporting our analysis.

References

1. Oracle Database Online Documentation 11g Release developing and using stored procedures. http://docs.oracle.com/. Accessed Mar 2016
2. Altinisik, M., Sozer, H.: Automated procedure clustering for reverse engineering PL/SQL programs. In: Proceedings of the 31st ACM Symposium on Applied Computing, pp. 1440–1445 (2016)

3. Bass, L., Clements, P., Kazman, R.: Software Architecture in Practice, 3rd edn. Addison-Wesley, Boston (2003)
4. Callo, T., America, P., Avgeriou, P.: A top-down approach to construct execution views of a large software-intensive system. J. Sof. Evol. Process **25**(3), 233–260 (2013)
5. Çatalyürek, Ü.V., Kaya, K., Langguth, J., Uçar, B.: A partitioning-based divisive clustering technique for maximizing the modularity. In: Proceedings of the 10th DIMACS Implementation Challenge Workshop - Graph Partitioning and Graph Clustering, pp. 171–186 (2012)
6. Çatalyürek, U., Kaya, K., Langguth, J., Uçar, B.: A partitioning-based divisive clustering technique for maximizing the modularity. In: Graph Partitioning and Graph Clustering. Contemporary Mathematics, vol. 588. American Mathematical Society (2013)
7. Chaparro, O., Aponte, J., Ortega, F., Marcus, A.: Towards the automatic extraction of structural business rules from legacy databases. In: Proceedings of the 19th Working Conference on Reverse Engineering, pp. 479–488 (2012)
8. Ducasse, S., Pollet, D.: Software architecture reconstruction: a process-oriented taxonomy. IEEE Trans. Soft. Eng. **35**(4), 573–591 (2009)
9. Eppinger, S., Browning, T.: Design Structure Matrix Methods and Applications. MIT Press, Cambridge (2012)
10. Guo, G., Atlee, J., Kazman, R.: A software architecture reconstruction method. In: Proceedings of the 1st Working Conference on Software Architecture, pp. 15–34 (1999)
11. Habringer, M., Moser, M., Pichler, J.: Reverse engineering PL/SQL legacy code: an experience report. In: Proceedings of the IEEE International Conference on Software Maintenance and Evolution, pp. 553–556 (2014)
12. Qingshan, L., et al.: Architecture recovery and abstraction from the perspective of processes. In: WCRE, pp. 57–66 (2005)
13. Mitchell, B., Mancoridis, S.: On the automatic modularization of software systems using the bunch tool. IEEE Trans. Soft. Eng. **32**(3), 193–208 (2006)
14. Murphy, G., Notkin, D., Sullivan, K.: Software reflexion models: Bridging the gap between design and implementation. IEEE Trans. Soft. Eng. **27**(4), 364–380 (2001)
15. Clements, P., et al.: Documenting Software Architectures. Addison-Wesley, Bostan (2002)
16. Parnas, D.L.: On the criteria to be used in decomposing systems into modules. Commun. ACM **15**(12), 1053–1058 (1972)
17. Eick, S., et al.: Does code decay? assessing the evidence from change management data. IEEE Trans. Soft. Eng. **27**(1), 1–12 (2001)
18. Sangal, N., Jordan, E., Sinha, V., Jackson, D.: Using dependency models to manage complex software architecture. In: Proceedings of the 20th Conference on Object-Oriented Programming, Systems, Languages and Applications, pp. 167–176 (2005)
19. Sangwan, R., Neill, C.: Characterizing essential and incidental complexity in software architectures. In: Proceedings of the 3rd European Conference on Software Architecture, pp. 265–268 (2009)
20. Sullivan, K., Cai, Y., Hallen, B., Griswold, W.: The structure and value of modularity in software design. In: Proceedings of the 8th European Software Engineering Conference, pp. 99–108 (2001)
21. Sun, C., Zhou, J., Cao, J., Jin, M., Liu, C., Shen, Y.: ReArchJBs: a tool for automated software architecture recovery of javabeans-based applications. In: Proceedings of the 16th Australian Software Engineering Conference, pp. 270–280 (2005)
22. Taylor, R., Medvidovic, N., Dashofy, E.: Software Architecture: Foundations, Theory, and Practice. Wiley, Hoboken (2009)

SeaClouds: An Open Reference Architecture for Multi-cloud Governance

Antonio Brogi[2], Jose Carrasco[1], Javier Cubo[1(✉)], Francesco D'Andria[3],
Elisabetta Di Nitto[4], Michele Guerriero[4], Diego Pérez[4], Ernesto Pimentel[1],
and Jacopo Soldani[2]

[1] Dept. Lenguajes y Ciencias de la Computación,
Universidad de Málaga, Málaga, Spain
{josec,cubo,ernesto}@lcc.uma.es
[2] Dept. Computer Science, University of Pisa, Pisa, Italy
{brogi,soldani}@di.unipi.it
[3] ATOS Research and Innovation, Barcelona, Spain
francesco.dandria@atos.net
[4] Dip. di Elettronica, Informazione e Bioingegneria,
Politecnico di Milano, Milano, Italy
{elisabetta.dinitto,michele.guerriero,diego.perez}@polimi.it

Abstract. We present the open reference architecture of the SeaClouds
solution. It aims at enabling a seamless adaptive multi-cloud management of complex applications by supporting the distribution, monitoring
and reconfiguration of app modules over heterogeneous cloud providers.

1 Motivation and Objectives of SeaClouds

Cloud computing is a model for enabling convenient and on-demand network
access to a shared pool of configurable computing resources that can be rapidly
provisioned and released with minimal management effort or service provider
interaction. Many private and public clouds have emerged during the last years,
offering a range of different services at SaaS, PaaS levels aimed at matching
different user requirements. Current cloud technologies suffer from a lack of
standardization, with different providers offering similar resources in a different
manner, which results in the vendor lock-in problem. This problem affects all
stages of the cloud applications' lifecycle, ranging from their design to their operation. Application developers must know the features of the services to be used,
and have a deep knowledge of the providers' API. To reduce the need of using
deep knowledge, we can find solutions based on the use of standards, such as
OASIS CAMP or OASIS TOSCA, DMTF CIMI, unified APIs, such as jClouds[1],
or solutions like Docker[2]. These solutions are indeed very different, for example,
whereas jClouds provides a cloud agnostic API library to provision and configure

---

This work has been partly supported by the EU-FP7-ICT-610531 SeaClouds project.
[1] https://jclouds.apache.org.
[2] https://www.docker.com.

© Springer International Publishing AG 2016
B. Tekinerdogan et al. (Eds.): ECSA 2016, LNCS 9839, pp. 334–338, 2016.
DOI: 10.1007/978-3-319-48992-6_25

secure communications with cloud virtual machines, container-based solutions like Docker allow describing and deploying applications and their dependencies through containers on machines with the corresponding engine. Furthermore, different vendors (e.g., Dell, BMC, Abiquo) are currently commercialising tools for the provisioning, management and automation of cloud applications. A promising perspective, opened by the availability of different cloud providers is the possibility of distributing cloud applications over multiple heterogeneous clouds.

To mitigate this heterogeneity and get a vendor-agnostic solution, independent tools and frameworks have emerged as the result of integrating, under a single interface, the services of multiple public and private providers [3–6]. These solutions offer a portable and interoperable environment where developers can describe their systems and select the resources that better fit their requirements. However, in all these attempts, platforms allow operating simultaneously with a single level of service to deploy applications, i.e., all the components of an application are deployed either at the IaaS level or all at the PaaS level (see, e.g., [1,2,7]). From this, with the goal of unifying cloud services, we propose a software architecture supporting the integration of IaaS and PaaS levels under a single interface. Then, this will allow developers to deploy their applications combining services offered by providers at any of these levels. In such a way, our proposal goes a step further in the software architecture and development of common APIs by unifying IaaS and PaaS services of different providers under the same interface, and using the TOSCA standard for the agnostic specification of applications' components and interdependencies. With such a proposal, we do not only reduce the need of vendor-specific knowledge to develop our applications for designing, deploying and operating them. In fact, such a homogenized API greatly improves portability and interoperability as well. This solution has been developed in the scope of the SeaClouds EU-funded research project[3]. This project aims to develop a new open source framework which performs Seamless Adaptive Multi-Cloud management of service-based applications.

2   The SeaClouds Platform: A Reference Architecture

SeaClouds is a software platform based on an open reference architecture to make more efficient the design, development, planning and management of complex business apps distributed on multi-cloud environments. It orchestrates services, platforms and infrastructures to ensure they meet the needs of cloud apps.

2.1   SeaClouds Functionalities and Open Reference Architecture

SeaClouds is a multi-cloud app management system based on standards and following the DevOps approach. The basic capabilities delivered to the developer via an innovative GUI are listed in the following.

---

[3] http://www.seaclouds-project.eu.

- **Discovery and Matchmaking**. It allows querying available cloud offerings (IaaS/PaaS) determining suitable ones based on app requirements.
- **Cloud Service Optimizer**. It optimizes the deployment topology of an application across multiple clouds to address non-functional requirements.
- **Application Management**. It supports efficient deployment and multi-cloud governance of a complex application on various cloud offerings (IaaS and PaaS) leveraging cloud harmonized APIs and platform-specific adapters.
- **Monitoring and SLA enforcement**. It provides monitoring and independent metrics to allow operators to monitor the health and performance of applications, hosted across multiple clouds.
- **Repairing**. It scales horizontally and vertically cloud resources to maximize the performance of each module of an application.
- **Application migration**. It provides a seamless migration of the app modules between dissimilar (but compatible) clouds, allowing application portability.

Figure 1 presents the reference architecture and the design of the SeaClouds platform. The platform features a **GUI** used by two main stakeholders: **Designers and Deployment Managers**, and it considers **Cloud Providers** offering cloud resources. From SeaClouds platform functionalities standpoint, we can identify five major components in the architecture, plus a RESTful harmonized and unified **SeaClouds API** layer used for the deployment, management and monitoring of simple cloud-based applications through different and heterogeneous cloud providers, and exploiting a **Dashboard**.

- **SeaClouds Discoverer**. It is in charge of discovering available capabilities and add-ons offered by available cloud providers.
- **SeaClouds Planner**. It is in charge of generating an orchestration plan considering the application topology and requirements.
- **SeaClouds Deployer**. It is in charge of executing deployment plans generated by the Planner, and supports the integration of both IaaS and PaaS.
- **SeaClouds Monitor**. It is in charge of monitoring that the Quality of Services (QoS) properties of the application are not violated by the clouds in which they were deployed; and of determining together with the Deployer, the reconfiguration strategies to trigger the repairing or migration actions.
- **SeaClouds SLA Service**. It is in charge of mapping the low level information gathered from the Monitor into business level information, Quality of Business (QoB), about the fulfillment of the SLA defined.

A distinguishing aspect of the SeaClouds architecture is that it builds on top of two OASIS standards initiatives: TOSCA (at design time) to specify the topologies and generate the plans, and TOSCA and also CAMP is supported (at runtime) to manage the building, running, administration, monitoring and patching of applications in the cloud. Also, an important advance of SeaClouds as regards other software architecture solutions is the fact of unifying IaaS and PaaS of multiple vendors. Specifically, we propose to use a provider-agnostic TOSCA-based model of the topology of applications and their required resources,

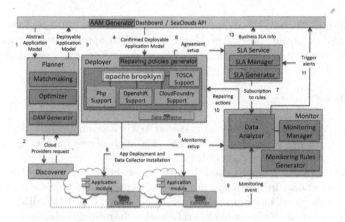

Fig. 1. Architecture of the SeaClouds Platform.

indistinctly using IaaS and PaaS services, which can be used for their deployment using (an extended version of) Apache Brooklyn.[4]

2.2   SeaClouds Implementation and Evaluation

The SeaClouds project has provided a solution which can be downloaded from the github repository[5]. The consortium identified Apache Brooklyn as the tool to deploy SeaClouds. To ensure a good level of quality assurance, a free Continuos Integration (CI) and Continuos Distribution was set up, travis-ci.org. SeaClouds platform is built using Java language, distributing the artefacts generated from the source code, like jar file, war file etc., to a well-know public managed maven repository hosted by Sonatype (free for opensource projects).

The SeaClouds solution has been evaluated in several examples, with the main focus on two real use cases: i) Atos Software application and ii) Nuro Gaming application[6], both consisting of several components (servers, database) and distributed in heterogeneous cloud providers (IaaS and PaaS).

3   Conclusions and Future Issues

We have presented the SeaClouds platform, which provides an open source framework to address the problem of deploying, managing and reconfiguring complex applications over multiple clouds. The SeaClouds solution has addressed the main functionalities presented in previous section. As future work, the consortium has agreed to create the SeaClouds Alliance in order to continue working on some aspects, such as the improvement of the unification of providers supported

---

[4] Apache Brooklyn: https://brooklyn.apache.org/.
[5] https://github.com/SeaCloudsEU/SeaCloudsPlatform.
[6] Deliverables 6.3.3 and D6.4.3 http://www.seaclouds-project.eu/deliverables.

by the deployment, and the reconfiguration covering replanning actions and data synchronization in database. Also, SeaClouds is an open source project, so it is open to receive more contributions and extensions from the community.

References

1. Elkhatib, Y.: Defining cross-cloud systems. ArXiv e-prints (2016)
2. Hossny, E., et al.: A case study for deploying applications on heterogeneous PaaS platforms. In: CloudCom-Asia (2013)
3. Gonidis, F., et al: A development framework enabling the design of service-based cloud applications. In: Advances in Service-Oriented and Cloud Computing (2014)
4. Pahl, C.: Containerization and the PaaS cloud. IEEE CLOUD (2015)
5. Pham, L.M., et al.: Roboconf, a hybrid cloud orchestrator to deploy complex applications. In: IEEE CLOUD (2015)
6. Sellami, M., et al: PaaS-independent provisioning and management of applications in the cloud. In: IEEE CLOUD (2013)
7. Zeginis, D., D'Andria, F., et al.: Scalable Computing: Practice and Experience (2013)

Author Index

Aaramaa, Sanja 238
Abujayyab, Mohammed 67
Abukwaik, Hadil 67
Agrawal, Ashish 291
Alexeeva, Zoya 84
Alshara, Zakarea 309
Altınışık, Metin 326
Angelov, Samuil 229

Bagheri, Hamid 274
Bahsoon, Rami 55
Batista, Thais 129, 185
Berruet, Pascal 210
Bex, Floris 22
Bignon, Alain 210
Boussaidi, Ghizlane El 149
Bouziane, Hinde Lilia 309
Brogi, Antonio 334
Bures, Tomas 113

Calero, Coral 39
Caljouw, Lambert 201
Cámara, Javier 274
Carrasco, Jose 334
Cavalcante, Everton 185
Cubo, Javier 334

D'Andria, Francesco 334
Dasanayake, Sandun 238
Di Nitto, Elisabetta 334
Dony, Christophe 309

Ersoy, Ersin 326

Galster, Matthias 229
Garlan, David 274
Gennari, Jeff 274
Gerostathopoulos, Ilias 113
Guerriero, Michele 334

Hassan, Adel 166
Heim, Robert 175
Holstein, Tobias 138

Jansen, Slinger 201

Kapto, Christel 149
Kautz, Oliver 175
Kaya, Kamer 326
Kazman, Rick 55
Kesraoui, Djamal 210
Knauss, Alessia 113
Kpodjedo, Sègla 149

Lago, Patricia 39
Legay, Axel 185
Leite, Jair 129

Malek, Sam 274
Markkula, Jouni 238
Me, Gianantonio 39
Meesters, Marcel 229
Mesli-Kesraoui, Soraya 210
Minku, Leandro 55
Mirandola, Raffaela 84

Naab, Matthias 102

Oivo, Markku 238
Oquendo, Flavio 3, 129, 185, 210
Oussalah, Mourad 166

Pérez, Diego 334
Perez-Palacin, Diego 84
Pimentel, Ernesto 334
Plasil, Frantisek 113
Prabhakar, T.V. 291

Queudet, Audrey 166
Quilbeuf, Jean 185

Riebisch, Matthias 247
Ringert, Jan Oliver 175
Rombach, Dieter 67
Rost, Dominik 102
Rumpe, Bernhard 175

Sadeghi, Alireza   274
Schenkhuizen, Jasper   201
Schmerl, Bradley   274
Schriek, Courtney   22
Schröder, Sandra   247
Seriai, Abdelhak-Djamel   309
Shatnawi, Anas   309
Skoda, Dominik   113
Sobhy, Dalia   55
Soldani, Jacopo   334
Soliman, Mohamed   247
Sözer, Hasan   326

Tang, Antony   22
Theunissen, Theo   265
Tibermacine, Chouki   149, 309
Toguyeni, Armand   210
Traonouez, Louis-Marie   185

van der Werf, Jan Martijn E.M.   22, 201
van Heesch, Uwe   265

Wietzke, Joachim   138
Wortmann, Andreas   175

Printed in the United States
By Bookmasters